THE COMMISSIONERS OF INDIAN AFFAIRS

The Defiance House Man colophon is a registered trademark of The University of Utah Press. It is based on a four-foot-tall Ancient Puebloan pictograph (late PIII) near Glen Canyon, Utah.

Library of Congress Cataloging-in-Publication Data

Names: DeJong, David H., author.
Title: The Commissioners of Indian Affairs : the United States Indian Office and the making of federal Indian policy, 1824 to 2017/David H. DeJong.
Identifiers: LCCN 2019040614 (print) | LCCN 2019040615 (ebook) | ISBN 9781607817727 (hardcover) | ISBN 9781607817499 (paperback) | ISBN 9781607817505 (ebook)
Subjects: LCSH: United States. Office of Indian Affairs—History. | United States. Bureau of Indian Affairs—History. | Indians of North America—Government relations.
Classification: LCC E93 .D346 2020 (print) | LCC E93 (ebook) | DDC 323.1197/073—dc23
LC record available at https://lccn.loc.gov/2019040614
LC ebook record available at https://lccn.loc.gov/2019040615

Errata and further information on this and other titles available online at UofUpress.com

Printed and bound in the United States of America.

THE COMMISSIONERS OF INDIAN AFFAIRS

The United States Indian Service and the Making of Federal Indian Policy, 1824–2017

David H. DeJong

The University of Utah Press Salt Lake City

CONTENTS

TABLES

PREFACE

The Commissioners of Indian Affairs

In 1969, Vine Deloria Jr., the eminent Sioux scholar and former executive director of the National Congress of American Indians, explained that while "some Indian people want desperately to get rid of the Bureau of Indian Affairs," others preferred the bureau increase its "services to help solve problems of long-standing." This ambivalence that Native people express with regard to the Bureau of Indian Affairs is complex and complicated.[1] The commissioner of Indian affair's sole purpose, Deloria concluded in his laconic manner of writing, was "to keep the members of the Interior and Insular Affairs committees of the House and Senate happy—not to serve Indians or even to run his own bureau." Until a new ideology governed the federal-Indian relationship, the Bureau of Indians Affairs would do no better than run "on one cylinder."[2]

The United States was founded on a myth constructed on the backs of founding documents, such as the Constitution and the Bill of Rights, that protected and encouraged the acquisition of land. In this narrative, indigenous peoples were temporary impediments to American expansion. But this myth was also premised on diplomacy and treaties that, while resulting in the loss of hundreds of millions of acres, also undergirded diplomatic recognition of tribal sovereignty and aboriginal property rights.[3] American expansion across the continent was "essentially the expansion of a system of property [transfer]," an integral aspect of the federal-Indian relationship. Indeed, the United States was the first nation in history to be founded on the principle that property translated into personal liberty, an idea that buttressed and perpetuated the desire to acquire the tribal estate.[4]

For philosophers such as John Locke, private property was a natural right. The enlightenment philosophers in turn were consumed by indigenous people and their lack of private property, which they blamed for Native people's lack of cultural and personal development. With an entire continent awaiting development, philosophers searched to define a means of appropriating indigenous lands. "Before they can be of any use, or at all beneficial to any particular man," Locke reasoned, the land had to be converted to private property.[5] Since God gave the physical resources to "men in common" along with a mandate to exercise dominion over the land, there had to be a means of appropriating both land and resources for individual development to ensure personal liberty. The means of securing liberty was individual labor, which converted the common estate into private property.[6] Inherent in this enlightened thinking were the concepts of Native land alienation and non-Native appropriation, which gave substance to Chief Justice John Marshall's doctrine of discovery in the *Johnson v. M'Intosh* decision.

A parallel concept of cultural and political integration of indigenous people rivaled that of land alienation. While early colonialists assumed Natives were barbarians on the low end of civilization-savagery continuum, federal policy focused on civilization and assimilation, two sides of the same coin of integration. Federal policy was predicated on Native savagery, which rationalized land alienation. In a practical sense, philosophers and policymakers debated whether Native people were to be integrated into or removed from American society. Treaties and parallel legislation often included provisions for land severalty in an effort to deconstruct tribal social and cultural ties to the land and force Native integration. Such a policy culminated in the passage of the General Allotment Act, the great pulverizer of indigenous property. Senator Henry Dawes (D-MA), the principal author of the allotment act, expressed the contemporary view when he exclaimed Native people had gone as far as they could, "because they own their land in common."[7]

PURPOSE

My original goal with the present study was to focus on the policy emphasis of each commissioner of Indian affairs up to the mid-1960s, which corresponds with the cessation of the "Annual Report of the Commissioner of Indian Affairs." To do this, I resolved to read each of the annual reports since its inception in 1824. Three years later I finished reading all of the reports, and as I neared the end, I concluded that the narrative would not be complete unless I continued it to the present-day. Since I had committed to using the annual reports to identify and follow specific policy strands that made up larger philosophical braids, I had to find a consistent and reliable source for identifying those strands after the mid-1960s.

Between 1965 and 1969, the Bureau of Indian Affairs produced an "Annual Progress Report" that proved somewhat useful. While after 1969 there was no shortage of secondary documents, I endeavored to follow policy strands in the official writings of the commissioners. I found that source in the press releases of the Bureau of Indian Affairs, the secretary of the interior, and the office of the assistant secretary for Indian Affairs. Recognizing there was some risk in relying on these sources, I found ample ways to supplement these releases by using federal statutes, congressional reports, federal court decisions, resources from the Office of Federal Acknowledgment, and other sundry sources.

To fulfill my goal of writing a comprehensive history of federal-Indian policy based on policy strands executed and enforced by the commissioners or assistant secretaries, I looked at how such strands over time were woven into (and driven by) broader philosophical braids. I sought to be broad in my treatment of philosophical braids and specific on policy strands affecting the ability of tribal nations to govern their citizens and protect their land and natural resources. It is not my intent to analyze the impact of policy on Native people per se but to evaluate such policy on tribal nations and, indirectly, on Native peoples. The product enables one to see the ebb and flow of strands comprising the philosophical braids embedded in policy over the past two centuries.

It is my contention that the United States had two overarching philosophical (macro) braids in executing policy. The first was the social and political integration of American Indians. The manifestation of this braid over the past two and a half centuries is visible in the policy strands of civilization (1776 to 1817), emigration (1817 to 1848), reservations (1848 to 1870), assimilation (1870 to 1929), acculturation (1929 to 1950), termination (1950 to 1968), and consumerism (1969 to present). How to achieve this philosophical goal and assert the political resolve to execute it has long been the challenge. Education was the fulcrum upon which this braid rested, even as it oscillated between rapid integration as illustrated in the boarding school experience and steady acculturation as exemplified in community schools and progressive education.

The second philosophical braid is reflected in federal land policy. Gaining access to tribal land and its resources has been the core of policy from the founding of the United States. This is represented by various policy strands, including the use of treaties (1778 to 1870) or agreements (1870 to 1911) to secure land cessions; the General Allotment Act, which opened the so-called surplus lands to sale and/or homesteading (1887 to 1934); the issuance of fee patents and the corollary competency commissions, which lead to further land alienation (1890 to 1930); the removal of trust restrictions (1890 to 1960); and termination and relocation (1950 to 1968). Notwithstanding a respite during the 1930s and early 1940s, a liberalized land policy predicated on issuance of fee patents continued into the latter 1940s and 1950s when termination ended the federal trust for scores of tribes.

Into these two braids—social integration and land alienation—all other federal policy strands were woven. For instance, federal policy tethered Indian irrigation projects and land alienation via severalty and termination. Development of transportation routes in Indian Country fostered economic development and opened Indian land to natural resource development, such as timber, oil, gas, and minerals. A policy of prohibiting Natives from participating in the turn-of-the-nineteenth-century Wild West Shows was intended to ensure that Natives did not revert to barbarism. Even healthcare was integral to integration and land alienation, as the moral honor of the nation mandated that Native people be healthy in order to give them a fair chance to stand as citizens of the republic.

The United States rarely remained committed to a specific policy strand for more than a generation, especially in the postbellum years when pendulum swings regularly occurred. While the braids of integration and land alienation remained, policy strands vacillated, often following the release of a study critical of federal policy or a significant court ruling. Examples include Helen Hunt Jackson's *A Century of Dishonor* (1880), the Supreme Court's devastating ruling in *Lone Wolf v. Hitchcock* (1903), Lewis Meriam's *The Problem of Indian Administration* (1928), the Hoover Commission's "Report on the Reorganization of the Executive Branch" (1948), and the Commission on Rights, Liberties, and Responsibilities of the American Indians' "The Indians: America's Unfinished Business" (1964). These pendulum shifts were largely void of a Native perspective and rare was the solicitation of an Indian voice.

These swings were in large measure premised on the continuing moral dilemma of what to do with the Indians. While the United States Congress—the Senate in particular—was constitutionally charged with ratifying treaties negotiated by the executive branch and funding the commitments made in such treaties, Congress initiated a significant shift in 1819 with the enactment of the Civilization Act, by which the legislative branch broadened its role in Indian affairs by appropriating gratuitous funds to civilize the Indians. The act represented a substantive shift in policy and was premised on the moral obligations of the nation to actively seek the integration of Native people into the American social fabric.

As western expansion encroached into Indian Country, a new moral dilemma arose. How was the United States to deal with tribes now sequestered within or adjacent to the several states? This moral question had tangible political implications and was resolved by a policy of emigration, the foundation of which was premised on saving the Indians from extermination by relocating them west of the Mississippi River. Unfortunately, the land cession that followed the Mexican War, combined with the independence of Texas and resolution of the Oregon Territory boundary in favor of the United States, created yet another moral and political crisis—the potential extermination of the tribes, the border tribes in the path of western emigration in particular. Yet another shift in policy premised on moral considerations resulted in the reservation policy as the alternative to extinction.

The reservation policy was both essential to prevent the extermination of Native peoples—particularly in the border states—and was another moral response tethered to further reduction of the tribal estate. As the West was populated and non-Indian communities surrounded reservations, and with the depletion of game and natural resources, the nation was moved to yet another moral solution to the "Indian problem" fostered by the failure of the federal government to control its citizens. With no new western territories into which the tribes could be settled, and with a new generation of reformers reeling from a national Civil War and seeking to salve the national honor in light of recent Indian massacres, a new policy of assimilation and incorporation was born. Birthed in the initial years of the Industrial Age, this policy—in effect as a specific strand for fifty years—focused on the forced and rapid assimilation of the Natives, with its concomitant land severalty, government-sponsored education, federal criminal jurisdiction, and abolition of the Indian landed-estate policy strands.

By the 1920s, another generation of reformers, secular humanists, began advocating change away from what they perceived as immoral—and perhaps even illegal—policies that not only failed to assimilate, but also despoiled the Natives of nearly ninety million acres of tribal real estate. An era of cultural pluralism with a thinly veiled acculturative underlining manifested itself in legislative enactments such as the Indian Reorganization Act, the Johnson-O'Malley Act, the Indian Arts and Craft Act, and others.

But these policies, too, were short-lived, as in the post-World War II years a wave of nationalism and conservatism born in opposition to Soviet-style communism swept the nation and renewed the rapid push to incorporate Native peoples into the American fabric. The result was a termination policy that was as harsh as it was ill-conceived. By the time it ended in 1968, scores of tribes and tribal groups had their political relationship with the United States severed, leading to an unprecedented level of distrust in Indian Country. A nation focused on civil liberties and the rights of minorities entered a new era of secularism. Acting under the guise of cultural pluralism, this benign secular moralism was predicated on consumerism, yet subtly undermined tribal traditions and culture.

This waxing and waning of policy was undergirded by moral and, to a lesser degree, political considerations and expediency. While policy followed the broad philosophical braids of integration and gaining access to tribal land and resources, the discreet strands manifested during each period best fit national political and social ideals. The result was a vacillating policy structurally influenced by an integrative goal driven by Christian charity (pre-1920s) and secular humanism (post-1920s). With the rise of tribal activism, Native peoples in recent decades have influenced policy strands facilitating economic and social advancement. While concurrently nudging Natives closer to mainstream America, this era resulted in a great increase in the exercise of tribal sovereignty. Nonetheless, this influence has been subservient to the well-entrenched and broader federal goals of incorporation and access to tribal resources.

Each commissioner of Indian affairs or assistant secretary intellectually or politically influenced these braids and strands, some more than others. While supportive of the tribal cause, Francis Leupp and John Collier still believed that the survival of tribes required economic development and exploitation of natural resources. Others—such as Thomas J. Morgan and Dillon Myer—were committed to a policy of rapid and enforced assimilation and termination of the federal-Indian relationship. Still other commissioners, such as Elbert Herring, George Manypenny and Cato Sells, worked to free aboriginal title to as much land as possible.

Certainly, the commissioners were not the final arbiter of policy. Congress and the president directed policy strands, only occasionally deferring to the Indian Office (also known as the Indian Service or Bureau of Indian Affairs, as it has been called since 1947). Once policy was determined, the Indian Office was left to implement the details. The department, as an executive agency under the authority of the secretary of war (1789 to 1849) and the secretary of the interior (1849 to present), was ultimately directed by the president, who greatly influenced policy. President Grant's Peace Policy, for instance, shaped policy for a generation, as did Andrew Jackson's emigration policy, Franklin Roosevelt's Indian New Deal policies, Dwight Eisenhower's termination and relocation policies, and Richard Nixon's policy of self-government.

The annual reports are filled with the minutia of policy and Indian affairs. Most commissioners spelled out policy strands the president intended to enforce or emphasize, or penned intellectual thoughts regarding policy matters. The initial reports dating to the period of emigration of the tribes were relatively short, at an average of 116 pages. As the nineteenth century progressed, these reports increased in length and detail, such that during the time of land severalty and the dissolution of the Five Tribes in Indian Territory, these reports averaged 1,029 pages (with the longest at 1,500 pages). By the 1930s and 1940s, during the period of reorganization, the reports were down to 50 pages, and those in the 1950s were less than 40 pages. Following the publication of the last annual report in 1964, the Bureau of Indian Affairs prepared an "Annual Progress Report on Indian Affairs" that averaged 18 pages, as shown in Table P.1.

Since 1816, the Indian Office has been directed by one superintendent of trade, three chief clerks, forty-three commissioners, seven acting commissioners, thirteen assistant secretaries, eight acting assistant secretaries, and one assistant to the secretary. There have been forty-two different commissioners (James Denver served two nonconsecutive periods), all of whom have been men:

six American Indians and thirty-six non-Indians. As for the assistant secretary for Indian Affairs, there have been eleven men and two women, all of whom have been American Indian or Alaska Native. These Native leaders have come from Oklahoma (five), the Midwest (three), Northern Plains (two), Pacific Northwest (one), Alaska (one), and the Southwest (one). Table P.2 lists the commissioners and assistant secretaries, including those in significant acting capacities.

The commissioners and assistant secretaries served under the direction of the secretary of war (1789 to 1849) and secretary of the interior (1849 to present). Some secretaries were quite active in directing Indian affairs while others were more passive, leaving the commissioners to work out policy. These secretaries are listed in Table P.3, including their dates of service and presidential administration(s).

Table P.1. Average Length of the Annual Reports, 1824–1969

Years	Strand	Average Page Length
1824–1848	Emigration	116
1849–1860	Reservation	286
1861–1881	Consolidation	449
1882–1904	Severalty	1,029
1905–1928	Assimilation	267
1929–1948	Reorganization	50
1949–1964	Termination	37
1965–1969	Self-Determination	18

Table P.2. Heads of the Bureau of Indian Affairs, 1824–2018

Commissioners of Indian Affairs				
Name	**State/Tribe**	**Begin Date**	**End Date**	**Title**
Thomas L. McKenney	Maryland	April 12, 1816	May 6, 1822	Supt. of Trade
Thomas L. McKenney	Maryland	March 12, 1824	August 16, 1830	Chief Clerk
Samuel S. Hamilton	Maryland	September 30, 1830	August 31, 1831	Chief Clerk
Elbert Herring	New York	August 12, 1831	July 10, 1832	Chief Clerk
1. Elbert Herring	New York	July 10, 1832	July 2, 1836	Commissioner
2. Carey Allen Harris	Tennessee	July 4, 1836	October 19, 1838	Commissioner
3. Thomas Crawford	Pennsylvania	October 22, 1838	October 29, 1845	Commissioner
4. William Medill	Ohio	October 29, 1845	June 30, 1849	Commissioner
5. Orlando Brown	Kentucky	June 30, 1849	July 1, 1850	Commissioner
6. Luke Lea	Mississippi	July 1, 1850	March 24, 1853	Commissioner
7. George Manypenny	Ohio	March 28, 1853	March 31, 1857	Commissioner
8. James W. Denver	California	April 17, 1857	December 2, 1857	Commissioner
9. Charles E. Mix	Connecticut	June 4, 1858	November 1, 1858	Commissioner
10. James W. Denver	California	November 9, 1858	March 12, 1859	Commissioner
11. Alfred B. Greenwood	Arkansas	May 4, 1859	April 16, 1861	Commissioner
12. William P. Dole	Vermont	March 12, 1861	July 6, 1865	Commissioner
13. Dennis N. Cooley	Iowa	July 9, 1865	November 1, 1866	Commissioner

Table P.2. Heads of the Bureau of Indian Affairs, 1824–2018 (*cont'd*)

Name	State/Tribe	Begin Date	End Date	Title
14. Lewis V. Bogy*	Missouri	November 1, 1866	March 4, 1867	Commissioner
15. Nathaniel G. Taylor	Tennessee	March 29, 1867	April 23, 1869	Commissioner
16. Eli S. Parker	Seneca Tribe	April 23, 1869	July 24, 1871	Commissioner
Henry R. Clum		July 24, 1871	November 20, 1871	Acting Commissioner
17. Francis A. Walker	Massachusetts	November 21, 1871	December 26, 1872	Commissioner
18. Edward P. Smith	Connecticut	March 17, 1873	December 11, 1875	Commissioner
19. John Q. Smith	Ohio	December 11, 1875	September 27, 1877	Commissioner
20. Ezra A. Hayt	New York	September 20, 1877	January 29, 1880	Commissioner
21. Roland E. Trowbridge	Michigan	March 2, 1880	March 19, 1881	Commissioner
Henry R. Clum		March 19, 1881	April 14, 1881	Acting Commissioner
22. Hiram Price	Iowa	May 6, 1881	March 21, 1885	Commissioner
23. John D. C. Atkins	Tennessee	March 21, 1885	June 14, 1888	Commissioner
24. John H. Oberly	Illinois	October 10, 1888	June 30, 1889	Commissioner
25. Thomas J. Morgan	Indiana	July 1, 1889	March 1, 1893	Commissioner
26. Daniel M. Browning	Illinois	April 18, 1893	May 3, 1897	Commissioner
27. William A. Jones	Wisconsin	May 3, 1897	January 1, 1905	Commissioner
28. Francis E. Leupp	New York	January 1, 1905	June 18, 1909	Commissioner
29. Robert G. Valentine	Massachusetts	June 19, 1909	September 10, 1912	Commissioner
Frederick H. Abbott		September 10, 1912	June 4, 1913	Acting Commissioner
30. Cato Sells	Iowa	June 4, 1913	March 29, 1921	Commissioner
31. Charles H. Burke	South Dakota	May 7, 1921	March 9, 1929	Commissioner
32. Charles J. Rhoads	Pennsylvania	July 1, 1929	April 20, 1933	Commissioner
33. John Collier	Georgia	April 21, 1933	March 5, 1945	Commissioner
34. William A. Brophy	New Mexico	March 6, 1945	June 3, 1948	Commissioner
William R. Zimmermann		June 3, 1948	March 10, 1949	Acting Commissioner
35. John R. Nichols*	New York	April 1, 1949	May 4, 1950	Commissioner
36. Dillon S. Myer	Ohio	May 5, 1950	March 19, 1953	Commissioner
W. Barton Greenwood		March 20, 1953	July 28, 1953	Acting Commissioner
37. Glenn L. Emmons	New Mexico	August 10, 1953	January 7, 1961	Commissioner
John O. Crow	Cherokee	January 7, 1961	July 31, 1961	Acting Commissioner
38. Philleo Nash	Wisconsin	September 26, 1961	March 15, 1966	Commissioner
39. Robert L. Bennett	Oneida	April 27, 1966	May 31, 1969	Commissioner
40. Louis R. Bruce	Oglala Sioux	August 8, 1969	January 20, 1973	Commissioner
Marvin L. Franklin	Iowa	February 7, 1973	December 4, 1974	Assistant to the Secretary
41. Morris Thompson	Athabascan	December 4, 1973	November 3, 1976	Commissioner
42. Benjamin Reifel*	Rosebud Sioux	December 7, 1976	January 28, 1977	Commissioner
Raymond Butler		January 28, 1977	September 19, 1977	Acting Commissioner
43. William E. Hallett	Red Lake Chippewa	December 14, 1979	January 20, 1981	Commissioner

Assistant Secretaries for Indian Affairs

Name	State/Tribe	Begin Date	End Date	Title
1. Forrest Gerard	Blackfeet	September 19, 1977	January 19, 1980	Assistant Secretary
2. Thomas Fredericks	Mandan-Hidatsa	June 18, 1980	January 20, 1981	Assistant Secretary
3. Kenneth L. Smith	Wasco	April 28, 1981	December 7, 1984	Assistant Secretary
4. Ross O. Swimmer	Cherokee	December 4, 1985	January 29, 1989	Assistant Secretary
William Ragsdale	Cherokee	January 29, 1989	June 20, 1989	Acting Assistant Secretary
5. Eddie Frank Brown	Yaqui	June 21, 1989	July 15, 1993	Assistant Secretary
6. Ada E. Deer	Menominee	July 16, 1993	November 9, 1997	Assistant Secretary
7. Kevin Gover	Pawnee	November 12, 1997	January 3, 2001	Assistant Secretary
James H. McDivitt		January 20, 2001	July 3, 2001	Acting Assistant Secretary

Table P.2. Heads of the Bureau of Indian Affairs, 1824–2018 (*cont'd*)

Name	State/Tribe	Begin Date	End Date	Title
8. Neal A. McCaleb	Chickasaw	July 4, 2001	December 31, 2002	Assistant Secretary
Aurene M. Martin	Bad River Chippewa	January 6, 2003	February 2, 2004	Acting Assistant Secretary
9. David A. Anderson	Lac Court Oreille Chippewa	February 2, 2004	February 12, 2005	Assistant Secretary
Jim Cason		February 12, 2005	March 5, 2007	Acting Assistant Secretary
10. Carl J. Artman	Oneida	March 8, 2007	May 23, 2008	Assistant Secretary
George T. Skibone	Osage	May 23, 2008	January 20, 2009	Acting Assistant Secretary
11. Larry J. Echo Hawk	Pawnee	May 22, 2009	April 27, 2012	Assistant Secretary
Donald Laverdure	Crow	April 27, 2012	October 9, 2012	Acting Assistant Secretary
12. Kevin K. Washburn	Chickasaw	October 9, 2012	January 1, 2016	Assistant Secretary
Lawrence S. Roberts	Oneida	January 1, 2016	January 20, 2017	Acting Assistant Secretary
Michael S. Black*	Oglala Sioux	January 20, 2017	June 28, 2018	Acting Assistant Secretary
13. Tara Maclean Sweeney	Inupiat	June 28, 2018		Assistant Secretary

* Not confirmed by the Senate

Table P.3. Secretaries of War and Interior, 1789–2017

Secretaries of War				
Name	**State**	**Start Date**	**End Date**	**President(s)**
Henry Knox	Massachusetts	September 12, 1789	December 31, 1794	Washington
Timothy Pickering	Massachusetts	January 2, 1795	December 10, 1795	Washington
James McHenry	Maryland	January 27, 1796	May 13, 1800	Adams
Samuel Dexter	Massachusetts	May 13, 1800	January 31, 1801	Adams
Henry Dearborn	New Hampshire	March 5, 1801	March 7, 1809	Jefferson
William Eustis	Massachusetts	March 7, 1809	January 13, 1813	Madison
John Armstrong	Pennsylvania	January 13, 1813	September 27, 1814	Madison
James Monroe	Virginia	September 27, 1814	March 2, 1815	Madison
William Harris Crawford	Virginia	August 1, 1815	October 22, 1816	Madison
John Caldwell Calhoun	South Carolina	October 8, 1817	March 7, 1825	Monroe/Adams
James Barbour	Virginia	March 7, 1825	May 23, 1828	Adams
Peter Buell Porter	Connecticut	May 26, 1828	March 9, 1829	Adams
John Henry Eaton	North Carolina	March 9, 1829	June 18, 1831	Jackson
Lewis Cass	New Hampshire	August 1, 1831	October 5, 1836	Jackson
Joel Roberts Poinsett	South Carolina	March 7, 1837	March 5, 1841	Van Buren
John Bell	Tennessee	March 5, 1841	September 13, 1841	Harrison
John Canfield Spencer	New York	October 12, 1841	March 3, 1843	Tyler
James Madison Porter	Pennsylvania	March 8, 1843	January 30, 1844	Tyler
William Wilkins	Pennsylvania	February 15, 1844	March 4, 1845	Tyler/Polk
William Learned Marcy	Massachusetts	March 6, 1845	March 4, 1849	Polk

Secretaries of the Interior				
Name	**State**	**Start Date**	**End Date**	**President(s)**
Thomas Ewing	Ohio	March 8, 1849	July 22, 1850	Taylor/Fillmore
Thomas McKean	Pennsylvania	August 15, 1850	August 26, 1850	Fillmore
Alexander H. H. Stuart	Virginia	September 16, 1850	March 7, 1853	Fillmore
Robert McClellan	Michigan	March 8, 1853	March 9, 1857	Pierce
Jacob Thompson	Mississippi	March 10, 1857	January 8, 1861	Buchanan
Caleb B. Smith	Indiana	March 5, 1861	December 31, 1862	Lincoln

Table P.3. Secretaries of War and Interior, 1789–2017 (*cont'd*)

Name	State	Start Date	End Date	President(s)
John B. Usher	Indiana	January 1, 1863	May 15, 1865	Lincoln/Johnson
James Harlan	Iowa	May 16, 1865	August 31, 1866	Johnson
Orville H. Brown	Illinois	September 1, 1866	March 11, 1869	Johnson
Jacob D. Cox	Ohio	March 5, 1869	October 31, 1870	Grant
Columbus Delano	Ohio	November 1, 1870	September 30, 1875	Grant
Zachariah Chandler	Michigan	October 19, 1875	March 11, 1877	Grant
Carl Schurz	Missouri	March 12, 1877	March 7, 1881	Hayes
Samuel L. Kirkland	Iowa	March 8, 1881	April 17, 1882	Garfield
Henry M. Teller	Colorado	April 18, 1882	March 3, 1885	Arthur
Lucius Q. C. Lamar	Missouri	March 6, 1885	January 10, 1888	Cleveland
William F. Villas	Wisconsin	January 16, 1888	March 6, 1889	Cleveland
John W. Noble	Missouri	March 7, 1889	March 6, 1893	Harrison
Michael H. Smith	Georgia	March 6, 1893	September 1, 1896	Cleveland
David R. Francis	Missouri	September 3, 1896	March 5, 1897	Cleveland
Cornelius N. Bliss	New York	March 6, 1897	February 19, 1899	McKinley
Ethan Allen Hitchcock	Missouri	February 20, 1899	March 4, 1907	McKinley/Roosevelt
James R. Garfield	Ohio	March 5, 1907	March 5, 1909	Roosevelt
Richard A. Ballinger	Washington	March 6, 1909	March 12, 1911	Taft
Walter L. Fisher	Illinois	April 17, 1911	March 5, 1913	Taft
Franklin K. Lane	California	March 6, 1913	February 29, 1920	Wilson
John B. Payne	Illinois	March 15, 1920	March 4, 1921	Wilson
Albert B. Fall	New Mexico	March 5, 1921	March 4, 1923	Harding
Hubert Work	Colorado	March 5, 1923	July 24, 1928	Coolidge
Roy O. West	Illinois	July 25, 1928	March 4, 1929	Coolidge
Ray Lyman Wilbur	California	March 5, 1929	March 4, 1933	Hoover
Harold L. Ickes	Illinois	March 4, 1933	February 15, 1946	Roosevelt/Truman
Julius D. Krug	Wisconsin	March 18, 1946	December 1, 1949	Truman
Oscar L. Chapman	Colorado	December 1, 1949	January 20, 1953	Truman
Douglas McKay	Oregon	January 21, 1953	April 15, 1956	Eisenhower
Fred A. Seaton	Nebraska	June 8, 1956	January 20, 1961	Eisenhower
Stewart L. Udall	Arizona	January 20, 1961	January 20, 1969	Kennedy/Johnson
Walter J. Hickel	Alaska	January 24, 1969	November 25, 1970	Nixon
Rogers C. B. Morton	Maryland	January 29, 1971	April 30, 1975	Nixon/Ford
Stanley K. Hathaway	Wyoming	June 12, 1975	October 9, 1975	Ford
Thomas S. Kleppe	North Dakota	October 17, 1975	January 20, 1977	Ford
Cecil D. Andrus	Idaho	January 23, 1977	January 20, 1981	Carter
James G. Watt	Colorado	January 23, 1981	November 8, 1983	Reagan
William P. Clark	California	November 18, 1983	February 7, 1985	Reagan
Donald P. Hodel	Oregon	February 8, 1985	January 20, 1989	Reagan
Manuel Lujan, Jr.	New Mexico	February 3, 1989	January 20, 1993	Bush
Bruce Babbitt	Arizona	January 22, 1993	January 2, 2001	Clinton
Gale A. Norton	Colorado	January 31, 2001	March 31, 2006	Bush
Dirk Kempthorne	Idaho	May 29, 2006	January 19, 2009	Bush
Ken Salazar	Colorado	January 20, 2009	April 12, 2013	Obama
Sally Jewell	Washington	April 12, 2013	January 20, 2017	Obama
Ryan Zinke	Montana	March 1, 2017	January 2, 2019	Trump
David Bernhardt	Virginia	April 11, 2019	——	Trump

1

ABORIGINAL INDIAN TITLE

The Meaning of Indian Country

Tribal sovereignty and the breadth of its application have been the topic of jurists and political theorists since the first European settler-states arrived in the Americas.[1] This discussion is no less passionate today, both within and without Indian Country, with the pendulum on the side of limited tribal sovereignty since the 1970s.[2] In recent decades, tribal nations have attempted to overcome the deleterious braids of two centuries of federal policy as executed by the U.S. Indian Service. This effort at nation-building has centered on rebuilding governing abilities and reacquiring land via purchase or legislative settlements. As tribes have placed land into federal trust, state and local governments have expressed concern over the extension of tribal jurisdiction, the exercise of which can have far reaching effects. These ramifications have social, economic, and political consequences for state, local, and tribal governments.

Since the 1990s, there have been challenges by local governments seeking to restrict the ability of the secretary of the interior to take newly acquired tribal land into trust.[3] These attempts to thwart land-into-trust were rejected by the Tenth Circuit Court in 2005 and the Eighth Circuit Court in 2007, but have not been brought before the Supreme Court for a definitive ruling.[4] In some cases, Congress has placed restrictions on newly acquired Native land by preventing its placement into federal trust status.[5] In other cases, the Department of Interior has frustrated this process. In 1998, the Shakopee Mdewakanton Sioux purchased 593 acres of aboriginal land near Minneapolis, Minnesota, and sought to place it in federal trust. Interior, concerned over jurisdictional, economic development, zoning, and political implications, denied the Shakopee's request.[6] Without trust status, the land remains subject to state and local taxation and jurisdiction.

FOUNDATION OF TRIBAL POLITICAL EXISTENCE

Nearly four hundred treaties between the United States and tribal nations recognized the territorial limits and sovereignty of the tribes. While scores of treaties resulted in land cessions and restrictions of enumerated political rights and authorities, such treaties were also recognition of tribal sovereignty. For instance, in *United States v. Winans*, the Supreme Court in 1904 examined Yakima fishing rights, holding that the tribe retained all rights not expressly surrendered via treaty.[7] While acknowledging that the external sovereignty of tribal nations has been curtailed, internal sovereignty—unless expressly restricted via treaty, act of Congress, or judicial interpretation—remains inviolate. Treaty scholar Vine Deloria Jr. explained that the "promise of self-government found in a multitude of treaties, the promises of protection by the United States from wrongs committed by its citizens, the promise that the tribes would be respected as nations on whose behalf the United States acted as a trustee before the eyes of the world, were all vital parts of the treaty rights which Indians believe they have received from the United States."[8]

Early in the federal-Indian relationship the United States acknowledged the governing authority of tribal nations. In *Johnson v. M'Intosh*, Chief Justice John Marshall concluded that European settlement of North America did not extinguish tribal sovereignty although it had "to a considerable extent" truncated it.[9] While impairing this sovereignty, the United States brought tribal nations under a protectorate, later described as a trust, relationship.[10] The 1804 Sac and Fox treaty with the United States illustrates this association. Under article 1 of the treaty, the tribes agreed to accept the protection of the United States and limit their political dealings with other foreign nations: "The United States receive the united Sac and Fox Tribes into their friendship and protection, and the said tribes agree to consider themselves under the protection of the United States, and of no other power whatsoever."[11] The Sac and Fox accepted a limitation of their economic and political intercourse with Great Britain in the old Northwest and agreed to compact exclusively with the United States in exchange for such protection.

Chief Justice Marshall, in the 1831–1832 Cherokee Nation cases, further characterized the extent of tribal sovereignty and delineated the basis of the federal trust relationship. While treaties provided the Cherokee Nation with the "protection of the United States," as a weaker political power the Cherokee Nation did "not surrender its independence—its right to self-government—by associating with a stronger and taking its protection."[12] Moreover, the court recognized the continuing political relationship between the United States and the Cherokee Nation—and by extension all tribal nations—as that of a "domestic, dependent nation."[13] Combined, the Cherokee cases form the theoretical underpinning of federal authority.

The internal sovereignty of tribal nations has always been carefully safeguarded by indigenous people and prior to 1819 was nearly inviolate. Then, Congress elected to modify its role in Indian affairs from a constitutionally mandated role of ratifying treaties (Senate) and appropriating funds to implement such treaties (House and Senate) to civilizing tribes by making gratuitous appropriations. Originally, prior to 1850, the only limitation on the internal authority of tribes was in their relationship with non-Indians.[14] Subsequent to 1850, treaties protected the internal

Table 1.1. Ten Largest Indian Reservations in the United States

Tribe	State	Size (in acres)
Navajo	Arizona, New Mexico, Utah	15,432,170
Tohono O'odham	Arizona	2,774,170
Pine Ridge (Sioux)	South Dakota	2,064,507
Cheyenne River (Sioux)	South Dakota	2,023,389
San Carlos (Apache)	Arizona	1,826,541
Wind River (Shoshone)	Wyoming	1,811,365
Fort Apache	Arizona	1,664,972
Hopi	Arizona	1,561,213
Crow	Montana	1,516,005
Standing Rock (Sioux)	North/South Dakota	1,248,334

Source: Getches, Wilkinson, and Williams, *Cases and Materials on Federal-Indian Law*, 1993.

authority of tribal nations over person and place, but federal legislation methodically restricted this jurisdiction with statutes such as the General Crimes Act (1854), Major Crimes Act (1885), General Allotment Act (1887), Assimilative Crimes Act (1898), Public Law 280 (1953), and the Indian Civil Rights Act (1968).[15] Despite such limitations, tribal nations remain distinct political communities with full rights of self-government.

Even where the United States extended authority over enumerated criminal acts in Indian Country, this jurisdiction is *concurrent* to that of tribal nations.[16] And while the United States asserts authority to intervene in certain tribal affairs, it has generally recognized the internal sovereignty of the tribes, although not always consistently. The rule remains: unless limited by treaty or a specific act of Congress, tribal nations are free of any state authority.

INDIAN COUNTRY

Although tribes granted enumerated rights and privileges to the United States, they reserved those not specifically relinquished. These rights, responsibilities, and privileges are exercised within Indian Country, a term that has legal as well as geographical expressions beyond the fact that it defines the territory still owned and governed by tribal nations. Collectively, tribal nations control 56.6 million acres of land in the United States, not including nearly 45 million acres owned by Alaska Natives.[17] Table 1.1 lists the ten largest tribal nations geographically, with five of these tribal reservations in Arizona. The Navajo Nation, at nearly 15.5 million acres, is the largest reservation in the United States, making it larger than nine eastern states, including West Virginia.

Despite restrictive legislative policies and judicial limitations on their ability to govern their territory and people, tribal nations are asserting a greater degree of sovereignty today than at any time in the past century. Consequently, an understanding of Indian Country and an examination of the federal-Indian law that governs it may be more pertinent today than ever before.[18] As tribal nations exercise and reassert authority, it is instructive to recognize what is and is not Indian

Table 1.2. Nine States with the Most Tribal Land in Acres

State	Indian Land (in acres)	Percentage of State
Arizona	20,178,234	27.7
New Mexico	8,152,895	10.5
Montana	5,551,343	5.9
South Dakota	4,522,325	9.2
Washington	2,568,791	5.6
Utah	2,319,373	4.3
Nebraska	2,185,211	4.4
Wyoming	2,010,928	3.2
Nevada	1,230,563	1.7

Source: Tiller, *American Indian Reservations and Trust Areas*, 1996.

Country, since it is in Indian Country that we find the effects of federal policy strands and philosophical braids. Over the course of the federal-Indian relationship, a body of jurisprudence has developed, a corpus of which is "founded in the political relationship between the United States and the tribal nations."[19] This corpus is not only rich and diverse but it is also dynamic, as tribes engage in nation-building and asseverate their inherent rights of self-government. Table 1.2 lists the states with the largest acreage of Indian Country where tribal nations are asserting sovereignty.

WHAT IS AN INDIAN TRIBE?

The federal judiciary has repeatedly held that Congress and the president have constitutional authority to determine whether or not a tribal nation and its territory is formally recognized and legally exists.[20] This authority is premised on the commerce clause of the United States Constitution, which states that Congress has the authority to "regulate Commerce ... with the Indian Tribes."[21] Consequently, Congress recognizes some tribal nations as political sovereigns but not others.[22] In large measure this stems from whether or not the United States has had a political relationship with a tribe, although in other cases it may result from specific federal statutes or congressional policies.

There is no single statute that defines what an indigenous tribe is, with some tribal groups composed of multiple tribal nations that resulted from the federal government consolidating tribes for purposes of administration or where war-decimated tribes joined together. The Oneida Indian Nation, for instance, took in a number of remnant tribes after the American Revolution, including the Brotherton, Stockbridge, and others. In other cases, such as at the Wind River (Wyoming) Indian Reservation (home to the Eastern Shoshone and Northern Arapaho Tribes), the federal government encouraged consolidation. The Salish and Kootenai (Montana) Tribes on the Flathead Indian Reservation are treated by the United States as a single administrative unit. The Gila River (Arizona) Indian Reservation, likewise, is home to the confederated Pima and Maricopa

Tribes who share a single governing body. While the United States amalgamated the tribes on the Flathead Reservation, on the Gila River Reservation the tribes voluntarily confederated together more than half a century before the United States annexed their territory via the Mexican Cession and Gadsden Purchase.

The United States also recognized some tribal nations in smaller administrative units called bands, usually in cases where a tribe held vast expanses of territory across multiple states. The Chippewa, for example, are scattered across two dozen reservations and communities from Michigan to Montana. The Sioux, made up of consanguineous bands, were administratively divided in the latter nineteenth century into more than half a dozen reservations, with each considered by the United States as a separate tribe for governing and administrative purposes.

The land held by federally recognized tribes and tribal members constitutes Indian Country, a term statutorily defined as the geographic area over which tribal nations exercise limited jurisdiction.[23] Indian Country is also the territorial base over which the United States government has a measure of control via treaties or statutory enactments and the federal trust responsibility. State and local governments have no authority in Indian Country unless specifically granted by treaty or act of Congress. The most egregious conveyance of state jurisdiction came via Public Law 280 (1953), by which Congress granted the states of California, Nebraska, Minnesota (except Red Lake), Oregon (except Warm Springs), and Wisconsin criminal and civil jurisdiction over Indian Country. Public Law 280 ran counter to the long-standing precedent of no state jurisdiction as prescribed in *Worcester v. Georgia*.[24] In 1958, Congress granted Alaska jurisdiction over Alaska Native communities within that state.[25]

ABORIGINAL TITLE

Tribal nations retain aboriginal title to their territory, meaning they are the original owners of the land with rights that are immemorial. They also hold land founded on their inherent sovereignty. The definition of Indian Country, however, applies only to federally recognized tribes and reservations and includes "all land within the limits of any Indian reservation under the jurisdiction of the United States Government, notwithstanding the issuance of any patent and, including rights-of-way running through the reservation."[26] Indian Country is further defined as "all dependent Indian communities within the borders of the United States whether within the original or subsequently acquired territory thereof, and whether within or without the limits of a State."[27] Moreover, it includes "all Indian allotments, the Indian titles to which have not been extinguished, including rights-of-way running through the same."[28]

During the U.S. tribal treaty period (1778–1871), there were three vehicles by which Native land was acknowledged. The first was formal recognition of aboriginal title, which was acknowledged in the first treaty the United States entered into with a tribal nation. In the September 1778 treaty with the Delaware Tribe, the United States made a clear and unambiguous endorsement of aboriginal title, guaranteeing "to the aforesaid nation of Delawares, and their heirs, all their territorial rights in the fullest and most ample manner, as it hath been bounded by former treaties."[29] Most treaties prior to 1850 included a similar admission of aboriginal title.

The second means of recognition came via the exchange of tribal lands. Numerous treaties acknowledged aboriginal ownership but required tribes to cede aboriginal territory for other land in the process. The removal treaties of the 1810s to 1840s are characteristic of this type of territorial validation. The Delaware removal treaty of 1818, for instance, called for the cession of all Delaware tribal land in Indiana and provided in-lieu land "upon the west side of the Mississippi" for the tribe.[30] The United States recognized these exchanged lands in the West as Delaware lands but demanded the tribe cede all of its aboriginal lands in Indiana in the process.

In similar fashion, the Choctaw removal treaty of 1830 called for the exchange of aboriginal Choctaw land in Mississippi and Alabama for in-lieu territory in the West. Article 2 of the Treaty of Dancing Rabbit Creek obligated "the President of the U.S. [to] cause to be conveyed to the Choctaw Nation a tract of country west of the Mississippi River, in fee simple to them and their descendants."[31] The Choctaw treaty, as with the Cherokee, Creek, and Chickasaw removal treaties, was unique in that the tribe not only had its aboriginal rights to the land recognized, but it also secured fee simple title to the land.[32]

The territory tribal nations reserved after ceding their aboriginal lands to the United States became the basis of Indian reservations. Article 2 of the 1818 Wea treaty provided that "The said Wea tribe of Indians reserve to themselves the following described tract of land." The accord then spelled out the boundary of the reservation, noting that the land would be held "by the said tribe as Indian reservations are usually held."[33] It is instructive that treaties recognized and guaranteed tribal ownership and possession of reserved lands, with tribes acknowledged as the rightful owners. By virtue of these "reserved" lands, tribes not only retained inherent rights of self-government and control over their land but also possessed sovereign authority over the resources of the land. These lands are the basis of the legal term Indian Country.

During the 1850s this definition of reserved land began to change, with reservations including lands set aside by acts of Congress as homelands for "tribal" Indians. On February 28, 1859, for instance, Congress recognized "a tract of land not to exceed 100 square miles" as a reservation for the Pima Tribe in Arizona, protecting and recognizing aboriginal Pima rights to the land upon which their villages and agricultural fields were located.[34]

A third means by which tribal lands were recognized was through the purchase of lands on behalf of a tribe, an action typically accomplished by act of Congress, presidential executive order, or a combination of these mechanisms. Many of the California rancherias, for instance, were purchased under the authority granted to the secretary of the interior by Congress under the provisions of the Indian Reorganization Act of 1934.[35] In 1930, the Supreme Court opined that land purchased on behalf of Native people was legally identical to an Indian reservation established by treaty, with both considered Indian Country.[36]

Some reservations were created or expanded by presidential executive order. The Pima Reservation in Arizona, for instance, was enlarged from its original 64,000 acres to its current 372,930 acres by a series of executive orders. The executive order issued by President Hayes in June 1879 both enlarged the Gila River (Pima-Maricopa) Indian Reservation and created the Salt River (Pima-Maricopa) Indian Reservation.[37] More than 23 million acres of Indian Country were set aside by executive order between 1855 and 1919, when Congress proscribed the practice of executive order reservations.[38]

Tribal property rights in executive order reservations mirror those on reservations recognized by treaty or act of Congress. In most cases, Congress confirmed Indian title in executive order reservations by enacting legislation for that purpose. In other cases, Congress used the power of the purse to implicitly recognize aboriginal title by continuing to fund services. In either case, reservations include lands reserved by treaty, set aside by act of Congress, or withdrawn from the public domain by presidential executive order. In instances where reservations were opened to homesteading, and if Congress did not intentionally and unambiguously disestablish the opened land from the reservation, all land—whether owned by tribal or nontribal landowners—remains part of the reservation.[39]

DEPENDENT INDIAN COMMUNITIES

The Pueblos of New Mexico, whose ownership of land was confirmed by Spanish land grants issued in the sixteenth and seventeenth centuries, fit the definition of "dependent Indian communities," which are not reservations in the traditional sense but are Indian Country nonetheless. In 1913, the Supreme Court stated that even though tribal land historically had been reserved by treaty, act of Congress, or executive order, there were other types of land that could meet the definition of Indian Country.[40] The federal courts have also held that a dependent community may include landless tribal communities that show dependence on the United States or that owned land that was once part of a reservation but later disestablished and subsequently reacquired.

A number of Native people also hold trust patents to public domain land allotments owned in severalty but with title held in trust by the United States. These allotments are outside the boundaries of a reservation and, therefore, differ from reservation allotments individual Natives received under the provisions of the General Allotment Act, which were made with the intent of dissolving the Indian political base by dividing the tribal estate in severalty. These trust allotments range in size from a handful of acres to several hundred acres and typically date to an 1875 federal statute allowing Natives to homestead on the public domain.[41] While the 1875 act allowed individuals who left their tribal existence to select an allotment, an 1884 statute authorized any Native to select an allotment under the provisions of the Homestead Act.[42] These allotments were placed in a twenty-five-year federal trust, with the land exempt from taxation, sale, or collateral for the duration of the trust period. Many of these allotment restrictions were extended by the president and/or then became permanent under the Indian Reorganization Act. While they are geographically scattered, these allotments remain Indian Country.

Reservations, dependent communities, and land allotments all constitute Indian Country. State reservations, which exist primarily in the eastern United States, are not statutorily Indian Country for purposes of federal law, although they are homelands for specific tribal groups.

The territory of these nonfederally recognized tribes are not part of Indian Country since the United States does not recognize their political existence and does not maintain a government-to-government relationship vis-à-vis these tribes or tribal groups.[43] While these tribes may be eligible to receive services from the state as a result of such state recognition, they do not receive social, educational, and health services or enjoy trust protection from the United States. Some of these individual Native peoples, however, may be eligible to apply for federal programs made available to American Indians, whether or not they are members of a federally recognized tribe.[44]

Indian Country, as a specific legally defined geographic area, affords reservation-based Native people rights that other Americans may not enjoy, rights that are based on their tribe's political relationship with the United States. As a result, a number of grassroots organizations have sprung up to oppose the concept of Indian Country. Citizen groups have recently organized in upstate New York to oppose the extension of tribal land and the exercise of tribal sovereignty over former reservation land because they perceive both as the "enemy of democracy."[45] Other citizen groups have opposed treaty rights, particularly hunting and fishing rights, believing tribal nations and tribal lands constitute a form of segregationist racism.[46] These groups fail to recognize that tribal nations are distinct political groups that have rights recognized and protected by treaty, statute, judicial ruling, and the U.S. Constitution, notwithstanding the vacillations in the strands of federal-Indian policy over the past two and a half centuries.

OKLAHOMA

Tribal nations in the former Indian Territory (Oklahoma) represent a unique situation. Commencing after the War of 1812, the United States began removing tribal nations from the East and Southeast into Indian Territory, pledging that neither the United States nor any state or territory would ever interfere in their affairs.[47] In the antebellum period, the Cherokee, Choctaw, Chickasaw, Creek, and Seminole Tribes were removed by treaty to Indian Territory, where they were succeeded by scores of tribes, including the Shawnee, Quapaw, Delaware, Pottawatomie, Kaskaskia, Sac and Fox, and Iowa. In the post-Civil War years, Congress used Reconstruction treaties to reduce the size of these reservations and relocated a number of western tribes into the territory, including the Modoc, Pawnee, Ponca, Comanche, Cheyenne, Arapaho, and Apache. Treaties executed just after the Civil War further reduced the territory of the tribes and, in 1889, the federal government severed the western portion of the territory from the eastern, creating Oklahoma Territory and opening it to non-Indian settlement.[48]

Prior to 1889, all of Indian Territory (except the panhandle) was considered Indian Country. Beginning that year and continuing into the early twentieth century, the United States forced tribal nations within the territory to accept agreements mandating land severalty, with all so-called surplus land sold to non-Indians and opened to settlement via the infamous Oklahoma land runs.[49] As the territory was settled by non-Indians, Congress abolished tribal governments and reservations, with allotments held in trust for twenty-five years. In time, many of these allotments were alienated due to taxation, mortgage foreclosure, fraud, or sale.[50]

The tribal nations in Oklahoma, however, continued to possess inherent rights of self-government and were never divested of their sovereignty. While a majority of the lands that were once part of their reservations are no longer Indian Country, the tribes, especially after the 1960s, exercised a level of jurisdiction over their remaining lands, most of which is owned by individual tribal citizens and held in fee simple by the descendants of the original allottees. Some of these individually owned tracts remain in trust or restricted status, meeting the definition of Indian Country.[51] As a result of severalty and the opening of reservations to homesteading, Indian Country within the state is checkerboarded, with tribes or individual tribal citizens owning scattered parcels of trust or restricted land. While the reservations no longer exist (except the Osage mineral reservation), the tribal nations exercise jurisdiction over these remaining parcels, but only if they are trust or tribal land.[52]

ALASKA NATIVES

The circumstances in Alaska differ from those of Oklahoma and the rest of the country. In Alaska, the United States recognized only a handful of tribal reservations with one—the Metlakatla Reserve on Annette Island—created by an act of Congress and eleven established by presidential executive order.[53] While there are "Indians" in Alaska (Athabaskan, Haida, Tlingit, and Tshimshian), the majority of the aboriginal people are Aleut and Inuit (Eskimo), although all Alaska Natives possess the legal status of American Indians. The United States government did not execute any treaties with Alaska Natives.

The United States did not recognize reservations in Alaska in large measure because the territory was so remote and non-Natives so few, limiting conflict over the land. In 1884, Congress established a territorial government with the Organic Act providing that no Alaska Native was to be "disturbed in the possession of any lands actually in their use or occupation or now claimed by them."[54] The act did not recognize land ownership but simply acknowledged aboriginal title.[55] When Alaska was admitted to the union in 1959, the Alaska Statehood Act prohibited anyone or entity from acquiring land "held by any Indians, Eskimos or Aleuts."[56] The statute expressly disclaimed any right the state might have to territory that "may be held" by Alaska Natives.

The discovery of oil on the North Slope hastened the matter of determining Alaska Native-owned lands. In 1971, after years of negotiation, Alaska Natives and the federal government agreed to a comprehensive land claims settlement act.[57] The Alaska Native Claims Settlement Act (ANCSA) identified Alaska Native-owned and occupied lands, compensated Alaska Natives for any land they might have lost, and allowed for the exploration and development of mineral resources by oil exploration companies.

The ANCSA also modified the relationship between Alaska Natives and the United States, but rather than creating reservations, the United States conveyed fee simple title to 40 million acres of land to village and regional corporations.[58] Individual Alaska Natives were issued stock in the corporations, thereby becoming shareholders in the regional corporations as well as in their individual village corporation. The amount of land each of the Alaska Native villages received was proportionate to the population of each. Villages with an enrollment between twenty-five and ninety-nine people could select 69,120 acres of land, while larger villages received increased acreage.[59] While the villages own the land and the surface features, the regional corporations own the subsurface minerals and oversee several dozen villages within the regional corporation's jurisdiction.

Title to the land received by Alaska Natives is in fee simple, but there are restrictions against alienation. Decisions by an Alaskan Native corporation to sell land do not require Department of Interior approval and there is no trust responsibility, although the federal restriction on the alienation of corporate stock suggests a continuing federal obligation. Despite the fact that Alaska Natives are "American Indians" for purposes of federal-Indian law—and their lands constitute dependent Indian communities—it is unsettled whether Alaska Native lands are Indian Country for purposes of law.[60]

TERMINATION

In the post-World War II years, Congress moved to terminate the government-to-government relationship and federal responsibility and involvement with Native people and nations. As early as 1944, Congress considered plans to end the federal-Indian relationship with some tribes and, two years later, enacted into law the Indian Claims Commission Act to settle outstanding tribal claims against the United States.[61] In 1947, Assistant Commissioner of Indian Affairs William Zimmerman categorized tribes into three groups based on the Bureau of Indian Affairs's (BIA) perception of those that were ready for withdrawal of federal services, those that could be withdrawn within ten years, and those requiring more than ten years before withdrawal of services. Combined with the Indian Claims Commission Act, the "Zimmerman Plan" became the basis of abrogating the federal trust obligation and terminating the political status of tribal nations. By so doing, these tribes became subject to state and local jurisdictions.

Congress expressed the philosophy of termination in House Concurrent Resolution 108 in 1953, declaring as a national policy the sense of Congress, "as rapidly as possible, to make the Indians within the territorial limits of the United States subject to the same laws and entitled to the same privileges and responsibilities as are applicable to other citizens."[62] Immediately, Congress enacted a series of bills preparing for termination, including repealing antiquated prohibitions against Natives owning guns or selling farm equipment. In 1954, Congress authorized the transfer of the Indian Medical Service from the BIA to the U.S. Public Health Service, with the goal of integrating Native medical care into the national healthcare system.[63]

With termination, Congress no longer viewed tribes in California, Florida, New York, Oregon, Texas, and other states statutorily identified as governments with whom the United States would interact. Between 1954 and 1966, Congress enacted specific termination acts affecting 117 tribes and tribal groups. Once these tribes and groups—as well as numerous scattered Native allotments—were terminated, the federal trust obligation ceased, census rolls were closed, land and resources were sold and divided in severalty (or placed into private trust), state jurisdiction was extended over the land, state and local taxation commenced, federal programs were discontinued, and the exercise of tribal sovereignty and jurisdiction was discontinued.[64]

Federal termination did not end the existence of the affected tribal nations, as they maintained their own rolls, regulated hunting and fishing rights within their territory, oversaw water resources, entered into contracts, received grants, or appeared in court.[65] In fact, federal recognition is not a prerequisite for maintaining tribal society, although it facilitates social and political consensus and enables tribes to receive federal protection of their land and resources and to lawfully resist state encroachment and interference. Where Congress enacted specific termination acts, the federal trust was terminated and there was no longer liability on the part of the United States for tribal affairs. By the 1970s and continuing into the 1980s, nearly all terminated tribes were restored to federal status.[66]

FEDERAL ACKNOWLEDGMENT

In cases where a tribe was never terminated—but also never federally acknowledged—there may be federal liability. In 1975, the Passamaquoddy Tribe sued the United States to force an action against the state of Maine for the loss of tribal territory dating to 1794. While the United States never acknowledged the Passamaquoddy as a tribe with whom it had a government-to-government relationship, the federal appellate court found that just because the United States had not recognized the Passamaquoddy did not mean that the Natives were not a "tribe." In fact, the court concluded that the Passamaquoddy was an "Indian tribe" within the meaning of the 1790 Nonintercourse Act—and despite the fact that the United States had never formally recognized the tribe, it had a trust obligation to protect the tribe's land.[67]

The Mississippi Choctaw Tribe is another example of a tribe maintaining its tribal nature despite the lack of federal recognition. When the Choctaw Nation was removed to Indian Territory in 1830, some Choctaw remained in Mississippi, where they maintained their way of life and continued to exercise the powers of limited self-government—despite not being federally recognized. The Choctaw's unique way of life and continued social and political existence imbued it with inherent sovereign powers and, in 1978, the United States formally recognized the Mississippi Choctaw as an indigenous tribe with whom it had a government-to-government relationship.[68]

A number of tribes have sought federal acknowledgment in recent decades even though the United States had never recognized them as tribes with whom the federal government had a trust responsibility. In 1978, Congress authorized the secretary of the interior through the Bureau of Indian Affairs to promulgate rules for determining how a tribe is to be recognized. The BIA then developed an acknowledgment process that placed the onus of recognition on the tribe. The acknowledgment process requires, among other criteria, a tribe or tribal group to prove a continuous existence and identification since at least 1900, demonstrate that is has been an autonomous entity throughout history and is a distinct community, and that it exercised political influence over its people.[69]

Since initiating the federal acknowledgment process, there have been several hundred tribes and tribal groups requesting recognition. In 1978, the Mashpee (Wampanoag) Tribe sought federal acknowledgment but was denied because it could not prove it was an Indian tribe within the meaning of the Nonintercourse Act of 1790.[70] In 2007, after thirty years of effort, the Mashpee successfully gained federal recognition, proving their continuous social, political, and economic existence under the criteria in § 83.7 of the federal acknowledgment process.[71] Unlike the Mashpee, however, the Lumbee of North Carolina has been denied recognition several times for failing to demonstrate its continuous existence as an Indian tribe. As these two examples indicate, the long, costly, and drawn-out process for recognition has made it difficult for a petitioning tribal group to prove it meets the criteria for federal acknowledgment. There are an estimated 200 unrecognized tribes, some of which were terminated in the 1950s and 1960s.[72] In 2018, Congress acknowledged 6 Virginia tribes—the Chickahominy Tribe, Chickahominy Tribe Eastern Division, Monacan Tribe, Nansemond Tribe, Rappahannock Tribe, and Upper Mattaponi Tribe.[73] As of 2018, there are 573 federally recognized tribes.

CONCLUSION

In 1831, Chief Justice John Marshall argued that the relationship between the United States and Indian tribes was unlike any other in the world. Marshall was perhaps prescient in his assertion. Today, Native people are citizens of their tribal nation and citizens of the United States and the state in which they live. If their tribe is federally recognized and they reside on the reservation, they are governed by tribal law and some federal statutes within Indian Country, but are otherwise governed by state law outside of Indian Country. The term Indian Country, therefore, is noteworthy since it determines whether a tribal government lawfully exercises its inherent rights of self-government.

Indian Country holds a unique status in the United States, with tribal nations exercising governing authority within their territory to the exclusion of state law. The primary application of federal law in Indian Country is in the exercise of enumerated criminal offenses, primarily under the Major Crimes Act. But due to the federal trust relationship, tribes are subject to federal administrative policies, including, among others, the National Environmental Protection Act, Archaeological Resources and Protection Act, and the Antiquities Act, giving the federal government a fair amount of authority in Indian Country.

While most Americans recognize the term "Indian reservation," and commonly perceive all Native land as reservations, there are other forms of Native land, including dependent communities and trust allotments. Combined, these tribal holdings constitute the essence of Indian

Country, a legal term that first appeared in federal-Indian law with the passage of the Nonintercourse Act of 1790. This legal nomenclature includes all land to which aboriginal title has not been extinguished. The modern definition stems from a 1948 federal statute updating and consolidating tribal real estate and leasing provisions.[74] Subsequent to 1948, the federal courts have consistently ruled that this statute applies to issues of federal and tribal jurisdiction.[75] Indian Country, therefore, is foundational to defining the territory over which tribal law governs.

What follows is a history of federal-Indian policy as it was intellectually, philosophically, and politically influenced and executed by the commissioner of Indian affairs or the assistant secretary for Indian affairs. This approach is unique in that it follows the main policy braids and strands as they were shaped by the men and women who have directed the Indian Office or modern Bureau of Indian Affairs.

2

"CIVILIZE OR EXTERMINATE?"

Formative Indian Policy, 1775–1849

In the weeks following the opening volley of the American Revolution, the Continental Congress took steps to diplomatically, militarily, and politically deal with tribal nations. While at war with Great Britain, the United Colonies expressed concern that the tribes in the interior east, especially the Iroquois and the Cherokee, Choctaw, Chickasaw, and Creek nations, might ally with Britain. On July 12, 1775, the Continental Congress adopted a series of policies, declaring the preservation of and friendship with the tribes to be of "utmost moment." To ensure peace, Congress authorized the creation of three Indian departments: a northern for the Iroquois and dependent tribes; a southern for the Cherokee and the other "civilized" tribes; and a central for the Shawnee, Delaware, and other tribes in the mid-Atlantic interior.[1]

The Continental Congress also authorized the negotiation of treaties of amity and alliance with tribes along the frontier. The first conference was held along the Mohawk River at German Flats, New York, in August 1775 with the Iroquois Confederacy.[2] A second was held at Fort Pitt in October 1775 with the Shawnee, Mingo, Ottawa, Delaware, and Wyandot.[3] The third conference was held in July 1779 at Fort Pitt with the Cherokee Nation.[4] These treaties and federal activities to control the western territory impacted tribal lands and pointed to a need for a federal department dedicated to executing and enforcing congressional policies. This relationship included managing and directing trade and intercourse with the tribes, as well as securing territory via treaties to satisfy the insatiable American demand for land and, in the process, creating and defining the American myth through which definitions of savagery and civilization enabled such land to transfer to the United States.[5]

During the prewar years, the colonies handled these matters severally, but with the commencement of the American Revolution, colonial leaders recognized that Indian affairs and the management thereof was a federal prerogative, although the debates of the Continental Congress indicate some states—South Carolina in particular—opposed federal control. As a whole, Congress agreed that the central government would "have the sole and exclusive right and power of . . . regulating the trade, and managing all affairs with the Indians, not members of any of the states."[6] Henceforth, the federal government asserted responsibility for conducting Indian affairs and, with the adoption of the Articles of Confederation in 1781, Congress affirmed a policy that was nearly verbatim to that approved by the Continental Congress: The United States asserted "the sole and exclusive right and power of . . . regulating the trade and managing all affairs with the Indians."[7]

This political relationship was premised on respect for tribal authority and in no way interfered with the internal tribal governing operations or intratribal affairs that were solely under the jurisdiction of the tribes. Beginning with the Articles of Confederation, the United States implemented a mechanism for politically interacting with the tribes, one that was built on the British and colonial American experience.[8] In time, the jurisdiction of the United States over tribal nations was inversely related to the federal government's recognition of tribal sovereignty. The more authority the United States assumed, the less it recognized in the tribal nations, notwithstanding the pledge the nation made to tribal nations in the Northwest Ordinance: "The utmost good faith" would always "be observed towards the Indians."[9]

THE PRELUDE: 1789–1824

In 1789, after the several states adopted the United States Constitution, Congress asserted exclusive authority to regulate Indian affairs. Pursuant to article 1, section 8, of the Constitution, Congress assumed sole responsibility to "regulate commerce with foreign Nations, and among the several States, and with the Indian tribes."[10] Using this pretext, Congress established the Office of Indian Affairs, more commonly referred to as the Indian Office. Diplomatic goals included protection of Native rights, control of the disposition of Native land, regulation of trade, control of liquor traffic, and punishment of crimes committed by Natives vs. non-Natives and vice versa.

Three years prior to the Constitutional Convention, Congress approved of an ordinance for the regulation of Indian Affairs, not only reaffirming federal authority to administer tribal affairs but also establishing two Indian departments, a northern for those tribes north of the Ohio River and west of the Hudson River, and a southern for tribes south of the Ohio River. Each of the departments was governed by a superintendent who reported to the secretary of war but attended "to the execution of such regulations, as Congress shall, from time to time, establish respecting Indian affairs."[11] The superintendents granted licenses to U.S. citizens to trade with the tribes and enforce federal regulations governing American subjects in Indian Country. They did not have authority over the tribes. Where such federal regulations could not be enforced without infringing on "the legislative rights of a state," the superintendent was to coordinate his activities with the state authorities.[12] When the U.S. Constitution superseded the Articles of Confederation in September 1789, Congress retained the departments and superintendents.[13]

President George Washington advised Congress to enact legislation authorizing the United States to deal lawfully with tribal nations, a request to which Congress acceded with the 1790 Nonintercourse Act. This act authorized the superintendent of the department to regulate trade, principally to enable the United States to govern its subjects in their dealings with the tribes.[14] The Nonintercourse Act required traders to secure federal licenses from the superintendent of the department to trade in Indian Country and mandated that purchases of tribal land by any person or state was unlawful unless conducted "under the authority of the United States."[15] Any citizen or inhabitant of the United States who murdered a Native or committed a criminal act in Indian Country would be punished in accordance with the laws of the nearest state or local district wherein the crime occurred.[16] The United States increased its presence in Indian Country only to the extent necessary to govern the actions of its citizens. While minimally intrusive on tribal sovereignty, Congress was methodically constructing the infrastructure necessary to expand this authority and secure additional tribal real estate.

Since the Nonintercourse Act expired after two years, Congress renewed and modified it in 1793, adding a policy strand promoting the civilization of the American Indians and authorizing the president to appoint agents to enforce regulations by residing among the Natives and furnishing them with "useful domestic animals and implements of husbandry."[17] Congress renewed the act in 1796 and 1799, and made it permanent in 1802.[18] The latter act for the first time authorized the president to establish a budget for Indian affairs, provided it did not exceed $15,000 per year.[19]

The supervision of the increasing number of Indian agents, superintendents, and other personnel resided with the secretary of war. To administer the growing trade with tribes, Congress in 1806 authorized the Office of Indian Trade, directed by a superintendent (John Shee, 1806–1807; John Mason, 1807–1816; and Thomas McKenney, 1816–1822), and appropriated $269,000 for trading purposes.[20] Housed in the War Department, the superintendent was the first full-time position in the federal bureaucracy devoted to tribal affairs, reporting directly to the president. While initially concerned with overseeing trade, superintendent Thomas McKenney gradually assumed responsibility for *all* matters pertaining to civilian Indian affairs.

To curb trader abuses, Congress in 1796 authorized government-run trading houses, or factories, along the western and southern frontiers and in Indian Country.[21] Government trading houses provided goods to the tribes at a cost such that "the capital stock furnished by the United States . . . not be diminished." Since the government did not seek to profit from trade, the goods theoretically would be available at reduced costs and preclude abuses in trading, which were not conducive to maintaining amity with the tribes. As important, private traders struggled to compete with British traders in the old Northwest, leading tribes to prefer British goods. This ran counter to the American political goal of reducing tribal ties to Britain, which in turn would weaken tribes by creating dependency on the United States. The latter was the principle objective of government trading houses. By undermining private traders, factories facilitated Native dependence on trade goods that further aided land cessions. In fact, Thomas Jefferson wrote in 1803 that the United States "push[ed] our trading houses . . . to see the good and influential individual [Indians] among them run in debt" so they would be "willing to lop . . . off a cession of land."[22]

The factory system had practical, economic, military, and political objectives, each of which enabled the new nation to better control the tribes and provide for their growing demands for trade goods. In theory, trading houses were void of fraud and abuse, although in practice they were not effective. With trade a lucrative business, private traders—forced out by the government—objected to the trading houses.[23] Traders asserted no small influence on federal policy, including directing land cessions and controlling trade with the tribes. Despite such opposition, President Jefferson established new trading houses in Ohio, Indiana, Illinois, Michigan, Alabama, and Tennessee, and along the Arkansas, Red, and Missouri Rivers in the Louisiana Territory. In all, twenty-eight government trading houses operated in Indian Country.[24]

After 1812, there was a growing consensus among entrepreneurs that government trading houses should be discontinued, in part because there were too few of them to adequately carry on trade. Moreover, there was sufficient private capital to conduct trade and the government monopoly violated a principle of free enterprise, not only in terms of the government management of such factories but also in the execution of the fur trade, which was an integral component of economic exchange. In 1822, Congress abolished the trading houses, although government licensing and supervision of traders continued.[25]

SUPERINTENDENT THOMAS L. MCKENNEY

Antecedent to the closure of the trading houses, President James Madison appointed War of 1812 veteran and Maryland Quaker Thomas L. McKenney as superintendent of Indian trade, a position he held from April 12, 1816, until the government monopoly ended on May 6, 1822.[26] As superintendent, McKenney expanded his role from simply overseeing the factory system to incorporating all aspects of Indian affairs. When John C. Calhoun became secretary of war in December 1817, he turned to McKenney to manage all Indian affairs. Six years later, on March 12, 1824, Calhoun rewarded his close friend by creating a "Bureau of Indian Affairs" within the War Department and appointed McKenney to a vacant clerkship within the department to direct the new office.

While the chief clerk position had the authority to supervise the expenditure of funds appropriated on behalf of the tribes, execute treaties, oversee schools, regulate trade, and distribute annuities—which were rapidly increasing due to treaty obligations—he did not have statutory authority to act.[27] Calhoun, recognizing the essential nature of government obligations to the tribes and the need to regulate trade as spelled out in the Nonintercourse Act, simply acted without congressional authorization. McKenney lamented this absence of authority, writing in his 1828 annual report to Secretary of War Peter B. Porter that Congress should enact "a simple law, connecting the responsibility of this branch of the public service with the Congress."[28] To gain approval, Porter called on two men with considerable experience in Indian Country: Lewis Cass and William Clark, who between them controlled Indian policy for nearly two decades. Both men traveled to Washington to assist McKenney in drafting regulations for consideration by

Congress. Their report was submitted on February 9, 1829, although Congress failed to act on it before adjourning.[29]

Notwithstanding a lack of statutory authority, McKenney expanded the role of the Office of Indian Affairs between 1824 and 1830. He was aided by the 1819 Civilization Act, a statute he almost single-handedly orchestrated through Congress by organizing humanitarians and church leaders in support of the bill. In 1818, the House Committee on Indian Affairs concurred, reporting the Indians would have to be "moralized or exterminated."[30] This civilization act authorized the president "to employ capable persons of good moral character, to instruct [the Indians] in the mode of agriculture suited to their situation; and for teaching their children in reading, writing, and arithmetic, and perform other such duties as may be enjoined, according to such instructions and rules the President may give and prescribe."[31]

But the act was much more than encouraging education and agriculture, the twin pillars of civilized life. Prior to enactment of the bill, Congress was content in its role of ratifying treaties (Senate) and appropriating funds to fulfill such conventions (House). The Treaty of Ghent, ending the War of 1812, proved a precipitating event in the enactment of the Civilization Act. With Great Britain no longer interfering in U.S. affairs, tribal nations could no longer turn to a European power for protection against the United States. Congress now asserted—with the assistance of McKenney and support of church leaders—a far greater role in Indian affairs, one that eventually opened the door to domination of the tribes. The House Committee report summed up the intent of the law in 1819: "Put into the hands of their children the primer and the hoe, and they will naturally, in time, take hold of the plough ... and they will grow up habits of morality and industry."[32]

The Indian Office now became the central clearinghouse for all matters pertaining to tribal affairs, the regulation of trade and intercourse, and the enforcement of integrative measures. Throughout the 1820s, a considerable portion of the department's activities focused on strands of emigration, civilization, Christianity, and execution of treaties, the latter being the principle means of satisfying the insatiable American demand for land.[33] On March 29, 1830, the Cass-Clark report and an accompanying bill were introduced into Congress, advancing the concept of a "Home Department" for Indian affairs.[34] In 1832, Congress partially satisfied McKenney's desire when it authorized the secretary of war to appoint a commissioner and empower him to have "direction and management" of all Native affairs.[35] McKenney, however, was not around to enjoy the legislative victory, as he was dismissed by President Andrew Jackson on August 16, 1830.

The initial decade of the Office of Indian Affairs was saddled with challenges as military personnel and Indian Office employees were both subject to the secretary of war. In fact, the War Department's military and Indian affairs goals were antithetical. The Northwest Ordinance, for instance, required the military to engage tribal nations as the old Northwest was settled, but the Indian Office was to check the settlement of the territory by protecting tribal people. These competing charges became more complicated and pronounced as the nineteenth century unfolded.

Consequently, conflicts over authority were inevitable when Indian Office personnel enforced provisions of the Nonintercourse Act and the Civilization Act seeking, at times, to prevent the emigration of the tribes, while military officers assigned to the agencies refused to accept orders from civilian officers or encouraged the Natives "by profuse distributions of money and presents" to emigrate west.[36] McKenney as father of the Indian Office assembled a cadre of laws and regulations, including the Civilization Act and establishment of the Indian Office, giving the United States far greater authority over the tribes that the Constitution allowed. In so doing, McKenney consolidated all tribal affairs into a single office dedicated to the braid of integration.[37]

THE EMIGRATION OF THE TRIBES: 1830–1849

On May 30, 1829, Secretary of War John H. Eaton warned General William Carroll that: "A crisis in our Indian affairs has arrived. Strong indications are seen in this in the circumstances of the legislatures of Georgia and Alabama extending their laws over the Indians within their respective limits."[38] Removal emerged as a policy strand after Georgia and the federal government in 1802 agreed to a compact by which the state gave up its western land claims in exchange for a federal pledge to extinguish all aboriginal title within the state. Presidents James Monroe and John Quincy Adams, however, refused to force the Cherokee out of the state unless it was of their own volition, with Adams informing Congress in 1828 that the United States had an obligation to the tribes.[39] On July 26, 1827, the Cherokee Nation adopted a new constitution and proclaimed itself a sovereign nation under federal protection not subject to state jurisdiction.[40] Georgia forthwith extended its laws over Cherokee territory and began forcing the Cherokee to exit the state. Alabama followed suit against the Creek Nation.[41]

While emigration of the tribes commenced in the years following the War of 1812 and continued throughout the 1820s, removal as an official congressional policy did not take shape until enactment of the Indian Removal Act in 1830, although President Jackson made it the defining policy in the election of 1828.[42] During this period of emigration, five men held the position of commissioner of Indian affairs: Samuel S. Hamilton (1830–1831); Elbert Herring (1831–1836); Carey Allen Harris (1836–1838); Thomas Hartley Crawford (1838–1845); and William Medill (1845–1849). Herring was the first commissioner to be appointed under the legislation authorizing the Bureau of Indian Affairs and Medill was the last while the Indian Office resided within the War Department.

The 1830s and 1840s were characterized by emigration of the tribes and a dramatic growth in the scope of the Indian Office. The election of Andrew Jackson in November 1828 did not bode well for tribes as the president-elect made no secret of his position on Indian affairs. In his first address to Congress on December 8, 1829, Jackson rejected the authority of the southern tribes to establish independent governments within the several states, arguing that they had possessory rights only and must emigrate west or submit to the laws of the state in which they resided.[43] As for treaties, Jackson called them an "absurdity" and declared that treating tribes as independent nations was a "farce."[44]

Jackson, using McKenney to drum up support for emigration, encouraged Congress to enact into law a bill authorizing the emigration of the tribes from the East and Southeast to lands west

Table 2.1. Heads of the Indian Office and Major Policies, 1816–1849

Name	Title	Years of Service	Main Policies
Thomas L. McKenney (D-R)	Supt. of Trade	6 years (1816–1822)	Trade, civilization, and lawful basis for Indian Office
Thomas L. McKenney (D-R)	Chief Clerk	6.25 years (1824–1830)	Trade, civilization, and lawful basis for Indian Office
Samuel S. Hamilton (D-R)	Chief Clerk	1 year (1830–1831)	Compilation of treaties, emigration of the tribes
Elbert Herring (D-R)	Chief Clerk	11 months (1831–1832)	Emigration of the tribes via bribery, civilization, create an Office of Indian Affairs and Commisioner of Indian Affairs (CIA)
Elbert Herring (D)	Commissioner	4 years (1832–1836)	Emigration of the tribes via bribery, civilization, create an Office of Indian Affairs and CIA
Carey Allen Harris (D)	Commissioner	2.25 years (1836–1838)	Treaties in the West, land cessions, land speculation, emigration of the tribes
Thomas H. Crawford (D)	Commissioner	7 years (1838–1845)	Emigration, manual labor schools, annuity reform
William Medill (D)	Commissioner	3.75 years (1845–1849)	Annuity reform, schools, restructure Indian Office, diplomacy in the West

of the Mississippi River. "Humanity and national honor demand every effort should be made to avert so great a calamity," the president rationalized, trusting the tribes would agree to emigrate. In this, the president followed the sentiments of Lewis Cass, William Clark, and McKenney, the latter of whom had a sudden change of opinion regarding the propriety of the tribes remaining in their homelands after a tour of Indian Country in 1827.[45] Both Houses of Congress introduced removal bills and debate commenced, with thousands of memorials and remonstrances protesting the bill.[46] In May 1830, Congress enacted into law the Indian Removal Act, calling for the voluntary removal of the tribes and Native people, making emigration an official policy strand in the braids of land alienation and integration.[47]

CHIEF CLERK SAMUEL S. HAMILTON

Removal fundamentally changed the way the federal government interacted with tribes and set into motion a modification and codification of the laws and regulations governing Indian affairs. Samuel S. Hamilton, a career War Department bureaucrat from Maryland who had served as a clerk in the Indian Office between 1824 and 1830, succeeded McKenney on September 30, 1830.[48] Hamilton's primary achievement as head of the Indian Office was his compilation of Indian treaties executed prior to 1825. In his only report to Congress, he lamented to Secretary of War John Eaton the difficulties in providing for annuities, an action that required twenty-one separate appropriation acts in 1830. A single act, Hamilton argued, would allow Congress and the Treasury Department to better account for the expenditures.

More telling was Hamilton's request to streamline the Nonintercourse Act to "adapt its provisions to the present state of our Indian relations."[49] The national media, however, viewed Hamilton as little more than a clerk, and most politicians did not believe he would remain in office long. Not surprisingly, Congress ignored Hamilton's recommendations, with Secretary Eaton asserting all authority within the department. When Lewis Cass replaced Eaton as secretary, he forced Hamilton to resign as chief clerk effective August 31, 1831.[50]

CHIEF CLERK ELBERT HERRING

Hamilton was replaced by Elbert Herring, who was appointed by President Jackson.[51] A Princeton graduate and a New York Democrat who became head clerk of the Indian Office on August 12, 1831, Herring—upon enactment of the 1832 statute authorizing a commissioner of Indian affairs—became the first commissioner on July 10, 1832. An intimate friend of Cass, Herring was a strong advocate of the strands of emigration, education, and the introduction of Christianity, policies he believed would substitute the social for the savage state and free aboriginal title.[52] Emigration of the tribes outside state boundaries where they could be isolated from corrupting influences, such as whiskey peddlers, Herring rationalized, was the only means of civilizing and saving Natives. "In the consummation of this grand and sacred object," he wrote in his first annual report, "rests the sole chance of averting Indian annihilation."[53]

Herring's policies governing the Choctaw Academy reflected his educational views. When Thomas Henderson, superintendent of the academy, requested departmental approval to establish manual trades at the school, the Choctaw leadership objected, not wanting their children to engage in manual tasks. Henderson, supported by Pottawatomie teacher Joseph Bourassa, argued a classical education offered little to the Native students and was a waste of time and resources. Bourassa informed Henderson that "most any trade will prove more beneficial in the first settlers of a country." It was not a "pen and book," Bourassa stated, that enabled Americans to be settlers, but the "axe and plough." Herring authorized the change in 1833 and then allowed other Indian schools to modify curriculum to add mechanical arts.[54] While praising the Choctaw model, Herring favored local schools over distant boarding facilities.

Elbert Herring was the epitome of where emigration of the tribes went awry. He believed bribing, withholding of annuities, providing compliant Native leaders with choice land reserves, and interfering in tribal politics were necessary and acceptable for the Indians' own good. Under his watch, emigration became a national embarrassment as "gross injustice and cruel treatment" towards the Natives drove thousands off their land, with their homes burned and families forced to flee for safety. Despite the lack of a Cherokee removal treaty, which proved especially embarrassing to President Jackson, the emigration of the tribes completely overwhelmed the Indian Office, compelling Secretary of War Lewis Cass to lobby for legislative changes to the Nonintercourse Act and a complete reorganization of the Indian Office in 1834.[55]

The first modification in administration occurred in 1832, when Congress, following Cass's recommendation, formally authorized the appointment of a commissioner of Indian affairs to replace the chief clerk of the Indian Office created by Calhoun.[56] While the commissioner reported to the secretary of war, he now acted under the color of law and was appointed by the president with the advice and consent of the Senate. Five days later, Congress appointed three commissioners to reconnoiter the country set apart for the emigrating tribes and report back to Congress on the status of emigration.[57]

Two years later, on June 30, 1834, largely in response to Cass's requests, Congress statutorily created the Bureau of Indian Affairs, expanding the authority of the commissioner.[58] Moreover, a new superintendency was established in St. Louis to govern "all Indian country not within the boundary of any state or territory west of the Mississippi river." Congress terminated a number of agencies in the East and established new agencies in the West, and codified all federal Indian regulations. Also important, the law provided protection for American Indians after they emigrated, although in practice such security was superfluous. A separate statute enacted that same day codified the trade and intercourse act and defined Indian Country as "all that part of the United States west of the Mississippi [River], and not within [a state or territory] to which Indian title has not been extinguished."[59] Thirty sections defined the jurisdictional extent of the department, granting enormous power to the Indian Office.

President Jackson consented to new regulations governing the payment of annuities (July 3, 1834) and superintendents, agencies, and subagencies (July 7, 1834), but was dissatisfied with Herring's performance as commissioner.[60] Despite the president's concerns over Herring's inefficiencies, he agreed to appoint Herring as the first commissioner of Indian affairs at the request of Cass. When Cass left the War Department in 1836, Jackson transferred Herring to a field position.[61]

COMMISSIONER CAREY A. HARRIS

At Jackson's request, Herring resigned as commissioner of Indian affairs on July 2, 1836, with the president appointing his close friend Carey Allen Harris, a Tennessee lawyer and chief clerk in the War Department, as commissioner.[62] Harris was handpicked by Jackson, who believed the commissioner would be acceptable to the administration of Martin Van Buren should he win the election in the fall of 1836. Harris served two years as commissioner (July 4, 1836, to October 19, 1838) executing a policy that, between 1829 and 1836, resulted in the cession of 93,401,637 acres of tribal land valued at $26,982,068.[63] Under his tenure, interpositions by the War Department resulted in frequent contacts and treaties with the western tribes, including the Sioux, Sauk and Fox, Kiowa, and Comanche. These inroads opened diplomatic exchanges and, at times, military actions west of the Mississippi River.[64]

The Indian Office also expanded its authority over tribal affairs, with Harris implementing five new regulations governing accounting of tribal annuities; the administration of superintendencies and the location of agencies; the acquisition of treaty goods, use of interpreters, and treaty negotiations; the licensing of traders and issuance of passports in Indian Country and Indian depredations; and the emigration of the tribes.[65] While not adopted as a regulation, Harris supported the organization of civil government in Indian Country west of the frontier and emphasized education as a tool of social control and change. Emigration, however, filled the majority of his annual reports.

While Harris's major contribution as commissioner was in enforcing the removal of the tribes, emphasizing speed and economy over the welfare of the Natives, the emigration of the Cherokee (North Carolina and Georgia) and Seminole (Florida) occupied much of his time—although it was in the emigration of the Creek and Chickasaw that the new commissioner displayed his true colors. Creek emigration in 1836 proceeded without the benefit of a treaty, in part because Harris was a partner in a speculation scheme in Creek land in Alabama. The following year, he threatened to withhold annuities and rations from the Chickasaw if they did not agree to immediate emigration.[66]

The appointment of Harris was unfortunate due to his avaricious nature and propensity to use his position to speculate on Indian contracts, in addition to his land speculation activities. By 1838, former President Jackson was informed of the treachery of Harris and he discreetly notified President Van Buren to be vigilant of all Indian Office accounts and activities. Harris, meanwhile, prohibited his clerks from reading any incoming field correspondence until his wife reviewed them. Before leaving office, Jackson had appointed Thomas H. Crawford to investigate the allegations of fraud, and Crawford's report contained damning evidence of wrong doing. When Van Buren demanded of Harris an explanation, he elected to resign, leaving office October 19, 1838, having become a political liability for the president.[67]

COMMISSIONER THOMAS H. CRAWFORD

On October 22, 1838, Van Buren appointed Thomas Hartley Crawford to replace Harris. A former state senator, lawyer, Princeton graduate, and Jacksonian Democrat from Pennsylvania, Crawford served seven years as commissioner under four presidential administrations. Crawford was a steady and forceful advocate for the emigration of the tribes, a process he referred to as simply a "change of residence effected under treaties."[68] One year into his tenure, Crawford detailed the difficulties of enforcing the emigration of the northern tribes by requesting Congress to renew its efforts to immediately remove Native people upon execution of a treaty. "The only expedient—the wisest, the best, the most practicable and practical" of all policies was to force emigration in order to minimize the "suffering" of the Indians.[69] Like other politicians of his day, Crawford perceived of removal in utopian terms, believing that only outside the influences of "bad and sordid men" would the Natives find a "home and a country free from the apprehensions of disturbance and annoyance."[70] To his credit, Crawford closely guarded against fraud and speculation in tribal lands.

In 1841, in response to the difficulties of removing the northern tribes, including the Menominee, Chippewa, Pottawatomie, and Ottawa in the Great Lakes area, and the Sauk and Fox in Iowa, Crawford proposed the creation of a northern Indian territory that he argued was judicious towards the health and well-being of the tribes. If Native people did not want to migrate to this territory, their only alternatives, Crawford argued, were seeking refuge in Canada or assimilating into white America. The latter was unlikely and the former posed national security risks should they seek to return to the United States. A separate territory in the north, however, would accommodate western immigrants crossing the central plains on the overland trails and would be "most beneficial."[71]

A northern territory would eliminate the primary complaints of the prairie tribes, which resisted emigration to the southern Indian territory (present-day Oklahoma, Kansas, and Nebraska). Crawford encouraged the Sauk and Fox to emigrate from Iowa (1841), the Wyandotte from Ohio (1842), several bands of Chippewa, Ottawa, and Pottawatomie from the southern Great Lakes (1842), and the Miami from Indiana (1842). The Menominee, western Oneida, Chippewa of Lake Superior, Iroquois in New York, and scattered bands of Pottawatomie and Ottawa near the southern Great Lakes remained. To the south, scattered bands of Seminole remained in Florida, numerous Choctaw still inhabited Mississippi, some Cherokee persisted in North Carolina, and scattered Creek continued to reside in Alabama.[72] Crawford, along with Secretary of War John Bell (an ardent emigrationist) sought the removal of fifty thousand northern Natives to a location northwest of Iowa. Crawford envisioned hardy non-Natives living in between the northern and southern Indian territories, strengthening national security by separating the concentration of tribes.[73]

During Crawford's tenure, the challenges incumbent with the emigration policy surfaced, with some tribes forced west under military arms, including the Cherokee Nation.[74] The Winnebago, who signed a treaty in 1837 committing the tribe to emigrate within eight months of ratification (June 15, 1838), proved a particularly difficult situation. In the spring of 1838, Crawford informed Secretary of War Joel R. Poinsett that the Winnebago's "pertinacity in resisting emigration made it judicious to commit their removal to General [Henry] Atkinson," who was instructed on February 28, 1839, to enforce emigration.[75] By 1840, the emigration of the tribe had yet to be accomplished, in large measure chief Wee-noo-shake pleaded, due to the fact "our wigwams are filled with sick." Agent David Lowry informed the aged chief that the Winnebago had pledged to emigrate not later than the spring of 1840, to which Wee-noo-shake responded, "We could not foresee that we would be now sick and dying."[76] Crawford consented to a year's delay but ordered all Winnebago annuities paid west of the Mississippi River in the Neutral Ground, a tract of land lying between Sauk and Fox lands to the south and the Sioux territory to the north. Tribal members residing east of the Mississippi River remained dependent on government subsistence.[77]

Another discouraging aspect of emigration was the poorly written language of the treaties. The Chippewa of the Saginaw agreed on January 14, 1837, to a treaty ceding their lands in Michigan, with the treaty supplemented by another convention on January 23, 1838. Article one of the latter treaty, ratified by the Senate on July 2, provided that such ceded land not be sold "at public or private sales, for a sum less than $5.00 per acre, for and during the term of two years from *commencement* of sale." After two years the remaining land could be sold for $2.50 per acre until all remaining tracts were sold. Article three, however, provided that any land remaining after five years from *ratification* of the treaty was to "be sold for such sum as it will command, provided that no such sale shall be made for less than seventy-five cents per acre."[78]

Confusion prevailed as settlers interpreted the convention as authorizing the five-year window to commence upon ratification by the Senate. This initiated the two-year window at $5.00 per acre on July 2, 1838; however, the sale of land did not begin until September 13, 1841. If treaty ratification initiated the sale of land then such a date would not allow for the two-year window of $5.00 per acre and would limit the period of sale at $2.50 per acre. Settlers were already entering upon the ceded Chippewa land and Crawford was concerned they would "insist the five years have expired" and secure title to the land under the preemption act of 1841.[79] While Crawford prevailed upon Congress to enact legislation amending the treaty, it refused. On August 18, 1843, Crawford requested Thomas Blake, commissioner of the General Land Office, to postpone land sales and then, beginning September 6, authorize sales at $2.50 per acre for three years. Blake concurred, but not before a sizeable portion of the ceded land was sold at reduced rates, diminishing the return to the tribe.[80]

Some ambiguities and indifference by the Indian Office and the federal government—if not intentional—were gross violations of the protections the United States assumed under treaty provisions and legislative enactments. An all too common thread exhibited by these actions was that of inattention by the trustee of tribal resources, especially those resources that were essential for the economic well-being of the tribes. This careless attitude was reflected at the highest levels of government: "From the very moment the general government came into existence to this time, it has exercised its power over this unfortunate race in the spirit of humanism and justice." This pronouncement by the Supreme Court reflected the growing paternalism of the United States and its rapidly shifting role in treating Natives as an inferior people.[81]

Significantly, the 1830s represented an important shift in federal policy, one that furthered dependence of the tribes on the United States. Large land cessions, such as the Chippewa cessions of 1838–1842, reflected more than just cessions; they also reflected a shift in tribal dependence. While prior to these cessions the tribes were dependent on the fur traders (making traders wealthy), after such cessions they grew increasingly dependent on the United States for government annuities. Fur traders who had grown wealthy from the fur trade now encouraged further cessions. Having the financial resources to purchase or speculate in such ceded lands, they now began to acquire additional land. Dependency on traders was one matter; dependency on the United States subjected tribes to federal social and political policies that interfered in their internal affairs.[82]

Directly associated with the strands of emigration was the braid of integrating and civilizing the Natives, with Crawford following the framework of manual labor schools bequeathed to him from Herring and Harris. Crawford viewed such schools as "the principal lever by which the Indians are to be lifted out of the mire of folly and vice."[83] As a member of the Pennsylvania state legislature that established a system of public schools, Crawford believed education constituted "one of the most important objects, if it be not the greatest, connected with our Indian relations. Upon it depends more or less even partial success in all endeavors to make the Indian better than he is."[84] Crawford's sanguine expectation was to send educated Natives, "qualified and zealously willing to instruct [their] brethren," back into Indian Country to serve as models "of truthfulness and general morality" and to further the federal objective of integration.[85] The manual labor system of education Crawford constructed governed the Indian school system well into the twentieth century.

Treaty-guaranteed annuities were a special concern for the Indian Office, not only because they continued to foster the separate status of Native people but also because they consumed a significant portion of the budget. In 1834, Congress directed the department to pay annuities to tribal chiefs rather than individual tribal members, in an effort to influence leaders to part with the land and support federal policies of civilization.[86] Challenges for the Indian Office and policymakers arose when the chiefs retained a portion of the money or dispersed it among political cronies.[87] The result was that annuities were not always well spent, generally did not benefit the tribe as a whole, and more often than not ended up in the hands of the traders who fostered dependency, thus ensuring future land cessions. Crawford complained that tribal leaders who received annuities were nothing "more than conduit pipes to convey [the money] into the pockets of their traders."[88] Too frequently annuities were used to purchase ardent spirits or similar items from traders, not only keeping the funds in the hands of the traders but also confining Native people to a cycle of debt. While annuities were associated with treaty provisions, they were also a strand that served the larger philosophical braid of land alienation.

COMMISSIONER WILLIAM MEDILL

Crawford resigned October 29, 1845, after Democratic president James K. Polk relieved him of his duties by appointing him to a federal judgeship. Polk chose a westerner with significant political authority as his new commissioner. William Medill, an Ohio Democrat, former congressman and Ohio state representative, took office October 29.[89] Medill was the recipient of patronage and a political appointee who had no prior knowledge of Indian affairs but who was given a free hand by Secretary of War William L. Marcy to conduct the department without interference. He was profuse in distributing patronage, eying a potential vice-presidential run in 1848.[90] During his tenure, the United States annexed Texas (1845), secured its rights to the Oregon Territory (1846), and acquired New Mexico and California (1848). The latter territories lacked Indian agents and federal authority over tribal affairs, with Congress reticent to confer such jurisdiction until it established civil government. Texas, meanwhile, insisted its admission to the Union proscribed federal jurisdiction over Indian affairs.

The Indian Office continued to operate under the 1834 reorganization act, with Medill advocating restructuring of the department and improving employee remuneration. He also sought to combine agencies and dispense annuities to heads of families, rather than to tribal chiefs, a proposition loathed by the traders. On March 3, 1847, Congress amended the Nonintercourse Act by granting discretionary authority to the president or the secretary to distribute annuities to heads of families or, with the consent of the tribe, to apply them "to such purposes as will best promote the happiness and prosperity of the [tribal] members."[91] While there was no reorganization of the field service, harsher penalties were issued for those selling whiskey to the Natives.

The federal statute was primarily intended to reduce the potential of annuities being used to purchase ardent spirits. Annuities, for instance, were not to be distributed to anyone who was inebriated or if "intoxicating liquor was within convenient reach." Tribal leaders were expected to use their influence to prevent the introduction of intoxicants into their territory.[92] Moreover, to eliminate the recurrence of Indians collateralizing their annuities, the act nullified any contract made by a Native who promised repayment in annuity funds. Individual debt was not payable on tribal annuities, much to the chagrin of the traders who were accustomed to collecting such debt from tribal funds.

The War Department immediately implemented the policy, seeking to curb the nefarious traffic in liquor. Medill opined that in so doing there had "never been a measure [more] productive of better moral effects."[93] He also advocated reducing annuities because they were the means by which the Natives came into "possession of resources, not the fruit of their own industry and frugality."[94] Unsurprisingly, the 1846 treaty with the Chippewa, Ottawa, and Pottawatomie contained a proviso reducing their annuities in proportion to their declining population.[95]

Politics trumped reform. After Zachary Taylor was elected president in 1848, the new (and first) secretary of the interior, Thomas Ewing, took office, reversed direction on annuities, and discharged a considerable portion of individual debt by tapping into tribal annuities. Ewing directed the commissioner to overturn the prohibition, suggesting that distributing annuities to all Natives diminished the authority and influence of the chiefs and created contempt for governmental authority.[96] In reality, Ewing was supportive of the traders, who stood to profit by lifting the prohibitions. The fact that it facilitated federal purposes was no small consideration for the shift, as it was easier to persuade a few chiefs than an entire tribe on the matter of federal policy. Neither Medill's successor, Orlando Brown, who was more concerned with government patronage, nor Luke Lea, who became commissioner in 1850, opposed the change. In fact, Lea believed the distribution of annuities to individuals worked against the government's efforts to implement policy through tribal leaders. If the latter were treated indistinguishably from other tribal members, their authority would be weakened, resulting in political disorder.[97]

Medill had great optimism for the tribes in Oregon, explaining that they were "of a different order from those with whom we have been in more familiar intercourse." Schools had already been established and many Native people looked "wholly to the soil for support," Medill optimistically reported in 1845.[98] The annexation of Texas that same year opened diplomatic relations with the Comanche, Wichita, and other tribes within the former Lone Star Republic, with Medill seeking congressional authority to establish a federal presence, a proposition Texas rebuffed.[99] Medill strongly advocated the introduction of manual labor schools by which knowledge of letters would go hand-in-hand with the practical employment of artisan tools and agricultural implements.[100] To this end, he discontinued nearly all of the Indian schools in the East and focused this strand in the West.

By the 1840s, the emigration of the tribes to the West resulted in two realties. To begin with, for the first time the United States was not in debt, as the sale of land brought the federal coffers in the black.[101] Moreover, some one hundred thousand American Indians were displaced, with emigration drawing to a close only after the U.S. Army offered to pay one hundred dollars to each emigrating Seminole remaining in Florida.[102] While initially contemplated by a new generation of bureaucrats and politicians as a way of creating an Indian utopia to foster integration outside the vices of frontier America, the emigration policy proved unsatisfactory and painful, with Medill rationalizing the growing national reproach. "Where in the context of civilization with barbarians, since the commencement of time, has it been less the case than with us?"[103] Any strife and bloodshed was the product of "natural and unavoidable causes." Despite such prejudices and disregard, Medill looked to the future when the past would be "measurably repaired."[104]

As emigration of the tribes ended, Medill initiated a new strand in the braids of integration and land alienation, one born in the context of frontier states—such as Arkansas, Missouri, and Iowa—opposing additional tribes adjacent to their borders. While emigration was designed to translocate the tribes outside of any state or territory, it resulted in dozens of tribes residing just west of the frontier states. To counter the growing concern, Medill proposed two large reservations along the frontier: one in the south (present-day Oklahoma, Kansas, and Nebraska) and one in the north (the Dakotas). Such a policy would support a "wide and safe passage [across the central Plains] for our Oregon emigrants," Medill noted.[105] As important, the continuous migration of Americans across the country cast doubts on the concept of an independent Indian Country outside the parameters of American settlement. Medill, however, would not be there to influence the emerging policy, as on June 30, 1849, at President Taylor's request, he resigned.

CONCLUSION

Before Medill left office, the Supreme Court validated the trajectory of federal policy and buttressed a vision for the future of federal-Indian policy. In 1846 the court ruled on a simple case that generated little attention at the time. In a case that dealt with the question of federal jurisdiction and whether the federal-Indian relationship was race based or political, the court issued a seemingly simple yet jarring ruling. In 1844, William Rogers murdered his brother-in-law Jacob Nicholson. Both men were non-Indians married to Cherokee women and were recognized as Cherokee citizens by the Cherokee Nation. The court assumed jurisdiction, holding that both men were "white men" who could not legally disassociate from the United States absent congressional authorization.

In reaching the decision of the court, Chief Justice Roger B. Taney held that the political affiliation of Rogers did not change the fact that he was not an Indian. In prior cases, the federal courts ambiguously used "race" to refer to Natives as a group with a common biological heritage and a common political identity. In holding divergent political and biological definitions, the court in 1846 redefined "Indian" and used the occasion to subject tribal nations to the authority of the United States. In so doing, the court referenced the 1834 Nonintercourse Act that declared "so much of the laws of the United States as provided for punishment of crimes committed within any place within the sole and exclusive jurisdiction of the United States, shall be in force in Indian Country." However, crimes "committed by one Indian against the person or property of another Indian" were exempt from jurisdiction.[106]

In peeling back the layers of jurisdiction, the court merged the status of Indian Country as federal land with the subjection of Native people to federal authority, giving rise a half century later to a theoretical framework of federal plenary power, which subjected tribal nations and Native people to overarching federal authority. Chief Justice Taney specifically argued that "the United States has adopted the principal . . . that the aboriginal tribes of Indians in North America are not regarded as the owners of the territory which they respectively occupy." Moreover, Taney argued Natives were subject to the overarching authority of the United States.[107] The legal underpinnings of near-complete federal control were in place. Congress was about to transform the federal-Indian relationship.

3

"HALFWAY ACROSS THE CONTINENT"

Beginnings of a Reservation Policy, 1849–1861

Congress envisioned emigration as the means of providing tribes with time to adjust to the inevitable social and cultural metamorphosis occurring with the geographic expansion of the nation. President Jefferson believed it could take generations before the American West would be settled, providing tribes ample time to adjust. Then, within a single decade the United States completed its continental expansion and in fewer than four generations the West was settled and the frontier closed.

Since the founding of the nation, Indian affairs had been a military matter. By the late 1840s, with the emigration of the tribes largely completed, Treasury Secretary Robert Walker urged Congress to establish a new department, building on the concept espoused by Lewis Cass and William Clark a decade earlier. "The duties now performed by the Commissioner of Indian Affairs are most numerous and important," Walker reasoned, "and must be vastly increased with the great number of tribes scattered over Texas, Oregon, New Mexico, and California, and with the interesting progress of so many of the tribes in Christianity, knowledge, and civilization."[1] These duties were not war related but appertained to peace and to what the federal government now perceived as domestic relations with the tribes. Chief Justice Taney's blueprint for federal policy was about to unfold.

To accommodate geographic expansion and the philosophy of governance advanced by those such as Walker, Congress in 1849 established the Department of the Interior to manage the internal lands and affairs of the nation.[2] With rapid American expansion across the continent, Congress now insisted on minimizing the foreign-nation status of the tribes by representing them not as foreign sovereigns but as domestic dependencies. By statute, Congress transferred

Table 3.1. Heads of the Indian Office and Major Policies, 1849–1861

Name	Title	Years of Service	Main Policies
Orlando Brown (W)	Commissioner	1 year (1849–1850)	Reservations and consolidation, agriculture, annuity reform
Luke Lea (W)	Commissioner	2.75 years (1850–1853)	Expand reservations, annuity reform, paternalism, expand Indian Office
George Manypenny (D)	Commissioner	4 years (1853–1858)	Reservations, severalty, cessions, annuity reform, commute annuities, General Crimes Act
James W. Denver (D)	Commissioner	8 months (1857)	Small reservations, severalty, manual labor schools
Charles E. Mix (D)	Acting Commissioner	6 months (1857–1858)	Reservations, severalty, annuities
James W. Denver (D)	Commissioner	4 months (1858–1859)	Manual labor schools
Charles E. Mix (D)	Commissioner	5 months (1858)	Reservations, severalty, agriculture
Alfred B. Greenwood (D)	Commissioner	1.75 years (1859–1861)	Reservations, severalty, treaties, update regulations, annuity as goods

the General Land Office, Patent Office, Pension Office, and Office of Indian Affairs into the new executive department.

The geopolitical expansion of the United States markedly changed the anticipated benefits of Indian removal. For one, the western tribes suddenly found themselves dealing with tens of thousands of American immigrants heading west, as well as the tens of thousands of eastern Indians now living in the West. The Cheyenne, Sioux, Arapaho, Kiowa, Comanche, Pawnee, Blackfeet, Ute, Shoshone, Navajo, Pima, and Apache people all encountered mass immigration, encroachment on their land, and decimation of their natural resources. While the recently removed tribes were militarily weakened and suffering from the ravages of emigration, the western tribes were militarily strong and as a whole had little interest in an agrarian lifestyle.[3]

As important, emigration was thought to have solved the legal dilemma of a sovereign (tribal nation) within a sovereign (the several states). The goal of emigration was to relocate the tribes outside of the jurisdiction of the states and territories. However, before emigration was completed, the whole scheme was compromised as the Indian frontier was engulfed within the newly organized territories of Kansas and Nebraska, notwithstanding a U.S. Supreme Court ruling upholding the rights of tribes to exist outside of state jurisdiction.[4] Neither was the removal treaty pledge of no state interference applicable, as almost immediately upon completion of emigration, settlers demanded organization of the frontier territories. With many of the border tribes politically and physically weakened and facing possible extermination, political expediency and good will combined to establish a new twist in the policy braid of integration: the reservation system.

Between 1849 and 1861 there were six commissioners of Indian affairs. Orlando Brown replaced William Medill in 1849 and served until 1850. He was succeeded by Luke Lea (1850–1853); George Manypenny (1853–1857); James W. Denver (1857 and 1858–1859); Charles Mix (1858); and Alfred

Burton Greenwood (1859–1861), each of whom added to the development of the reservation policy. The antebellum era also reflected a period of high turnover in civilian officers managing Indian affairs, in large part because the commissioners lacked experience and they were all recipients of the spoils system.

COMMISSIONER ORLANDO BROWN

The first commissioner of Indian affairs within the Department of the Interior was Orlando Brown, a southern Whig and Princeton graduate from Kentucky, who was appointed commissioner by President Zachary Taylor on June 30, 1849.[5] Brown was a humanitarian, believing the only means to save the Indians from extinction was to place them on reservations where they could be taught the art of civilized life, a euphemism for engaging in agriculture, assimilating American values and ideals, and adopting Christianity.[6] "The best of all knowledge [and] religious truth" was in the Native's "duty towards God and their fellow human beings."[7]

At the same time, Brown believed the United States owed American Indians a debt because the nation displaced them from the land and now enjoyed possession of it.[8] It would take only a few years, Brown was convinced, for Native people to "be fully able to maintain themselves in prosperity and happiness under any circumstance of contact or connection with our people."[9] As evidence of the tribes' capacity for self-government, Brown pointed to the success of the Cherokee, Choctaw, Chickasaw, and Creek nations, each of which "adopt[ed] written constitutions upon the model of our own, by establishing and sustaining schools, by successfully devoting themselves to agricultural pursuits, by respectable attainments in the learned professions and mechanics, and by adopting the manners and customs of our people so far as they are applicable to their own condition."[10]

Much to the chagrin of Brown, Interior Secretary Thomas Ewing directed the policy of the Indian Office and dispersed political patronage, paying little attention to corruption among traders. Politically and filially connected with and beholden to the traders, Ewing went so far as to pay off the Indians' debt using tribal funds. As for Brown, he labored to expand the scope of the Indian Office, lamenting the fact that in 1849 the department was administered as it had been fifteen years earlier. Brown specifically pointed out the office was inefficiently run with antiquated regulations that did not fit the western tribes. He enumerated these tribes in great detail in his 1849 report, requesting seven independent superintendencies (four east of the Rocky Mountains and one each for New Mexico, Utah, and California) to provide "immediate and rigid supervision" of tribal affairs in areas where discretionary authority was lacking.[11]

Brown petitioned President Taylor to increase the number and remuneration of the Indian agents, which totaled eleven, believing additional agents and increased salaries would hasten integration of Natives. A reticent Congress approved of just one superintendency in the Oregon Territory and three new agents, rejecting any new agencies in New Mexico and California until the issue of civilian government was resolved.[12] While the Compromise of 1850 provided direction on civil government, policy decisions in the Southwest would have to wait for Congress in 1854 to adopt the Kansas-Nebraska Act and its corollary concept of popular sovereignty before additional agents were hired and agencies were established.

Following Ewing's direction, Brown intended to negotiate treaties with tribal nations on the plains in order to establish reservations, protect immigrants, and distribute gifts. Congress was too late in appropriating funds for the treaties in 1849 and, when the $200,000 appropriation was made the following year, it was too late to bring the tribes together. While the treaty was held at Fort Laramie in September 1851, Brown was not there to witness it. As for the border tribes, Brown believed their reservations should be consolidated and the Natives concentrated on "smaller districts" where they could be taught agricultural and other civilized pursuits, fulfilling both braids of policy.[13] And while Ewing paid traders for tribal debts, Brown advocated that future treaty annuities and gifts to Natives be in the form of "farming utensils, provisions, etc., in lieu of money."[14]

COMMISSIONER LUKE LEA

Unfortunately for Brown, he was associated with Whig corruption stemming from Ewing paying annuities to traders satisfying tribal debt, forcing President Taylor to seek his resignation. Brown served as commissioner for exactly one year, submitting his resignation on May 22 and leaving office July 1, 1850. Taylor then appointed Mississippi politician Luke Lea to replace Brown effective that same day.[15] As with Brown and, for that matter, all of the commissioners of the era, Lea had no experience in Indian affairs but was politically motivated and connected. Then a most fortuitous event occurred for Lea: eight days after he took office, President Taylor died, with Vice President Millard Fillmore assuming the presidency and immediately initiating a reorganization of the executive cabinets. By the end of July, Ewing resigned as secretary, with Alexander H. H. Stuart replacing him and granting Lea free reign on all matters pertaining to Indian affairs.[16]

Lea followed the lead of his predecessors and did not question the superiority of white America, arguing that "[w]hen civilization and barbarism are brought [together] they cannot coexist." Contention over land and settlement ensued because of the Indian's "own perverse and vicious nature." Their "haughty pride" and "wild energies," Lea explained, required tempering by "the more ennobling pursuits of civilized life."[17] In stark contrast, Lea was convinced that Native people had "all the elements essential to [their] elevation" and only needed "proper development . . . to tread with equal step and dignity the walks of civilized life."[18] Lea did not question, nay he was not allowed to question, the paternalism and ethnic superiority of white America.

Following Medill and Brown's efforts, Lea fleshed out the reservation policy, in large measure due to the rapid continental expansion of the United States. In Texas and New Mexico tribal wars raged, in California gold seekers threatened the very existence of Native people, and the border state tribes faced extermination. The Natives had to be placed in locations where they could be "controlled and finally compelled, by sheer necessity, to resort to agricultural labor or starve," Lea wrote in his first annual report. "There should be assigned to each tribe, for a permanent home, a country adapted to agriculture, of limited extent and well-defined boundaries, within which all should be compelled constantly to remain until such time as their general improvement and good conduct" warranted their release.[19]

Lea advised President Fillmore and Secretary Stuart to allow the Menominee Tribe to remain in Wisconsin on a reservation that "will not be required by our emigrating population for many years to come." In 1848, the Menominee had agreed by treaty to immigrate to western Minnesota Territory. Two years later, a Menominee delegation visited the western frontier but expressed dissatisfaction with the land and a reluctance to remove.[20] President Fillmore conceded two extensions but Lea recommended the president authorize the department to negotiate a new treaty by which the Menominee would relinquish their Minnesota lands and accept a diminished reservation in Wisconsin.[21] Lea also favored allowing the Ottawa and Chippewa in Michigan to remain where they were and, while the U.S. Army continued to encourage the emigration of the Florida Seminoles, he advocated allowing the scattered tribal members to remain where they were in south Florida.

Lea supported expanding the Indian Office, seeking new superintendencies and agencies in Texas, New Mexico, Utah, and California, as well as on the Great Plains. Unlike Brown, who found no interest in Congress to extend civilian government and authority over Indian affairs due to the unsettled nature of slavery in the western territories, Lea discovered fertile ground, especially after Congress approved of the Compromise of 1850. With the issue of slavery momentarily resolved, Lea prepared a bill to reorganize the Indian Office and Representative Robert W. Johnson (D-AR) introduced it on February 20, 1851. Seven days later, Congress approved of the act and Lea immediately implemented it.[22]

The act repealed all existing superintendencies east of the Rocky Mountains and created three new ones: the northern superintendency, which included Wisconsin and Michigan; the southern superintendency, which encapsulated the border tribes in Kansas and Nebraska territories, as well as Indian Territory; and the central superintendency, which covered everything else in the West. Eleven agents making $1,500 annually replaced existing Indian agents, and Lea hired five additional agents at a salary of $1,000, with four assigned to New Mexico and one to Utah Territory. For the first time the provisions of the Nonintercourse Act were extended over tribal nations in the West residing north of the Gila River.

With congressional authorization, Lea dispatched treaty commissioners to Oregon Territory and to California to negotiate treaties of cession and amity (twenty-two in Oregon and nineteen in California).[23] Local opposition, however, led the Senate to reject thirty-nine of the treaties, with only the Rogue River and Umpqua treaties in Oregon ratified.[24] Lea advocated for Congress to appropriate sufficient fiscal resources to properly conduct tribal affairs in the far West. In New Mexico, the "untamed habits" of the tribes—Lea reasoned capriciously—rendered "its acquisition a misfortune and its possession a reproach to the Government."[25] Only with appropriate resources could the territory be civilized.

Lea convened the most significant treaty of the day, the September 17, 1851, treaty of Fort Laramie. While not all of the Plains tribes were party to the convention, the Teton Sioux, Assiniboine,

Mandan, Arikara, Gros Ventre, Crow, Cheyenne, and Arapahoe all agreed to defined territories and consented to western immigrants passing safely along the Oregon Trail.[26] The treaty reflected the priorities of Lea and Congress in that it fostered matters of national interests over the well-being of the tribes.

Lea and Stuart refined the reservation policy, viewing the measure as an alternative to extinction. "The question must now be fairly met," Stuart wrote in 1851. "A temporary system can no longer be pursued. The policy of removal, except under peculiar circumstances, must necessarily be abandoned." The "only alternatives are, to civilize or exterminate them."[27] Forthwith Lea, influenced by national railroad interests (Platte River route) and advocates of organizing Nebraska Territory, sought to clear the frontier of its indigenous inhabitants, including those who had emigrated a few years prior. A reticent Congress was not yet ready to authorize treaties until the matter of slavery in the territories was decided, so the negotiation of new treaties of limits would have to wait.

Notwithstanding congressional restraint, Lea advocated modification of existing treaties, believing they had been "made from time to time to meet the emergency of particular occasions."[28] He also argued in support of treaties of cessions to reduce the extent of reservations. Concentrating Native people on smaller reserved lands was not only central to assimilation but it was also the means of satisfying the demands of western progress. The 1851 Dakota treaty Lea negotiated resulted in a cession of 10 million acres of Minnesota prairie, leaving the Mdewakanton Sioux a small reservation ten miles in length along the Minnesota River.[29] Adding the Mendota Sioux treaty cession of 13 million acres, Lea and Minnesota superintendent of Indian affairs Alexander Ramsey negotiated on behalf of the traders in opening the southwestern quarter of Minnesota Territory to settlement.[30]

Appreciating that treaties were the supreme law of the land and had to be faithfully executed, the commissioner supported modifying tribal annuities, arguing they should be paid to the traders in fulfillment of tribal debt, continuing the oscillating policy governing annuities.[31] The federal debt due tribes by midcentury was significant, with nine treaties of cession obligating the United States to pay tribes $2,396,600 at 5 percent interest. In lieu of making investments, Congress appropriated funds each year of $1,742,240 for nine treaties as of 1852. That same year, the United States held in trust for tribes $4,344,000, payable at 5 percent interest. When combined with yet another schedule of annuities, the United States paid $478,280 annually to the tribes. Yet, many tribes never saw their funds because federal payments were paid directly to the traders, an evil Lea supposed "had to be endured" since the "system is fastened upon us."[32]

Lea believed annuities were "a curse to [the Indians] rather than a blessing," since such payments encouraged indolence and idleness. He suggested investing treaty annuities in secured federal bonds with the interest paid annually in order to awaken the tribal "spirit of enterprise" and encourage self-reliance.[33] He endeavored to convert existing treaty annuities, as well as all future annuities, into "a few plain, necessary, and assimilative provisions" such as tools, agricultural implements, and home-building items.[34]

COMMISSIONER GEORGE MANYPENNY

Lea remained commissioner until the inauguration of Franklin Pierce as president and resigned March 24, 1853. George W. Manypenny, an Ohio businessman and newspaper publisher who "was a man of energy, intelligence, and honesty who won the enmity of western politicians for his courageous resistance to fraudulent claims against Indian annuities," replaced Lea and assumed office on March 28, 1853.[35] Serving under Interior Secretary Robert McClelland, Manypenny was both a strong leader and an advocate for the welfare of the Natives.[36]

Manypenny refined the reservation system by interjecting a new strand in policy: allotting in severalty communal reservation lands. Further emigration of the tribes was no longer feasible since settlers now surrounded the tribal territories established under the removal policy. This was particularly the case in Kansas and Nebraska, which were rapidly settled. To remove the tribes farther west would result in needless suffering. "These tribes have been removed, step by step, from mountain to valley, and from river to plains, until they have been pushed half way across the continent," Manypenny exclaimed. "They can go no further."[37] Rather than consolidating tribes on several larger reservations as his predecessors had done, Manypenny lobbied for reducing the size of existing reservations and then allotting them in severalty. Where there were no reservations, such as in the Southwest, Manypenny exhorted Congress to use treaties to colonize the tribes in suitable locations where they could sustain themselves.[38]

Manypenny believed warfare and depredations would never be terminated by military force unless the Natives were annihilated. But extermination was neither practical nor moral, so the only option was to refine the reservation policy by reducing tribal land holdings, fixing permanent boundaries, and allotting the land in severalty, a concept the commissioner exposited on in great detail in 1855. "He must have a home; a fixed, settled, and permanent home," as soon "there will be no place to remove the Indian population."[39] A permanent home was the only moral action compatible "with the obligation of justice and humanity."[40]

In his first annual report, Manypenny disclosed a number of policy changes and described the two-month excursion he took to visit the frontier tribes, which he found both "alarmed" and "excited" at the prospect of further encroachment. The tribes opposed the further sale of land, but were open to such a possibility if they could remain on the land they then occupied and remain self-governing. Manypenny actively sought congressional authority to negotiate treaties with the western tribes in order to establish "well defined and permanent relations of amity."[41] In 1853, he reported to Congress that the Chippewa still owned valuable mineral land in Minnesota that the United States should acquire as soon as practical. The cession that followed benefitted the North Shore Mining Company of Reuben Carlton and his partners, who immediately developed the copper in the Arrowhead region of the territory.[42]

The commissioner was perhaps the most practical head of the Indian Office with regard to the idealized world reformers envisioned for Native people, recognizing their desire and right to remain on their ancestral lands. Appreciating the progress many of the border tribes had made in adapting to Euro-American ways, Manypenny acknowledged much work remained.

"As a Christian government and people, our obligations and duties are of the highest and holiest character, and we are accountable to the Maker of all men for the manner in which we discharge them."[43] Permanency of reservation lands would cultivate good effects and establish both "friendship and neighborliness" among Native and non-Native people.[44]

In concert with the prevailing attitudes of his day, Manypenny was committed to the proposition that in order to survive, American Indians had to assimilate American values and ideals. In 1856, he peered into the future and envisioned railroads transporting settlers who built towns and established farms. "When that time arrives, and it is at our very doors... where will be the habitation and what the condition of the rapidly wasting Indian tribes of the plains, the prairies, and of our new States and Territories? As sure as these great physical changes are impending, so sure will these poor denizens of the forest be blotted out of existence, and their dust be trampled under the foot of rapidly advancing civilization."[45] There was no alternative but to take steps "to designate suitable tracts or reservations of lands... for permanent homes" for the tribal nations.[46] A policy of expedient and convenient emigration was no longer an option.

Manypenny doubted the veracity of issuing annuities to individuals rather than tribal leaders, believing that the authority of leaders was diminished, in the process facilitating political disorder. This was not without merit, as tribal leadership was frequently undermined as individuals were decoupled from traditional social and political bonds. But Manypenny went a step further, arguing annuities were obstacles to civilization as they crippled and counteracted the "efforts made to domesticate and civilize" Natives.[47] As did Lea before him, Manypenny recommended Congress make annuities payable in goods, stock animals, and agricultural implements.[48] He refused to pay annuities to traders who took advantage of the Indians. In the treaties he negotiated, Manypenny placed all annuities under the discretion of the president and included a prohibition against individual debt being paid out of tribal funds.[49]

Manypenny's primary goal was to secure cessions of land from each of the tribes along the frontier in Kansas and Nebraska in order to facilitate the organization of civil government and settlement of the land. In March 1853, Congress appropriated funds for treaty councils and Manypenny headed west in August, although no treaties were negotiated. With the passage of the Kansas-Nebraska Act in 1854 and the anticipated opening of the land to settlement, Manypenny engaged in clearing the frontier of its aboriginal title, inserting land severalty provisions into all of the treaties. In spring of 1854, he negotiated nine treaties with the border tribes, beginning with the Ottoe and Missouria, opening the door to severalty and commutation of permanent annuities. In rapid succession, he negotiated similar treaties with the Omaha; Delaware; Shawnee; Ioway; Sauk and Fox (of Missouri); Kickapoo; the Kaskaskia, Peoria, Wea, and Piankeshaw; and the Miami.[50] In the thirty-six-month period of July 27, 1853, to August 7, 1856, Manypenny negotiated fifty-two treaties, as shown in Table 3.2, clearing 113,635,710 acres of aboriginal title.[51]

Manypenny inserted himself into the midst of a flourishing debate over the proper home of the Indian Office. In August 1854, a party of Sioux warriors awaiting annuity distribution at Fort Laramie, stole and butchered a cow belonging to a group of Mormon settlers heading across the plains. Rather than follow the protocols of the Nonintercourse Act, which would have reimbursed

Table 3.2. Indian Treaties between July 27, 1853, and August 7, 1856

Title	Location	Date	Land Ceded (in acres)	Ratified
Kiowa, Comanche, and Apache	Indian Ty.	7/27/1853	——	Yes
Rogue River	Oregon Ty.	9/10/1853	9,180,000	Yes
Cow Creek Umpqua	Oregon Ty.	9/19/1853	452,000	Yes
Ottoe and Missouria	Nebraska Ty.	3/15/1854	1,840,000	Yes
Omaha	Nebraska Ty.	3/16/1854	5,776,000	Yes
Delaware	Kansas Ty.	5/6/1854	1,588,000	Yes
Shawnee	Kansas Ty.	5/10/1854	1,400,000	Yes
Menominee	Wisconsin	5/12/1854	382,500	Yes
Ioway	Kansas Ty.	5/17/1854	95,200	Yes
Sauk and Fox of Missouri	Kansas Ty.	5/19/1854	95,360	Yes
Kickapoo	Kansas Ty.	5/19/1854	618,000	Yes
Piankeshaw, Wea, Peoria, Kaskaskia	Kansas Ty.	5/30/1854	904,640	Yes
Miami	Kansas Ty.	6/5/1854	299,360	Yes
Creek	Indian Ty.	6/18/1854	——	Yes
Seneca and Shawnee	Indian Ty.	8/23/1854	60,000	No
Quapaw	Indian Ty.	8/12/1854	96,000	No
Chippewa (Superior)	MN, MI, WI	9/30/1854	7,160,000	Yes
Choctaw and Chickasaw	Indian Ty.	11/4/1854	——	Yes
Rogue River	Oregon Ty.	11/15/1854	9,150	Yes
Shasta and Umpqua	Oregon Ty.	11/18/1854	1,600,000	Yes
Umpqua and Callapooya	Oregon Ty.	11/29/1854	2,880,000	Yes
Ottoe and Missouria	Nebraska Ty.	12/9/1854	——	Yes
Nisqually, Puyallup, etc.	Washington Ty.	12/26/1854	2,286,160	Yes
Willamette Valley Tribes	Oregon Ty.	1/4/1855	7,500,000	Yes
Duwamish, etc.	Washington Ty.	1/22/1855	——	Yes
S'Klallam	Washington Ty.	1/26/1855	——	Yes
Makah	Washington Ty.	1/31/1855	——	Yes
Wyandot	Kansas Ty.	1/31/1855	——	Yes

the immigrants for their loss from Sioux tribal annuities, the immigrants instead went to the army, which dispatched Lt. John L. Grattan, an interpreter, and twenty-nine soldiers to seek return of the stolen cow. Grattan and all with him were killed in an ensuing battle, resulting in a war with the Sioux in 1855.[52] While chagrined at the loss of life, Manypenny opined to Secretary McClelland that the army had no jurisdiction to arrest or even try Natives.[53] But neither did the Indian Office, leading Manypenny to advance the concept of the department having "direct control of the means necessary" to enforce its rules and regulations. By "careful attention and kind and humane treatment," Indian Office forces could exert greater influence on Native people "than bayonets and gunpowder."[54] Congress did not concur, and it would be another quarter century before it would grant the department authority to hire its own police force. In the meantime, critics branded the reservation system "the legalized murder of a whole nation."[55]

While Congress did not extend the jurisdiction of the Indian Office to police Indian Country, it did in March 1854 clarify the intent of the trade and intercourse act of 1834 to temporarily govern frontier conditions in an act commonly called the General Crimes Act.[56] The 1834 statute

Table 3.2. Indian Treaties between July 27, 1853, and August 7, 1856 (*cont'd*)

Title	Location	Date	Land Ceded (in acres)	Ratified
Chippewa (Mississippi)	Minnesota	2/22/1855	14,000,000	Yes
Winnebago	Minnesota	2/27/1855	690,540	Yes
Gila Apache (Mimbres)	New Mexico Ty.	6/9/1855	9,600,000	No
Walla Walla, Cayuse and Umatilla	OR/WA Ty.	6/9/1855	4,012,800	Yes
Yakima, etc.	Washington Ty.	6/9/1855	10,828,000	Yes
Nez Perce	OR/WA Ty.	6/11/1855	15,480,000	Yes
Mescalero Apache	New Mexico Ty.	6/14/1855	9,680,000	No
Choctaw and Chickasaw	Indian Ty.	6/22/1855	—	Yes
Des Chute, Upper and Lower	Oregon Ty.	6/25/1855	8,110,000	Yes
Quinault and Quilehute	Washington Ty.	7/1/1855	—	Yes
Flathead, Pend d'Oreille	Washington Ty.	7/16/1855	14,720,000	Yes
Navajo	New Mexico Ty.	7/18/1855	—	No
Ottawa and Chippewa	Michigan	7/31/1855	—	Yes
Chippewa (Sault Saint Marie)	Michigan	8/2/1855	—	Yes
Chippewa (Saginaw/Swan/Black)	Michigan	8/2/1855	—	Yes
Shoshone	Utah Ty.	8/7/1855	—	No
Ute (Capote)	New Mexico Ty.	8/8/1855	—	No
Comanche	Texas	8/30/1855	—	No
Ute (Mohuache)	New Mexico Ty.	9/11/1855	—	No
Apache (Jicarilla)	New Mexico Ty.	9/12/1855	—	No
Blackfeet and Flathead	Nebraska Ty.	10/17/1855	—	Yes
Molalla	Oregon Ty.	12/21/1855	—	Yes
Stockbridge and Munsee	Wisconsin	2/5/1856	1,681,920	Yes
Menominee	Wisconsin	2/11/1856	46,080	Yes
Creek and Seminole	Indian Ty.	8/7/1856	—	Yes

Total Land in Acres Ceded via Ratified Treaties: 113,635,710. Source: DeJong, *American Indian Treaties.*

declined federal authority over an "Indian committing any offense in the Indian Country . . . who has been punished by the local laws of the tribe" or where by treaty such exclusive jurisdiction was reserved by the tribe.[57] Notwithstanding, the perpetrator of any act of arson or assault with intent to kill committed against the person or property of another within Indian Country was to be tried and punished by federal law, whether Native or non-Native. In the chaotic environment of the frontier in Kansas and Nebraska territories, Congress sought, if only temporarily, to preclude any further violence or lawlessness.

COMMISSIONER JAMES W. DENVER

Manypenny served all four years of the Pierce administration and left office on March 31, 1857, just days after James Buchanan was inaugurated as president.[58] He was replaced by James W. Denver, a former California state representative and member of the House of Representatives (D-CA) during the 34th Congress (1855–1856). President Buchanan appointed Denver commissioner of Indian Affairs on April 8, 1857, and he took office nine days later, serving until December 2, 1857, when he resigned to serve as governor of Kansas Territory.[59] After serving as governor for a year, Denver was reappointed as commissioner on November 9, 1858, and served until March 12, 1859. In between his two terms, chief clerk Charles E. Mix served as interim commissioner and then commissioner for five months.

While Denver's tenure as commissioner was too brief to significantly impact any policy strands, he did advance the developing reservation system and its corollary, land severalty. More telling was his time as a representative from California and governor of Kansas Territory, during which he advocated a transcontinental railroad across the central plains and opposed the extension of slavery into Kansas. In both cases, he sought further reductions to tribal land holdings in both the border territories and across the plains.

Denver vociferously supported manual labor schools, arguing it was "more important that the Indian be taught to till the soil and to labor in the mechanical shops, than to have even a common school education."[60] He added to the oscillating debate on annuities, writing that "the great body of the Indians can be managed only through the chiefs." With this in mind, Denver favored paying annuities directly to the chiefs, rather than to individuals, as the latter reduced the stature of the chiefs in the eyes of the Natives to the level of a "common Indian," which in turn "increased lawlessness" and the "number of outrages."[61] In practice, Denver opposed annuities altogether, writing to Congressman A. H. Stephens (Whig-GA): "There seems to be no likelihood of a termination of this pauper system but with the extermination of the whole race."[62]

Denver, influenced by chief clerk Charles Mix, encouraged President Buchanan to consider modifying three policy strands: establish smaller reservations, encourage the Natives to cultivate the soil, and convert annuities from cash to agricultural implements.[63] But the commissioner and his father-in-law (Matthew Rombach) took advantage of his position and speculated in Indian land along the frontier, with Denver appointing numerous land agents to secure tribal allotments and, where practical, large tribal tracts. He resigned on March 12, 1859, and returned to California.

COMMISSIONER CHARLES E. MIX

In the midst of Denver's term, a most influential man served as commissioner. Charles E. Mix had been appointed chief clerk of the Indian Office in 1850, serving a total of eighteen years in the position. He was appointed commissioner of Indian affairs by President Buchanan on June 4, 1858, but avoided and was uncomfortable in the limelight of the commissionership, preferring a behind-the-scenes role where his influence was authoritative. With his appointment as chief clerk, Mix drafted at least a dozen treaties, met visiting tribal delegations, handled daily correspondence, and supervised staff, leaving his stamp on all aspects of policy. While he signed the 1858 annual report (and the 1867 report), Mix drafted or edited most of the Indian Office's annual reports in the late 1850s and 1860s.

Mix's philosophy of the reservation policy and his impact on its development is exemplified in the 1858 annual report. The United States had acquired via treaty 581,163,188 acres of land from tribal nations at a cost of $49,816,344 and, after deducting survey and sales expenses, netted an estimated $100,000,000 upon sale of the land.[64] But Mix presumed there were three "fatal errors" that marked policy. The removal of Native people from "place to place as our population advanced" fostered resentment and hostility, something Mix had witnessed firsthand in his years in the Indian Office. Then there was the misjudgment of assigning too much land to the tribes and allowing them to hold it in common, rather than in severalty. And the policy of granting large annuities, Mix concluded, discouraged industry and promoted indolence and profligacy. These policies prevented Natives from being "domesticate[d] and civilize[d]."[65]

The establishment of the Pima Reservation in New Mexico Territory (present-day Arizona) in February 1859, typified all three of these alleged indiscretions. In 1857, Denver impressed upon Interior Secretary Jacob Thompson and President Buchanan the need to protect the Pima and Maricopa villages, through which the national mail lines traversed. These routes, Denver declared prophetically, "will induce and increase white settlements that may conflict with [the Indians] rights." Protection from encroachments was absolutely necessary, especially since the tribes supplied "large quantities of breadstuff" for the territory.[66] The Pima claimed six million acres of aboriginal land, but the establishment of the reservation was limited to one hundred square miles, encapsulating only their agricultural fields and villages. The 1859 reservation, consistent with Mix's philosophy, kept the Pima within their aboriginal territory but limited the size of the reservation to sixty-four thousand acres. And rather than provide the Pima and Maricopa with an annual annuity, Mix provided $10,000 worth of tools, agricultural implements, seed, blacksmithing equipment, etc.[67]

Mix's lasting legacy was in his role as chief clerk, where he issued a compilation of rules and regulations for Indian Office employees entitled *Office Copy of the Laws, Regulations, etc., of the Indian Bureau, 1850*. This compilation particularized the authorities of the Indian Office as defined by federal statutes (primarily the Nonintercourse Act, as amended) and departmental regulations, and included copious administrative forms and information that served as a canonical guide for departmental employees for decades. Among its more salient features, the manual defined the administrative measures for handling trade, illustrated how to account for such trade, described how to handle depredations, and provided detailed guidelines for prohibiting ardent spirits. Because the emigration of the tribes represented a significant function of the Indian Office, an entire section described emigration matters from contract pay for officers, agents, and physicians, to employing interpreters and conductors. Eighteen ready-to-use forms were provided to implement emigration policies.[68]

Regulations defined the administrative structure of the Indian Office, including the scope and jurisdiction of superintendencies and agencies. Regulations issued by Secretary of War Joel R. Poinsett, in June 1837, for instance, described the role of the department in negotiating treaties. The Indian Office was to "determine the time and place at which the Indians should be convened in council" and, where practicable, convene such conferences in Indian Country.[69] The major part of the manual dealt with licensing traders and restricting liquor in Indian Country.[70]

Mix resigned as commissioner on November 1, 1858, having served fewer than 150 days as commissioner, and returned to his role as chief clerk. He remained in the Indian Office until he retired from government service in 1869, with more than 30 years with the department. When he resigned, the Indian Office calculated that Mix had served 1,579 days (4.3 years) as acting commissioner, having labored under twelve commissioners, earning a legacy as a man of "integrity and efficiency."[71]

COMMISSIONER ALFRED B. GREENWOOD

On May 4, 1859, President Buchanan appointed Alfred B. Greenwood as acting commissioner, a position for which the former three-term congressman (D-AR) neither sought nor was prepared to administer.[72] A Georgian by birth and a former agent implementing Cherokee emigration, Greenwood was well known in the House of Representatives for his support of the Kansas-Nebraska Act, popular sovereignty, and southern principles. As commissioner, Greenwood relied on the expertise of Mix and, like his predecessors, supported the reservation policy and its corollary, land severalty. He was the fifth commissioner of the decade to support updating Indian Office regulations, a task Congress finally authorized in February 1859.

While Greenwood accepted the inevitable assimilation of Native people, he acknowledged it would come "by slow degrees" and only after their sequestration. As did Mix and Denver before him, Greenwood supported the application of tribal annuities to purchase stock animals and farm implements.[73] He also believed the reservation policy needed modification, especially in California, Washington, and Oregon. While no additional treaties were negotiated with the California tribes, Greenwood bargained for two treaties with tribes in Kansas: one with the Sauk and Fox and one with the Kansas Tribe.[74] His support of the reservation policy was particularly pronounced on the southern plains. When the Pike's Peak gold rush began, tens of thousands of miners crossed Cheyenne land, hunting game and disrupting Cheyenne life. When the Cheyenne retaliated, the miners called for military protection or took matters into their own hands. In fall of 1859, Greenwood advised Congress to negotiate a new treaty with the tribe in order to restore peace.[75] The Cheyenne, Greenwood wrote, "must entirely change their habits, and, in fixed localities, look to the cultivation of the soil and the raising of stock for their future support. There is no alternative to providing for them . . . but to exterminate them, which the dictates of justice and humanity alike forbid."[76]

As sectional differences intensified, Greenwood and Interior Secretary Jacob Thompson (another Southerner) faced increasing skepticism from Northern Republicans who distrusted Greenwood's proslavery sentiments after the commissioner criticized missionaries among the Cherokee for "interfering with the institution of slavery."[77] When Greenwood and Thompson diplomatically reached out to the Creek and Cherokee nations, the Republicans saw a Southern conspiracy. Henceforth, neither Greenwood nor Thompson was considered trustworthy. Thompson resigned on February 8, 1861, and Greenwood followed shortly thereafter.

CONCLUSION

In the 1850s, the commissioners of Indian affairs were united in their views that there was no alternative to the reservation system short of extermination.[78] As the decade drew to a close, and with Civil War looming, the United States had yet to fully implement the reservation policy. While the policy arguably worked in Kansas and Nebraska, it had yet to root in the far West. In California, the implementation of the policy or lack thereof proved an embarrassment, and in Washington and Oregon territories action was essential "to save the race from extermination."[79] On the Great Plains, the policy was a complete failure, as tribes were without defined reservations. Where they were established, such as among the Ponca Tribe, the policy resulted in "destitution and desperation," with the Indian Office failing to provide treaty goods to sustain the tribe.[80] In Texas, locals either demanded the complete removal of the Natives or exterminated them. Some 1,415 Natives fled to land leased from the Choctaw and Chickasaw nations in Indian Territory in order to protect their families.[81]

On the verge of Civil War, Thompson summed up the prevailing situation by noting that while the same general relationship existed between tribal nations and the United States government, there were in fact two categories of tribes. There was one with whom the United States had treaty relationships and one with whom the United States did not. The former was further subdivided into annuity tribes without recognized rights to particular reservation lands and annuity tribes with recognized title guaranteed "forever." While recognized title tribes held land communally and/or in severalty (fee or aboriginal title), those within the border states were completely surrounded by settlers, and the western tribes remained isolated. The latter group included tribes in Arizona and California, and on the central plains. It was with these tribes, perhaps the majority in the country, that the United States sought to pursue policies "as circumstances may render expedient," subordinate to the legislative prerogative of Congress and as sanctioned by the federal courts.[82]

As the decade closed, sectional differences over slavery and state's rights divided the country. As a Southern Democrat, Greenwood was drawn into this dispute and resigned on March 4, 1861, refusing to serve in the administration of Republican president Abraham Lincoln. Instead, Greenwood joined the Confederacy and served as a delegate to the Confederate Congress (1862–1865), during which time he sought to recruit the Cherokee and Choctaw nations to join the Confederacy.[83] Ominously, a new political battle was brewing over the administration of Indian affairs, with many policymakers and reformers advocating the return of the Office of Indian Affairs to the auspices of the War Department. In February 1859, both the House and Senate narrowly rejected the transfer, temporarily postponing such action.[84]

4

"TO CONQUER BY KINDNESS"

Civil War and Peace Policy, 1861–1881

In 1861, Secretary of the Interior Caleb Smith informed President Lincoln that Indian affairs were "in a very unsettled and unsatisfactory condition."[1] The Southern states were in open rebellion, Indian Territory had fallen under Confederate control, and tribes in the West were restless. Fear and threat of violence permeated the border tribes, as well as the tribes in Indian Territory. In the Southwest, the Navajo and Apache depredated New Mexico Territory. Confederate troops occupied southern Arizona, including the agricultural fields, grain mill, and food supply in the Pima villages. In Minnesota, the Dakota War erupted and the western trails across the central plains were closed to immigrant traffic.

Throughout the West, federal policy broke down, resulting in two military massacres of the Cheyenne, as well as the massacre of Captain William Fetterman and his U.S. Army troops in the Powder River country of Montana. Confederate diplomats encouraged the southern tribes to ally with the Confederacy, British-Canadian emissaries encouraged tribes along the Upper Missouri River to cause mischief, and the withdrawal of federal troops from the West encouraged lawlessness. Not surprisingly, Interior Secretary James Harlan warned President Johnson in 1865 that "gentlemen of high position, intelligence, and personal character" were advancing a policy of "total destruction of the Indians." Such a policy "no enlightened nation can adopt or sanction ... without a forfeiture of its self-respect and the respect of the civilized nations of the earth."[2]

By the mid-1860s, the West was awash in conflict, demonstrating that the idealized world envisioned by the reformers in the antebellum period not only failed to materialize but also threatened peaceful relations throughout the West. Union general Ulysses S. Grant was elected president in 1868 and initiated a Peace Policy intended to unite the nation and heal the ravages of war. The president's policy of "conquest by kindness" extended an invitation to Christian churches to appoint men of character and integrity as Indian agents. Military conquest also accelerated in the postwar years and by 1880 most tribes were sequestered on reservations and, despite an occasional outbreak, the West was generally quiet by the early 1880s.

At the same time, a new breed of reformers influenced Indian policy. Born in the Freedman's Bureau of the postbellum era, these reformers advocated social policies and came armed with the knowledge and experience of how to incorporate a people—the freedmen—into the American social fabric. The Senate in the 1870 Indian appropriation act even debated whether the United States exercised an "excess of sympathy for the negro race [and] an utter destitution of it for the Indian race." Regardless, the solution to both was integration. This bipartisanship was both a continuation of previous efforts to integrate Native people and a mixture of new efforts.[3] These efforts included a bevy of social programs and policies, all predicated on the virtue of labor. This concept of free labor and self-support permeated all late nineteenth and early twentieth-century policy efforts.[4]

In the years following Civil War, the *Annual Report of the Commissioner of Indian Affairs* increased in length and detail, illustrating several important strands.[5] The federal government had established administrative control throughout Indian Country, with superintendencies and agencies dotting the West. While many of these administrative units were underfunded, the fact remained that there was a growing federal presence. Moreover, there was a shift in policy away from treating tribes as sovereign nations and towards a de facto policy of wardship, with treaty making ended in 1871. Tribes were increasingly sequestered and natural resources were extracted from tribal lands in violation of Indian rights. This was especially the case in the 1870s, as scores of tribes capitulated to the federal presence, with the extraction of natural resources to fuel the emerging industrial revolution sweeping the country. Federal policy was premised on expediency, with the goal of accomplishing the greatest national good in the least amount of time at the lowest possible cost.

During the 1860s and 1870s, ten men served as commissioner of Indian affairs, including the first American Indian—the Seneca aide-de-camp to General Grant, Ely S. Parker. The first commissioner of the era was William P. Dole (1861–1865); followed by Dennis N. Cooley (1865–1866); Lewis V. Bogy (1866–1867); Nathaniel Green Taylor (1867–1869); Ely S. Parker (1869–1871); Francis A. Walker (1871–1872); Edward P. Smith (1872–1875); John Q. Smith (1875–1877); Ezra A. Hayt (1877–1880); and Roland E. Trowbridge (1880–1881).

COMMISSIONER WILLIAM DOLE

President Lincoln nominated William Palmer Dole, a former Whig in the Indiana legislature and an 1860 Republican Convention delegate, as commissioner on March 8, 1861.[6] Dole was confirmed by the Senate on March 12 and assumed office immediately. While he had a genuine concern for Native people, Dole had no prior experience in Indian affairs, relying on chief clerk Charles Mix

Table 4.1. Heads of the Indian Office and Major Policies, 1861–1881

Name	Title	Years of Service	Main Policies
William P. Dole (R)	Commissioner	4.3 years (1861–1865)	Reservations, severalty, need treaties to extinguish aboriginal title
Dennis N. Cooley (R)	Commissioner	1.25 years (1865–1866)	Military authority, prevent taxation, treaties, reconstruction, control trade
Lewis V. Bogy (D)	Commissioner*	4 months (1866–1867)	Trading contracts, treaties
Nathaniel G. Taylor (R)	Commissioner	2 years (1867–1869)	Peace treaties, peace commission, reduce reservations
Ely S. Parker (R)	Commissioner	2.25 years (1869–1871)	Peace Policy, reservation policy, and treaty making
Francis A. Walker (R)	Commissioner	13 months (1871–1872)	Confine to reservations, federal funds, wardship, state authority
Edward P. Smith (R)	Commissioner	3.75 years (1872–1875)	Peace, wardship, federal jurisdiction, citizenship
John Q. Smith (R)	Commissioner	1.75 years (1875–1877)	Consolidation, severalty, federal jurisdiction
Ezra A. Hayt (R)	Commissioner	2.3 years (1877–1880)	Indian police, severalty, boarding schools, efficiency
Roland E. Trowbridge (R)	Commissioner	1 year (1880–1881)	Consolidation, severalty

* Not confirmed by the Senate.

and therefore being heavily influenced by Mix's views on the reservation policy and the evolving consensus on land severalty. But Dole also brought his own unique interests to Washington, believing the United States had to negotiate treaties with all tribes, viewing such conventions as the primary means by which the United States controlled tribes.[7]

In 1861, Dole urged Secretary Smith to negotiate treaties with tribes in the Southwest, a region in which Congress refused to negotiate treaties based on the prevailing theory that Spain and Mexico had already extinguished aboriginal title.[8] This policy was "radically wrong," Dole argued, as treaties were the only legal mechanism to extinguish aboriginal title and protect land for Native people.[9] It was senseless to argue whether or not Spain or Mexico had extinguished aboriginal title, Dole stated. Tribes had a moral if not a legal right to the land. A year later, Dole reiterated the need for treaties, arguing a failure to utilize them would be disastrous to the tribes.[10] To his credit, the Indian Office negotiated fifty treaties during Dole's tenure, with the Senate ratifying half of them.

Dole informed Smith that there were two means to establish peace in the West. The first was to set aside land from the public domain and appropriate funds to provide for the Natives and enable them to "commence their new mode of life under favorable conditions." The second was to acknowledge that the western tribes held aboriginal title just as the eastern tribes did and then negotiate treaties to extinguish this title and appropriate funds for tribal adjustment to civilized life. Either option, Dole argued, resulted in the same expense. The difference was the recognition of aboriginal title and the use of treaties to extinguish tribal claims to land not reserved by treaty.

Moreover, treaties would preclude Native people from supposing they were separated from their land "by [an] irresistible power" and "robbed of their hunting grounds, crowded upon scanty reservations, and compelled to subsist upon its bounty."[11] It was illogical to Dole to deal with some tribes and not others since they both held identical tenure to the soil.

In California, Dole was committed to "a complete change in the management" of tribal affairs. Thousands of Natives had been driven from their homes into the deserts or mountains, with many indentured under state law, a practice "subject to enormous and outrageous abuses." Others were "hunted like wild and dangerous beasts of prey, [with] the parents ... 'murdered,' and the children 'kidnapped.'"[12] There were but four reservations in the state—Mendocino, Smith River, Tule River, and Round Valley—encompassing just 31,761 acres.[13] The California tribes, Dole explained, had the "most righteous claims" to the land, yet they were dispossessed and reduced to "vagabonds to steal or starve." Considering the tribes once held "undisputed possession of this beautiful domain," the United States "ought not to withhold the little which by every consideration of humanity and justice, they may ... so imperatively and rightfully demand."[14]

While anxious about tribal rights, Dole just as feverishly worked to break up reservations into smaller territories and into individually held allotments.[15] His attention to eliminating large reservations and replacing them with smaller ones upon which many tribes could be confined, foreshadowed the consolidation policy that gained favor after the Civil War. Such a construct enabled the Indian Office to better manage, educate, and control the Indians. Consequently, Dole urged Congress to authorize the negotiation of new treaties calling for further emigration of the border tribes in Kansas and Nebraska territories due to the devastation they faced in the wake of the Civil War, with an estimated ten thousand Native people driven from their homes and left to wander.[16] Congress approved of such treaties in 1863.

With the anticipated end of the Civil War, Dole predicted, "[m]ost, if not all of the [tribes] will gladly exchange their present homes for a home in [Indian] territory." Any force on the part of the United States to affect such a result, however, would be viewed by the tribes as "a wanton and disgraceful breach of national faith." To encourage the tribes to emigrate once more would require adjustments to existing treaties with the Five Tribes, and because the latter allied with the Confederacy, Dole proposed the United States should adjust their treaties as a punitive measure for those allying with the Confederacy while allegedly protecting the rights of those who did not.[17] While he negotiated a treaty with the Creek Nation in 1863, providing for the cession of 700 square miles (448,000 acres) for such relocated tribes, the Senate failed to ratify the convention.[18]

In the Southwest, the U.S. Army forced the Navajo and Apache to Bosque Redondo in eastern New Mexico rather than negotiate treaties reserving territory in their homelands. But what the tribes needed were treaties that recognized aboriginal title before they ceded land to the United States.[19] Continued confinement at Bosque Redondo, Dole offered, would require an appropriation "counted by millions" if the tribes were not provided with the means of earning a living. Dole encouraged Congress to establish a reservation for the Navajo in their own country as both a humane gesture and as a matter of good policy.[20] Meanwhile, he criticized military control of Bosque Redondo, with General Grant turning the military reservation over to the Indian Office.

Dole was apprehensive of federal policy being "governed by the course of events, rather than by the adoption of a well-settled policy."[21] While encouraging land severalty, he sought to direct policy towards tribal members based on their "good conduct, and … disposition to abandon the[ir] ancient customs … and engage in the more rationale pursuits of civilization."[22] Consequently, he advocated additional resources be made available for Indian affairs. In lieu of annuities, which he blamed for Native reliance on "charity rather than on their own exertions," Dole favored providing tools, pointing to the agriculturally rich Pima in central Arizona and their success in adapting to market forces by providing food to much of the territory and U.S. military posts.[23] In acknowledgment of the success and importance of the Pima's agricultural pursuits, Dole provided them with one hundred muskets and ten thousand rounds of ammunition so they could defend the territory.[24]

Dole also sought to insulate the tribal nations in Indian Territory, tribes for which the United States had treaty obligations to protect. At the commencement of the war, he informed the Five Tribes (Cherokee, Choctaw, Chickasaw, Creek, and Seminole) that the United States had no intention of interfering with their internal affairs and that he had requested the War Department to protect them in the event war spilled over into Indian Territory.[25] Escalation of the rebellion in the East, however, led to the withdrawal of federal troops from the West, leaving Indian Territory vulnerable to Confederate overtures. In spring of 1861, each of the Five Tribes signed treaties of alliance with the Confederacy, which in turn negotiated treaties of amity with the Seneca, Comanche, Delaware, Shawnee, Tonkawa, Osage, and Quapaw Tribes.[26]

While some in Congress—Senator James Harlan (R-IA) in particular—advocated organization of civil government in Indian Territory, Dole did not, believing it violated treaties the tribes had with the United States. To create such a government would be a "gross breach of national faith." Notwithstanding, he argued the Five Tribes "should be required to receive within the limits of their country other tribes with whom they are on friendly terms."[27] While Dole was able to preclude territorial organization, he was unable to stop punitive postwar treaties and the reduction of the Five Tribes' land base in Indian Territory.[28]

Dole's ideas regarding the reservation policy focused on isolating the tribes from nontribal communities. In areas settled by homesteaders, Dole suggested the practicality of consolidating tribes. In Michigan, for instance, he supported locating all the tribes "upon a single suitable reservation" where an agent could model and care for them. He advanced the same concept at the Green Bay Agency for the Menominee, Oneida, Stockbridge, and Munsee tribes. And for the New York tribes (Iroquois), Dole believed their churches, schools, homes, agricultural pursuits, and devotion to thrift qualified them, "aside from … treaty stipulations," to be freed from the government trust relationship.[29] For all other tribes, Dole reiterated a common theme of his administration: the United States either had to use overwhelming force to "compel conformity on the part of the Indians" or "induce the[m] to negotiate … treaties" reserving small tracts of land. The latter option was self-evident to Dole, who could "hardly realize that the former is seriously advocated."[30] Recognizing that much of the arid West was unsuitable for agriculture absent irrigation, Dole worked to insert treaty provisions for stock animals, which he believed were more suitable for the wants of the Natives and adaptable to the arid West. That it was a form of social nudging towards a civilized occupation was self-evident.[31]

By the mid-1860s, reformers grew tired of Dole's approach and attacked the Indian Office for not doing enough to integrate the Natives. John Beeson (a Methodist pastor), Henry Whipple (an Episcopal priest), and John Pope (U.S. Army general), resurrected the concept of transferring the Indian Office back to the War Department.[32] In a February 1864 letter to Secretary of War Edwin Stanton, Pope proposed to overhaul the Indian Office, arguing "that our Indian policy has totally failed of any humanizing influence over the Indians."[33] Pope was determined that the United States abandon the treaty system and refused to recognize aboriginal title. While "a radical change in our Indian policy," Pope believed Indian affairs should be returned to military control "without the interposition of Indian agents."[34] He also supported removing the tribes—"with or without their consent"—to a single isolated reservation and then terminating the payment of annuities. To further ensure the peace and transformation of the Natives, Pope proposed disarming all of them and abolishing their tribal organizations to hasten integration.

Dole initially ignored Pope's proposal but was forced to respond after it was published in the *Army and Navy Journal*. Dole acknowledged mistakes may have been made in the Indian Office but focused more on the failed military policies at Bosque Redondo where the U.S. Army forced the Navajo and Apache to live under military rule. In New Mexico, "military operations have been almost continuous" while in Indian Territory "it was seldom necessary." The difference was the use of treaties and an acknowledgment of aboriginal title, both of which were matters of respect.[35] As for forced consolidation, Pope's "scheme of colonization was fraught with insuperable difficulties and objections." Where, Dole asked, could Native people "deprived of their arms," reside in the West and survive? And how would peace be maintained between hostile tribes? Dole argued for the establishment of three large territories into which the tribes might be consolidated, but beyond this there were too many differences to expect the tribes to coexist on a single reservation. The use of boarding schools, rather than day schools, was the only "hope for permanent good to the Indians."[36] But even this would be accomplished only by "the patient, persevering effort … [of] reclamation and civilization."[37] Dole's oversimplification of policy was met with skepticism and then dismissed.

In the months that followed the massacre of Cheyenne women and children at Sand Creek, Dole shouldered the burden of criticism and, with the appointment of Senator Harlan as secretary of the interior, fell into disfavor with the party. While Harlan did not assume office until May 1865, he critiqued the Indian Office and its policies at every opportunity. Within weeks of President Lincoln's assassination in April 1865, Dole was forced from office, resigning July 6.

COMMISSIONER DENNIS N. COOLEY

President Andrew Johnson nominated Dennis Nelson Cooley, a transplanted New Englander living in Iowa, as commissioner of Indian affairs on July 9.[38] A trusted colleague of Harlan, Cooley served as commissioner from July 1865 to October 1866, with Secretaries Harlan and Stanton, General Pope, and President Johnson directing all policy matters. The Johnson administration, focused on Reconstruction and impeachment, ignored Cooley's call for reform.

Harlan and Stanton favored rapid dispossession of the Indians and the establishment of small, isolated reservations. As a practical matter, during Cooley's administration, the Indian Office was subject to the policies of the War Department. In his 1865 annual report, Cooley noted: "Where Indians are hostile, the civil authority is to be held in abeyance until measures taken by the military authorities for quieting the outbreak have been concluded." In circumstances "where the Indians are generally quiet and peaceable, the military are to render assistance when appealed to by the agents."[39]

Cooley advised sweeping changes in the administration of the Indian Office, including asking Congress for authority to strictly control traders and set a schedule of values on trade goods to preclude merchants from taking advantage of Natives. He also sought authority to punish agents who had an interest in, or were involved in, the profits of trading posts. To overcome cattle theft—especially in Indian Territory—Cooley pressed legislative authority to prosecute rustlers. Beyond this, he sought to reorganize the Indian Office and increase the remuneration (with a graduated schedule) of the agents and provide them with housing where it was not available. To combat an increasingly difficult situation for border tribes who had received land in severalty under treaty provisions, Cooley requested the Justice Department to intervene and preclude state taxation.[40]

Among Cooley's more significant proposals, which included Harlan's backing, was the immediate organization of civil government in Indian Territory. As part of this effort, he pushed for the relocation of the border tribes into Indian Territory and he recommended the Senate ratify a series of treaties that he had submitted to Secretary Harlan. Based on the outcome of these treaties, Cooley would then revise or add agents. He also argued the United States should purchase land for the California Indians and then formally extinguish their aboriginal title, and he recommended the pro rata distribution of tribal funds for those—such as some of the Pottawatomie—who had become U.S. citizens.[41]

As moderate Republicans, Harlan and Cooley faced an uphill battle in effecting policy change due to radical Republican control of the Congress and their focus on Reconstruction. Harlan, while still in the Senate, encouraged his colleagues to adopt what came to be known as the Harlan Bill (S. 459). In February and March 1865, the Senate debated the bill calling for civil government in Indian Territory under the principles of the Northwest Ordinance of 1787. Such a bill was not without opposition. As Senator Lafayette Sabine Foster (R-CT) correctly argued, it "changes our whole Indian policy." Harlan defended the bill, which also included consolidation of the tribes in Indian Territory, stating its primary purpose was to establish civil government for the purpose of opening the territory to settlement. Foster was presciently unconvinced: "The moment the Territory is organized our people will go upon the Territory, and there will be no power to stop them."[42]

Harlan refused to acquiesce, declaring the tribes in Indian Territory had forfeited their rights by allying with the Confederacy. Senator Jacob M. Howard (R-MI) concurred with Foster, viewing the bill as "a complete revolution of the principles which lie at the bottom of our Indian policy."

"Hitherto the United States have not assumed to possess political power over the Indian tribes," Howard argued in defense of tribal authority, but "have regarded the Indian tribes in most respects as independent nations [as] consecrated by a clause in the Constitution of the United States."[43] While the Senate voted seventeen to nine in favor, the House of Representatives did not consider it, and the bill died.[44] Congress, nonetheless, made clear its intent to dramatically modify policy.

Having failed to advance civil government while in the Senate, Harlan, as secretary of the interior, worked to advance the concept as a matter of administrative policy. He was adamant that the United States no longer was obligated to abide by the antebellum treaties signed with the Five Tribes. After all, the tribes joined the Confederacy, a "perfidious" act of "unprovoked war."[45] In August 1865, Harlan instructed Cooley to proceed to Indian Territory, meet with the tribes to negotiate treaties authorizing civil government, and inform them that Congress had authorized the president to abrogate their treaties, but that he was inclined to treat the tribes "with forbearance and liberality" if they cooperated.[46] While Cooley met with the Cherokee, Choctaw, Chickasaw, Creek, Seminole, Osage, Seneca, Quapaw, Shawnee, Wyandotte, Wichita, and Comanche at a treaty conference held at Fort Smith, Arkansas, in September 1865, the best he could muster was a treaty of amity, with the tribes arguing they had not been empowered by their people to make any concessions except peace and friendship.[47] The Senate refused to ratify the convention as it did not include any provisions for civil government.[48]

Failing to secure Reconstruction treaties with the Five Tribes in 1865, Cooley called them to Washington, D.C., in January 1866 to continue negotiations, holding firmly to the position that most of the Indians had not only supported the Confederacy but also forfeited their rights under treaties with the United States.[49] Throughout the winter and spring of 1866, Cooley, Colonel Ely Parker, and southern superintendency head Elijah Sells outlined four provisions that they insisted had to be included in the Reconstruction treaties. These included the proper manner of "adjusting affairs between the loyal and disloyal" Natives, providing compensation to those loyal by their disloyal brethren, properly identifying the role "of the freedman in relation to the tribe," and requiring a cession of land from each of the tribes to be used for relocating border tribes into Indian Territory.[50] While civil government remained elusive, the voluntary relocation of additional tribes into Indian Territory took a step closer to materializing.

Cooley oversaw numerous treaty negotiations, executing forty-two treaties between June 8, 1865, and August 29, 1866—twenty-two of which were ratified by the Senate. Twenty of the treaties were left unratified by the Senate or were never submitted for its advice and consent, as shown in Table 4.2.

Cooley requested authority to negotiate treaties with the tribes in Kansas and in Idaho and New Mexico Territories. While authorized to negotiate with the tribes in Kansas, he was prohibited from doing so in New Mexico, and those he negotiated in Idaho Territory remained unratified. In New Mexico, the Senate held firmly to its position that aboriginal title had already been extinguished by Spain and Mexico, and treaties were unnecessary. In an effort to curb lawlessness, Cooley advocated a code of laws to punish criminals committing violent acts, whether such crimes were Indian vs. Indian, Indian vs. white, or white vs. Indian.

Table 4.2. Treaties Negotiated between June 1865 and August 1866

No. Tribe	Date	Location	Purpose	Ratified
1. Ute	June 8, 1865	Utah Territory	Cession	No
2. Choctaw	June 19, 1865	Choctaw Nation	Peace/friendship	No
3. Cherokee	June 23, 1865	Choctaw Nation	Peace/friendship	No
4. Chickasaw	July 14, 1865	——	Peace/friendship	No
5. Northern Paiute	August 12, 1865	Oregon	Amity/cession	Yes
6. Apache, Kiowa, Arapaho, and Comanche	August 15, 1865	Kansas	Peace	No
7. Cheyenne/Arapaho	August 18, 1865	Kansas	Peace	No
8. Seneca, Shawnee, Osage, Quapaw, Cherokee, Choctaw, Chickasaw, Creek, Seminole	September 13, 1865	Arkansas	Peace	No
9. Southern Paiute	September 18, 1865	Utah Territory	Cession	No
10. Osage	September 29, 1865	Kansas	Cession/friendship	Yes
11. Minniconjou Sioux	October 10, 1865	Dakota Territory	Friendship	Yes
12. Lower Brule Sioux	October 14, 1865	Dakota Territory	Friendship	Yes
13. Cheyenne/Arapaho	October 14, 1865	Kansas	Peace/commerce	Yes
14. Cheyenne, Apache, Arapaho	October 17, 1865	Kansas	Confederation	Yes
15. Kiowa/Comanche	October 18, 1865	Kansas	Peace/friendship	Yes
16. Two Kettle Sioux	October 19, 1865	Dakota Territory	Peace/friendship	Yes
17. Blackfeet Sioux	October 19, 1865	Dakota Territory	Peace/friendship	Yes
18. San Arc Sioux	October 20, 1865	Dakota Territory	Peace/friendship	Yes
19. Yanktonai Sioux	October 20, 1865	Dakota Territory	Peace/friendship	Yes
20. Hunkpapa Sioux	October 20, 1865	Dakota Territory	Peace/friendship	Yes
21. Oglala Sioux	October 28, 1865	Dakota Territory	Peace/friendship	Yes
22. Yanktonai Sioux	October 28, 1865	Dakota Territory	Peace/friendship	Yes
23. Weber River Ute	October 30, 1865	Utah Territory	Cession/removal	No
24. Warms Springs	November 15, 1865	Oregon	Allotment	Yes
25. Blackfeet, Blood, Piegan, Gros Ventre	November 16, 1865	Montana Territory	Cession/friendship	No
26. Bannock	Spring 1866	Idaho Territory	Cession	No
27. Shawnee	March 1, 1866	Washington,D.C.	Cession	No
28. Seminole	March 21, 1866	Washington,D.C.	Peace/cession	Yes
29. Pottawatomie	March 29, 1866	Washington,D.C.	Amend 1861 treaty	Yes
30. Bois Forte Chippewa	April 7, 1866	Washington,D.C.	Peace/cession	Yes
31. Owyhee Shoshone	April 21, 1866	Idaho Territory	Cession/friendship	No
32. Choctaw/Chickasaw	April 28, 1866	Washington,D.C.	Peace/cession	Yes
33. Brule/Oglala Sioux	June 27, 1866	Dakota Territory	Friendship/commerce	No
34. Cheyenne	June 27, 1866	Dakota Territory	Friendship/commerce	No
35. Creek	July 4, 1866	Washington,D.C.	Peace/cession	Yes
36. Delaware	July 4, 1866	Washington,D.C.	Peace/cession	Yes
37. Cherokee	July 13, 1866	Washington,D.C	Peace/cession	No
38. Crow	July 16, 1866	Montana Territory	Friendship/cession	No
39. Assiniboine	July 18, 1866	Montana Territory	Friendship/cession	No
40. Cherokee	July 19, 1866	Washington,D.C.	Amnesty	Yes
41. Mandan, Arikaree, Gros Ventre	July 27, 1866	Dakota Territory	Peace/friendship	No
42. Uintah Ute	August 29, 1866	Colorado Territory	Peace/friendship	No

Source: DeJong, *American Indian Treaties*, 158–59 and 181–82.

The issue of taxation of allotted lands in Kansas proved to be an especially embarrassing situation for the department. Miami, Kaskaskia, Wea, Peoria, and Shawnee tribal members securing land in severalty under treaty provisions found themselves losing their land to Kansas tax forfeiture laws. In 1860, the Kansas Territorial government enacted a statute authorizing taxation of allotted tribal lands upon issuance of a patent from the United States. The following year, the Kansas Enabling Act expressly prohibited any impairment of the "rights of person or property now pertaining to the Indians of said Territory, so long as such rights shall remain unextinguished by treaty between the United States and such Indians."[51] Before any Native land became subject to state taxation, the president had to concur, but only after he received the consent of the tribe. "It was certainly not understood by the Indians when making their treaties that the mere fact of their accepting lands in severalty should per se break up their tribal relations," Cooley explained in 1866.[52] Taxation was no small matter, as it implied citizenship and, by virtue of the 1866 Civil Rights Act, U.S. citizens would not be "capable of taking part of any treaties to be hereafter made with their people." With tribal lands being alienated to forfeiture, Cooley asked Harlan to request the United States Attorney General to intercede on behalf of the tribes.[53]

In December 1866, the U.S. Supreme Court weighed in on the matter of taxation of both allotted and tribal lands in two separate cases. In *The Kansas Indians*, the Supreme Court overturned the decision of the Kansas Supreme Court, ruling the state statute unconstitutional. The court opined that the 1817 Shawnee treaty unambiguously declared their land would not be liable for taxes so long as the Shawnee owned it.[54] In 1854, the Shawnee and United States negotiated another treaty providing for allotment in severalty. Because the treaty was silent on the taxation issue, Kansas concluded it did not intend to extend the exemption. The treaty, however, did provide that land taken in severalty included the typical "guards and restrictions as may be advisable for their protection."[55] The same restrictions governed the severalty process for the other tribes in question.

Justice David Davis penned the opinion of the court, concluding state taxation was null and void and in violation of federal treaties that guaranteed Native landowners the same rights as their brothers holding land in common. Moreover, the court concluded that "if the tribal organization of Indian bands is recognized by the political department of the National Government as existing; that is to say, if the National Government makes treaties with, and has its Indian agent among them, paying annuities and dealing otherwise with 'head men,'" then the state is not authorized "to regard the tribal organization as gone, and the Indians as citizens of the state . . . subject to its laws."[56] On the same day, the court ruled in *The New York Indians* that the state cannot tax Native land, reaffirming that tribal lands are not subject to taxation.[57]

Harlan fell into disfavor with the radical Republicans and left office August 31, 1866, having failed to gain civil government in Indian Territory. Orville H. Brown succeeded him, and forthwith Cooley resigned as commissioner of Indian affairs, effective November 1, 1866. While his tenure was brief, Cooley resisted the transfer of the Indian Office to the War Department and negotiated treaties with the tribes in Indian Territory, opening the lands of the Five Tribes to border state tribes who might agree to relocate onto the ceded lands.

COMMISSIONER LEWIS V. BOGY

Lewis Vital Bogy, a Missouri Democrat, replaced Cooley, and, as with Secretary Orville Brown, opposed Radical Reconstruction. To Bogy's detriment, Brown supported the traders in their quest to be paid out of tribal funds, and Bogy awarded lucrative trading contracts to members of his family in St. Louis. It was not long before he too fell into disfavor.[58] While he served as commissioner of Indian affairs from November 1, 1866, to March 4, 1867, the Senate refused to confirm his appointment. In an attempt to bypass the Senate, Brown appointed Bogy as a special agent to oversee Indian trade goods purchased and authorized by contract. Bogy remained in this position until the Senate Judiciary Committee concluded that Brown exceeded his authority in making the appointment. Bogy, whose wife was the great-granddaughter of Marie Chouteau, the matriarch of St. Louis traders and whose family members signed dozens of treaties and traded with the tribes over the course of a century, was too vulnerable politically.[59] The Senate formally rejected Bogy as commissioner on March 12, 1867.

COMMISSIONER NATHANIEL G. TAYLOR

With the Senate's refusal to confirm Bogy, President Johnson nominated Nathaniel Green Taylor, a moderate Republican and former Tennessee representative, as commissioner. Taylor, a Methodist-Episcopal preacher and attorney, was a principled man committed to securing peace with the western tribes. The Senate confirmed him on March 29, 1867, notwithstanding Brown's support for General Henry H. Sibley as commissioner of Indian affairs and his keeping Bogy on as a special agent with a higher annual salary than Taylor's. While the Senate Judiciary Committee condemned the action of Brown as unconstitutional, Taylor murmured to President Johnson that Bogy was interfering with his duties as commissioner. Brown held firm, quickly losing support in Washington, D.C. In the end, Brown and Bogy capitulated, with Bogy resigning in June, having never drafted an annual report for the Indian Office.[60]

Taylor served as commissioner of Indian affairs until April 23, 1869, setting into place the principles of the Peace Policy, a strand governing Indian affairs in the 1870s. He was a strong proponent of the Jeffersonian ideal of yeoman farmers that eventually bore fruit with the passage of the General Allotment Act in 1887. A man of probity, Taylor was committed to the reforms of the Indian Office, although his "convictions on Indian perfectibility often got in the way of his grasp of the . . . situation."[61]

In January 1867, the Joint Special Committee of Congress issued a report spearheaded by Senator James R. Doolittle (R-WI) that was a stark reminder of the deteriorated state of tribal affairs, Native hostility in particular. This 542-page "Condition of the Indian Tribes" (the "Doolittle Report") authorized by Congress in 1865 was published just weeks prior to the Joint Committee Report on the Fetterman massacre.[62] Together, these reports underscored the widespread challenges facing tribal affairs, including a growing concern that Native people—excluding those in Indian Territory—were rapidly dying of disease and warfare and that they desired peace.[63]

The Doolittle report asserted that disease, intemperance, war, and encroachment on Native land were the primary causes of ill-health in Indian Country. Indian wars in particular were largely the result of the aggressive actions of lawless whites on the frontier. Absent a change in policy, Doolittle hyperbolized, the Natives were on a path to extinction. While the report was filled with allegations of fraud and corruption, and painted a less than rosy picture of Indian Country, it did not reflect the true conditions of the tribes. It did, nonetheless, awaken a national conscience and usher in a new phase of policy: a humane Christian Peace Policy that, while short-lived, was instrumental in hastening the land severalty policy and further diminishment of Indian Country.

A month after release of the report, President Johnson—in an attempt to establish peace in the West—appointed Brigadier General Alfred Sully, Major General John B. Sanborn, Nathaniel B. Buford, Colonel Ely S. Parker, J. F. Kinney, and G. P. Beauvais as commissioners to visit the scene of the Fetterman massacre (Battle of the Hundred Slain) in the Powder River Basin of Wyoming. This military fiasco occurred when Lieutenant Colonel William J. Fetterman and eighty soldiers marched from Fort Phil Kearney into an ambush set by Lakota, Cheyenne, and Arapaho warriors. The committee was directed to evaluate the underlying causes of the incident and formulate a policy that the United States could implement to secure peace in the West.

The committee concluded that the annihilation of federal troops resulted from the construction of a military wagon road through Lakota country between Fort Laramie and the gold fields of Montana, an action the Lakota viewed as a declaration of war.[64] As for continued hostilities south of the Platte River, Taylor argued that the chief cause was the action of Colonel John Chivington and the Colorado militia, which massacred Cheyenne men, women, and children in 1864.[65] This was further complicated by General William Scott Hancock and his troops marching through Cheyenne and Sioux country in April 1867, destroying villages, burning possessions, and degrading terrified occupants.[66] The committee recommended the establishment of two reservations where the tribes could live in safety, learn to farm, and adapt to modern civilization, thus furthering the integration braid.

In July 1867, Congress authorized President Johnson to establish a peace commission to ascertain more broadly the causes of hostility in the West, negotiate treaties of peace, and establish reservations for the tribes east of the Rocky Mountains.[67] In the Senate debate, some members of Congress believed the United States spent $1 million for every Native killed and another $1 to $2 million to defend the frontier from tribal attacks. Senator John B. Henderson (R-MO) was quick to conclude that "if we can make peace with the Indians we had better do it."[68] Senator Samuel C. Pomeroy (R-KN) was more candid: the solution was for "the Indian [to] take his place among other men and accept the march of civilization . . . or there is nothing except his destiny that awaits him, which is extinction."[69]

President Johnson appointed a seven-man commission—four civilians and three military officers—to establish peace, with the civilian members including Taylor as chairman, Sanborn,

Senator Henderson, and Samuel F. Tappan. Military members included Terry, Lieutenant General William T. Sherman, and Major General William S. Harney, all experienced in Indian affairs. Congress directed the commission to establish peace via treaties and secure the overland trails and railroad lines. If peace could not be gained through civil means and the establishment of reservations, it was to be enforced by military action, with four thousand civilian volunteers authorized for service.[70] That fall, the commission negotiated treaties of peace with the Southern Cheyenne, Southern Arapaho, Kiowa, Comanche, and Kiowa-Apache at Medicine Lodge Creek, Kansas.[71] The following year, the commission traveled to Fort Laramie and negotiated treaties of peace with the Crow, Northern Arapaho, Northern Cheyenne, and the Sioux.[72] Additional peace treaties were negotiated with the Navajo, Ute, Shoshone, and Bannock Tribes.[73] In the commission's report to Congress, Taylor explained that the treaties were an attempt "to conquer by kindness."[74] "The Indians," the commissioner argued in 1867, "as now situated can [only] be saved from extinction by consolidating them, as rapidly as it can be done, upon large reservations."[75] Native people must accept civilization, learn to engage in agriculture, give up their Native ways, and integrate into American society. Annuities and any other vestige of the past that set Natives apart were to be abolished and civilian—not military—control implemented. Overall the report was little more than a tirade against the Indian "system" and the evils incumbent with it, rather than a well-grounded document. Nonetheless, it accomplished its purpose, as it fueled humanitarian reforms.

A year later, Taylor was more candid in his zealous assessment of the situation. Native people had to adapt to new realities. "If the savage resists, civilization, with the ten commandments in one hand and the sword in the other, demands his immediate extermination." While the work would be slow, "aside from extermination," confinement to reservations was the only solution. The long-term solution was both simple and yet complex: "The whites and Indians must mingle together and jointly occupy the country, or one of them must abandon it."[76] The Peace Commission laid down the gauntlet: without peace the military would enforce compliance.

The battle for control of Indian affairs was heightened when the House of Representatives again supported a bill returning Indian affairs to military control.[77] The Senate, however, refused to concur, supporting the status quo. In June 1868, a majority of the Peace Commission—including Sherman—broke with the rest and favored military control of Indian affairs but agreed that the final decision on the matter should be prefaced on whether the United States intended "to have war or have peace."[78] While the Peace Commission, of which Taylor was president, supported a transfer, Taylor opposed such a move. The national debate on the transfer back to the War Department was rich and was supported by the army, which demanded full control; newspapers across the West supported such action.[79]

Taylor was a staunch opponent of the Indian Office returning to the auspices of the War Department and in his 1868 report he devoted nine pages and outlined eleven reasons why the Indian Office must remain in Interior. If the object of federal policy was peace, then the Interior Department should control Indian affairs; if the object was war, then the War Department should govern. The causes of hostilities with the western tribes, Taylor stated, included the presence of the military to arouse "feelings of hostility and ... sentiments of resistance."[80] If war continued, Taylor estimated the annual costs at $50 to $150 million. Military management, Taylor explained, "has proven a failure" and "must ... always prove a failure," as the cost of "each dead Indian [is] about one million dollars each."[81] As important, it was "inhumane and unchristian ... to destroy a whole race by such demoralization and disease as military government is sure to entail upon our tribes."[82]

In Taylor's mind, the solution was for Congress to create a department exclusively for the management of Indian affairs led by a cabinet head reporting directly to the president and Congress.[83] To ensure peace, "the best policy to pursue towards the tribes ... is to treat with them, recognize their rights, relieve their fear of suffering, remunerate them for that which they have been deprived, and provide for their concentration upon tracts of country guaranteed to them." Taylor supported the propriety of treaty arrangements with the tribes in Nevada, Arizona, New Mexico, and Washington territories—especially with those tribes "inhabiting or claiming rich agricultural districts or mining districts."[84]

Taylor devoted five pages in his report to the intellectual question of "Shall our Indians be Civilized and How?" In his answer to the former, Taylor supposed the United States was morally obligated to the braid of integration and, as to the latter, he remarked it was "better to feed the Indians than fight them." Once fed, they could be educated and Christianized. "In the difference of language today lies two-thirds of our trouble," the commissioner exclaimed. The "sameness of language" would lead to "sameness of sentiment and thought [and] customs and habit."[85] In this, Taylor was prescient in adding to the groundwork for boarding schools and the prohibition of speaking indigenous tongues.

As commissioner, Taylor advocated that the tribes should be settled on three large reservations: one north of Nebraska and west of the Missouri River; one in Indian Territory; and one in the Southwest for tribes west of the Rocky Mountains.[86] This could best be accomplished by treaties recognizing tribal rights and extinguishing aboriginal title. The reserved lands could be guaranteed and, while Taylor advocated such policy, the impeachment of President Johnson and the political posturing in Congress over Reconstruction all but relegated Indian affairs subordinate to other political interests.

The peace that Taylor so passionately believed in quickly vanished. In summer of 1868, Sherman ordered General Phil Sheridan to compel Cheyenne removal into Indian Territory, and "to kill if necessary."[87] The peace was shattered in the fall, first by the Battle of Beecher's Island and then in November when General George Armstrong Custer attacked Black Kettle's band of Southern Cheyenne camped along the Washita River, killing 103 Cheyenne, including the peaceful Black Kettle.[88] A $500,000 congressional appropriation for the Indian Office to establish reservations was instead transferred to the War Department, and Taylor lost credibility. The Peace Commission was disbanded and the tenuous peace established by treaty in 1867–1868 vanished. On April 23, 1869, Taylor left office.

COMMISSIONER ELY S. PARKER

In fall of 1868, Ulysses S. Grant was elected president, with Indian affairs playing a prominent role in national politics. Grant sought to develop a policy based on his experience with postwar Reconstruction, seeking to adapt to Indian affairs a free-labor concept that was the basis of the Freedman's Bureau.[89] Before he took office, the "Society of Friends" visited with Grant and persuaded him of the benefits of a policy of kindness premised on Indian agents appointed by the Quakers, a pacifist people. After taking office in March, Grant agreed to implement the framework of this Peace Policy and nominated his friend and Civil War aide-de-camp Ely Samuel Parker as commissioner of Indian affairs. Parker was a member of the Seneca Nation of New York, a hereditary Grand Sachem of the Iroquois Confederacy, and a civil engineer by profession who once studied law but was denied the bar in New York because, as an American Indian, he was not a U.S. citizen.[90]

In 1865, Parker was sent at General Grant's request to negotiate treaties with the Five Tribes, signing the Choctaw, Chickasaw, and Seminole Reconstruction treaties of 1866. The following year, again at General Grant's request, he drafted a plan "for the establishment of a permanent and perpetual peace," advocating Indian affairs return to the War Department's control and the placement of agencies under army officers, an action he believed would curb abuses in Indian Country. He also recommended a board of inspectors to monitor Indian Office expenditures and funds.[91]

Parker was the first American Indian commissioner of Indian affairs, earning Senate confirmation on April 16, 1869, and taking office April 23 after resigning his military commission. He enthusiastically endorsed Grant's Peace Policy and plan to appoint Quakers as agents. While prior to his appointment he favored military officers assigned as agents (and military control of the Indian Office), after Grant initiated his Peace Policy, he supported civilian agents. By the end of the year, there were eighteen Quaker agents in Indian Country.

Parker began his first annual report with a rhetorical question: "What shall be done for the amelioration and civilization of the [Indians]?"[92] In response, he noted a $2 million congressional appropriation to maintain peace with the tribes, an accomplishment that could only be realized by the "wise and humane" policy of appointing agents nominated by various churches to aid Natives in developing a "healthy Christian civilization."[93] To initiate this endeavor, Parker supported Grant's appointment of eastern philanthropists to a newly-created Board of Indian Commissioners to oversee expenditure of tribal funds, propose policy considerations, and establish peace in the West. While Parker was committed to civilian control, if Natives refused to live peaceably on reservations, he pledged to turn them over "to the control and supervision of the military."[94]

The ten-man Board of Indian Commissioners was empowered by Grant to review Indian Office records and investigate allegations of fraud. While the board's primary purpose was to oversee Indian Office funds to ensure they were properly expended and to recommend social policies that would nudge Native peoples towards civilization and Christianization, Parker requested the board to review the legal status of Natives and ascertain what rights and responsibilities they had under existing treaties. He also charged the board to investigate whether treaty making should continue and what might be the best method of fulfilling the reservation policy.[95]

Parker advocated ending the treaty system since Native people were fast becoming "wards of the government." Treaty making perpetuated the "myth of Indian independence," and it was time for the United States to "cease the cruel farce" of dealing with the tribes as political sovereigns, although justice and humanity necessitated that existing treaties be faithfully executed.[96] The Board of Indian Commissioners concurred, noting that while there was a "shameful record of broken treaties and unfulfilled promises," the United States government should abandon the treaty system "as soon as any just method can be devised to accomplish it." Unlike Parker, the board recommended abrogating existing treaties, a position with which the president concurred.[97]

The cessation of treaty making had broad social and political ramifications. Many treaties and much federal diplomacy referred to the tribes as "nations" or referred to specific tribal territory as their "country." The United States defined Native people as belonging to nations when it sought land cessions from them. With the end of treaty making, however, the United States began to refer to specific tribal nations as wards of the government, asserting plenary authority over them. This was no small transformation of the federal-Indian relationship, and it increasingly attached social and political benefits to the United States.[98]

Parker expressed disdain for the "wild and roving tribes," such as the Apache, Ute, Kiowa, Comanche, and Sioux, with the latter christened the "most powerful and warlike tribe" in the nation.[99] He supported "a territorial form of government followed by . . . admission into the Union as a State," for Indian Territory.[100] And with the U.S. acquisition of Alaska from Russia in 1867, Parker's 1869 report included the first descriptions of Alaska Natives.[101] While President Grant opened Indian agencies to Quaker agents, by 1870, Parker was convinced the appointments were so successful that, after Congress proscribed military officers from serving as agents, he invited other church denominations to appoint agents and "engage in the great work of civilizing the Indians."[102]

The reservation policy was both a continuation and a modification of the antebellum policy. When Parker requested the Board of Indian Commissioners to critique the reservation policy with the goal of refining it, the board responded: "The policy of collecting the Indian tribes upon small reservations . . . and within the limits of a large reservation, eventually to become a State of the Union . . . seems to be the best that can be devised. Many tribes may thus be collected in the present Indian Territory. The larger the number that can be thus concentrated the better for the success of the plan."[103]

Interior Secretary Jacob Cox enthusiastically supported this recommendation, with Columbus Delano, who succeeded Cox in 1870, seeking to relocate "the entire Indian population in the country, excluding Alaska and those scattered among the states," into Indian Territory. According to Delano's arithmetic, 172,000 American Indians living on 96,155,785 acres of land resided outside of Indian Territory, or 558 acres per capita. Within Indian Territory, he enumerated 60,000 Natives residing on 44,154,240 acres, or 630 acres per person. If the entire population could be induced to immigrate to Indian Territory, Delano reasoned, there would be 180 acres per capita—"ample area of land to afford them all comfortable homes."[104]

The Board of Indian Commissioners that Parker once supported initiated his resignation when board chairman William Welsh accused him of unscrupulous dealings in the purchase of Indian goods. While the House of Representatives cleared him of any wrongdoing, Parker resigned on July 24, 1871, declaring his enemies "waxed rich and fat from the plundering of poor Indians." He left office stating it was "no longer a pleasure to discharge patriotic duties."[105]

COMMISSIONER FRANCIS A. WALKER

In Parker's stead, Grant nominated Francis Amasa Walker as commissioner, a position he assumed on November 21, 1871.[106] Between July 24 and November 21, chief clerk Henry R. Clum served as acting commissioner and prepared the 1871 annual report. Clum's summary report was just eight pages, considerably shorter than the reports that preceded or followed his. Clum considered the Apache, Kiowa, and Comanche the most difficult tribes to manage, noting that several bands of Lakota Sioux had gone to Montana to follow Sitting Bull. "Unless carefully managed, these seceders," Clum prophetically penned, "may cause great trouble to the Government."[107]

Clum noted for the first time in any annual report that Native people were decreasing in number, a conclusion also reached by the Doolittle Commission.[108] While those tribes "most advanced in civilization" were increasing in numbers, Clum believed that the United States had an obligation to preserve the "less advanced" tribes "from utter extinction." The means to accomplish this remained social: education, private property, individual labor, Christianity, and citizenship. Clum joined a long list of commissioners urging Congress to update the 1834 Nonintercourse Act and sought congressional approval allowing the Indian Office to assert criminal jurisdiction over Indian vs. Indian crimes in Indian Country.[109]

Francis Walker was an intelligent Boston economist who arrived as commissioner via a congressional failure to appropriate funds for the U.S. Census Bureau, where he was employed. Rather than lose him from federal service, Grant nominated Walker as commissioner of Indian affairs until the census was completed. While Walker had no prior experience in Indian affairs, he was confirmed by the Senate on December 16, 1871, with the *New York Times* editorializing, "He did not seek the office, the office sought him."[110] To eastern humanitarians, Walker was a breath of fresh air, as the Peace Policy they supported had been slow to root and they were convinced Walker could jumpstart the policy. The national press viewed Walker's appointment as a "complete overthrow of a most gigantic system of robbery, hypocrisy, greed, and cruelty."[111]

Humanitarians admired the new commissioner for his views on the moral obligation of the government to care for Natives, while at the same time he proved acceptable to westerners because of his pragmatic views and willingness to use military force if necessary. The tribes "must yield or perish," he wrote in his only annual report. "Can any principle of national morality be clearer than that, when the expansion and development of a civilized race involves the rapid destruction of the only means of subsistence possessed by members of a less fortunate race, the higher is bound as of simple right to provide for the lower some substitute for the means of subsistence which it has destroyed?"[112] If tribes resisted, "use of the military constitutes no abandonment of the 'peace policy,' and involves no disparagement of it."[113]

Walker the intellectual philosopher waxed poetically that "with wild men, as with wild beasts, the question whether in a given situation one shall fight, coax, or run, is the question merely of what is easiest and safest." Consequently, Walker enhanced a social policy of protecting and feeding those who "went right" and harassing and scourging those who "went wrong."[114] Recognizing Native people as the aboriginal owners of the continent entitled them to more than 160 acres of land and as much temporary assistance as needed to adapt to a civilized life, Walker nonetheless proposed "a rigid reformatory discipline" to keep them from falling into pauperism and a life of crime. To prove workable in practice, Walker sought to implement a social policy of confining Natives to their reservations to learn the habits of civilization with a federal right to "arrest and return them whenever they wandered away."[115]

The practical aspect of this policy strand was educating children in modern civilization. To ensure this occurred, the federal government had to capitalize tribal funds in permanent endowments and then place them in trust for the civilization of the Natives. While reservations still provided game and fish for most Natives, in time these resources would wane and the tribes would have to adapt to agriculture, "however rude and primitive at first." For tribes without reservations, Walker argued, the United States would have to provide an endowment equal to treaty reservations. "We have received the soil from them, and we have extinguished their only means of subsistence," and in exchange the United States had a moral obligation to provide for those "who have been impoverished that we might be rich."[116]

Walker was a realist, recognizing the inevitability of western settlement. He informed the humanitarians in 1872 that they should "not feebly and futilely" attempt to arrest the western migration across the continent. The strength of western emigration could "hardly be measured," he stated. The best the humanitarians could hope for was "to snatch the remnant of the Indian race from [the] destruction before it."[117]

To ensure Native people survived, Walker sought to bring them under federal protection. According to his estimate, there were 300,000 Native people in the country. Of these, 180,000 were in treaty relations; 40,000 had no treaties but lived on executive order reservations; 25,000 had no reservations but were under the care of an Indian agent; and 55,000 had no treaty or reservation, and were not under the control of the Indian Office. Those without reservations but under the care of an agent were primarily in California and the 55,000 not under any control or treaty were bands of Lakota Sioux and allied tribes on the northern plains.[118] The Indian Office would have to work to bring those tribes under its control.

COMMISSIONER EDWARD P. SMITH

While Walker received little to no negative press during his tenure as commissioner, he elected to resign on December 26, 1872, to join the faculty of Harvard University. President Grant then nominated Edward Parmalee Smith as commissioner on March 12, 1873, with the Senate confirming him five days later.[119] A Congregational minister from Connecticut, Smith had previously worked with the American Missionary Association as an agent at the Chippewa Agency in Minnesota prior to his appointment as commissioner and quickly became the face of Grant's Peace Policy.

In his first report, Smith referred to dealing with the tribes as sovereign political powers as "anomalous." There were "over sixty-five independent nations within our border, with whom we have entered into treaty relations as being sovereign people," he wrote in 1873, "and at the same time the white agent is sent to control and supervise these foreign powers and care for them as wards of the Government." This made little sense to Smith. "All recognition of Indians in any other relation than strictly as subjects of the Government should cease."[120] While not a new sentiment, Smith was forthright in his assessment of the transformation of sovereign nation definition to domestic wards.

A corollary matter growing out of the "fiction in Indian relations," were the payments of cash annuities to individuals, which Smith judged were lost, squandered, or wasted, tending to "brutalize more than civilize." It was better for Natives to receive land from which they could earn a living, "if compelled by hunger," than to receive annuities that "perpetuate idleness and poverty."[121] In short, what Native people needed, the commissioner asserted, were individual property rights, and land severalty was the only means to separate "an individual from a herd." Associated with private property was the protection of life and property brought about by the administration of law. It was imperative that the federal district courts administer justice to Natives for criminal acts committed in Indian Country, notwithstanding treaty provisions to the contrary.[122] These social policies would encourage further progress towards self-support and free labor.

As did Walker before him, Smith was adamant that Native people be confined to their reservations, particularly the powerful plains tribes, such as the Sioux, Arapaho, Cheyenne, Kiowa, and Comanche. These tribes freely depredated local towns, emigrants, and transportation routes, and for Smith this was an issue of the tribes assuming a "hostile attitude toward the Government."[123] As for the Lakota Sioux, Smith requested a military force "sufficient to enable the agents to enforce respect for their authority." While he stated in 1874 that "it is not probable that as many as 500 Indian warriors will ever again be mustered at one point for a fight," he was concerned that the nontreaty bands of the Lakota were living off their reservation in disregard of the authority of the United States government.[124]

Smith advised Congress to authorize a $25,000 payment to the Lakota in exchange for foregoing their treaty-protected Nebraska hunting rights. He supposed that miners in the sacred Black Hills—still part of the Great Sioux Reservation—would depart after realizing minimal mineral wealth and he recommended the president not force any sale of or open the Black Hills to settlement.[125] A year later he changed his mind. "The occupation and possession of the Black Hills by white men seems now inevitable but no reason exists for making this inevitability an occasion of wrong or lasting injury." Instead, the government should feed the Sioux and, in exchange for preventing their starvation, demand "something of theirs in return." But first he argued the survey of the Black Hills to ascertain what eight hundred square miles of "gold fields are worth to us" and what three thousand square miles of "timber, agriculture, and grazing lands are worth to them"—then simply fored the sale.[126]

The new commissioner was only slightly more practical in other policy matters. He supported establishing reservations in Southern California for the mission Indians who were landless and living as trespassers on their own land. These tribes deserved the protection of their rights, in large measure due to the Senate's failure to ratify any of the 1851–1852 California treaties.[127] As a show of strength to the Kiowa, Comanche, and Cheyenne warriors raiding in Texas, Smith ordered seventy select captured leaders to Fort Marion (San Augustine), Florida, as prisoners of war, an action he predicted as having a positive effect "upon others of the tribe." He continued supporting churches nominating men as Indian agents, although he tempered his zeal by noting such agents were far from perfect even if they were "a better class of officers than could otherwise be had by political nomination."[128]

Smith supported manual labor schools, suggesting "four or five years of this appliance of civilization cures one-half of the barbarism" in Indian Country.[129] But such social policies alone would not solve the challenge of Native people becoming U.S. citizens—Smith stated passionately—because of "the fiction of sovereignty" and the "domestic dependent nation" status that precluded them from changing their nationality unless agreed to by "both parties to [their] tribal treaty."[130] In 1874, and again in 1875, Smith outlined a multi-step process of "qualified citizenship" for Native people that included the prerequisites necessary to becoming a U.S. citizen, such as federal criminal law governing Indian Country and state jurisdiction for all offenses outside of Indian Country, both of which seemed logical to reformers as both undermining tribal authority and nudging Natives closer to integration. Smith also advocated authority to extend state court jurisdiction over reservations and the use of federal marshals within Indian Country. Only with the organization of civil government—especially in Indian Territory, where Smith believed it should be forced on the tribes—could Indian Country blossom, with citizenship following land severalty and distribution of tribal funds.[131] To emphasize the policy, Smith supported citizenship for some tribes as early as 1874 and recommended that all Natives in New York and some of the tribes in Minnesota, Michigan, and Wisconsin be immediately granted U.S. citizenship and then made subject to the state in all matters.[132]

The adoption of such qualified citizenship, Smith acknowledged, would not "secure civilization" but would merely prepare the way "for a rationale effort in that direction." To ensure success, tribes had to be permanently placed on reservations "affording water, timber, grass and soil upon which a white man could make a living." They would need larger annual appropriations from Congress in order to facilitate this transition from barbarism to civilization. This could take as few as five years, Smith optimistically reported, if done properly. Finally, Indian agents had to be "competent for the business at hand," meaning they had to be "men who had faith in their fellowman" and who believed (and could model such behavior) that Natives could become U.S. citizens. With these essentials, Smith was optimistic beyond "a shade of doubt ... that the Indians of the country can be reclaimed from barbarism and fitted for citizenship."[133]

Among Smith's last actions as commissioner, he sent directions to the Indian agents in Dakota Territory on December 6, 1875, ordering them to notify Sitting Bull and his followers to return to their reservations before January 31, 1876, or face military consequences. Five days later, on December 11, 1875, Smith resigned as commissioner under scrutiny for accounting discrepancies while he served as Chippewa agent in 1871. Although exonerated, he became the object of yet another investigation regarding fraud at the Red Cloud Agency in 1875 and chose to resign rather than face charges. He died aboard a ship bound for West Africa twelve days before General George Custer discovered on June 25, 1876, that the plains tribes were still capable of mustering more than five hundred warriors.

COMMISSIONER JOHN Q. SMITH

Senator John Sherman (R-OH) recommended President Grant nominate fellow Ohioan John Quincy Smith to replace Edward Smith as commissioner of Indian affairs. The Senate confirmed Smith on December 11, 1875, and he assumed office immediately. J. Q. Smith continued the reforms begun by his predecessors, although with a hint of malice towards Native people. In the opening of his only annual report, Smith was apologetic that "the management of Indian affairs is always attended with much of difficulty and embarrassment." Why, he asked rhetorically? While in the other branches of the public service "the officers of the Government conduct business mainly with civilized and intelligent men," in the Indian Office they dealt with "an uncivilized and unintelligent people, whose ignorance, superstitions, and suspicion materially increase the difficulty both of controlling and assisting them."[134] Such froward thinking skewed Smith's actions and fueled the growing sentiment that Native people were no more than wards of the government to be dealt with as the exigency demanded.

Smith proposed no new policy ideas, although he added a few unique strands. While he pleaded for increased remuneration for agents, he focused on the inadequate and delayed congressional appropriations, which "induced large numbers [of Indians] to go north and join the hostile bands under Sitting Bull." Multiple times in his opening salvo he underscored the failure of Congress to enact spending bills in a timely manner, with each delay causing cost increases, transportation delays, and lost goodwill.[135] From his perspective, the "next twenty-five years are to determine the fate of a race." There were no new hunting grounds and the frontier—"an almost incessant struggle, the Indians to retain and the whites to get possession"—was quickly fading.[136]

Smith advanced three policy considerations. All tribes had to consolidate on three large reservations. All of the tribes in Kansas, Nebraska, Dakota, Wyoming, Montana, Colorado, New Mexico, Arizona, and Nevada were to be relocated to Indian Territory. Tribes in Wisconsin, Minnesota, and the Pembina Chippewa from Dakota were to emigrate to the White Earth Reservation in northern Minnesota. All other tribes in the Pacific Northwest were to be sent to the Yakima Reservation in eastern Washington. Most of the present reservations were "almost worthless for agricultural purposes," Smith supposed, or were "too small to subsist the Indians by hunting." All were too "remote and difficult of access," leading to great expense in delivering goods and services to the tribes. But above all, "nearly all are surrounded by white settlers," and when this happened the "white men usually prevail" in owning the land. By consolidating the tribes "the difficulties surrounding the Indian question will vanish."[137] Such simplistic thinking based on practical exigencies only compounded policy matters and added to the lack of goodwill in Indian Country, thwarting policy by those who carried it out on the ground.

While land severalty was not a new policy, Smith encouraged passage of a general allotment act that would require all heads of families to accept "a reasonable amount of land" to work and hold inalienable for a minimum of twenty years (and possibly as long as fifty years), with any right of alienation only to another tribal member thereby keeping all land in Native ownership. Closely associated with severalty was the imposition of law in Indian Country such that Natives held "the same relation to law that a white man does." In another reflection of the influence of the Freedman model applied to Indian Country, Smith argued if citizenship could be granted to the freedmen after the Civil War, it could be granted to Native people as well.[138]

Smith's assertion was no small matter in light of passage of the Fourteenth Amendment to the United States Constitution in 1868. The amendment declared "all persons born or naturalized in the United States and subject to the jurisdiction thereof, are citizens of the United States and the state wherein they live." While the Senate debated the application of the amendment to American Indians in 1866, it voted three to one against such application, concluding Native people did not owe allegiance to the United States and as "quasi foreign nations" were not completely subject to the jurisdiction of the United States.[139] In 1870, the Senate Judiciary Committee further analyzed the amendment, concluding that the constitutional phrase "Indians not taxed" when determining apportionment was a clear exclusion of the amendment to Native people.[140] The political question of where tribal nations stood politically vis-à-vis the United States—wards of the government or semiautonomous nations—was far from transparent, as federal policies continued to emphasize wardship and plenary authority.

The commissioner was especially critical of the lack of political organization in Indian Territory. The governmental affairs in the territory were "complicated and embarrassing," Smith wrote in 1876. "The idea that that Territory is to consist forever of a collection of little independent or semi-independent nationalities is preposterous."[141] Public policy demanded Indian Territory be reduced in size "for the occupancy of other tribes of Indians or of white people." Treaties or not, the government had to do what was in the tribes' "own best interests." As to the form of government, Smith followed the same course of territorial organization as did his predecessors.[142]

During Smith's tenure he oversaw the removal of the peaceful Ponca Tribe from their treaty-protected reservation in Nebraska into Indian Territory and the Chiricahua Apache from southeastern Arizona to San Carlos, where embers of hostility smoldered for another decade under Geronimo's leadership. In an event that shocked the country, General Custer and his troops were killed in battle with the Sioux and Cheyenne in the Little Bighorn River valley in Montana, where the number of hostiles increased to over ten thousand. With the election of Rutherford B. Hayes as president in November 1876, Smith's days were limited and the new secretary of the interior, Carl Schurz, requested his resignation on September 20, 1877.[143]

COMMISSIONER EZRA A. HAYT

Schurz set a high standard in filling the position of commissioner of Indian affairs. After William Welsh of the Board of Indian Commissioners declined the position, Schurz turned to Ezra A. Hayt, a New Jersey businessman who had served on the Board of Indian Commissioners before President Grant asked for and received his resignation over political infighting and the results of an inspection into contract food supplies for Indian agencies. While a board member, Hayt had personally investigated multiple allegations of abuse within the Indian Office, often sharply criticizing the department.[144] Hayt took office on September 20, 1877, although the Senate did not confirm him until December 12, when his confirmation was unanimous.

Hayt penned three annual reports, with the first defining the policies he intended to implement and the second and third report cards on his progress. In his 1877 report, he defined a number of policy strands that he believed were prerequisite to the civilization of the Natives and efficiency of the Indian Office. While not novel concepts, Hayt zealously prosecuted such policies. The primary need of Indian Country was law. "Civilization has loosened, in some places broken, the bonds which regulate and hold together Indian society in its wild state," the commissioner aptly theorized. But at the same time, it "has failed to give the people law and officers of justice in their place."[145] This was a disgrace to the nation, Hayt stated, as he sought to ameliorate the matter. His plan included subjecting Natives to federal law. The use of an Indian police force would go a long way in institutionalizing law among tribes. In May 1878, Congress concurred and authorized the Indian Office to hire 50 officers and 430 privates.[146]

Hayt advocated "the endowment of the Indians with lands" held in severalty as a means of promoting knowledge of agriculture and self-preservation, exhorting Congress to authorize a general allotment of tribal lands.[147] Without land in severalty—including a patent to the land—"the fear that [the land] will some day be taken from him will operate as a serious hindrance to his progress."[148] Patenting land to individuals would allow the government to create "separate and individual interests, which are necessary . . . to induce him to follow civilized pursuits."[149]

In the interim, the commissioner advanced consolidation of reservations and agencies as a matter of fiscal efficiency. He drew up a bill in 1878 proposing to consolidate thirty-six reservations in Oregon, Colorado, Iowa, Kansas, Nebraska, Wisconsin, Minnesota, Washington, and Dakota down to nine, while at the same time opening up to settlement 17,642,455 of the 21,922,507 acres on these reservations. This would net "a large reduction of the expense attending to the civilization of the Indian," better protect their rights, and, by using the interest gained from the sale of such land, fund their civilization "in lieu of direct appropriations."[150] Hayt estimated an additional annual savings of $120,000 by reducing twenty agents down to nine, as well as trimming other support staff. Further consolidation was "not only possible, but expedient and advisable," the efficiency-minded Hayt reported. He immediately drew up a plan to consolidate the tribes in Arizona, New Mexico, and Colorado, and proposed to reduce the seventy-four existing agencies down "to a very limited number."[151]

The social policy of Hayt was not novel, but the techniques he adopted were. Under his leadership both Hampton Normal Institute and Carlisle Manual Labor Boarding School were established, with the latter set up by Captain Richard Henry Pratt as an experiment with 40 adult Cheyenne, Kiowa, and Arapaho prisoners-of-war sent to Fort Marion, Florida, in 1875.[152] A year later, Pratt was so sure of success that he convinced the Indian Office and War Department to establish a school at Carlisle, Pennsylvania, for 158 children from the northern plains.[153] By 1884, there were 81 boarding schools and 76 day schools in the government school system.

Hayt was practical enough to point out the shortsighted policy of Congress in not funding schools to the level of commitments made in treaties. In the 1867 Treaty of Medicine Lodge Creek, for instance, the Kiowa and Comanche agreed to reside on a reservation in exchange for a school and competent teacher "for every thirty children between the said ages [6–16]."[154] By 1878, there was just one boarding school at the Kiowa-Comanche Agency, which accommodated 75 children, with "another 425 children waiting their turn."[155] Hayt recommended Congress appropriate not less than $200,000 for the construction of additional schools and the maintenance of existing facilities. A reticent Congress refused, providing $80,000 in 1880. By underfunding schools, Congress effectively pushed Native youth to the periphery of American society.

Hayt rounded out his policies by seeking to complete a series of administrative measures to reclaim the Natives from "a debasing paganism." These social measures represented an assault on indigenous people and included mandating civilized clothing ("the blanket must give way"), institutionalizing marriage, requiring labor in exchange for rations, prohibiting the sale of arms, and establishing penal settlements for "the more turbulent and troublesome." For the first time in an annual report a commissioner noted the propriety of improving sanitary conditions, instituting a new social paradigm to the strand of integration.[156]

Hayt was the last commissioner involved with the Peace Policy, a policy he never fully embraced philosophically, preferring economy and efficiency. In 1878, he boasted that he had replaced thirty-five agents, which was "of great benefit to the service."[157] He also rebuffed a renewed push to return Indian affairs to military control, a position he opposed on the discriminatory grounds that it could enable the Catholics to boast that they should be allowed to serve at every Indian agency. Although the Bureau of Catholic Missions opposed military control, many Catholics favored it.[158] While the popularly elected House of Representatives approved of such a plan in 1876 the Senate again failed to support the bill and it died.[159]

The most moving events of the Hayt administration were the highly emotional removal of the Ponca Tribe, as well as the military excursions against the Northern Cheyenne and the Nez Perce. The Ponca had been wrongly removed in 1877, after Congress in 1868 ceded their Nebraska reservation to the Sioux without Ponca consent. Hayt recognized the injustice and recommended Congress correct it. When Congress refused, Chief Standing Bear, in January 1879, led a number of his people on a trek back to their Nebraska homelands from their reservation in Indian Territory. While the Ponca were captured near Fort Robinson, Nebraska, and awaited return to Indian Territory, local Omaha citizens took up their cause and filed suit on behalf of Chief Standing Bear in the U.S. district court, which that same year ruled in *Standing Bear v. Crook* that American Indians were "persons under the law" and had rights to sue for a writ of habeas corpus in federal court.[160]

Judge Elmer Dundy not only ruled that Native people were "persons under the law" but he also ordered the Ponca released. In May 1880, a Senate Select Committee investigated the failed Ponca removal and recommended passage of a bill with $50,000 to assist the tribe in returning to Nebraska and restoring their homes; a parsimonious Congress refused.[161] President Hayes then appointed a commission to investigate the matter and provide guidance on what justice and humanity required, with the commission concluding the Ponca had a valid claim based on their 1858 and 1867 treaties to their reservation lands in Nebraska.[162] In March 1881, Congress relented and allowed the Ponca the choice of residing in Indian Territory or Nebraska.[163] In the process, the tribe was divided, with a northern and southern band.

Hayt was forced to resign in January 1880, in part due to Northern Cheyenne Chief Dull Knife's escape from Indian Territory, Chief Joseph's Nez Perce attempted escape to Canada, and the Ute massacre of agent Nathan Meeker, and in part because of allegations that he spent too much time promoting his own business interests rather than executing those associated with the Indian Office. He became a liability to both President Hayes and Secretary Schurz, who asked for his resignation effective January 29, 1880. Hayes then recommended his college friend and former three-term congressmen Roland E. Trowbridge (R-MI) as commissioner of Indian affairs on February 20, 1880.

COMMISSIONER ROLAND E. TROWBRIDGE

Roland Trowbridge, known for his honest character, was confirmed by the Senate on February 27, 1880, and assumed office on March 2. Like most commissioners before him, Trowbridge had no experience in Indian affairs. Frequently ill, he accomplished little as commissioner, resigning March 19, 1881, as the Hayes administration drew to a close. With Trowbridge too ill to prepare the 1880 annual report, the duty fell to acting Commissioner E. M. Marble, whose report included no new policy revelations; it did highlight the fact that over 314,398 acres in Indian Territory and 168,340 acres outside of the territory were in agricultural production, an increase of 10 percent from the prior year. Moreover, over 78,000 head of cattle had been distributed to tribes on the northern plains, in Indian Territory, and among the Apaches.[164]

While government schools were growing and "full of encouragement," a parsimonious Congress limited development of new schools. Nonetheless, Marble reported eighteen new boarding schools were constructed and another thirteen were in the planning stages.[165] And while the House Committee on Indian Affairs approved of a bill conferring over Indian Country state and territorial law governing murder, manslaughter, arson, rape, burglary, larceny, and robbery, the Senate failed to act on the bill and it died.[166]

The remainder of the 1880 report covered day-to-day administrative issues that were becoming increasingly more complex and yet more common with the near-complete federal domination of the tribes and introduction of scores of new social policies. Not only did this include land severalty, consolidation of reservations, depredations, sale of tribal lands, railroad rights-of-way, and exploitation and protection of tribal resources, but it also included the introduction of additional Indian Office personnel such as field matrons and agency farmers.[167] Four weeks after his resignation, Trowbridge died. He was replaced by acting Commissioner Henry Clum, who served until April 14, 1881.[168]

CONCLUSION

Ponca removal ignited a new round of reform in the Indian Office. In 1881, as a direct result of Chief Standing Bear's lecture given in Boston, Massachusetts, in November 1879, an impetus for reform came from an unlikely place. Helen Hunt Jackson was so moved by Standing Bear's story that she penned a disjointed compilation of broken treaty promises and unjust treatment of Native people that became Indian Country's equivalent of *Uncle Tom's Cabin*. In *A Century of Dishonor*, Jackson wrote: "The question of the honorableness of the United States' dealing with the Indians turns largely on a much disputed and little understood point." This point centered on the nature of the Indian rights to the land on which "they were living when this continent was discovered."[169] In the next 342 pages, Jackson quoted from Grotius, de Vattel, Kent, Hobbes, and numerous Supreme Court decisions in seeking to definitively answer the question. She then gave seven specific examples of wrongs perpetrated by the United States against tribes. "The story of one tribe is the story of all," Jackson wrote, and "varied [only] by difference of time and place."[170]

At her own expense, Jackson delivered a copy of her fragmented history to every member of Congress. "What an opportunity for the Congress of 1880 to cover itself with a lustre of glory, as the first to cut short our nation's record of cruelties and perjuries! the first to attempt to redeem the name of the United States from the stain of a century of dishonor!" Recognizing it would be fruitless to attempt to fix the problem in "one sudden stroke of legislative policy" by making "all Indians at once citizens of the United States," Jackson strongly supported land severalty with the issuance of patents as the key to Native survival.[171] Only with private property could Native people invest in their land and develop the skills necessary to survive in modern American. Jackson struck a sympathetic chord with reformers and the general public and her message spread rapidly with the end goal of citizenship. Congress did not accept the challenge.

The Peace Policy came to a quiet close by 1880. While it employed church-appointed agents and favored "conquest by kindness," the policy did not bring about the harmony President Grant envisioned. Instead, the Indian Office worked to further reduce tribal land holdings, a source of great conflict with Native people. The department also stepped up its efforts to socially transform Natives into agriculturalists and stockmen. Although not yet national policy, land severalty continued on a reservation-by-reservation basis. Land that remained unallotted was sold and, in theory, Native people would be treated just as any other American and become subject to the laws of the state in which they resided.

The reformed reservation policy, like the removal policy before it, did not result in the idyllic world envisioned by reformers. In their eyes, tribal nations held too much land and controlled too many resources that industrial America demanded. American Indians would not have the luxury of gradually adapting to mainstream cultural norms as the West was settled, as change was not only rapid but inevitable. To reformers, the only way to halt the loss of Indian land and preserve Native people was to allot in severalty all tribal lands, with a fee patent issued to protect individual ownership. By the early 1880s, a shift in policy occurred, one focusing on the strands of land severalty and citizenship, which facilitated the twin braids of integration and land alienation. It would prove to be destructive, both in terms of further land alienation and social disintegration.

5

"PART OF THE GREAT FAMILY"

Allotment and Citizenship, 1881–1904

The reformed reservation policy, as its antecedent emigration roots, did not bring about the integration of American Indians as envisioned by humanitarians; neither did it improve the overall quality of life for Native people. Indeed, the 1870s witnessed scores of tribes relocated to Indian Territory and scores of others losing land and resources in the rush to allot in severalty the border state reservations. At the outset of a new decade, one that put postbellum Reconstruction and federal military occupation of the Southern states behind it and turned towards industrialization of the nation, a new generation of reformers influenced policy. Beginning in the 1880s and continuing into the 1920s, these reformers—the Women's National Indian Association (1881), the Indian Rights Association (1882), and Lake Mohonk Conference (1883)—encouraged the United States to embark on a concerted effort to assimilate American Indians and dissolve the authority of tribal governments. In 1887, the reformers achieved success as land severalty became the central strand of federal action, initiating a policy that decreased the tribal land base from one hundred-thirty-eight million acres to fewer than forty-eight million.[1] Off-reservation industrial boarding schools expanded across the West and the Indian Office unified and standardized curriculum. The federal government asserted criminal jurisdiction over Natives and tens of thousands of Native people were granted American citizenship. A cadre of social programs administered by the Indian Office attacked the cultural integrity of tribal nations and worked to undermine the political survival of their governments.

Six men served as commissioner of Indian affairs between 1881 and 1904. Hiram Price served from 1881 to 1885, and was followed by John D. C. Atkins (1885–1888), John H. Oberly (1888–1889), Thomas Jefferson Morgan (1889–1893), Daniel Browning (1893–1897), and William A. Jones

Table 5.1. Heads of the Indian Office and Major Policies, 1881–1904

Name	Title	Years of Service	Main Policies
Hiram Price (R)	Commissioner	4 years (1881–1885)	Courts of Indian Offenses, severalty, self-reliance, criminal jurisdiction
John D. C. Atkins (D)	Commissioner	3.25 years (1885–1888)	Agreements of cessions, allotment act, banned languages in schools
John H. Oberly (D)	Commissioner	9 months (1888–1889)	Compulsory school attendance, federal jurisdiction
Thomas J. Morgan (R)	Commissioner	3.75 years (1889–1893)	Temperance, abolish reservations, autonomy of individual, opposed Wild West shows
Daniel Browning (D)	Commissioner	4 years (1893–1897)	End sectarian funding, public schools, civil service for all positions, army officers as agents
William A. Jones (R)	Commissioner	7.75 years (1897–1905)	Short hair, end rations, work or starve, leasing, abolish Indian Territory

(1897–1905). These men presided over the unparalleled expansion of federal paternalism in and over Indian affairs, and under their leadership the bureaucracy of "federal fathers and mothers" firmly established and enforced the guardian-ward relationship with Native people.[2] By the twentieth century, Congress had court-sanctioned plenary authority over American Indians and tribal affairs.

COMMISSIONER HIRAM PRICE

Hiram Price, a Pennsylvania native living in Iowa, was the first commissioner of the era. A former five-term Republican congressman from Iowa, Price was nominated to the position by President James A. Garfield and his friend, Interior Secretary Samuel J. Kirkland, who sought a man for the commissionership who might quiet the national uproar caused by Helen Hunt Jackson's *A Century of Dishonor*. Kirkland, anxious for his friend to assume office, appointed Price chief clerk on April 13, enabling him to serve as acting commissioner until the Senate confirmed his nomination on May 6, 1881.[3]

Price defined his policy strands in the first of his four annual reports, supporting "a thorough and radical change" of policy. "The greatest kindness the government can bestow on the Indian is to teach him to labor for his own support." There were only two options, Price declared, "civilization or extermination. . . . One of the two must die."[4] The latter was not an option, so the solution was simple. "The Indian must be taught to work for his support, and to speak the English language, or he must give place to people who do."[5] A key component was for the government to end the "evil" of cash annuities and use social nudging to encourage integration and enhance free labor.[6]

The challenge for Price was how to accomplish this without partiality. Tribes that resisted and warred against the United States tended to be fed and provided for, Price lamented, while "the peaceable and industrious Indians" received little support, giving "the appearance of rewarding vice and punishing virtue."[7] The solution was self-reliance, the lynchpin of Price's administration.

The means of self-reliance was to extend to all tribes the provisions of land severalty. "Within a few years" severalty would erase the so-called Indian problem and turn Native people into "a blessing instead of a curse."[8]

The existing policy of severalty, however, was governed by treaties that were "crude and imperfect, with no provisions for a title which affords sufficient protection to the Indians."[9] Some treaties provided for issuance of a fee patent while others did not, and patents were an essential component of severalty as they confirmed ownership. Where treaties proscribed fee patents, the General Land Office refused to issue patents, arguing only Congress could make that determination. According to reformers, fee patents would foster "individuality, responsibility, and a desire to accumulate property," with frugality and industry following.[10] While not all Native people were ready to accept severalty, Price was convinced that "where prepared for it, the Indian should have a home of his own."[11] Existing treaties, however, were dubious when it came to fee patents, illustrating the lack of overall thought in the severalty policy.

Severalty was not just driven by the Indian Office. The Board of Indian Commissioners recommended land severalty in its first annual report in 1869, followed by the Women's National Indian Association in 1881 and the newly formed Indian Rights Association a year later. The latter organization tethered the federal social programs of education and law to policies of assimilation and citizenship, an approach that drove policy for two generations. Herbert Welsh, founder and president of the Indian Rights Association, was a lifelong advocate of severalty, believing it was the only means of weaning Native people from barbarism.[12]

A corollary measure to severalty was an 1875 statute that allowed Natives to secure a homestead on the public domain under the provisions of the Homestead Act.[13] This, too, was an integration tool, as the Native homesteader would be surrounded by non-Indians. The challenge for Native homesteaders was the $1.25 per acre filing fee. While some desired to avail themselves of the provisions of the act, "their poverty and improvidence" made it difficult to pay the necessary fees.[14] Moreover, many Natives were seminomadic, making it difficult to fulfill the residency requirement of the allotment act. Other questions complicated public domain homesteads. For instance, could wives of Natives who held reservation allotments take public domain allotments?[15] Price sought congressional authorization to either waive the filing fee or to have the government pay it on behalf of the Native homesteader. Congress refused to consider the bill.

By 1881, the Indian Office had made 5,972 allotments and issued 2,793 fee patents—all done under treaty provisions.[16] To extend severalty, reservations would have to be surveyed and in recognition of this, Price requested from Congress $100,000 to facilitate allotment and define reservation boundaries. Congress granted the Indian Office $5,000, leading Price to lament that the "principal obstacle" to expanding severalty was "the fact that there are no appropriations available for the surveying of reservations."[17] Congress once again advanced a policy but did not appropriate the necessary funds to put it into effect, demonstrating that congressional parsimony was just as much to blame for failed policy as Native resistance.

Lack of surveys was a further embarrassment because of the increasing number of conflicts resulting from boundary disputes. When coal was discovered along the southern boundary of the

San Carlos district of the White Mountain Apache Reservation in eastern Arizona, prospectors poured into the country, disputing the unsurveyed boundary.[18] Price advanced appropriation requests to survey and monument the reservation to no avail. To heal the rift caused by mineral discoveries, he proposed leasing tribal land for mining purposes, with the royalties used to support the Apaches, a proposition the departmental solicitor denied due to a lack of statutory authority for leasing tribal land.[19]

Education was the crown jewel for Price, who asserted educational appropriations were entirely insufficient. If the American people "are to demand that Indians shall become white men within one generation, the Indian child must have other opportunities and come under other influences than the reservations can offer." These opportunities included the English language and off-reservation boarding schools, where children could "breathe the atmosphere of a civilized . . . community."[20] The government had an obligation to "provide the safest, surest, and most equitable means to induce the Indian to abandon the manners, customs, and traditions of his fathers," Price wrote in 1882, "and accommodate himself to the new and better way."[21]

The industrial boarding schools (Hampton, Forest Grove, and Carlisle) were the nucleus of the social transformation of Native students. These schools were doing "pioneer work" and, while there was no precedent for such educational philosophy, Price sought to expand the number of such schools, citing Richard Henry Pratt's philosophy of free labor that "even the youngest pupils might have some kind of manual training daily."[22] The Indian Office supported Pratt's idealized outing system whereby students attending Carlisle Institute were dispatched to live with and work for local non-Indian families between school terms so they might learn to "do something for [themselves]" and adopt the art of civilization.[23]

Price lamented the fact that the federal government contributed less to the education of Native children than did the state of Rhode Island for theirs.[24] To fulfill treaty obligations, the Indian Office should have made available $708,000 for 417 schools and requisite staff; Congress provided $44,000.[25] The shortfall led the department to encourage religious denominations to join with the government in educating children, with more sectarian schools opening each year.[26] With the growth of education, Price established a position of Superintendent of Indian Schools to unify curricula, a position that in future years proved effective in directing educational philosophy and providing young white women their first opportunity to work in the federal system, in the process feminizing the Indian Service.[27]

In a further effort to assimilate, Price encouraged the appointment of medical doctors at the agencies both to undermine the authority and influence of shaman and to treat the growing list of illnesses. If Native conceptions of medicine could be replaced with modern medicine, Price reasoned, "a long stride would be made in the work of civilization."[28] To eliminate vices associated with alcohol, Price proposed complete prohibition within twenty miles of Indian Country. "Fire should not be permitted near a powder magazine," he declared, "nor whisky [*sic*] near an Indian reservation."[29]

Price exhorted Congress to update the Nonintercourse Act, a statute that was entirely insufficient for the day. Enacted in 1834, Congress intended the statute to regulate the fur trade and prohibit the introduction of liquor in Indian Country. By the late nineteenth century, the fur trade was inconsequential and, while liquor was still a concern, the act allowed for removal of intruders from Indian Country, but a fine could be imposed only upon a second offense. Price encouraged Congress to amend the statute to allow fines upon the first offense, but while the Indian Office prepared a bill for legislative action, Congress failed to act.[30]

In 1881, Price unsuccessfully collaborated with Congressman Edwin Willits (R-MI) to introduce H.R. 755, which purported to extend the jurisdiction of the federal courts over Indian Country. The following year, Price again advanced legislation, arguing the sooner Native people came "to understand that no ancient custom, or tribal regulation, will shield [them] from just punishment for crime," the better off they would be.[31] Price and the reformers advocated jurisdiction in part to stem the near dictatorial power of Indian agents, who often controlled the application—or lack thereof—of policy at the local level.

When Congress failed to enact legislation, Interior Secretary Henry Teller directed Price to formulate rules for Courts of Indian Offenses. Established by departmental order in April 1883, these courts enabled local Indian agents to appoint Native judges to enforce Indian Office regulations against various dances, long hair, gambling, polygamy, theft, destruction of property, and social and cultural practices associated with death.[32] Judges were appointed by agents from the Indian police force but Congress did not provide funding to support them, making it difficult for agents to organize such courts. Moreover, many Natives were "unwilling to leave their farms and business occupations when they [knew] that their only reward [as a judge] may perhaps be a loss of influence and popularity among the tribe."[33] As a parallel measure, Price advocated that, as territories were admitted to statehood, Congress should confer on them civil and criminal jurisdiction over Indian Country, with the only exception if treaty provisions precluded such action.[34] Despite a number of proposals to establish law, there was no consensus on the form of such law, other than that federal law should govern capital crimes.[35]

Indian police continued to increase in number, with 84 officers and 786 privates by 1881.[36] In addition to preserving order, attempting to suppress liquor traffic, arresting offenders, driving out timber thieves, and transporting truant children to school, officers and privates were expected to be in a monogamous marriage, wear civilized clothing, keep their hair cut short, and exhibit good moral behavior. In 1883, despite such offenses being under the authority of Indian agents, Price broadcast the use of such officers as one of the four main tenets in solving the "Indian problem."[37]

That same year, the U.S. Supreme Court accepted a case from Dakota Territory that materially modified criminal jurisdiction in Indian Country and forced Congress to act. The case involved the murder by Crow Dog of Brule chief Spotted Tail within the Rosebud Sioux Reservation. The territorial court tried, convicted, and sentenced Crow Dog to death for his crime. Local attorneys working on behalf of Crow Dog, however, sued for a writ of habeas corpus into the Supreme Court, which opined that there was no clear expression of a congressional intent to subject Natives to federal jurisdiction and the United States had no authority over Native offenders committing crimes in Indian Country.[38] Neither the 1868 Sioux treaty nor the 1876 Sioux agreement granted such authority to the United States and Congress never extended or purported to extend such jurisdiction. Crow Dog was a free man. A year later, in direct response to the court's ruling,

Congress appended a paragraph to the 1885 Indian Appropriation Act conferring on the United States jurisdiction over seven enumerated crimes—murder, manslaughter, assault with intent to kill, rape, arson, burglary, and larceny.[39]

Much as the reformers in the postbellum era viewed the Civil War as paying for the national sin of slavery, the reformers in the late 1870s and early 1880s looked to the federal government for a moral high ground in relationship with tribal nations. The lamentable "Indian problem" was a threat to national honor. During Price's tenure, reformers organized the Women's National Indian Association, the Indian Rights Association, and the Lake Mohonk Conference of Friends of the Indians to atone for national sins perpetrated against Native people. Reform, stimulated in part by Chief Standing Bear and inspired by Jackson's *A Century of Dishonor*, was dedicated to doing away with "pauperizing" reservations that encouraged dependency by emphasizing land severalty, education, citizenship, and assimilation. Samuel Armstrong of Hampton Institute, himself a reformer, compared reservations to the institution of slavery, arguing both impeded free labor via social separation. While Price had little to do with the creation of such organizations, the policy strands he espoused reflected those of the new reformers.[40]

COMMISSIONER JOHN D. C. ATKINS

With the election of New York Democratic governor Grover Cleveland to the presidency in November 1884, Price resigned and left office on March 21, 1885, being replaced by John DeWitt Clinton Atkins, a Tennessee politician, former Confederate general and member of the Confederate Congress, and a six-term Representative (D-TN).[41] Atkins took office on March 21, 1885, becoming the first Democrat to hold the office since the Buchanan administration, resigning when the Indian Rights Association attacked his credibility and accused him of nepotism in filling positions in the Indian Office.

Atkins implemented a number of far-reaching changes. In his first annual report, he outlined a series of priorities, beginning with a renewed focus on agriculture. "It requires no seer to foretell or foresee the civilization of the Indian race [tied to] a knowledge and practice upon their part of the act of agriculture." Indeed, those "who are in ignorance of agriculture are also ignorant of almost everything else."[42] In his 1887 report, Atkins described agriculture as one of the three stages in the hierarchy of civilization, the other two being "the adoption of the dress of the white man" and "the education of their children."[43] Such a hierarchy built on the classification system of Swedish scientist Carl Linnaeus who classified humans in 1758 into categories: Europeanus (whites), Americanus (red, choleric, stubborn, and free), and Africanus (black, crafty, sly and careless).[44] To facilitate agriculture as one expression of European civilization, Atkins secured from Congress $25,000 to employ practical farmers to assist agency farmers, believing yeoman farming would induce tribal people to adopt civilized homes and, therefore, hasten civilization.[45]

In his inaugural report, Atkins favored a "practical policy" of severalty that both encouraged the abandonment of tribal relations and fostered "personal independence." The excess land after severalty could be sold to homesteaders, with the funds applied toward the education of children on the reservation.[46] Atkins argued a series of severalty musts. Natives must "abandon tribal relations ... give up their superstitions ... forsake their savage habits ... learn the arts of civilization ... learn to labor ... rear their families as white people do ... know more of their obligation to the Government and to society ... learn to work for a living, and they must understand that it is their interest and duty to send their children to school."[47]

While a general land severalty bill was approved by the Senate in 1886, the House failed to act on it.[48] A year later, however, Congress enacted, and President Cleveland signed the General Allotment Act into law. In his annual report, Atkins dedicated seven pages to the law, including a section-by-section analysis of its provisions. In exchange for an allotment, the allottee would secure a trust patent with the title held in federal trust and inalienable and free of any encumbrances for twenty-five years. Upon receipt of a trust patent, the landowner became subject "to the civil and criminal laws of the State or Territory" in which he resided.[49] Each landowner was under the equal protection of the laws of the United States and each was granted ipso facto citizenship. For those having already taken an allotment, they were granted U.S. citizenship on the date of the act (February 8, 1887).[50] Following a humanitarian mantra, Atkins proclaimed that severalty would end the pauperizing practice of tribal relations, with agriculture and education gradually accomplishing the goal of civilization and enabling "the Government to leave the Indian to stand alone."[51] This overly simple—and socially destructive—philosophy not only undermined the social structure of tribalism but it also initiated the fractionalization of Native land that remains today.

The General Allotment Act was not a panacea, however, as Atkins recognized the difficulties of implementing it. Competent agents were needed to assist the Natives in selecting allotments and the government would have to avoid "too great [of] haste" in allotting reservations. The Indians needed good, productive land, with the size of the allotments dependent on locality. Title to the land would vest in the United States for twenty-five years with the option of extending the trust period if circumstances dictated. The public "must not be impatient" by the absence of alacrity on the part of Natives, Atkins remarked, and advocates of severalty were cautioned not to expect "too immediate and pronounced success." "Character, habits, and antecedents cannot be changed by an enactment" and severalty was not the consummation but the "introduction and invitation" to civilization.[52]

The Five Tribes in Indian Territory were exempt from severalty due to their unique land ownership following their emigration from the Southeast. While Atkins held a high opinion of the Five Tribes, he was critical of their exemption. The tribes should "set freely and promptly an example [to the] advance[ment of] the civilization of their savage brethren," he wrote in 1886.[53] Each member of the Five Tribes, he judged, should be allotted 160 acres per head of family and 80 acres to each dependent minor, with the surplus sold and opened to homesteading. These tribes "have no right to obstruct civilization and commerce and set up an exclusive claim to self-government." The Congress and the president "are the supreme guardians of these mere wards," Atkins argued, and must "administer their affairs as any other guardian."[54]

A year later, and subsequent to the passage of the General Allotment Act, Atkins was more vociferous. The decision whether or not to accept severalty was not the Five Tribes' to make. The American people will not "meekly submit to what is manifestly an insubordinate and unpardonable meddling" with the policy of the United States. If the Five Tribes refused to accept land severalty, they would "set an example to all other tribes derogatory to the influence which the Government is entitled to wield over them."[55]

With tribes in the western portion of Indian Territory (the Oklahoma district) subject to allotment, and with the contemplated allotment of the Five Tribes, Atkins considered a general concentration of unallotted tribes in Indian Territory. The states of Kansas, Missouri, Texas, and Arkansas, however, opposed any further consolidation of Native people in the territory. Atkins, nonetheless, continued to advocate such a policy, believing it was advantageous that "the Indians . . . be together in a more compact form."[56] He also argued for a more general concentration policy, including amalgamating the tribes in Michigan, Wisconsin, and Minnesota on the Red Lake and White Earth Reservations in Minnesota, placing the tribes in the Pacific Northwest on the Yakima Reservation in central Washington, and selecting one or two reservations in the desert for the southwestern tribes.[57]

Congress continued its assault on Indian land, seeking to take from tribes that which was "worthless to them [since] they did not know how to cultivate [the land]."[58] On May 15, 1886, Congress created a commission to negotiate with the tribes in Minnesota and Oregon, as well as in the territories of Dakota, Montana, Idaho, and Washington, for the purpose of reducing the extent of their reservations and providing for allotment in severalty. Under the terms of ten agreements, tribes ceded more than twenty-five million acres to the United States, with the largest single cession—17.5 million acres—from the Fort Peck, Fort Belknap, and Blackfeet Tribes. Table 5.2 lists the agreements and tribes involved.

Atkins further expanded the Courts of Indian Offenses and encouraged Congress to provide statutory authority to correct certain defects in the Major Crimes Act. Under existing statute, for instance, the United States paid for the prosecution of Indian criminal cases when reservations were within the geographic boundaries of a state. In the territories, however, local citizens were responsible for these costs. Moreover, Atkins urged Congress to extend the provisions of the act to Indian Territory and to subject the Five Tribes to it.[59] He also lobbied Congress to establish federal district courts in Indian Territory to deal with "the reckless destruction of human life, particularly in the Cherokee and Choctaw nations," and to handle non-Indian criminal acts that were left unprosecuted because legal loopholes made reservations—Indian Territory in particular—criminal refuges.[60] In order to protect Native land titles, Atkins requested legislative authority to record Indian deeds and conveyances, of which there were 10,755 pages worth as of 1887.[61]

Atkins followed Price in the field of medicine, encouraging Congress to construct hospitals, of which there were only four by 1890. Such facilities were social institutions in that they could "weaken the hold of ancient superstitions and traditions" of the medicine man and place tribal people beyond their reach.[62] In the field of education, he implemented an "English only" policy to prevent "the waste of valuable time by Indian children" leaving barbarism for civilization.[63] While

Table 5.2. Indian Agreements of Cession, 1886–1887

Reservation	Tribe(s)	Date
White Earth	Otter Tail and Pembina Chippewa	August 11, 1886
Red Lake	Chippewa	August 11, 1886
Leech Lake	Pillager and Winnibigoshish Chippewa	September 17, 1886
Fort Berthold	Gros Ventre, Arikara, Mandan	December 14, 1886
Fort Peck	Assiniboine and Sioux	December 28, 1886
Fort Belknap	Gros Ventre, Assiniboine, Blackfeet	January 21, 1887
Spokane	Spokane	March 18, 1887
Coeur d'Alene	Coeur d'Alene	March 26, 1887
Sand Point	Lower Pend d'Oreille	April 21, 1887
Jocko	Flathead, Kootenai, Upper Pend Oreilles	April 27, 1887

Source: DeJong, *American Indian Treaties*, 203–5.

sectarian schools preferred to use Native languages, Atkins opposed these practices, believing they prejudiced Native children against government schools. English was "the language of the greatest, most powerful, and enterprising nationalities under the sun" and its use would hasten civilization.[64]

By 1887, the Indian Office counted 166 federal and 61 sectarian schools operating in Indian Country. Of the former, 68 were boarding facilities, 90 were day schools, and 8—Carlisle, Chilocco, Genoa, Hampton, Haskell, Lincoln, Salem, and St. Ignatius—were industrial boarding schools. "I take no part in the controversy as to which is the best method of having Indians educated, whether on or off reservation," Atkins argued, but "what for a time was an experiment [manual labor or industrial boarding schools] no longer admits of uncertainty."[65] Of the industrial schools, Hampton and Carlisle served to train Native leaders to return to their reservations and teach in day and boarding schools, although statistically only 8.4 percent of Carlisle and 11 percent of Hampton graduates went into government schools as teachers or matrons/disciplinarians.[66] To give focus and attention to the growing educational activities of the Indian Office, Atkins appointed John Oberly as the first superintendent of Indian schools and conferred on him authority to set curriculum and school regimentation. That Natives were capable of being educated was well established. What the Indian Office sought from Congress was the political will to accomplish the objective.

The Indian Office continued its quest for citizenship, even when the federal courts were reticent. When John Elk, a Winnebago from Nebraska, voluntarily left his tribe and registered to vote in Omaha, he was denied suffrage due to his tribal ethnicity. Elk argued that under the Fourteenth Amendment he was a "person born or naturalized in the United States" and, therefore, entitled to citizenship and suffrage. Chief Justice Roger Taney, however, opined that "Indians born within the territorial limits of the United States, members of, and owing immediate allegiance to one of the Indian tribes, although in a geographical sense born in the United States, are no more 'born in the United States and subject to the jurisdiction thereof,' within the meaning of the first section of the 14th Amendment," than foreign diplomats whose children were born within the country.

Elk—and Native people in similar capacities—could not become a citizen of the United States unless and until Congress specifically provided for his naturalization.[67] American Indians could not voluntarily separate themselves from their tribe, take up residence among non-Indians, and become citizens unless the United States and the tribe consented.

In New Mexico, the Pueblo people constituted a unique situation. While the Supreme Court in 1877 held that the Pueblo people were not "Indians" within the meaning of the Nonintercourse Act and, therefore, not subject to the police powers of the act, there was ambiguity as to whether they were citizens.[68] The Indian Office treated the Pueblo people as wards of the government, with federal agents stationed in the villages. "On the one hand," Atkins lamented, "we have the opinion of a United States judge that the Pueblo Indians should be treated as citizens of the United States [and] on the other, we find the Department to have uniformly treated them as wards of the nation."[69] The ambiguity surrounding the Pueblos would continue until the 1924 citizenship act.

COMMISSIONER JOHN H. OBERLY

Atkins resigned on June 14, 1888, and was replaced by one of the few men nominated as commissioner of Indian affairs because of his qualifications and experience: John H. Oberly, an Illinois native, and former superintendent of Indian schools. President Cleveland nominated Oberly in September and the Senate confirmed him on October 10, 1888. The new commissioner advanced several educational policies, including compulsory school attendance, although parents retained the option of sending their children to government or private schools, as long as the latter "furnished the elements required by civilized life and conformed to a uniform standard prescribed by the Government." Teachers, Oberly argued, needed tenure and ought to be exempt from partisan appointments.[70]

While Oberly was committed to education, a parsimonious Congress limited him to a maximum budget per school of $10,000, both for construction and furnishings. Congress further precluded the Indian Office from applying new appropriations to add to or alter existing schools, a prohibition that "prevented the Bureau from furnishing suitable and adequate school buildings and accommodations." This limitation required a statutory adjustment, the commissioner informed Interior Secretary Henry Teller, as it was impossible to construct schools—even with public bids—under such fiscal restraints.[71]

Industrial education was increasingly the focus of the Indian Office: "From the day of its birth the child of civilized parents is constantly in contact with civilized modes of life—of action, thought, speech, dress, and is surrounded by a thousand beneficent influences that never operate upon the child of savage parentage." In the current school system, Oberly exclaimed, "the Indian child cannot receive an adequate idea of civilized home life." To correct this deficiency, the commissioner advanced the concept of large off-reservation boarding schools being surrounded by pods in which staff would instruct girls in domestic chores and teach boys in agricultural, industrial, and mechanical trades, with both boys and girls jointly cultivating gardens.[72]

Table 5.3. Indian Service Personnel, Select Years, 1877–1897

Year	Education	Agents/Clerks	Other	Total
1877	114	98	513	725
1883	267	121	1,255	1,643
1889	708	117	1,514	2,339
1893	1,326	128	1,665	3,119
1897	1,936	141	1,840	3,917

Source: Adams, *Education for Extinction*, 61.

Not surprisingly, of all Indian Office positions, the greatest growth occurred within the field of education, increasing from 114 positions in 1877 to 1,936 twenty years later. Federal school-related positions constituted about 16 percent of Indian Office employees in 1877, whereas by 1897 they constituted about 50 percent. As school personnel increased, more consideration was given to how such employees were selected and the ways standards could be routinized. A majority of Indian Service teachers were young, single women, both because they were less expensive than male teachers and because teaching was becoming feminized. Table 5.3 illustrates the growth in personnel.

Oberly encouraged Congress to increase the responsibilities of the superintendent of Indian schools. While Congress in June 1888 granted the superintendent authority to employ and discharge staff, Oberly did not believe the legislation went far enough: "All matters connected with all branches of Indian education" should be placed under the superintendent, including "disbursing school moneys, making school contracts, paying school salaries, etc."[73] While Oberly advocated such, Congress was reticent to grant such authority.

During Oberly's administration, the Protestant-dominated Indian Rights Association and Lake Mohonk Conference expressed concern that the Indian Office discriminated against Protestant schools in favor of the Catholics, believing the Bureau of Catholic Missions received a disproportionate share of school contracts.[74] Oberly defended the Indian Office against such charges, noting that government schools accommodated just one-quarter of the students, making contract schools essential. Moreover, the Catholics "expended larger sums of money than any other denomination," since they received a disproportionate number of school contracts. While the Bureau of Catholic Missions had thirty-eight contracts for 2,068 children, Protestant denominations had just twelve contracts serving 500 children. When the reformers met for the annual Lake Mohonk Conference in 1888, they pointed to the disparity and concluded that the only prudent course was for the government to control all education. The Indian Office "has no right to leave this burden to be carried by the churches," the conference delegates concluded, despite "the necessity [being] great and the neglect absolute." Congress concurred.[75]

Natural resource exploitation in Indian Country also became a contested matter in the late 1880s, with Oberly facing questions related to illegal harvesting of tribal timber in northern Minnesota and Wisconsin. At issue was who owned these resources and whether it was lawful to harvest dead and down timber. The Menominee Tribe in 1888 harvested 8.3 million board feet of dead and down timber, and on the Lac Court Oreille, Bad River, Lac du Flambeau, and Fond du Lac Chippewa Reservations, the tribes contracted for and cut 190,206,080 board feet of timber at a net gain of $428,221.[76] While the Indian Office allowed timber contracts to proceed on allotments on which the United States issued fee patents, allottees were forbidden to dispose of timber on their land, and Indian Office regulations required them to reserve enough for "domestic and farm purposes."

As for dead and down timber, the Indian Office issued regulations authorizing the cutting and sale of such timber but only by the allottee; they were prohibited from cutting or selling live timber. The question was: Who was the lawful owner of the timber? Did the landowner or the federal government own the natural resources? Based on Supreme Court interpretation, Native land tenure was one of occupancy only, with the allottee having a right to clear and improve the land and to use or sell the timber so cut for improving his allotment. "When cut or severed for sale alone," Oberly stated, "and not as an incidental use to the occupancy, the right and title to the timber is absolute in the name of the United States" as the underlying holder of the remaindermen.[77] As such, no timber could be cut or marketed by Native people on their reservations "except as might be necessary to clear land for cultivation."[78]

Oberly requested of Congress legislation authorizing tribes to cut and market dead and down timber so as to bring "into productive use timber, which, if left alone, will soon become of no value to the Indian, the Government, or any one else."[79] He also requested of Congress authorization to lease land, an action the U.S. Attorney General again determined to be illegal unless authorized by a treaty or specific statute. "Many tribes would benefit [and] would derive a revenue from their surplus grass," Oberly argued in support of such authorization, "which would lessen their dependence upon Government appropriations."[80] Again, Congress did not act.

Throughout the decade, the Indian Office continued to increase in size, surpassing 2,200 employees (531 of which were Natives) by 1888. With the increase came the challenges associated with political patronage, a system that seemed to guarantee that appointees would lack qualifications for working in Indian Country. Patronage was an "evil [that] can be corrected in no other way than by abandonment," Oberly argued.[81] Maintaining patronage would obstruct improvements in the Indian Office and prevent it from securing competent employees. In an attempt to hire qualified persons, Oberly instituted an in-depth questionnaire for prospective employees that ran the gamut of alcohol usage to marital status. Three persons acquainted with the applicant were required to complete a separate seventeen-point character-matter questionnaire. Oberly also adopted minimum standards for all positions, believing that only with such changes could the "Indian question in all its most perplexing features . . . be translated from a demoralizing political question into a not dangerous social question."[82]

Land severalty, with its companion focus on citizenship, remained the fulcrum of all policy. In 1888, the Indian Office issued 3,349 allotments totaling 349,124 acres on the Lake Traverse, Yankton, Absentee Shawnee, Eastern Shawnee, Seneca, Wyandotte, Fond du Lac, Crow, Winnebago, and Siletz Reservations. Elsewhere, severalty progressed slowly, with considerable opposition in Indian Country. Many Native people believed tribal ownership was the only means of preventing the dissolution of tribal relations and forestalling their "absorption into the body politic." Another segment of the tribal population opposed severalty on the grounds that it "would immediately open to public settlement long-coveted Native lands."[83] Still, a third group favored allotment, but feared severalty would be forced upon them before they were ready, driving them into "vagabondage." The Indian Office, nonetheless, accelerated severalty as the means of taking the Indian "out of the reservation."[84]

Oberly facilitated the extension of federal judicial authority in Indian Territory. In 1888, seven bills were introduced into Congress seeking to legislate federal authority over the territory. While not initiated by the Indian Office, the Supreme Court weighed in on the constitutionality of the Major Crimes Act. In a case originating on the Hoopa Valley (California) Reservation, the court in *United States v. Kagama* was asked to consider whether the federal government could constitutionally assert jurisdiction over crimes involving Natives from the same tribe when the crime was committed within their reservation.

The Indian Office favored such an interpretation, with the Supreme Court concluding that federal jurisdiction was constitutional even though the United States recognized via treaties the "semi-independent position" of the tribes. Congress had the "right and authority ... to govern [the tribes] by acts," the court concluded, even as it nudged tribes closer to full congressional plenary power. The court also opined that since states had no authority over tribes, and Natives in tribal relations owed "no allegiance to the States and receive from them no protection," federal authority was necessary. Due to their wardship status, the court declared that the United States had to protect the tribes and that such protection was a national obligation based on the tribes' dependent status. In affirming such authority, the court transformed Chief Justice John Marshall's 1831 simile characterizing the tribal-federal political relationship as "*resembl[ing]* that of a ward to his guardian" into a definitive "Indian tribes *are* the wards of the nation" status.[85] Territorial courts had no jurisdiction over Native crimes in Indian Country, but federal authority was upheld.[86]

Commissioner Oberly fell victim to the very patronage system against which he railed. He submitted his resignation on June 6, 1889, and left office on June 30. Although incoming Republican Interior Secretary William Vilas retained the Democratic-nominated Oberly—and the reformers supported him—the election of President Benjamin Harrison assured change. While the Indian Rights Association advocated Harrison retain Oberly—and thus establish a precedent that commissioners could be carried over from administration to administration—it was unable to persuade the president.[87]

COMMISSIONER THOMAS JEFFERSON MORGAN

From Indiana, Thomas Jefferson Morgan replaced Oberly as commissioner on July 1, 1889.[88] An educator, Baptist minister, and Civil War veteran (who served under Benjamin Harrison in the 70th Indiana Infantry), Morgan earned the support of reformers by announcing: "The chief thing to be considered in the administration of this office is the character of the men and women employed to carry out the designs of the Government."[89] A frequent guest of the Lake Mohonk

Conference, Morgan spelled out in his first report "a few simple, well-defined, and strongly cherished convictions." These included the strands of abolishing reservations; assimilating Native people as citizens of the United States and the state in which they resided; recognizing the individuality of tribal people; conforming Natives to "the white man's ways," or allowing the advancing civilization to crush them; requiring all Native children to attend school; breaking up tribal relations; and enforcing "the autonomy of the individual."[90] Beginning with Morgan, the Indian Office made the home the center of social reorganization.

Morgan characterized these policy strands as settled, and set out to treat Natives not as members of "nations or tribes, but as individual citizens."[91] In 1891, he clarified his philosophy by noting that "no two reservations are exactly similar, and no two tribes present the same condition." Nonetheless, he emphasized policy centered on a reorientation of family life, including legalizing marriages, defining heads of households, instituting a new definition of what a home was and how it was to be constructed. Marriage, with its strong social and legal constructs, was the key to ending Native independence on the United States by transforming men into a role of primary responsibility for providing and caring for their families. What was once the domain of local governing bodies to dictate was now a federal responsibility.[92]

With regards to the different tribal languages, manners, customs, religions, and environments, Morgan admitted that "any theory which ignores these essential facts and attempts to deal with them en masse must, of necessity, be radically and fatally defective."[93] Notwithstanding his enlightened views, Morgan executed policy focused on ten essentials:

1. Comprehensiveness of execution.
2. Definiteness of aim (citizenship).
3. Clarity to "bridge a thousand years of tedious evolution."
4. Adaptation of means to the ends by providing the Indians with good agricultural lands so they could thrive.
5. Justice or paying Native people what was due, but demanding of them what was necessary.
6. Firmness of land severalty, with the caveat that if an individual refused to sustain himself on the land then it was survival of the fittest.
7. Respecting their humanity by treating them with justice and generosity.
8. Radicalness in the application of severalty and education for all.
9. Stability until the "work is accomplished."
10. And time, which depended on the will of the government, execution of policy by Indian Office employees, conversion by missionaries, and the respect of citizens surrounding tribes.

If these strands could be carried into effect, the transformation might be completed within a single decade.[94]

The commissioner developed lengthy descriptions of the various means to accomplish the ends. For instance, in 1891 he devoted twenty-nine pages of his annual report to the political status of Native people. A year later, he dedicated seven pages to describe the legal status of Natives.[95]

In response to these inquiries, he subscribed to late nineteenth-century political philosophy: American Indians could not on their own volition become citizens unless Congress statutorily granted them citizenship or it was provided via treaty. At the same time, the United States had an obligation to displace "the fiction of regarding Indians as independent people" and instead had to "treat them as wards."[96] As for what constituted an Indian, Morgan adopted a liberal, rather than a clinical construction. He acknowledged tribal custom—not ethnological definition—governed; and he was careful in defining Natives, being mindful that a restrictive legal definition might invalidate treaties and lead to equitable claims against the United States. By Morgan's account, persons of mixed blood were Native, lest claims be levied against the government for paying annuities to persons not legally identified as Indians.[97]

A product of his day, Morgan accepted the evolutionary bias that human beings evolved from savagery to civilization, but he also acknowledged education could hasten this process. In fact, Morgan was "the most significant national figure" in the field of Indian education in the nineteenth century.[98] To this end, education was the only means to Americanize and save Native children. Morgan mandated that children be given Christian names and, although Native surnames could be retained, English translations of tribal names were inadvisable.[99] Schools and curriculum were further standardized, and rules promulgated, with Morgan actively involved in the National Education Association.[100] Industrial training was provided to more students, even though such skills were increasingly obsolete by the 1890s, and all children were equipped for patriotic citizenship. The goal was the disintegration of the tribes, with Native people educated "not as Indians, but as American citizens."[101] With adequate funding, Morgan optimistically argued, it would take only two or three years for all Native children to be on the road to civilization, with nothing of the children's past to be maintained.[102] Congress could not be counted on to appropriate the funds necessary, with the result that most government schools required students to work in order for the facilities to remain self-sufficient.

Morgan also identified a growing challenge: returned boarding school students who learned a trade or technical skill had limited opportunities to apply their skills upon return home. To remedy the situation, the Indian Office encouraged such students to seek homes and work outside of their reservations.[103] Morgan asked Congress to increase educational funding with a view of "bringing as large a number as possible" under its civilizing influences. Congress again failed to oblige and Morgan attributed parsimony and restrictions on school construction for limiting his plan. While overall appropriations for schools increased from $1,348,015 in 1889 to $2,291,650 in 1892, Morgan's request for a $315,000 increase in 1893 was rejected, and he received just $30,735, even though tribal leaders pleaded for more and better schools.[104] Additional funds were required to counteract the rising incidence of disease at the schools, boarding facilities in particular.[105] Above all, the Indian Office advocated off-reservation boarding schools as the means of bringing children "into more vital contact with civilization" and veiling the commissioner's goal to end the domination of sectarian education by the Bureau of Catholic Missions. In 1892, Morgan refused to enter into new contracts with sectarian schools, arguing that a separation of church and state required the government to refrain from funding such schools.[106]

Land severalty remained the parallel braid of the integration policy, with Morgan seeking to remedy challenges in its application. If severalty were to occur, then tribes demanded an equal division of all reservation land and a halt to the sale of any surplus lands. Moreover, tribes demanded women receive the same acreage as men. Morgan dismissed the former as "beyond the actual needs of the Indians" but supported the latter since some tribal marriages were dissolved with women left landless. Reservations were the common property of the tribe, Morgan argued, and "each member had an equal right therein." Such a modification would remove a principle inequity of the General Allotment Act. Congress concurred and, in February 1891, amended the act to provide a "fair and equitable division of tribal property."[107]

While Morgan did not advise the sale of so-called surplus lands until "the Indians have been located upon and [are] absolutely secured in their individual holdings," he hastened on with surveying reservations, scheduling allotment, and issuing patents. In 1890, 12,071,380 acres of tribal land were restored to the public domain or sold as surplus.[108] Between 1889 and 1892, more than forty reservations were in the severalty or patenting process. Commissions to initiate allotment or negotiate further cessions were active among the Chippewa in Minnesota; the Pottawatomie and Kickapoo in Kansas; the Sioux in Dakota Territory; the Coeur d'Alene in Idaho; the Puyallup, Warm Springs, and Colville Reservations in Washington; the Cherokee Nation (Outlet lands) in Indian Territory; the Shoshone in Wyoming; the Shoshone and Pyramid Lake Paiute in Nevada; the Navajo in New Mexico; the Turtle Mountain Chippewa in North Dakota; and the Round Valley and Mission Indians in California. Morgan warned against moving "too suddenly and violently," as the harm to the Natives would not be "counterbalanced by the benefit conferred."[109] In 1892, he published a state-by-state schedule of allotment in Indian Country, advocating the application of severalty to all tribes—except the Five Tribes in Indian Territory—and completing the process by the mid-1890s.[110]

To reform Indian agencies, Morgan directed employees to exemplify good role models and refrain from imbibing alcohol, with those refusing to comply dismissed. In 1892, Congress supported Morgan's temperance movement by prohibiting alcoholic drinks, including beer, in Indian Country.[111] In line with temperance, Morgan opposed Indian participation in the Wild West shows, believing such events were economically, physically, and morally "pernicious," "degrading," and "antagonistic to [the influence] of the schools."[112] He did, however, support an Indian village at the 1892 World Exposition to illustrate a "view of the Indian as he appeared when America was discovered," as long as the center stage of the exhibit was an industrial boarding school complete with thirty pupils and a teacher to "give a graphic and impressive showing of what the Government is trying to do for the Indians in the way of education and civilization and of the capacity and readiness shown by the Indian to improve the opportunities thus offered him."[113] Both extremes fostered stereotypes that prevailed throughout the twentieth century.[114]

As part of the 1891 amendments to the General Allotment Act, Congress not only equalized allotments but also authorized for the first time the leasing of land, both allotted and tribal.[115] Staunchly opposed by Senator Henry Dawes (D-MA), who feared the collapse of severalty if Natives leased their allotments instead of working them, Congress nonetheless approved of a leasing policy. Within two years, local agents controlled the leasing of tribal lands and by 1894 leasing regulations were further relaxed, with the result that additional land was leased to non-Native farmers and ranchers. In 1890, the first of the infamous land runs occurred in Oklahoma Territory and, while irrigation provisions dated to 1864, Morgan developed policy for irrigating tribal lands.[116] Traders were put on notice that the time for federal licensing was nearing an end and the free market was at hand. Morgan planned the abolition of Indian agencies and he hired and dispatched to Indian Country field matrons to teach Native women to manage their home and care for their children. In light of the Wounded Knee Massacre at Pine Ridge and the Ghost Dance movement on the Northern Plains, Morgan supported a transfer of the Sioux agencies to the War Department for control and discipline, but with the caveat the Indian Office retain civil authority.[117] He viewed any other use of the military with apprehension.[118] And after years of advocating change, the Indian Office in 1892 secured regulations governing the punishment of crimes and misdemeanors committed by Natives in Indian Country, and for the first time reservations were apportioned into judicial districts to handle matters of original and appellate jurisdiction.[119]

COMMISSIONER DANIEL BROWNING

With the election of Democrat Grover Cleveland to a second term as president in fall of 1892, Morgan's days as commissioner were numbered. He resigned on January 10, 1893, and left office on March 1, being replaced by Cleveland appointee Daniel Browning. Morgan left office steadfast in his advocacy of Americanization of Native people. "This great nation, strong, wealthy, aggressive, can signalize its spirit of fairness, justice, and philanthropy in no better way, perhaps, than by making ample provision for the complete education and absorption into the national life of those who for more than one hundred years have been among us but not of us," Morgan waxed poetically. "Where in human history has there been a brighter example of the humane and just spirit which ought to characterize the actions of a Christian nation superior in numbers, intelligence, riches, and power, in dealing with those whom it might easily crush, but whom it is far nobler to adopt as part of its great family?" he challenged.[120]

A former judge from Illinois, Browning was among the least qualified to serve as commissioner, taking office on April 18, 1893, with *The New York Times* editorializing that Assistant Commissioner Frank Armstrong was "the best informed man on Indian affairs."[121] Browning came to office with no interest in Indian affairs and did not initiate any new policies during his tenure, simply continuing status quo.[122] The closest he came to articulating a personal philosophy was in his final report: "The main effort now is, and for many years must be to put the Indian upon his allotment, get him to support himself there, protect him from encroachment and injustice, and educate and train his children in books and industries." If a Native would agree to this, "the Government assists him in building a house, gives him a team, agricultural implements, wire for fencing, and grain for seeding, and the supervision and counsel of a practical farmer to aid him in the cultivation of his crops."[123] That most Natives did not seek this government assistance was immaterial to the discussion. Not surprisingly, Browning opposed Indians working in Wild West shows, although he permitted some entertainers—Buffalo Bill and Pawnee Bill—to take Natives on tour but only under strict controls and penalty of bond forfeiture.[124]

Pursuant to an act of Congress dated July 13, 1892, President Cleveland in June 1893 began detailing Army officers to all Indian agent vacancies and by the end of the year, twenty-seven of the fifty-seven agencies were under the authority of military officers.[125] Stimulated in part by the Ghost Dance and as a matter of economy, such agents were largely replaced by the late 1890s. As part of Cleveland's reforms, civil service was extended to all positions in the Indian Office except "laborers or workmen and persons who have been nominated for confirmation by the Senate." Believing that Natives were at a disadvantage "in competing with his more favored white brother," Browning appointed them "without examination or certificate by the Civil Service Commission, to all positions," except those of superintendent, teachers, and physicians. By 1896, there were 1,434 Native employees and 645 non-Indian employees in the Indian Service, excluding schools, where 1,365 were non-Indian and 705 were Indian. The average salary of the former was $622.45, while that of the latter was $211.06.[126]

Browning was committed to a "vigorous practical education to fit [the Indians] for the average walks of life."[127] While he initially supported parental choice before sending children to off-reservation boarding schools, by 1896 he instituted the Browning Rule, which held that government schools were to be filled before mission schools. To end the rivalry and competition between schools over students, Browning defined the geographical boundaries from which schools could draw students, both for government and contract schools. This was ostensibly to protect the health of children by keeping them "within the climate and latitude to which they are accustomed."[128] He also argued there was no need for additional off-reservation industrial schools and that such schools were to hereafter "be regarded as advanced schools," meaning students were to be limited to those who first attended on-reservation schools and had completed their course of studies. Table 5.4 lists the industrial schools in 1893, along with their average attendance.

The effort to terminate federal support for sectarian contract schools accelerated during Browning's tenure, not due to any effort of the commissioner but per legislative fiat. In the 1894 Indian Appropriation Act, Congress—influenced by the Lake Mohonk reformers—directed the secretary of the interior to investigate the propriety of discontinuing federal funding for contract schools and whether "the same can be done without detriment to the education of Indian children."[129] In 1895, funding for sectarian schools was reduced 20 percent to $463,505 from $537,600. The following year, Congress limited sectarian funding to 80 percent of the previous year ($370,796 from $463,505), and a year later limited such funding to 50 percent ($257,928). By 1896, only the Bureau of Catholic Missions ($198,228), Miss Howard School ($3,500), Lincoln Institute ($33,400), Hampton Institute ($20,040), Point Iroquois ($660), and John Roberts School ($2,160) received federal funding.[130] The result was the government became the sole provider of education in Indian Country, notwithstanding a small number of sectarian schools that remained.

Browning advocated for children to be placed in and made the responsibility of local public schools, believing that their "strange language and uncouth customs" were barriers that such schools

Table 5.4. Active Off-Reservation Industrial Boarding Schools, 1893

School	Year Established	Average Attendance
Carlisle, PA	1877	731
Chemawa, OR	1880	248
Fort Stevenson, ND	1883	153
Chilocco, OK	1884	224
Genoa, NB	1884	340
Albuquerque, NM	1884	222
Haskell, KN	1884	538
Grand Junction, CO	1886	98
Santa Fe, NM	1890	118
Fort Mojave, AZ	1890	118
Carson, NV	1891	80
Pierre, SD	1891	120
Phoenix, AZ	1891	105
Fort Lewis, CO	1892	63
Fort Shaw, MT	1892	136
Perris, CA	1893	90
Flandreau, SD	1893	86
Pipestone, MN	1893	38
Mount Pleasant, MI	1893	36
Tomah, WI	1893	77
Total	20	181

Source: *Annual Report of the Commissioner of Indian Affairs, 1893*, 9.

would break down.[131] Overall, there were 16,584 students enrolled in government schools, 319 in public schools, 253 in mission schools, and 5,580 in contract schools.[132] Browning reported that a total of 22,736 students were enrolled in schools, although there were over 38,000 eligible students, meaning 40 percent neither were in nor had access to school.[133] Graduates of boarding schools were eligible to be employed in the schools as assistant teachers or day school teachers without regard to civil service so long as they were of good moral character and of physical soundness.[134] The Indian Office increasingly filled its positions with Native employees, including matrons, cooks, laundresses, farmers, mechanics, and in smaller numbers, teachers, nurses, and doctors.

Land severalty and the opening of reservations to homesteading continued at a rapid pace, with Congress appointing additional commissions to negotiate with tribes for a further reduction of their land base.[135] In 1893, the Indian Office issued 7,258 patents, with 4,342 issued in 1894 (plus 804 homestead patents), 3,865 in 1895 (excluding 1,895 homestead patents), and 2,364 in 1896. While on-reservation Native people faced discrimination in taking an allotment, Native homesteaders on the public domain faced severe discrimination as their non-Indian neighbors contested their homesteads, with the Natives more often than not losing their land because they failed to understand public land laws and the manner of perfecting title.[136] Under Browning's watch, the first reservations were opened to homesteading, including the Yankton Sioux (May 21, 1895), Kickapoo (May 23, 1895), Siletz (July 25, 1895), and Nez Perce (November 18, 1895).[137]

With a strong national commitment to develop the nation's natural resources to fuel the burgeoning industrial revolution, Browning requested permission to employ an irrigation engineer to work with the tribes in developing their irrigable lands. More pointedly, the Indian Office leased additional tribal and allotted land, although Browning opposed "indiscriminate leasing of allotted lands" since it "defeat[ed] the purpose for which allotments were made." He directed Indian agents to not lease such land if the allottee possessed "the necessary physical and mental qualifications to enable him to cultivate his allotment either personally or by hired help."[138] In 1894, Congress amended the 1891 leasing act by increasing the period of agricultural leases from three to five years for allotted lands.[139] That same year, the Indian Office approved of nearly three hundred leases of allotted land, and in 1893 and 1894, it approved of more than fifty tribal leases covering 3,279,691 acres of land, with Osage (831,188 acres), Uintah (650,000 acres), Crow (846,000 acres), and Shoshone (283,691 acres) leases representing 79.6 percent of all tribal land leases.

In the rush to allot land and make it productive, the Indian Office executed a number of illegal leases. In Nebraska, the Flourney Livestock and Real Estate Company leased 50,000 acres from Winnebago allottees for $0.15 to $0.50 per acre and then subleased the land to non-tribal ranchers and growers for $0.25 to $2.50 per acre.[140] Browning ordered Winnebago agent William Beck to warn Flourney and his sublessees that such leases were null and void since they had not been approved by the Indian Office. Flourney, in the meantime, secured an injunction from the U.S. District Court in Nebraska, although the U.S. Court of Appeals upheld the Interior solicitor's bill of complaint, holding the leases null and void. Only after the War Department issued Beck twenty Springfield rifles to arm the Winnebago police force and the Nebraska congressional delegation interceded was a compromise reached, with Flourney and the sublessees allowed to harvest their crops and remove their improvements. Browning then initiated a no-middleman policy, with the allottees entitled to the fair market value of any lease.[141] By 1898, 112,000 of the 140,000 acres on the Omaha and Winnebago Reservations in Nebraska were under leases.[142]

The Flourney matter embodied one of the challenges with severalty, namely, who had the authority to lease the land. Severalty also raised the matter of the legality of liquor sales to allottees who had received patents to their land and were U.S. citizens. In 1890, the U.S. District Court for Washington concluded that Puyallup tribal members who received allotments were U.S. citizens and no longer bound by the police authority of the Indian Office. A similar case from Grande Ronde (Oregon) Agency held that allotment confirmed citizenship and freed allottees from provisions of the Nonintercourse Act, which banned the sale of alcohol to Indians.[143]

Browning adopted the view held by Morgan that, as long as the trust period was still in effect, the allottee was subject to federal statutes governing Natives.[144] Citizen Indians, Browning argued, remained for a time "in a state of tutelage and wardship, and the Indian agent placed over him is continued for the purpose of executing the duties of the Government."[145] Browning favored a liquor case being appealed to the Supreme Court so that the high court might issue a definitive answer. Otherwise, the government was temporarily "helpless to relieve the Indians of the danger to which the attitude of the lower courts ... expose them."[146] A year later, the Federal Court of Appeals in San Francisco upheld the police authority of the federal government over allottees.[147]

Concurrently, Browning labored to see the passage of a bill introduced by Congressman George Meiklejohn (R-NE), which would extend the prohibition of alcohol to all Natives, including "any Indian to whom allotment of land has been made while title to the same shall be held in trust by the Government." While the House approved of the bill in 1895, the Senate failed to consider it and it died. A year later, another bill was introduced but again failed to gain passage.[148]

Land severalty complicated Indian affairs in ways beyond whether Native citizens were subject to the policing authority of the Indian Office. In 1894, the department announced new rules relative to the rights of children from Native women married to white men. In 1888, Congress approved of a bill granting citizenship to any such women; however, the statute did not address the children of such unions.[149] In March 1894, Charles Penney, agent at the Pine Ridge Sioux Agency, inquired of Browning whether children of such marriages (with both parents citizens) were entitled to per capita payments. Browning arbitrarily ruled that a Native woman in such a marriage "separate[d] herself from her tribe and becomes identified with the people of the United States."[150] As such, her children were U.S. citizens and no longer "deemed members of the tribe [with a] right to share in the property of the tribe." The exception was upon the death of the mother, at which time her interests in tribal property reverted back to the tribe with her children having no interest in the property "except as they might take by representation of the mother on her death." Otherwise, there was nothing to inherit, since the tribe was "the universal heir of such member."[151]

COMMISSIONER WILLIAM A. JONES

Browning left office May 3, 1897, six weeks after Republican president William McKinley took office. In April, McKinley nominated William Arthur Jones as commissioner, with the Senate confirming his appointment on May 3. Jones was a successful businessman and former educator from Wisconsin who had been active in McKinley's election bid and was rewarded with the appointment of commissioner of Indian affairs.[152] He took office upon Senate confirmation.

While continuing the policies of his predecessors, Jones brought efficiency to the Indian Office, at times personally supervising bid openings for annuity or treaty goods. He enforced the practice of renaming Native children with Christian names, although his 1902 circular directed agents to ensure names be as close to their tribal counterpart as possible, both for simplicity and to facilitate legal matters such as inheritance, census taking, and dissolution of tribal affairs. Jones also saw dress as part of the civilizing process and noted with satisfaction that, out of 187,966 Natives under government supervision, 111,703 dressed wholly in civilized clothes and 44,558 in part, demonstrating that the Indians were "casting aside the blanket of barbarism" and the government's efforts at reorienting the domestic life of Native people were gaining ground.[153]

In a further effort at social modification, Jones ordered all Indian agents to induce men to cut their hair, believing it would "hasten their progress toward civilization."[154] Any Native employed by the Indian Office who refused to be shorn was denied rations. For returned boarding school students who declined, they were refused employment or annuities until they acquiesced. Facial paint was prohibited, as were dances and feasts as they had a "deleterious effect" on the moral training of students and interfered with school attendance.[155] Concurrently, Jones refused to grant permission to any person or company proposing to take Natives on Wild West or exhibition tours.[156] Exceptions included exhibits at the annual World Expositions, where the Indian Office displayed student arts and crafts and industrial skills, as well as the government school efforts to "train the Indians in our line of work and thought."[157]

Jones shifted his policy positions in 1900, when he described at length "obstacles to self-support." Noting that rations were a vestige of the reservation system, but also admitting the physiographic conditions on the reservations were such that agriculture was generally a failure, Jones outlined a policy of ending rations. During the transition period he acknowledged there would be no effective means of self-support for many Natives and the government had a moral obligation to provide for those in need. He was confident that Natives would once again be self-sufficient since they were "originally and until a comparatively recent period . . . self-supporting."[158] In 1900, he estimated that 45,270 Natives were supported by daily rations, with 17,876 individuals from the Sioux Reservations claiming them under the provisions of their 1876 agreements.[159] Jones issued directives to Indian agents charging them to deny rations to able-bodied Indians who refused to work. Returned school students were "to depend entirely upon their own resources." Natives were "little, if any, nearer the goal of independence than [they were] thirty years ago, and if the present policy is continued, [they] will get little, if any, nearer in thirty years to come."[160] Policy was a complete failure, Jones admitted, with the government spending more than $240 million over the past century in an effort to civilize the Indians.[161] Ending rations, Jones suggested, would encourage agricultural endeavors, facilitate independence, and draw to a close the government's involvement in Indian affairs.

A parallel policy strand was the discontinuation of annuity payments. In 1900, the United States paid various tribes $1,507,542.68 in annuities, ranging in per capita payments of $255.00 down to $0.50.[162] Most annuities were "too small to accomplish either good or harm," but some were "so large to be useful for good or powerful for evil." Annuities "induce[d] pauperism and scandal and crime," and, as such, Jones argued, the government should "provide for the[ir] gradual extinction" by appropriating sufficient funds to maintain tribes for a period of time and then dividing the annuity principle per capita. While such a policy might relegate some to poverty, the long-term benefit would be the realization of the "work or starve" policy.[163]

The annuity principle—$33,317,455.09 in 1900—was no small sum, resulting in annual interest income of $1,646,485.96 and an annual payout of over $1,500,000. But this payment was made to only a handful of tribes that had treaty-guaranteed annuities, leaving most tribes emptyhanded. Jones remained steadfast: abolish rations and annuities and the government would be relieved "of an enormous debt" and "the entire Indian question" would be settled within a single generation.[164]

The commissioner admitted that the abolition of annuities and rations would be difficult with Natives confined to "reservations and [holding] everything in common." The solution was land severalty and the leasing of allotments. In 1900, a vacillating Congress again authorized five-year agricultural and grazing leases to govern the more than two thousand leases of allotted lands.[165] More than 2.25 million acres of unallotted tribal lands were also leased, as leasing was rapidly becoming the rule rather than the exception.[166] The remedy was to hasten forward with severalty and compel Natives to farm their land. But this worked only if the land was irrigable and the soil was conducive to cultivation. Moreover, if the landowner "has no capital to begin on, it must be given him; a house must be built, a supply of water must be assured and the necessaries of life furnished, at least until he can get a start and his labor become productive."[167] In 1902, Jones issued leasing regulations that required every "adult able-bodied Indian not engaged in some permanent business or occupation" to reserve not less than forty acres of cultivable land from his own allotment for "cultivation by himself, which shall always be exempt from leasing." Adult males not disqualified by physical or mental conditions were "required to work or manage a part of their allotment."[168]

The third obstacle Jones defined was education. "The present Indian educational system ... is not calculated to produce the results so earnestly claimed for it and so hopefully anticipated." Children were selected to attend boarding schools not based on merit or "reason of mental fitness," but solely on the fact they were Native. These children found themselves "translated from a state of poverty [on the reservation] to one of affluence" while at school. They were fed, clothed, and lodged at no personal expense. The schools became what Jones coined "a modern Aladdin," where the student had "only to rub the Government lamp to gratify his desire."[169] Education had become "a right, not a privilege." "Not having earned his education," Jones reasoned, "it is not appreciated; having made no sacrifice to obtain it, it is not valued."[170] So, what to do? "Throw the Indian on his own resources." It was not the government's role to "enlighten the soul" but to "educate the mind." A student's education should be one of self-support, with the individual "removed from a state of dependence to one of independence." This gradualist policy of assimilation required "the breaking up of tribal customs, manners, and barbaric usages," and was premised on time as the key ingredient.[171]

While early in his administration Jones subscribed to the theory of taking Natives to civilization (i.e., off-reservation boarding schools), in his later years he was persuaded that "the strength and foundation of Indian education must be the reservation boarding schools," where parents could witness the education of their children, an action that itself was instructive. It was in on-reservation schools that Natives would witness the "power and influence" of the United States, which the Indian Office believed would appeal to the father through his children and "awaken smoldering sentiments for the betterment of him and their condition."[172] And since the "average Indian cannot successfully compete with the average white man," the "overwhelming majority of Indians must be farmers, stock raisers, and laborers," a sentiment that overlooked those who were qualified for advanced study (i.e., Dr. Charles Eastman, Sioux, and Dr. Susan LaFlesche, Omaha).[173] Jones focused the attention of educational policy to this end. There was no place in government schools for "higher mathematics, geometry and astronomy." The money "spent by the Government on the dullard, or the physically weak boy or girl ... is practically wasted."[174] The brightest youth, on the other hand, would "leaven" the whole and elevate and civilize Natives more than any policy seeking the intellectual education of the whole.

Jones continued to fill schools at all costs—even after an Indian Office health survey indicated that many children were infected by disease while at school, in large measure because of overcrowding.[175] Inspector William McConnell spent four years investigating government school conditions, discovering at the Blackfeet Agency tubercular children enrolled in overcrowded school dormitories and healthy children sleeping three or four to a bed, often with pulmonary and lymphatic tubercular children. No child slept alone. Nonetheless, Jones reported 89 percent of the students in the Indian school system returned home in good health and instructed agents to "fill the schools to the limit of their capacity."[176]

The commissioner's educational policy was premised on the supposition that a parent "had no moral or legal right to stand in the way of his child's advancement."[177] It mattered not which school the child attended so long as he attended one. Parental consent had no place in the process, with Jones recommending to Congress that it grant him such authority. "A compulsory school law will hasten the final accomplishment of the Government plan of absorption of tribes and extinguishment of reservations."[178] While the disposition of the adults might be set, Jones believed it was his duty "to train the next generation [to be] stronger morally and physically," and this could best be accomplished by compulsory attendance at government schools.[179]

By the turn of the twentieth century, the question of health gained national exposure, with the twin scourges of tuberculosis and trachoma ravaging Indian Country. While Jones did not ignore these concerns, it was incidental to the work of severalty and education.[180] In 1904, he issued a policy directive that agency physicians were to thoroughly examine children before releasing them to school, with any child suspected of illness to remain home. When physicians sought to organize an Indian Medical Service as a means of improving treatment, Jones discouraged them, believing the Indian Office would soon be abolished as the Natives received patents to their land and federal supervision ceased.

In addition to education for citizenship, land severalty remained the fulcrum of policy. Using the authority of the Curtis Act, Congress extended severalty to the Five Tribes, which heretofore had fended off division of their land.[181] This extension was the culmination of years of work and the fulfillment of the government's desire to incorporate the Five Tribes—and their successful model of self-government that demonstrated tribes could govern themselves—into the general populace of the nation. Acting through the Dawes Commission, Congress forced the Five Tribes to accept—under threat of unilateral federal action—agreements authorizing land severalty.[182] The Curtis Act also extended federal district court jurisdiction in Indian Territory over all persons, regardless of the parties. All tribal courts were abolished, and the Five Tribes were precluded from enforcing tribal law. The act further mandated a census of each of the tribes in advance of severalty and the dissolution of Indian Territory. The Indian Office immediately assumed authority over all of the schools and orphan asylums in territory. In May 1900, at Jones's request, the United States abolished the Osage tribal government.[183]

Land severalty was a priority of Jones. During his term, federal commissions reached agreements for additional cessions and extended land severalty to the Fort Hall Shoshone-Bannock Reservation, the Uintah and White River Ute, the Crow (the single largest cession at 1,137,500

Table 5.5. Indian Agreements, 1896–1902

Reservation	Tribe(s)	Purpose	Date
Wind River	Shoshone-Arapaho	Cession	April 21, 1896
Choctaw/Chickasaw	Choctaw/Chickasaw	Allotment and abolish gov't	April 23, 1897
Creek	Creek	Allotment and abolish gov't	September 27, 1897
Seminole	Seminole	Allotment and abolish gov't	December 16, 1897
Uintah	Ute	Cession	January 8, 1898
Fort Hall	Shoshone-Bannock	Cession	February 5, 1898
Lower Brule	Sioux	Cession	March 1, 1898
Rosebud	Sioux	Cession	March 10, 1898
Creek	Creek	Allotment	February 1, 1899
Crow	Crow	Cession	August 14, 1899
Yankton	Sioux	Cession of Pipestone quarry	October 2, 1899
Seminole	Seminole	Close tribal roll	October 7, 1899
Missouria/Ottoe	Missouria/Ottoe	Land Claims	November 20, 1899
Creek	Creek	Allotment	March 8, 1900
Cherokee	Cherokee	Allotment	April 9, 1900
Stockbridge-Munsee	Stockbridge-Munsee	Distribute annuities	December 8, 1900
Chickasaw	Chickasaw	Royalties for education	April 11, 1901
Rosebud	Sioux	Cession	May 6, 1901
Lower Brule	Sioux	Cession	May 6, 1901
Klamath	Klamath	Cession	June 17, 1901
Grande Ronde	Grande Ronde	Cession	June 27, 1901
Rosebud	Sioux	Cession	September 14, 1901
Devil's Lake	Sisseton/Wahpeton	Cession	November 2, 1901
Kaw	Kansa	Per capita distribution	February 15, 1902
Red Lake	Pembina Chippewa	Cession	March 10, 1902
Choctaw/Chickasaw	Choctaw/Chickasaw	Allotment	March 21, 1902
Fort Berthold	Gros Ventre, Mandan, Arikara	Cession	June 25, 1902
Creek	Creek	Allotment	June 30, 1902
Kaw	Kansa	Allotment	July 1, 1902
Cherokee	Cherokee	Allotment and abolish gov't	July 1, 1902
Creek	Creek	Allotment	July 26, 1902

Source: DeJong, *American Indian Treaties*, 195–218.

acres), the Grande Ronde Tribes, the Yankton, Lower Brule, Rosebud and Devil's Lake Sioux, Red Lake Chippewa, the Fort Berthold Tribes, and with each of the Five Tribes. By 1902, Jones could report dozens of agreements, most of which called for allotment and/or land cessions, as shown in Table 5.5.

Allotment and the sale of surplus land was one matter, but the sale of allotted land was another. Peoria and Miami allottees, as well as Citizen Band Pottawatomie and Absentee Shawnee allottees, continued to sell their land under the congressional acts of August 15, 1894, and June 7, 1897.[184] By 1899, the Peoria and Miami had sold 6,645 acres, and the Citizen Pottawatomie and Absentee Shawnee had sold 52,915 acres. Jones in 1899 sought permission to authorize the latter tribal members who took allotments under the 1887 General Allotment Act the same "privilege" of selling their land as those who took allotments under an 1872 act. In 1900, Congress granted such authority and, within a year, Citizen Pottawatomie and Absentee Shawnee land sales swelled to 90,447 acres.[185]

As severalty concluded on specific reservations, they were opened to homesteading. On June 17, 1902, the Fort Hall Reservation was opened to settlement, and that same year Jones made plans to open the Walker River Paiute Reservation in Nevada.[186] In 1904, Congress authorized removal of all restrictions on the sale of allotted land to members of the Five Tribes.[187] Jones also approved of rules authorizing the sale of inherited land, but only after local Indian agents advertized and secured sealed bids for the purchase of those allotments. In the first six months of such regulations, 44,494 acres of inherited land was sold at a rate of 6,810 acres per month. In the subsequent nine months, sales increased 20 percent per month to 8,182 acres.[188]

The rapid sale of land proved so detrimental that Jones called for an overhaul of the realty process. While he favored sales, Jones was concerned that Native people were not using the revenue from the sale of inherited land to improve their allotments. He estimated that less than 20 percent of such income was invested in home improvements, with the remainder alienated to creditors and swindlers.[189] To ameliorate the situation, Jones recommended to Interior Secretary Ethan Allen Hitchcock that he authorize the Indian Office to restrict the disposition of the proceeds from inherited land sales by requiring heirs to place the funds into a federal bank account with restrictions on maximum monthly withdrawals (ten dollars), a proposition the assistant U.S. Attorney General opined was lawful. On September 16, 1904, the rule was approved and applied to all inherited land sales. Between September 15, 1903, and June 30, 1904, 122,222 acres of inherited land were sold, 51 percent of which was in Oklahoma Territory.[190]

By 1900, 5,736,504 acres had been allotted to 55,996 Indians from eighty-eight different reservations.[191] As tribal lands fell before the juggernaut of severalty, Jones reduced the number of agencies from sixty-one, in 1897, to twenty-two by 1904. In place of agents, Jones assigned bonded school superintendents to oversee reservation affairs, seeing them as agents of efficiency, since they oversaw the education of children and were in a position to carry out "the idea of self-support inculcated into the child while at school."[192]

As he neared the end of his tenure, Jones reported: "Reservations are being broken up. Inherited lands are being sold, and sturdy American citizens are buying them and settling among the Indians, and following the wake of all comes the public school, where in time the white and Indian will mingle."[193] The Supreme Court facilitated severalty and the further diminishment of tribal authority in *Lone Wolf v. Hitchcock*, a decision by which the court assumed a hypothetical national emergency to establish the plenary power doctrine of Congress to act lawfully on behalf of tribes without their consent, as long as such action was in good faith.[194]

The *Lone Wolf* decision originated in the congressional ratification of the 1892 Kiowa-Comanche-Apache agreement that called for the allotment and sale of surplus reservation land. Under the 1867 Treaty of Medicine Lodge Creek, any future land cessions required the approval of three-quarters of all adult males within the tribes.[195] The 1892 agreement called for a cession of 2.15 million acres but did not meet the treaty threshold of three-quarters of adult male consent. Congress was determined to ratify the agreement, with Kiowa chief Lone Wolf seeking to enjoin it.

Drawing heavily on the 1886 *Kagama* ruling, the court, in an opinion written by Justice Edward Douglas White, argued Congress had always enjoyed plenary authority over tribes since they were dependent communities. In reality, Congress did not always enjoy such authority, only asserting such jurisdiction in a slow, methodical manner until the late nineteenth century, when it progressed rapidly. In reaching this decision, the court assumed Congress could lawfully and unilaterally change the form of Native property from land to money. "Indian tribes are wards of the Nation," White opined in a ruling that has hobbled Indian Country ever since, and the action of Congress "was solely within the domain of the legislative authority and its action is conclusive upon the courts." Moreover, since the action of Congress was political, the court assumed the legislative branch acted in "perfect good faith." Any redress the tribes might have would be with Congress, not the federal courts. With tribes exercising little substantive power, they were unable to intervene.

Jones was ecstatic, arguing that to wait for tribal consent could delay by fifty years the time to "do away with the reservations." A year prior, and antecedent to *Lone Wolf*, the court upheld the right of Congress to enact policies that were "political and administrative" in nature, including the extension of unprecedented federal authority over the Five Tribes in Indian Territory.[196] Combined, the *Lone Wolf* and the *Cherokee Nation* cases usurped tribal authority and demonstrated the lengths to which a Congress intent on abolishing reservations and integrating Native people would go.

Jones was committed to the strand of social and political absorption of Native people into American society, regardless of the cost. He summed up his deepest convictions in a letter to Interior Secretary Ethan Allen Hitchcock: the Native "must practice what he has been taught or starve."[197] As he prepared to leave office, Jones recognized that policy was more complicated than just severalty and education. But solutions would have to be left to his successors. In poor health, Jones resigned effective January 1, 1905.

CONCLUSION

The philosophical braid of individualization and integration of Natives was firmly entrenched by the end of Jones's tenure as commissioner of Indian affairs. This philosophy was by no means a product of Jones but was one that had been constructed throughout the development of the federal-Indian relationship and took a more tangible format in the initial decades of land severalty. The "great family" of Americans had to include the American Indians in every facet of the meaning, and the commissioners of Indian affairs made that social tenet the focus of policy—regardless of the impact on the everyday life of those living in scattered enclaves across the country.

By the turn of the century, federal-Indian policy had transitioned to a "domestication of politics," with a burgeoning bureaucracy focused on paternalistic (and maternalistic) social policies. The federal government had become firmly entrenched as the agency responsible for education, with sectarian schools marginalized. Land was not only allotted in severalty but was also alienated as rapidly as feasible. The familial structure of Indian Country had shifted, with a new focus on free labor and the home as the center of Native life.

In so executing a policy of forced social and political integration and land alienation, Congress, the courts, and the executive branch, acting through the Indian Office, exerted unprecedented pressure on tribes and Native people. In their haste to accomplish these goals, the United States fictionalized Indian affairs to meet the political exigencies of the day. Tribes found themselves under dire pressure and struggled to resist the transformative processes.

6

"THE NEW MAGNA CHARTA"

Carrying Civilization to the Indians, 1905–1928

By the end of William Jones's term, Protestant reformers had reached the zenith of their influence on federal policy. In the first years of the new century, these reformers unsuccessfully defended Kiowa chief Lone Wolf in his fight to protect Kiowa-Comanche-Apache land in Oklahoma Territory. Following other political and legal setbacks, their eminence waned. Beginning with Francis Leupp in 1905, the old reformers discovered a new era dawning and they were increasingly on the outside looking in. The strands of severalty, education, and citizenship remained assimilative after 1905, reaching a pinnacle during the Cato Sells' administration (1913–1921). In the midst of a growing secularization of government, the seeds of progressive change were sewn in the late 1920s.

Just four men served as commissioner of Indian affairs between 1905 and 1928, beginning with Francis E. Leupp (1905–1909), and followed by Robert G. Valentine (1909–1912), Cato Sells (1913–1921), and Charles Burke (1921–1929). These men advocated truncating the Indian Office even as they expanded federal paternalism over Indian affairs and exploited the alienation of Native land and resources. Their policies suggested both a lowering expectation of Native people and their relegation to the periphery of American social, political, and economic life.

COMMISSIONER FRANCIS E. LEUPP

President Theodore Roosevelt nominated Francis Ellington Leupp, a New York City attorney and former member of the Indian Rights Association and the Board of Indian Commissioners, in fall of 1904 to replace Jones as commissioner, assuming office on January 1, 1905.[1] Leupp had

Table 6.1. Heads of the Indian Office and Major Policies, 1904–1928

Name	Title	Years of Service	Main Policies
Francis E. Leupp (R)	Commissioner	4.5 years (1905–1909)	Sectarian education funds, on-reservation schools, fee patents, Burke Act, cultural pluralism
Robert G. Valentine (R)	Commissioner	3.25 years (1909–1912)	Efficiency and economy, healthcare, natural resource development, severalty, public schools
Cato Sells (D)	Commissioner	7.75 years (1913–1921)	Competency commissions, severalty, fee patents, stock raising, irrigation, public schools
Charles Burke (R)	Commissioner	7.75 years (1921–1929)	Education, survey each home, resource exploitation, citizenship, sale of land

the trust and ear of the president on matters pertaining to Indian affairs, in part because, as a member of the Indian Rights Association, he advocated integrative reform for and investigated corruption throughout Indian Country.[2] While he supported the Dawes Commission and joint statehood for Oklahoma and Indian territories, he was often at odds with the Indian Rights Association, leading Leupp to resign from the board in 1898. During his tenure on the Board of Indian Commissioners (1896–1897) he was an outspoken critic of Richard Henry Pratt and his educational methods at Carlisle Industrial School. In June 1897, Interior Secretary Cornelius N. Bliss requested and received Leupp's resignation from the board.

Leupp was a prolific writer and speaker on policy matters. In his first annual report he devoted a dozen pages to his "outlines of an Indian policy," a theoretical framework that guided him throughout his four-year term. "The commonest mistake made by his white wellwishers in dealing with the Indian," Leupp began in his folksy manner of writing, "is the assumption that he is simply a white man with a red skin." "The truth is that the Indian has as distinct an individuality as any type of man who ever lived, and he will never be judged aright till we learn to measure him by his own standards."[3] Leupp praised Native people for their positive traits. That they "have not been wholly ruined is the best proof we could ask of the sturdy traits of character inherent in them."[4] Leupp was determined that the deterioration progress no further.

Believing little could be done to change adults, Leupp had great hope for "the youthful generation who are still measurably plastic."[5] He opposed the off-reservation boarding schools modeled after the philosophy of Pratt and lamented the "mistake, in the process of absorbing the [Indians], of washing out of them whatever is distinctly Indian. Our aboriginal brother brings, as his contribution to the common store of character, a great deal which is admirable."[6] Day schools were "the outposts of Indian civilization," Leupp argued as he shuttered a number of off-reservation boarding schools and increased the number of day schools.[7] The salient question was "whether we are to carry civilization to the Indian or carry the Indian to civilization?"[8] By constructing schools on the reservations, the Indian Office would bring parents and grandparents "within the sphere of influence of which every school is a center," while at the same time curtailing government dependency and social cruelty in forced assimilation by advancing the idea of gradualism.[9] Boarding schools—especially those located off reservation—were an educational anomaly because they gratuitously furnished the total education of the students at no expense to them. "In plain English, they are simply educational almshouses," which did not cultivate a spirit of independence and self-reliance. History failed to record a more egregious "wrong perpetrated upon a weaker by a stronger."[10]

Leupp coined his educational approach as revolutionary, viewing it as the means of restoring the health and well-being of Native children. Simple country schools were adequate for the purpose, as the monumental boarding schools costing tens of thousands of dollars were "institutional" in routine, fostered a "herding practice," and facilitated "the development of germ diseases."[11] Day schools, when they were "no longer needed exclusively for Indians," could be turned over to the counties as public schools. At the juncture of turnover, Leupp argued for inserting into the transfer deed a guarantee that for "ninety-nine years any Indian who wishes an education there may have his tuition free."[12] That day schools, with their annual per capita costs of fifty dollars (just 20 percent of the cost of boarding facilities), would economize the budget was no small consideration.[13]

The matter of efficiency became a major policy consideration by the progressive-minded Roosevelt. In 1905, the president convened the Committee of Department Methods to identify modifications necessary to conduct government affairs on the most modern business model. To encourage the committee, the president used a typical example from the Indian Office. A local agent requisitioned a seven-dollar stove in the fall, certifying its need in keeping the infirmary warm during the coming winter. "The transaction moved like a glacier with dignity to its appointed end," Roosevelt explained, as the stove arrived in good order. The agent acknowledged receipt by writing, "The stove is here. So is spring."[14]

The matter of sectarian education, a controversy dating back more than a decade, was settled during Leupp's tenure.[15] In 1904, after the Indian Office used tribal monies to fund nine sectarian schools, Congressman John Stephens (R-TX) introduced legislation, premised on the belief that such funds were public dollars, precluding the use of tribal monies for such schools. The bill failed to make it out of committee, and the following year Leupp outlined a policy of funding sectarian schools. With the president's support, and predicated on an attorney general's opinion, Leupp applied tribal trust funds to the support of such schools, but only when tribal members requested it. The federal prohibition on public money "did not extend to moneys belonging to the Indians themselves," Leupp argued, as he outlined thirteen factors governing the use of such funds, capping per capita expenditures at $108 per year.[16] The attorney general opined there were two sources of funds for education: tribal trust funds and tribal treaty funds, both of which were annually appropriated by Congress. While the former could be administered as the tribes requested, the latter could be considered public funds and, until the Supreme Court provided a definitive answer, were not to be used for sectarian purposes.[17] In 1908, the Indian Office received unqualified direction when the Supreme Court determined that treaty obligations were not public but were, in fact, tribal funds. "It seems inconceivable," the court explained, "that Congress should have intended to prohibit [the Indians] from securing religious education out of their own cost if they desired it."[18] Tribes, at their own request, were free to use treaty and trust funds for religious or nonreligious school purposes.

Table 6.2. Allotment and Fee Patents, 1905–1908

Year	Allotments	Fee Patents Issued	Competencies approved
1905	1,828	493	N/A
1906	3,067	4,027	N/A
1907	10,643	3,363	753
1908	5,365	10,461	2,050

Source: *Annual Report of the Commissioner of Indian Affairs*, 1905–1908.

As other commissioners before him, Leupp advocated "severing forever" the ties that bound Natives to their tribes. Tribal allegiance was to be a vestige of the past, with civilization dependent on the free labor of the individual, not the tribe. "As fast as an Indian of either mixed or full blood is capable of taking care of himself" he was to be "set upon his own feet."[19] Leupp escalated severalty and issued a record number of patents. Admitting that there was "a great demand for [Native] lands by the whites," Leupp advanced severalty to the fullest, as demonstrated in Table 6.2. During his tenure, the Wind River, Rosebud, Coeur d'Alene, Blackfeet, Flathead, Fort Peck, and Spokane Reservations were opened to sale or homesteading.[20]

That Congress granted citizenship to allottees, while at the same time holding their land in trust, did not go unnoticed by reformers and policy makers. In 1905, the Supreme Court heard and decided a case regarding alcohol use by allottees. The question was: Did the police authority of the Indian Office govern Native people who were citizens yet were treated as wards of the government? In *A Matter of Heff*, the Supreme Court held that an Indian who was a citizen was not a ward and was not subject to the police authority of the Indian Office. The court struck down the conviction of a non-Indian selling liquor to an allottee, arguing the United States was not under any "constitutional obligation to perpetually continue the relationship of guardian and ward." The United States could terminate its guardianship at any time, with Native people subject to all rights and privileges of citizens.[21]

The Indian Office argued that as long as it held land in trust it could exercise police authority over liquor matters on an allotment. While the court implied that citizenship was fundamentally incompatible with guardianship, Leupp held the opposite view. Congress agreed with the passage of the Burke Act in 1906, which postponed citizenship for allottees until after the issuance of a fee patent, materially aiding the Indian Office. Amending the General Allotment Act, the act authorized the secretary of the interior to issue a fee patent to any Native deemed competent, with the twenty-five-year trust period terminating upon issuance of competency. All restrictions as to sale, encumbrance, and taxation were removed with issuance of the fee. While prior to the act Natives became citizens upon acceptance of severalty, subsequent to it citizenship was bestowed only upon issuance of a fee patent. Until such time, allottees remained subject to the policing authority of the Indian Office.[22]

The Burke Act created a legal loophole by authorizing legal instruments called competencies, even if it did not define how to implement this process or to whom it should apply. Leupp expressed concern with the task of ascertaining the competency of applicants, noting that some field agents interpreted short hair as the test of competency, while others considered a school education as sufficient. As for Leupp, "the safest test is the industry and thrift of the applicant."[23] Between 1906 and 1908, the Indian Office relied on the field agents and superintendents to determine competency, with six out of ten Natives declared competent, and alienated their land.[24] Not until late in his tenure did Leupp establish competency criteria. In 1907, there were 881 applications for competency with 753 approved (85.5 percent). The following year, the Indian Office approved 2,050 out of 2,281 applications (89.9 percent).[25] While Leupp advocated state and local governments exercising jurisdiction over allotted lands, the Supreme Court on February 25, 1907, opined that state courts had no jurisdiction over such lands since the United States had an interest in ensuring that they "inure[d] during the trust period for the sole use and benefit of allottees."[26]

Leupp mirrored his predecessors when it came to the sale of inherited land. In 1905, he reported the sale of 212,437 acres of inherited land, netting $3,450,596 to the heirs, and between 1903 and 1908, the Indian Office authorized the sale of 519,040 acres for $7,740,502.[27] Leupp encouraged such sales, although he amended governing regulations to include placement of the funds into national banks secured by bonds.[28] In addition to inherited land, the Indian Office in 1908 authorized the sale of 7,990 acres of noncompetent land and 10,716 acres of other land.[29]

By 1906, reservations that could support agriculture without irrigation had largely been allotted in severalty. The remaining reservations were arid and required irrigation to make them farmable. While tillable reservations were allotted in 80- to 320-acre parcels, Leupp argued that severalty on arid southwestern reservations range from "not less than 5 or more than 40 acres of irrigable land." Eighty acres of land was "more than [a Native grower] can utilize," Leupp reasoned, "especially as, owing to lack of funds, the costs of irrigation is almost prohibited."[30] Leupp did not believe Native people had reserved rights to water and that none of them had the wherewithal to make a "beneficial and continued use" of water under state prior appropriation laws.[31] He further argued that Congress should empower allotting agents to take into account "the attitude, character of the soil, climate, productive possibilities, proximity to markets, as well as the habits of the tribe" when making allotments.[32]

Leupp was not altruistic, but his progressive thinking led him to recognize that severalty could work against Indian interests. Too little thought was given to the character of Native people, he argued, when allotments were made. While critical of severalty, he suggested that "not enough regard is paid to the ultimate welfare of those whites who will ultimately succeed to a large part of the allotments." Moreover, not all Natives desired to farm and not all reservations were tillable. To force "agriculture on such Indians . . . would undoubtedly spoil a lot of good [Indians] in order to make a few poor farmers."[33] The solution was small, manageable allotments with rights to water.

As the Indian Office made plans to allot arid reservations, Leupp turned to matters of irrigation. To date, most funds spent on irrigation projects were tribal funds, such as the Crow Irrigation

Project, which was funded with tribal trust and treaty funds. The reservation policy had largely relegated Native people to a lifestyle of subsisting on rations or foraging on non-Indian neighbors, Leupp stated, even as times were changing, with the "irrigation by white settlers who were continually crowding into the Indian Country [making] the available waters a consideration of first importance."[34] Passage of the 1902 Reclamation Act further compounded matters and increased the urgency of protecting Indian water.[35]

The commissioner asked the new U.S. Reclamation Service to assist the Indian Office in constructing irrigation facilities, although he feared that work done by the former would lead to "the abandonment of any special right secured to the Indian under the law creating his status as a property holder." Moreover, he was concerned that Indians would only have "the possibility of acquiring a right under the doctrine of beneficial use" rather than an assured right.[36] As lands transferred to the jurisdiction of the states, Leupp stated, "the water rights should go with them." Forthwith, he directed his office to have the water rights of each allottee determined before their land became alienable and the water right subject to prior appropriation laws.[37] He encouraged Congress to enact legislation enabling Natives to sell a portion of their land with the proceeds used for paying the costs of reclamation. Congress obliged.[38]

Leupp's concern for irrigation of arid lands and rights that Native people had to water was answered in 1908 when the Supreme Court ruled in *Winters v. United States* that land reserved to tribes and tribal members had a reserved right to the water necessary to make the land productive.[39] In upholding the rights of the Fort Belknap Gros Ventre and Assiniboine to the waters of the Milk River in Montana, the court held that reservations were tribal homelands and that no tribal nation would have agreed to reside on a reservation unless it was implied that it had rights to water. In issuing a decision with far-reaching impacts, the court advanced the idea that tribes had unquantified rights to water that extended to future uses, a concept that was at odds with state prior appropriation rights. The date a reservation was established reflected the date of the reserved right to water, meaning tribes generally had the senior right on a stream even if they did not have wet water. While the court ruled in favor of tribal rights, neither Leupp nor the Indian Office thought much of it, with the commissioner believing Native people had lost whatever rights to water they might have once held. While the reserved rights doctrine was a victory for Indian Country, the fact was that non-Indians held the water to which the Indians were entitled. Not having the political strength to defend and protect their water, tribes struggled to put the water to use, a struggle that continued throughout much of the twentieth century.[40]

Indian Office cooperation with the Reclamation Service was in line with the general policy Leupp pursued "of obliterating, as rapidly as conditions will permit, the barriers between the several bureaus of our common Government."[41] Secretary Ethan Allen Hitchcock supported Leupp's plan of consolidation in April 1907, with irrigation plans approved by the Reclamation Service and the Indian Office before being authorized by the secretary. Leupp then established the Indian Irrigation Service, headquartered in Los Angeles under the leadership of Charles Real Olberg, with chief engineer William Code tasked with funneling all Indian irrigation activities to the Reclamation Service to ensure "large economies of effort and expenditure."[42] Notwithstanding

Table 6.3. Indian Office Irrigation Expenditures, 1905–1908

Year	Expenditures
1905	$185,000
1906	$179,500
1907	$152,000
1908	$125,000

Source: *Annual Report of the Commissioner of Indian Affairs, 1905–1908.*

his emphasis on irrigation, in each of Leupp's years in office, irrigation expenditures declined, as shown in Table 6.3.[43]

Leupp's overarching goal was to put the Indian Office out of business by extending coordination with other government agencies. It made little sense, he stated, to have both an Indian Forestry Service and a U.S. Forest Service. The same was true of the Indian Medical Division, which paralleled the Public Health Service.[44] By 1908, Leupp had contracts in place or in progress with the U.S. Reclamation Service, U.S. Forest Service, and the U.S. Department of Agriculture's Bureau of Animal Husbandry and Bureau of Plant Husbandry. He also sought to turn all land matters over to the General Land Office. In view of this intergovernmental cooperation, Leupp reorganized the department and sought to employ a "higher class of men to wind up the affairs of the Indian Service."[45]

While Leupp intended to dissolve the Indian Office, in reality he increased its size and scope, with the number of central office employees increasing from 132 to 227. The work of healthcare, education, allotment, and the dissolution of tribal property required Leupp to expand the overall department to over 5,500 employees. Notwithstanding this growth, the Indian Office had difficulty hiring employees, with nearly half (47 percent) of the persons selected to fill vacancies declining them due to parsimonious salaries.[46] Leupp's "policy of shrinkage" failed to materialize.

The distribution in severalty of tribal funds was a corollary to land severalty, with Leupp drafting a bill to divide all tribal moneys per capita. Until this was accomplished, "our progress towards [solving the Indian problem] is bound to be limping rather than strong."[47] In 1907, Congressman John Lacey (R-IA) worked with Leupp to introduce legislation authorizing such distribution, with the bill enacted into law on March 2, 1907.[48] But in final passage, Congressman Charles Burke (R-SD) amended the bill to apply only to those Natives requesting their pro rata share of the funds. The amended statute authorized tribal members to petition for their share of tribal funds but only if they were deemed competent to manage their own affairs. While pleased with the prospects of distributing tribal funds, Leupp was disappointed the act did not grant discretion to the president as to whom and when to distribute the funds. In applauding the act as an important step, Leupp attempted to silence his critics who feared the law would cause Natives to lose their fiscal and physical resources. "I would rather myself take the chance of an Indian here and there disappointing the confidence placed in him," Leupp haphazardly explained, "than to see his manhood shrivel up under the influence of its nonuse."[49]

In line with his "policy of shrinkage," Leupp sought to emancipate Natives from government supervision. When the Indian Office declared an individual competent to own land and control his money, Leupp directed his name be stricken from the tribal roll, thereby reducing the number of federal dependents.[50] An ancillary policy was that of finding employment for Natives outside of the reservations where they could "make a living as white men do."[51] In 1905, Leupp established an employment bureau administered by Charles E. Dagenett (a member of the Peoria Tribe) and within a year over six hundred Indians were working in the open market for the Southern Pacific and Santa Fe railroads; irrigation districts (including construction of Roosevelt Dam and repairing breaches in the Colorado River at the point it discharged into the Salton Sink); the sugar beet industry on the Northern Plains; and other farm and general labor across the West. Within two years, nearly fifteen hundred individuals were working outside of their reservation.

The Board of Indian Commissioners was critical of Leupp's employment policy, arguing it ran counter to the home-building policy of the social reformers of the late nineteenth century. The effect of Leupp's employment policy on family life could only be malicious, the board asserted in 1905.[52] Leupp countered that Natives were inferior to whites and were not as capable of doing similar work. Labor conducive "for people at a lower stage of civilization" meant largely manual labor. "The experiment of putting them into the places of highest responsibility has, except in rare instances, not worked so successfully."[53]

Yet, Leupp was discouraged because so many Natives with a "home-keeping instinct" refused higher wages and more favorable work off reservation to remain at home where jobs were scarce.[54] In 1908, Congress, at Leupp's behest, provided for Indian preference in employment in what generally became known as the Buy Indian Act.[55] But even federal preference had little impact on employment at the highest levels, as Native people were relegated (mostly) to the lower echelon of employment.

The Indian Office also sought to increase its control over liquor traffic in Indian Country, a matter that was a social and political challenge for Leupp. Heirship land sold to non-Indians, for instance, brought into question the matter of whether the land was still Indian Country and subject to federal liquor statutes or treaty prohibitions.[56] A federal district court ruled that Indian Country only included land "that is generally occupied by the Indians. . . . If it is in possession of the Indians by allotment or otherwise, it remains . . . Indian Country." If the land left Indian ownership, it was no longer Indian Country.[57] In an effort to bypass the court's decision, Leupp inserted liquor prohibitions into the deeds of inherited land sales. Only after an Interior solicitor opined that such provisions "would [cause] the purchaser trouble [and result in] the Indian grantee get[ting] a less price for his land" did Leupp notify the agencies to withdraw such prohibitions.[58]

More compelling for the Indian Office—and a result of the rapid push for assimilation—was the Supreme Court's *A Matter of Heff* ruling that the sale of alcohol to Indians who received land in severalty was not only legal but federal acts restricting such sales or use were also unconstitutional.[59] The United States was under no obligation to continue a guardian-ward relationship. Severalty freed Natives from federal supervision. They were no longer wards of the government and were fully subject to the laws and authority of the state. Leupp disagreed, arguing that severalty and trust patents did not divest the United States of the fee and, as long as the title was held in trust, the federal government maintained jurisdiction. He immediately requested of Congress funds to further suppress liquor in Indian Country.[60]

The Indian Rights Association was increasingly critical of Leupp's land policies and actions, in particular his attempt to mandate patents for parents who refused to send their children to school. Leupp in turn believed the association was meddling in his management of the Indian Office. With the election of William Howard Taft as president in 1908, Leupp resigned effective Inauguration Day. He subsequently withdrew his resignation and remained commissioner until June 18, 1909, when he resigned much to the delight of his critics.[61]

After he vacated office, Leupp published several books, including *The Indian and His Problem* (1910) and *In Red Man's Land* (1914).[62] He also relished the fact that he shifted Indian Office philosophy away from the religious to the secular by expressing tolerance for tribal religious beliefs and customs and supporting protection for Native arts and crafts, as well as cultural sites.[63] While committed to land severalty, education, and citizenship, Leupp's views on cultural pluralism were progressive and, before leaving office, he recommended to President Taft as his successor fellow progressive and then Assistant Commissioner Robert Grosvenor Valentine.

COMMISSIONER ROBERT G. VALENTINE

President Taft agreed with Leupp's recommendation and appointed Robert G. Valentine commissioner effective June 19, 1909. A graduate of Harvard and native of Massachusetts, Valentine came to the Indian Office in 1905 as Leupp's personal secretary and was committed to "speed, economy and efficiency" in the Indian Office.[64] Healthcare, utilization of natural resources, industrial education, and severalty were his priorities.

Valentine began his tenure by lamenting the lack of medical care in Indian Country. "The physical wellbeing of the Indians is an essential consideration in all plans." This was not heretofore sufficiently recognized, he observed in his inaugural report, with the result that government schools improperly prepared students as laborers or tradesmen.[65] A year later, he further underscored the importance of healthcare, arguing that: "The reduction of the death rate is not the primary interest. It is working rather to increase the vitality of the Indian race and to establish for it a new standard of physical wellbeing."[66] As important was the protection of non-Indians who now lived in close proximity of the reservations as they were opened to homesteading.

Valentine attacked tuberculosis and trachoma, securing from Congress a $12,000 special appropriation in 1910 and another $40,000 for promotion of disease prevention a year later. Where possible, he ordered a house-to-house sanitary inspection by physicians to gain an understanding of the extent of ill-health in Indian Country.[67] At his request, President Taft addressed Congress and requested $253,000 for a complete medical diagnostic of Indian Country. "The present conditions of health on Indian reservations and in Indian schools are, broadly speaking," the president informed Congress, "very unsatisfactory."[68] Congress granted the president $90,000, even though 22.7 percent of American Indians were trachomatous and they had a tuberculosis incidence rate of 46.9 per 1,000, quadruple that of white America and nearly a third higher than the African American rate.[69]

To check the spread of tuberculosis, Valentine directed medical supervisor and tuberculosis expert Dr. Joseph A. Murphy to prepare an educational campaign focused on the causes and prevention of the disease. He then sent this to all Indian Office employees, distributed it to Indian school children, and provided it to all adults who could read. To control the epidemic at government schools, Valentine mandated more nutritious food, improved sanitary conditions in the classrooms and dormitories, sterilization of dishes, fumigation of the physical plants, traveling health exhibits, classroom instruction, tuberculosis camps and sanitaria, and banned shared towels.[70] That the Indian Office belatedly addressed the concern did not atone for its inattention.

He then adopted a three-pronged attack on ill-health in Indian Country by embarking on an all-out campaign against tuberculosis and trachoma, the twin scourges of Indian Country. Valentine initiated preventive health education using regular inspections of the schools and he intensified regard for the physical well-being of children enrolled in schools. His efforts were rewarded in 1912 when Congress authorized the Public Health Service to conduct a comprehensive evaluation of the status of health in Indian Country.[71] The findings of the Public Health Service substantiated what Valentine already knew: health conditions were appalling. Nearly seventy-five thousand Natives had trachoma (and nearly 30 percent of school children) and the tuberculosis rate was "very greatly in excess of that of the white race."[72] More disturbingly, disease appeared to be spread at schools and then transported to the reservations when the students returned home.[73]

The Indian Office was quick to blame intemperance as the chief culprit of poor health, believing it was responsible for "direct and incalculable injury" to Native people. As did Leupp before him, Valentine sought to enforce treaty clauses prohibiting the introduction of alcohol onto ceded lands, especially in Minnesota, where he employed treaty provisions that kept two-thirds of the state dry.[74] While he ultimately abandoned this policy after President Taft, on February 16, 1911, modified treaties in Minnesota to eliminate this prohibition, Valentine unsuccessfully requested of Congress legislation restoring prohibition on ceded lands.[75] An active Supreme Court, however, did act, upholding the authority of Congress to preclude the sale or introduction of alcohol in Indian Country as "both within the power of Congress and [a] proper regulation for the protection of the Indian wards."[76] The court also declared that the Indian Office had jurisdiction over the regulation or prohibition of intoxicating beverages on individual allotments—even if the allottee was a U.S. citizen—but only during the trust period.[77] In line with this political theory, Valentine sought to prohibit the use of peyote (*lophophora williamsii*), believing it made "the Indian contented with his present attainments" and "cut off from him the possibility of healthful aspirations."[78]

Valentine advocated policies that encouraged the utilization of natural resources, especially development of the estimated $73 million in timber reserves owned by tribes and individuals.[79] "The policy for the economic and social emancipation of the Indians from the protection of the Government requires that they . . . should find their prosperity and development upon the basic industry of the utilization of the land," underscoring John Locke's theory of land ownership and individual labor as the keys to human development.[80] Land served as both a braid in the integration of the Indians and a conservation matter that required tribal people to adapt or be crushed by the advancing tide of western expansion. To enforce such a policy strand, Valentine believed it was time to commute perpetual annuities since they encouraged "a strong tribal bond and [were] a bar to individual progress." To foster self-reliance, Congress authorized the commissioner to negotiate for the commutation of annuities with the tribes.[81] Valentine then dispatched agents to the nations of the Iroquois Confederacy, the Pawnee, Wisconsin Oneida, Pottawatomie (Prairie Band and the Wisconsin and Kansas bands), and the Sauk and Fox of Oklahoma and Iowa, reaching commutation agreements with the Potawatomie and Sauk and Fox bands.[82]

At the same time, the Indian Office held in trust over$9,500,000 in individual Indian money (IIM) accounts representing funds earned from the sale of land, leases, mineral royalties, timber sales, etc. Between 1902 and 1911, the single largest contributor to the IIM accounts came from the sale of 133,245,000 barrels of oil extracted from more than 22,000 mineral leases, which accrued over $6,344,000 in royalties. The single largest beneficiary was the Osage Tribe, with royalties totaling over $1,900,000.[83] As the Indian Office collected funds on behalf of the lessees, they were placed into the IIM accounts. As additional leases were executed, and with each new timber contract signed and with more youth working in the outing program, the larger and more complicated the accounting became. In an effort to reduce the Indian Office's fiscal obligations, Interior Secretary Richard A. Ballinger in 1911 issued departmental orders placing all traders and lenders on notice that henceforth the Indian Office would no longer guarantee credit and that any credit so extended was at the sole risk of the lender.[84]

Valentine believed the overall work of the Indian Office was educational.[85] He perceived agency farmers and field matrons as the lynchpin behind the efforts to promote social integration by "pushing the work [of farming and domestic sciences] in every possible way."[86] His annual reports included luminous accounts of the work accomplished by agency farmers at multiple agencies, including Crow, Pala, Pima, Fort Hall, Otoe, Nevada, and others. Across Indian Country progress in agricultural endeavors was at various stages. "If the Indian can only retain possession of his land there is little to fear that he will not be able to support himself," Valentine optimistically reported, with agriculture the "essential basic point of present educational policy."[87] In conjunction with the U.S. Department of Agriculture, the Indian Office established experimental farms in Indian Country and encouraged tribal communities to establish annual agricultural fairs geared toward preparing "the Indian for the lifting of the Government's hand."[88]

The commissioner was committed to the integration of education with that of local public schools. "In Indian Country, Indian and white will inevitably have to live closely together," he philosophized in 1909, "and every effort should be made to bring about a state of such neighborliness."[89] In 1910, Congress granted the department authority to admit white children into government boarding schools on the condition they paid tuition. At the Fort Lapwai boarding school, Valentine experimented with Native children attending local white schools and white children attending government schools, with neither child charged tuition. A total of seventy-five white children attended such schools.[90] Valentine further decentralized schools and continued to place children in public schools, with more than eleven thousand in such schools by 1911.[91] According to Valentine, public schools were the way out for Native children. To this end, he quietly shelved the standard government school curriculum and replaced it with that of local public schools.[92] In the process, he transferred a number of government schools to the states as a means of further integrating education.[93]

But severalty remained the fulcrum of federal policy, and Valentine was no exception in its application. The primary feature of severalty remained "the abolition of old tribal relations and the treatment of every Indian as an individual. . . . The basis of this individualization," Valentine argued, "is the breaking up of tribal lands into allotments."[94] However, he adopted a fresh method of severalty that was tested on the Pala Reservation in California. To date, severalty divided reservations into individual parcels that did not consider tribal village structures and patterns. At Pala, agents allotted land to preserve the villages, which were surrounded by small individual gardens along the creek on the valley floor. Conversely, at Umatilla (Oregon), severalty did not reflect existing village patterns but progressed with the intent of dispersing the Indians. "Naturally, as a rule they did not [scatter]," Valentine observed. "Procedures along these lines [Pala example] will go far to put an end to the old cry 'the Indians will not live on their allotment.'" To perfect this social engineering, Valentine ensured each cluster of allotments included a school, a trading post, and "a good center for church work."[95]

Valentine did not accept all of the platitudes of severalty, writing that the 1891 leasing provisions cut short the promise of allotment since Natives "were able to take the line of least resistance by leasing their lands to white farmers and by continuing to live quite after their former fashion."[96] "Leasing as it has been practiced is, as a general rule, a positive detriment to the Indians" he surmised, and it "raise[d] some of the gravest questions of policy with which the Indian Office ha[d] to deal."[97] If a tribal grower had too much land and not enough capital, "it may be advisable for him to lease the surplus," although the real question was whether to lease or sell. "If he can get a good price, it is frequently better for him to sell and have capital value of his surplus land to put into substantial improvements on his retained farm."[98]

By 1912, 300,930 Natives were under federal supervision, with about one-third (120,876) having yet to secure land under the severalty policy. Some 103,417 individuals had trust patents for their land, 70,904 held fee patents, and 1,926 had gained a fee patent for a portion of their land.[99] Overall, 32,413,553 acres of land had fallen before the severalty juggernaut, with 39,503,388 acres left to be allotted. The tribal land base in 1912 totaled 71,916,941 acres, with 82,060 irrigated and 1,018,303 irrigable but lacking water. An additional 755,210 acres were dry farmed. More than 18,747,356 acres were opened to homesteading, with 5,432,942 acres disposed of by 1912.[100] The Indian Office issued 6,167 fee patents in 1912, totaling 638,870 acres. Over 215,186 acres of allotted incompetent land was sold, as were 809,978 acres of inherited land.[101] Twenty-two reservations were opened to homesteading, as shown in Table 6.4.

With so much patented land alienated, Valentine grew increasingly concerned over granting additional fee patents. "There is ordinarily so little legitimate reason for Indians alienating their lands, and the disposal of their farms so effectually thwarts the policy of the Government in

Table 6.4. Reservations Opened to Homesteading as of 1912

Reservation	Original Acres	Allotted	Opened	Surplus Sold
Cheyenne River	2,874,811	785,611	1,615,000	445,919
Coeur d'Alene	598,500	104,077	224,410	207,356
Colville	2,800,000	51,653	1,500,000	156,283
Crow	4,712,960	478,702	1,116,000	533,081
Devil's Lake	230,400	137,381	104,000	90,390
Flathead	1,433,600	228,227	1,126,588	287,791
Fort Berthold	2,912,000	116,213	1,900,000*	76,984
Grande Ronde	61,440	32,983	26,302	26,022
Kiowa/Comanche/Apache	2,968,893	546,376	2,429,202	784,924
Lemhi	64,000	N/R	N/R	N/R
Lower Brule	472,550	176,083	176,560	59,177
Navajo	8,205,440	328,963	506,000	N/R
Red Lake	3,200,000	320	256,152	243,719
Rosebud	3,228,160	1,579,915	1,554,000	1,279,459
Round Valley	102,118	42,106	65,000	16,813
Southern Ute	1,094,400	72,651	523,079	301,777
Spokane	153,600	64,794	5,781	5,544
Standing Rock	2,672,640	1,273,169	2,582,140	349,431
Uintah	2,039,000	99,367	1,004,285	276,977
Wichita	743,610	152,714	586,468	155,241
Wind River	2,342,000	223,236	1,438,633	128,298
Yuma	45,889	7,880	7,756	7,756

* Approximate
Source: *Annual Report of the Commissioner of Indian Affairs, 1912*, 132–34.

developing self-support," he stated, that issuing fee patents would "be utterly at cross purposes with the other efforts of the Government to encourage industry, thrift, and independence."[102] While Leupp approved of 97.5 percent of patent requests, Valentine approved just 63.7 percent (3,491 of 5,478), in large measure because of the establishment of competency commissions and the rejection of blood quantum as a favored criterion for approval.[103] The sale of land, nonetheless, was so great that Valentine resorted to hiring additional staff to process the real estate transactions.

As for the question of who owned ceded land that had yet to be homesteaded or sold, the Indian Office in 1911 declared that aboriginal title remained unextinguished "until the date of entry or sale." As such, the tribes retained use of and benefited from any royalties on the land until such time as the final sale.[104] Due to rapidly expanding mineral development in Indian Country—especially coal and oil—the Indian Office in 1912 declared that it would no longer allot land until the U.S. Geological Survey declared whether the land contained coal or other mineral wealth, or whether such land could serve as a potential reservoir or power site.[105]

In Oklahoma, Congress facilitated land alienation via legislation. By 1912, 51 percent (8,000,000 out of 15,794,400 acres) of the allotted land of the Five Tribes could lawfully be alienated.[106] This legislation, Valentine admitted, "was to enable Indians to change holdings in land which they would not need as land into another form of property which they could utilize to improve and cultivate the land which they kept."[107] As elsewhere, allotted land in Oklahoma remained nontaxable during the trust period, notwithstanding the efforts of the state to subject it to state and local ad valorem taxation.[108]

By 1911, Valentine's health—as well as his zeal—gave out, and he was homebound for two months. Multiple field investigations, repeated congressional inquiries, land and resource scandals, and personal attacks took such a toll on Valentine that he explained, "If I could get angels with flaming swords to run the reservations and inspectors with two flaming swords to watch the Superintendents, I could do better."[109] In 1912, Valentine was charged by the House of Representatives with improprieties and on September 10 he resigned. "The mental wear and tear, the struggle between all kinds of opposing forces, some good, some bad, were so great," Valentine told the gathering at the Lake Mohonk Conference, that even though he prided himself on having "skin seven times the span of the hand in thickness," he could no longer bear "all the attacks from right, left, behind and before."[110] Frederick H. Abbott assumed the role of acting commissioner, remaining until June 4, 1913.[111]

COMMISSIONER CATO SELLS

In 1913, newly elected President Woodrow Wilson turned to Cato Sells, an Iowa Democrat and Texas banker, to serve as commissioner.[112] While he had no experience in Indian affairs, Sells assumed the head of the department on June 4, 1913, committed to expediting competency hearings and emancipating Natives from federal protection. He took office concurrent with several bills introduced into Congress calling for completion of severalty, abolition of the Indian Office, and termination of federal guardianship within ten years.[113] While these bills failed to be enacted, Sells did his part to hasten emancipation, outlining his goals in his first annual report: "The government is the guardian of this vast Indian estate. How this property is to be conserved for the benefit of the Indians and how they shall be taught to make the best possible use thereof so that they may ultimately take their rightful place as self-supporting citizens of the Republic are the greatest problems confronting this bureau."[114] He immediately accelerated the process of releasing allottees from government supervision using the authority of the Burke Act, which enabled the president to declare Natives competent, and the Act of February 14, 1913, which authorized any Native twenty-one years of age and older and of less than one-half Indian blood to dispose of any right or title in an allotment, whether it was held in fee, trust, or restricted status.[115]

In his inaugural report, Sells delineated a policy of determining heirs of decedents so that their lands could be sold "to improve the allotments of the heirs." Such sales would encourage the "settlement of white people in the Indian Country . . . materially increasing the value of the lands retained by the Indians" and lead to the establishment of "free schools, churches, good roads, and other agencies of a modern and progressive community."[116] To facilitate heirship work, Sells requested additional resources from Congress to expedite the determination of heirs and sale of land. He also hastened on with a policy of "individualizing Indian property" and removing "restrictions from the Indian as fast as he demonstrates competency."[117]

Sells lamented that there were only three severalty agents in Indian Country when there once had been eighteen.[118] Three years later, he outlined his "Declaration of Policy" that liberalized the determination of heirs and increased the number of certificates of competency, which multiplied the issuance of fee patents and unrestricted control of individually held land.[119] "'The cardinal principle of this declaration revolves around this central thought," Sells emphasized, "that an Indian who is as competent as an ordinary white man to transact the ordinary affairs of life should be given untrammeled control of his property [thereby releasing] from guardianship of the Government a very large number of Indians who are qualified to mingle on a plane of business equality with the white people."[120]

This Indian "Magna Charta" included a declaration of placing annuities and per capita payments in the hands of competent Natives. "Under the new policy I have thought it advisable to be more liberal in this respect, even at the risk of some of the money being squandered . . . so that they might 'learn by doing.'"[121] In 1918, the commissioner added that such a policy was "the only way the Indians will ever learn to stand on their own feet as competent citizens of the community."[122] He speedily applied this policy strand to all tribal nations except seventy-five thousand Navajos, Hualapais, Hopis, and Apaches in Arizona who Sells determined were "not qualified to withstand the competitive tests that would follow a withdrawal of federal guardianship."[123]

Sells pledged to "not be outdone by anyone who would hasten Indian progress."[124] He used new congressional authority to partition inherited trust allotments (regardless of competency) and issue fee patents to competent heirs, trust patents to incompetent heirs, or to sell the land.[125] By 1920, the Indian Office had issued 225,000 allotments and, between 1917 and 1920, Sells made good on his "Declaration of Policy" by issuing 17,376 fee patents, twice the volume of the previous nine years combined, as shown in Table 6.5.[126]

As the Indian Office declared Natives competent to manage their own affairs and conferred citizenship on them, they and their land were released from government supervision. To illustrate this transformation, Sells initiated a "last arrow" ceremony demonstrating the progress of those the Indian Office declared competent and to whom it delivered fee patents. Before a gathering of tribal members at the local agency, a Native would appear from a tipi in indigenous dress, shoot an arrow into the distance, reenter the tipi, and then reemerge in civilized dress. This final act as an "Indian" was consummated when the individual was given a plow, a purse, an American flag, and a badge representing citizenship, all illustrating his status as an American. The first ceremony occurred at the Yankton Sioux Agency and was followed by ceremonies at the Crow, Shoshone, Coeur d'Alene, Fort Hall, Sisseton, Fort Berthold, and Devil's Lake agencies.[127] In no small sense of irony, Sells served at a time when the first twenty-five-year trust patents were set to expire, agreeing to extend by ten years the trust patents on select reservations.[128]

Corresponding with the policy of declaring individuals competent and authorizing the sale of their land was the effort by Sells to fully utilize natural resources. Timber, oil, and gas were exploited, and land not being utilized by allottees for grazing or farming was leased to non-Indians. Sells

Table 6.5. Fee Patents Issued under the Act of May 8, 1906

Year	Patents Issued	Acres	Total Number Pre-Declaration (Post)
1907–1912	6,352	1,239,900	6,352
1913	520	67,477	6,872
1914	1,148	152,405	8,020
1915	940	124,114	8,960
1916	934	130,980	9,894
1917	**2,203**	**265,550**	**(2,203)**
1918	**4,379**	**704,269**	**(6,582)**
1919	**4,368**	**553,376**	**(10,950)**
1920	**6,426**	**938,419**	**(17,376)**
1907–1920*	4,880	636,411	4,880
Total	32,151	4,812,791	32,151

* Not listed by year but listed in the table
Bold = Under Declaration of Policy
Source: *Annual Report of the Commissioner of Indian Affairs*, 1920, 172.

informed the superintendents of the agencies that it was "an economic and social crime . . . to permit thousands of acres of fertile land . . . to lie in unproductive idleness."[129] In 1913, he toured western reservations and lamented that of nine million acres of agricultural land, tribal growers were cultivating only six hundred thousand.[130] "Our utmost efforts [are] beyond the physical capacity of the Indian to bring under cultivation all the surplus land on the different reservations," Sells announced. Hence, "aggressive steps have been taken with the view of leasing as much of this surplus land as possible, on liberal terms, [permitting] long leases."[131] Special efforts were made to lease large blocks of irrigable land on the Gila River, Colorado River, Crow, Blackfeet, Fort Hall, and Fort Peck Reservations. By 1920, forty thousand agricultural leases encumbered 4.5 million acres of Native land.[132]

To his credit, Sells recognized that irrigation projects were one means of protecting water rights, especially after Wyoming and Utah threatened to revoke Indian water rights unless the water was put to beneficial use by the end of the decade. A year later, Sells moved the Indian Irrigation Service office from Los Angeles to Washington, D.C. While acknowledging the Winters Doctrine of reserved rights, Sells did not believe that tribes held such rights other than on unallotted land—and then only until such lands were allotted and fee patents issued, at which time the water was subject to state prior appropriation laws.[133] Under Western law, rights to water were respected only if the water was put to a beneficial use. After passage of the Reclamation Act, Sells was convinced that beneficial use of water on Native lands was essential, lest such rights be terminated. "If this is not done," the commissioner argued, individuals "will be in danger of losing their water rights and forfeiting the same to subsequent appropriators of the water."[134] Under the guise of protecting water rights, Sells leased additional land. At the Uintah Agency in Utah, the Indian Office leased twenty-five thousand acres "in order to save the [water] rights thereto."[135] In Arizona, Sells leased over twenty-five hundred acres on the Gila River Indian Reservation for agricultural purposes for similar reasons.[136]

Sells was committed to the premise that Natives pay their share of the reimbursable portions of irrigation project construction.[137] With eight thousand Natives irrigating their allotments, Sells advocated legislation authorizing him to charge the beneficiaries for their prorated share of such projects. Congress obliged with passage of the 1915 Indian Appropriation Act, which authorized the Indian Office to charge individuals an apportioned amount of the irrigation investment against their share of tribal funds.[138] More than one hundred irrigation projects were operational by 1916, with 607,962 acres of allotted land and 176,334 acres of unallotted land under a project. Another 836,413 acres of Native land was susceptible of being irrigated.[139] The goals of such projects were to "stimulate crop production" and bring land into productive use, hastening the day when Natives would be set free of government supervision.[140] At the same time, Sells was the first commissioner to acknowledge that irrigation projects benefitted non-Indian growers who acquired or leased tribal lands.

To stimulate self-support, Sells sent a series of circular letters to the agencies, encouraging the development of farming, stock raising, and ranching.[141] Continued cooperation with the USDA Bureau of Plant Industry facilitated the development of new crops, such as Pima long staple cotton, developed at the Pima Sacaton Experimental Farm administered by the U.S. Department of Agriculture. While Sells acknowledged tribal growers were at a disadvantage in that they lacked the capital to make agricultural equipment and seed purchases, he nonetheless terminated the practice of distributing farm implements, wagons, harnesses, and stock, replacing it with reimbursable loans or requiring growers to "pay cash for what they get."[142]

For the tribes on the Great Plains that held expansive grazing lands, Sells emphasized self-support via stock raising and ranching. There were more than fifty million acres of grazing land in Indian Country, Sells reported. To encourage self-support, he promoted improving stock through selective breeding. In 1914, Congress provided the Indian Office with $1.5 million to purchase stock for tribal ranchers, with additional funds appropriated each year by Congress to increase and improve herds.[143] Sells allowed non-Indian grazing leases to expire and, between 1915 and 1917, his efforts resulted in great success. While ranching was "given an impetus never before undertaken," drought, American entrance into World War I in 1917, and the severe winter of 1920–21 interrupted its success, with tribal herds significantly reduced and ranches decreased.[144]

Sells also oversaw the final liquidation of the Cherokee, Choctaw, Chickasaw, Creek, and Seminole nations in Oklahoma. These tribal nations owned 19,525,966 acres before they were forced to accept land severalty and dissolution of their governments. Of this real estate holding, the Dawes Commission allotted 15,794,400 acres to 101,209 people on the tribal rolls, and sold or leased another 2,178,174 acres for mineral development.[145] By June 30, 1914, all legislative and judicial governance of the Five Tribes was dissolved, with only limited executive authority remaining to close out final business. Of the 101,209 allottees, 36,967 had restrictions on the sale of their land, with the restrictions against alienation for the remainder removed under the Act of May 27, 1908. This legislation allowed intermarried whites, freedmen, and all Native people of less than one-half Indian blood to sell their land, while those between one-half and three-quarter blood were authorized to sell all but their 160-acre homestead. Federal restrictions against alienation

Table 6.6. Noncompetent and Inherited Land Sales, 1903–1920 (Excluding Five Tribes)

Year	Noncompetent Sales*	Acres	Inherited Sales**	Acres
1903	N/A	N/A	Unknown	44,494
1904	N/A	N/A	1,236	122,222
1905	N/A	N/A	978	90,215
1906	N/A	N/A	643	64,448
1907	N/A	N/A	820	106,359
1908	92	7,991	768	91,302
1909	235	34,060	753	102,708
1910	520	82,656	873	129,360
1911	494	56,198	638	79,665
1912	324	34,391	392	43,652
1913	208	20,778	109	10,798
1914	529	45,526	418	45,241
1915	422	34,429	393	68,245
1916	583	54,959	324	35,762
1917	588	69,849	655	75,892
1918	662	74,126	438	49,216
1919	463	57,947	507	57,450
1920	1,206	147,047	1,000	155,794
Totals	6,326	719,957	10,945	1,372,823

* Under the acts of March 1, 1907; May 29, 1908; June 25, 1910; and February 14, 1913.
** Under the acts of May 27, 1907; May 8, 1906; May 29, 1908; June 25, 1910; and February 14, 1913.
Source: *Annual Report of the Commissioner of Indian Affairs, 1920*, 169.

remained for all Natives who were three-quarter blood or greater.[146] By the end of Sells's tenure, the Indian Office released from all restrictions 14,872 individual land holdings, 1,068,205 acres in aggregate.[147]

Nationally, the Indian land base diminished from 118,484,302 acres in 1888 to 72,660,316 acres in 1920, with 37,158,655 acres allotted and 35,501,661 remaining tribal land.[148] Of the latter, 18,571,285 acres were in Arizona and part of the Navajo, Hopi, Hualapai, and Apache Reservations.[149] Land sales continued their upward trajectory throughout Sells's administration, as shown in Table 6.6.

Despite the dissolution of tribal governments in Oklahoma, the Indian Office continued to exercise great latitude over tribal property and persons. While committed to the idea that the Indian Office would cease to exist, Sells discovered that its authority was increased by scores of administrative responsibilities, with the scandals related to property and life of the Five Tribes becoming a national embarrassment.[150] In 1914, Sells issued rigid regulations governing probate among the Five Tribes, and the following year he removed twenty-five hundred probate judges and required several thousand probate workers to give account of their work.[151] When Congress directed the Indian Office to refrain from representing minors unless they held restricted land, the Oklahoma state legislature abrogated Sells's probate rules and the looting of the Five Tribes resumed.[152] By 1920, Sells reported that the number of federal field clerks and probate attorneys had diminished due to lack of funding and because of an "increased number of removals of restrictions."[153] It was only a matter of time, the commissioner explained, before the Five Tribes would be "capable of handling their own affairs." During Sells's tenure, the Five Tribes alienated 3,578,934 acres (18.3 percent) of their land.[154]

Sells accelerated placement of children into public schools. As reservations were allotted and surplus and heirship lands sold, non-Natives moved onto the land and constructed homes, schools, and towns. "This process of disintegration of the Indian reservations is a splendid example of the elimination of the Indian as a distinct problem either for the Federal or the State governments," Sells boasted. "The most distinctive element aiding in this growth is the public school," which would enable "advanced" students to remain on their allotments with the "backward" parents having the option of sending their children to federal boarding schools.[155] Excluding the Navajo and Papago (Tohono O'odham), who lacked sufficient schools, Sells believed the government school system was "very close to a turning point" with regards to enrollment. The federal school population peaked in 1915 and diminished each year thereafter.[156] In 1920 alone, Sells closed eleven schools, transferring all children to local public schools, with 10,828 children then enrolled in such schools.[157] In 1918, during wartime exigencies, Sells closed Carlisle Indian School, with the facilities turned over to the War Department.[158]

As part of his Declaration of Policy, Sells ordered all government schools to deny enrollment to children whose parents could afford to pay for their education and who had the opportunity to attend a public school.[159] Two years later, he mandated that any child of a Native parent who held fee-patent title to his land attend public schools unless there were extenuating circumstances precluding such attendance.[160] For those in the government school system, the goal was unchanged: develop "sufficient industrial efficiency to enable the returned boy or girl to derive happiness and comfort from a home created by individual efforts."[161] As a precursor to students transitioning into public schools, Sells deployed a uniform school curriculum in 1916 that was tied to that of public schools.[162] Reservation-based day schools sought to hire married couples in an effort to model a civilized family.[163]

The status of health continued to be substandard. Sells was concerned that there were 25,000 tubercular Natives, but hospital facilities for only 300. This was unacceptable, so the commissioner requested additional funds from Congress to construct new hospitals. Congress obliged and as the Indian Office constructed new facilities, they became increasingly more popular. By the end of 1915, there were 52 hospitals with a bed capacity of 1,567.[164] To combat disease, Sells assigned medical specialists—including tuberculosis and trachoma experts—to the Indian Medical Service staff. But the reduction of infant mortality was the main focus of Sells's healthcare policy and he encouraged—with limited success—women to birth their babies in government hospitals.[165] In 1916, he instituted the "Save the Babies" campaign. "If we have an Indian policy worthy of the name, its goal must be an enduring and sturdy race, true to the noblest of its original inhabitants and virtues and loyalty, sympathetic with our social and national life."[166] Despite a shortage of physicians during and after World War I and continuing health concerns, Sells boasted in 1918 that Native people were no longer a vanishing race.[167]

Above all, Sells was an ardent prohibitionist who prosecuted liquor law violations in Indian Country with fervor. In 1915, he invoked article 7 of the 1855 Chippewa treaty to close over one hundred saloons on Chippewa-ceded lands in Minnesota.[168] Elsewhere, he faced challenges in regulating liquor sales. In New Mexico, the Supreme Court had ruled decades earlier that Pueblo lands did not constitute Indian Country under the Nonintercourse Act and were, therefore, not subject to federal liquor prohibitions.[169] In 1913, however, the Supreme Court considered anew whether Pueblo lands were Indian Country and if the introduction of liquor was within the policing authority of the Indian Office. The court this time opined that Congress was competent to prohibit the introduction of intoxicating liquors into the Pueblos since it had the authority and duty as guardian to care for and protect all "dependent communities," adding a new definition to the term Indian Country.[170]

In 1916, the Supreme Court added scope to prohibition laws by overturning the 1905 *Heff* decision that held allottees were U.S. citizens and not subject to federal prohibition laws. Under the *Nice* ruling, the court held that the General Allotment Act did not sever tribal relations or remove federal protections and the Indian Office could regulate and prohibit the introduction, sale, and manufacture of intoxicating drinks. Notwithstanding severalty, Congress retained its power "to regulate or prohibit traffic in intoxicating liquor with tribal Indians, whether on or off an Indian reservation."[171] As important, the court implied that citizenship was no longer incompatible with tribal existence.

World War I and the prohibition cases were an impetus for federal citizenship, which once was thought to be incompatible with guardianship. By 1918, there were numerous classes of Native citizens: those whose trust or restricted fee patents had expired prior to May 8, 1906; those who had received fee patents to their land; those governed by treaty provisions; and members of the Five Tribes.[172] In 1918, Sells noted that more than eight thousand Natives were admirably serving in the Armed Forces during the Great War. Quoting from the Supreme Court's *Nice* decision, he declared that citizenship and guardianship could coexist and that wartime service had an immediate benefit on Native people in terms of equal opportunities and responsibilities. It was time to confer citizenship on all American Indians.[173]

By 1920, Sells faced increased criticism from reformers for being "too liberal" in emancipating the Indians from federal supervision. Thousands of Natives had lost their land, with Sells expediting competency tests for others. When John Barton Payne replaced Interior Secretary Franklin K. Lane, he saw little benefit in citizenship, informing Sells that it could be a "very long time" before Natives were truly competent. Payne revoked Sells's practice of blanket issuances of competency. Henceforth, each individual case would be evaluated on its own merit.[174]

COMMISSIONER CHARLES H. BURKE

Sells resigned on March 29, 1921, having served all eight years of Woodrow Wilson's administration. With the inauguration of Warren G. Harding as president, Charles Henry Burke, a native of New York who grew up in Dakota Territory and later served in the House of Representatives (R-SD), where he authored the Burke Act, replaced Sells. Harding initially considered J. George Wright, superintendent of the Five Civilized Tribes Agency in Oklahoma, as commissioner but instead nominated Burke in March 1921, with Burke taking office May 7.[175] Burke continued the assimilationist policies of Leupp, Valentine, and Sells, but his tenure was marked by intense scrutiny, which set the groundwork for significant policy changes in the 1930s.[176]

Burke assumed office at a time of public discord over the direction of Indian affairs. Supporters of integration argued that Native people were not being emancipated rapidly enough, while a growing cadre of reformers, such as John Collier, argued that it was time to abandon assimilation and emancipation and protect the integrity of tribal nations. Interior Secretary Albert Fall dominated the first two years of Burke's tenure, with the secretary not only controlling policy but also undermining the protection of tribal rights. Fall supported recognition of squatter rights on Pueblo lands in New Mexico, attempted to carve out a national forest from the Mescalero Apache Reservation that adjoined his New Mexico ranch, ordered the opening of executive order reservations to oil and gas exploitation, and favored disbursement of all tribal money and property on a per capita basis.[177] In March 1923, Fall resigned and was replaced by physician Hubert Work, who gave Burke greater control of Indian affairs.

Burke viewed the work of the Indian Office as one of education and, in 1923, he outlined his goals: "Every eligible Indian child in school every day" and "Every Indian school filled to its limit."[178] He enumerated twenty-five thousand children not in school, eighteen thousand of whom were eligible to attend but not enrolled due to insufficient schools.[179] Two-thirds of these eligible students were from the Navajo, Hopi, Hualapai, and Papago Tribes in Arizona. Burke committed to constructing no new schools except for the Navajo and Papago. "I am not willing to overlook the future to provide schools for these Native Americans," he wrote. A year later, he requested additional resources from Congress for children to attend public schools, except the Navajo and Papago, the former of which were spread out over some thirteen million acres and had treaty stipulations guaranteeing schools and teachers, while the latter lived in small scattered villages on 2.8 million acres of Sonoran Desert in southern Arizona.[180]

When Congress enacted legislation making school attendance compulsory, the Indian Office adopted the truancy laws of the states for its schools.[181] Where distance or conditions made attendance problematic, children were placed in boarding or other schools as designated by the commissioner. To fill government schools and maintain efficiencies, Burke extended day schools to grade six and added grades eleven and twelve to the larger off-reservation boarding schools. "Adoption of this policy constitutes a recognition of the fact that if Indian young people are to compete with those of other nationalities they must have equal educational opportunities."[182] Within a year, 391 students were in the higher grades, 315 of whom were from Kansas tribes and, by 1928, there were 747 students in the higher grades.[183] In addition, there were 10,340 students in public schools, with the Indian Office paying 737 school districts $311,000 in tuition.[184] In 1927, after congressional appropriations failed to enable the Indian Office to further expand educational opportunities, Burke deployed a "new platoon" system under which children attended school three-quarters of the day and spent one-quarter in institutional work, even as he argued "too much institutional routine labor" was "detrimental to educational advancement."[185] To encourage healthier lifestyles, the commissioner added free time to the school schedule in 1927.[186]

Burke faced difficult policy decisions in part due to congressional parsimony, as reflected in the passage of the Snyder Act of 1921, which attempted to limit funding for the Indian Office to eight specific categories.[187] Throughout the 1920s, educational appropriations failed to meet demand, leading the commissioner to ignore compulsory attendance laws. Funding for public schools also diminished, leaving children without educational facilities. As for healthcare, the task was daunting. In 1927, Burke lamented that the Indian Office failed to maintain "pace with the progress elsewhere along health, educational, industrial, and social lines."[188] Annual turnover among Indian Office physicians was 56 percent and for skilled nurses it was an astonishing 122 percent. "The Indian medical and nursing service should be stabilized," Burke argued in 1927 in his most moving and pointed annual report. Nurses were on call twenty-four hours a day with little social life, inadequate living quarters, low salaries, and dismal working conditions.[189]

Not surprisingly, the overall health of Native people was poor, with trachoma and tuberculosis continuing as the twin scourges. While in theory the Indian Medical Service "countenanced no fads and trust[ed] no fanciful theories [and its] policy is to make use of all scientific knowledge," the reality was starkly different.[190] "The time has come," Burke announced, "when preventative medicine . . . must be applied to the solution of the health problems of the Indian Service."[191] When Burke asked the American Red Cross to survey health conditions in 1922, he was disheartened to learn that disease and poor health were more rampant than he initially thought.[192] But, whereas he intended to use the report "to seek such provisions as are now lacking to accomplish a higher average of Indian health," when the report was released, he failed to seek additional resources from Congress. Consequently, he banished the report from the public record and had chief medical director Robert E. Lee Newberne rebuke Elinor Gregg, Florence Patterson, and Augustine Stoll, the three public health nurses involved in the study, out of concern that the report would add to the criticisms of the Indian Office.[193]

In 1924, Burke announced that improving healthcare was his number one priority: "Public health is purchasable" and "under adequately funded health efforts, a decrease in illness and in the death rate can be attained."[194] In July he deployed his Southwestern Trachoma Campaign, with three teams consisting of a special physician, two nurses, an orderly, and an interpreter, fanning out across the Southwest. The units focused on the Navajo, Hopi, Hualapai, and Apache Tribes in Arizona, with 19 percent of the 38,111 Natives testing positive for trachoma.[195] Two years later, he reorganized the Indian Medical Service and placed it in the hands of Public Health Service physician Marshall C. Guthrie. In a further effort to improve health, Burke implemented a series of five-year plans to upgrade homes and instituted a series of scientific studies to assess the status of every Native home on each reservation. The analysis was to be a barometer of civilization.[196]

Utilization of natural resources remained an integral objective of the Indian Office, with Burke continuing and expanding the policy of his predecessors. He requested additional resources to improve management of tribal forests as a means of promoting educational and industrial work

Table 6.7. Sale of Inherited and Original Allotted Land and Fee Patents Issued, 1921–1928

Year	Land Sales	Acres	Fee Patents Issued
1921	1,268	135,893	1,692
1922	1,006	104,814	911
1923	1,328	171,715	625
1924	1,286	125,099	913
1925	N/A	112,638	N/A
1926	1,203	126,051	322
1927	1,284	141,422	272
1928	1,268	151,414	242
Total	8,643	1,069,045	4,977

Source: *Annual Report of the Commissioner of Indian Affairs, 1921–1928.*

and protecting national resources. Forestry and severalty went hand-in-hand, and as tribal land was allotted, surplus lands were sold. In many cases these lands were timber lands, which were often harvested.[197]

Inherited and original allotted land continued to be alienated in the 1920s. In his inaugural report, Burke reported that 135,893 acres of patented land had been sold, in large part because the Indian Office continued to issue fee patents under Sells's Declaration of Policy. "This practice, however, has been discontinued," Burke announced in 1921, with the result that "there has been a great falling off in the number of land sales and in acreages sold."[198] Burke acted in part due to Congress pushing emancipation. Congressman Melville C. Kelly (R-PA) argued: "The reservation system may have served a good purpose in compelling the Indians of other days to forsake their wild, nomadic ways. But its day is long passed. . . . The sooner the whole tribal system and the reservation policy is abandoned the sooner we will write *finis* to one of the bloodiest pages in American history."[199]

Burke favored emancipation but his "stricter policy" of issuing patents was necessary "to more fully protect [the Indians'] interests."[200] Despite such rhetoric, Burke authorized an average annual sale of 133,630 acres of allotted land during his tenure, as shown in Table 6.7.

Burke hastened on with land severalty, with over 97,000 acres allotted on the Gila River Indian Reservation in 1921. The following year, the Indian Office allotted 554,613 acres on the Blackfeet Reservation and a year later allotted 1,904,000 across the northern plains and in the Southwest, followed by 169,953 acres in 1924, 594,697 acres in 1925, 13,177 acres in 1926, 207,932 acres in 1927, and 101,234 acres in 1928 scattered throughout Indian Country.[201] At the same time, Burke extended the trust period on hundreds of allotments, largely due to public discontent over the rapid alienation of Native land.[202] The Indian Office also added land for homeless Natives and made large additions to the Navajo, Walker River, and Acoma Reservations.[203] For those who refused to work their allotments, Burke issued regulations authorizing the agency superintendent or officer in charge to execute leases and, using departmental rules issued in 1922, made executive order reservations subject to the General Leasing Act of 1920.[204] In 1924, in an effort to further develop oil and gas, the department issued new regulations governing mineral leases, including extending such leases in perpetuity as long as resources were mined in paying quantities.[205]

Burke condemned Native ceremonials, especially religious dances he deemed immoral. In 1921, he issued Circular 1665 and banned most ceremonies, including the Hopi Snake Dance and the Plains Sun Dance, making such offenses subject to fines and imprisonment. Two years later, in a letter widely circulated, he demanded Native people devote "more serious attention to their home interests, particularly in the planting and harvesting seasons," and prohibited them from participating in traditional and ceremonial dances more than once a month.[206] Burke believed such activities were inappropriate for modern life, antithetical to assimilation, and a vestige of the past. This attack on religious freedom was not lost on a new generation of reformers, some of whom—such as the American Indian Defense Association—saw a disregard for Indian rights.[207]

Burke's tenure brought about the most cherished goal of the old reformers—U.S. citizenship. While more than half of Native people had gained citizenship via marriage, treaty provisions, acts of Congress, fee patents, or involvement in World War I, by 1924, many yet remained without the franchise.[208] In 1924, Congress enacted into law the Indian Citizenship Act, conferring the federal franchise on all American Indians.[209] But citizenship did not arrive as the reformers had once envisioned. It did not mean that tribal citizenship and tribal rights were forfeited, as many Native people had treaty-protected rights that could not easily be ignored. Thus, when federal citizenship arrived, it came in the form of dual citizenship—American citizenship and recognition of tribal citizenship.[210] Burke lamented this fact, noting that since the act provided citizenship without impairing tribal rights, the "trust or restrictions upon Indian property will continue."[211] In line with citizenship, Burke sought to extend the jurisdiction of the Major Crimes Act to include bigamy, incest, adultery, and breaking and entering, although Congress refused and the states were precluded from doing so.[212]

While advocating dissolution of the Indian Office, Burke consolidated agencies and assumed increased authority over Native people and their property.[213] Annual appropriations from Congress failed to meet their needs, however, especially medical and educational. Congress granted Burke just 80 percent of his requested budget for the years 1922 to 1929.[214] Despite the reclassification act that raised salaries for Indian Office employees, the department shed 534 positions in 1925, although 190 were added to staff new schools in the Southwest.[215] The Welch Act of 1928 further raised federal salaries, giving Burke increased optimism for higher qualified and better compensated employees.[216]

Even more of a concern for Burke was a series of reports highlighting the poor treatment and conditions of Native people and the negligence of the Indian Office. The most prominent of these was an 872-page indictment by the Institute for Government Research entitled "The Problem with Indian Administration," or the "Meriam Report," which described deplorable conditions in health, education, economics, resource management, and federal administration.[217] "Taken as a whole," Lewis Meriam wrote, "practically every activity undertaken by the national government for the … Indians is below a reasonable standard of efficiency." Moreover, "it seems as if the government assumed that some magic in individual ownership of property would in itself prove ... educational." In reality, severalty "for the most part operated in the opposite direction," leading Meriam to caution the Indian Office to exercise restraint in issuing fee patents. [218]

A second study focused on irrigation projects and was authored by engineers Porter J. Preston (Bureau of Reclamation) and Charles A. Engel (Indian Office). The engineers analyzed Indian irrigation projects and discovered that only 16.9 percent (117,189 acres) of the total irrigated land under such projects was cultivated by Natives. On the Wapato (Yakima) Irrigation Project just 6 percent of the land (4,661 acres) was cultivated by tribal citizens. On the Blackfeet Reservation just 0.006 percent (44 acres) was cultivated by Native growers, and on the Flathead Reservation just 1.3 percent (452 acres) of the project was cultivated by tribal members.[219] Forty percent of Native land nationwide under an irrigation project and cultivated by Native people came from the Uintah (Utah) and Gila River (Arizona) Reservations.[220] Irrigation projects, designed to foster economic development and self-sufficiency, had largely failed to benefit Native people. "It cannot be said that there has been any serious and sustained effort on our part to make farmers of the Indians," Preston and Engel concluded. The government's fundamental mistake was in assuming severalty would transform the Indians into farmers.[221]

By the late 1920s, the Indian Office and Burke faced intense criticism for their conduct in Indian affairs. Burke's support of the Bursum Bill in 1922, which proposed to protect non-Indian squatter rights on Pueblo lands in New Mexico, exacerbated matters.[222] Burke submitted his resignation on March 9, 1929, five days after Herbert Hoover took office as president. His resignation corresponded to a fundamental shift in federal policy. The integration policies advocated by the Indian Service and Congress for more than a half century had proven unsuccessful. American Indians were burdened by administrative controls and denied basic constitutionally protected rights. Tribes had lost nearly eighty million acres of land and their cultural heritage and existence were at stake.[223]

CONCLUSION

The 1920s proved to be a time of great discord, which planted the seeds of change that followed in the 1930s. Many of these changes were championed by John Collier and the American Indian Defense Association and resulted in a radical departure from established policy. Change began with the election of President Herbert Hoover in 1928 and was hastened on by the election of Franklin D. Roosevelt in 1932. The impetus proved to be the American Red Cross report, several tuberculosis reports, and the Meriam Report, the latter shattering the premise of the colloquial assimilation strands that had governed the previous half century. In this respect, the Meriam Report proved to be as important an impetus for change as Helen Hunt Jackson's *A Century of Dishonor* had been a generation earlier.

7

"LAST CHANCE FOR THE INDIANS?"

Reorganization and New Deal, 1928–1948

The Progressive Movement was a philosophical catalyst for a change in policy. The publication by the Brookings Institute of *The Problem of Indian Administration* and the Great Depression provided an economic framework and rationalization for modulating policy, with the former advocating either fitting Natives "to merge into the social and economic life" of the nation or allowing them to live outside of it "with a minimum standard of health and decency."[1] The Indian Office needed a strong visionary to direct the shift enumerated by the Brookings Institute in its analysis of Indian affairs, which colloquially came to be called the "Meriam Report" after its principle author, Lewis Meriam. But while policy strands changed, the braids remained, albeit less pronounced.

As the scandal-plagued 1920s drew to a close, the critics of Indian policy grew vociferous, encouraging President Hoover to initiate reform.[2] One particularly outspoken individual was John Collier who, in 1920, experienced his "Red Atlantis" in Taos, New Mexico, and three years later organized the American Indian Defense Association to command protection of tribal social, cultural, and political rights. Yet another generation of reformers was proving to be more secular and liberal minded than their predecessors. As the leading voice of the reformers, Collier viewed the actions of the Indian Office as disdainful and disrespectful of tribal rights and culture, both of which he believed not only had a right to exist but also were imperative for the survival of modern industrial America.[3]

The Depression-era policy strands initiated a transformation in social and political attitudes that had far-reaching consequences, setting into motion the self-determination policies of the late twentieth century. This movement towards self-governance advanced, notwithstanding a post-World War II effort to terminate the political relationship between tribal nations and the United

Table 7.1. Heads of the Indian Office and Major Policies, 1929–1948

Name	Title	Years of Service	Main Policies
Charles J. Rhoads (R)	Commissioner	4 years (1929–1933)	Levitt Act, cancelled reimbursable loans, land sales, natural resource protection, reorganized Indian Office, day schools, closed boarding schools
John Collier (D)	Commissioner	12 years (1933–1945)	Indian Reorganization Act, end land severalty and land sales, resource development, Pueblo Land Consolidation Act, land for landless Indians, CCC-Indian Division, Johnson-O'Malley Act, Indian Arts and Crafts Act
William Brophy (D)	Commissioner	3.25 years (1945–1948)	Navajo-Hopi Rehabilitation Act, Indian Claims Commission, resource development, community schools, restored opened land to tribal status, preparation for termination

States and rapidly integrate Native people once and for all into the national social and political fabric. Between 1929 and 1948, just three men served as commissioner of Indian affairs, beginning with Charles Rhoads and his "co-commissioner" Henry Scattergood (1929–1933), followed by John Collier (1933–1945), and William Brophy (1945–1948).

COMMISSIONER CHARLES J. RHOADS

Upon his election as president in 1928, Republican Herbert Hoover accepted the resignation of Charles Burke as commissioner and transferred longtime assistant commissioner Edgar Meritt to the Bureau of the Budget. Charles James Rhoads recommended to the president his longtime friend Joseph Henry Scattergood as commissioner of Indian affairs, but Hoover instead selected Rhoads, who accepted on condition that the president support alterations in federal policy advanced by the Meriam Report. Rhoads was appointed commissioner of Indian affairs on April 18, 1929, and took office on July 1. His first action was to appoint Scattergood as assistant commissioner.

Rhoads and Scattergood were well-respected Pennsylvania Quakers and members of the old guard Indian Rights Association, with Rhoads a former president of the association.[4] Interior Secretary Ray Lyman Wilbur took an active role in Indian affairs, spelling out his position in the simple statement of freeing the Indians of government wardship: "The Red man's civilization must be replaced by the white man's and he must give up his role as a member of the race that holds aloof, while all others enter into our own melting pot."[5] He pledged an end of the Indian Office within a generation.

Rhoads, meanwhile, worked with Matthew K. Sniffen of the Indian Rights Association, Lewis Meriam of the Brookings Institute, and John Collier of the American Indian Defense Association to prepare a series of policy considerations that were sent by Wilbur to Lynn Frazier (R-ND), chairman of the Senate Indian investigating subcommittee of the Committee on Indian Affairs, five months after taking office.[6] Wilbur and Rhoads implored Frazier to consider a series of reforms, including cancelling reimbursable debts assessed against Native growers and changing land severalty in its entirety. The latter policy should be abandoned, Rhoads argued, due to the difficulties and challenges in administering it.[7] He also asked the Senate to investigate the matter of guardianship of Native property, in particular the challenges with federal control of tribal resources. While it was important not to undermine individual responsibility, it was equally important not to attenuate tribal authority over unallotted lands. Consequently, taking a cue from the Meriam Report, Rhoads suggested that Congress consider authorizing tribes to incorporate for purposes of administering tribal real estate while at the same time empowering them to control their own lands and resources. He also recommended that Congress establish an Indian court of claims so that tribes might seek redress of treaty and trust violations, and that Congress evaluate irrigation policy and consider turning over to the Reclamation Service all Indian irrigation projects.[8]

The Indian Office earned mixed results on Rhoads's policy requests. There were 205 irrigation projects on the Indian Office's books, although only 80 were active. On these, the department had expended $37,104,000 on construction and another $10,284,000 on operation and maintenance. Construction repayment on reimbursable loans, however, totaled a paltry $1,271,000 and operation and maintenance charges netted just $3,400,000.[9] While 754,000 acres of land were under an irrigation project, just 387,552 acres were actually irrigated. Of these, Native growers irrigated less than one-third, or 124,316 acres. Lessees irrigated 103,578 acres (27 percent) and non-Indians irrigated 159,658 acres (41 percent) of fee land, meaning non-Indian growers irrigated over two-thirds of the land under irrigation projects.[10]

The Indian Office utilized gratuitous appropriations, tribal funds, and reimbursable loans for individuals when constructing irrigation projects, but this created indebtedness and, in some instances, established per acre assessments that exceeded the value of the land. "The policy is to place these irrigation projects on a sound economic foundation," Rhoads remarked in 1930, "so that the individual Indians will feel that their land is not encumbered with onerous obligations." Some Natives refused to utilize the irrigation system because they did not wish to "be involved in the reimbursable obligation."[11]

As a matter of policy, the Indian Office endeavored to furnish irrigation facilities for arid lands allotted in severalty. At the same time, it "weigh[ed] the economic advantage of joint storage and canals systems."[12] Joint works facilities, such as those on the Flathead and Gila River Reservations (San Carlos Irrigation Project) were intended to be assimilative while at the same time spreading the costs of irrigation projects across Indian and non-Indian growers. Anticipating the eventual absorption of Native people, Rhoads in 1931 directed the Indian Office to evaluate and classify irrigation projects and to recommend continuation, abandonment, or transfer to local irrigation districts. Cancelling reimbursable debts so Natives could farm the land without encumbrances facilitated final absorption.[13]

For lands within active irrigation projects as of June 1932, tribal growers owned 239,885 acres and non-Indians owned 191,423 acres. Of the former, Native growers irrigated 133,134 acres of trust land and leased to non-Indians 106,751 acres of trust land. For the latter, non-Indians farmed

Table 7.2. Character of Landownership under Indian Irrigation Projects, 1932

Character of Ownership	Acres under Constructed Ditches	Acres under Construction	Acres Not Constructed	Total Acres in Project
Tribal	14,612	14,640	24,730	53,982
Deceased Trust Patent	78,330	63,722	48,010	190,062
Living Trust Patent	91,412	88,456	73,805	253,673
Deceased Restricted Patent	6,466	6,745	7,444	20,655
Living Restricted Patent	10,235	9,533	6,965	26,733
Patented Indian owned	4,826	6,094	6,530	17,450
Non-Indian owned	185,243	87,986	22,409	295,638
U.S. Owned	2,435	1,139	430	4,004
Total (23 projects)	393,559	278,315	190,323	862,197
87 minor projects				170,674
Grand Total				1,032,871

Source: *Annual Report of the Commissioner of Indian Affairs*, 1932, 20.

175,731 acres of fee patented land, with 15,692 acres of Indian fee patented land classified as non-Indian land.[14] More telling was the breakdown of land under ditches and irrigated as of July 1, 1932, which is shown in Table 7.2. Non-Indian–owned land accounted for 47 percent of the acres under constructed irrigation ditches.[15]

Congress responded to reimbursable loans for irrigation projects by cancelling all debt against Native lands incurred before June 7, 1924, the date it authorized construction of Coolidge Dam and the San Carlos Irrigation Project for the benefit of the Gila River Indian Reservation.[16] The act specifically required the Gila River Indian Community to repay reimbursable debts in the amount of $312,000 for irrigation works outside of the project (and soon-to-be decreed) lands on the reservation. Another $1.37 million in reimbursable debt for land falling within the San Carlos Irrigation Project, however, was cancelled.[17] Since there were other tribes facing similar challenges with reimbursable irrigation debt, Rhoads prepared a list and submitted it to Congress, requesting its consideration of a bill cancelling all irrigation debt. Congress concurred with Rhoads's assessment and, on July 1, 1932, cancelled or adjusted all Native reimbursable debt.[18]

Both the Preston-Engel irrigation report and the Meriam Report had recommended cancellation of reimbursable debt, noting the inequity of converting gratuitous appropriations to reimbursable expenses that discouraged farming. In many cases, Natives were unable to repay the construction debt and yet were obligated to pay the Operations and Maintenance assessments.[19] As for irrigation reimbursable debt, the Leavitt Act, as it became known, deferred the collection of all reimbursable debt and assessments of construction costs or charges against Native land until such time that aboriginal title was extinguished. A House Committee on Indian Affairs explained that "the progress of many Indians is retarded by old debts held against them by the Government and incurred under circumstances which dictate adjustment as a matter of simple justice." Such debt decreased the value of the land and interfered with securing the credit "necessary to make the Indian self-supporting through farming."[20]

Table 7.3. Sales of Original and Inherited Allotted Land, 1930–1932

Year	Original Allotments	Acres	Inherited Allotments	Acres	Total Acres
1930	290	35,773	596	72,742	108,515
1931	206	19,132	438	50,663	69,795
1932	265	26,316	300	45,368	71,684
Total	761	81,221	1,334	168,773	249,994

Source: *Annual Reports of the Commissioner of Indian Affairs, 1930–1932.*

Rhoads also requested Congress to reconsider guardianship of Native property. He was critical of, but not opposed to, severalty, even though the government seemed to assume "some magic in individual ownership of property" would prove assimilative.[21] In 1930, he described the task of the Indian Office as enabling Natives to become "independent, self-supporting, self-respecting member[s]" of their communities.[22] Over his four-year tenure, Rhoads allotted 459,329 acres to 2,819 individuals, with 1,664 allotments totaling 249,018 acres issued in 1932 alone.[23] Simultaneously, he recommended to President Hoover the extension of all expiring trust patents, and each year the president extended such patents, delaying alienation of land.[24] Notwithstanding such extensions, Rhoads continued to approve land sales, as shown in Table 7.3, much to the chagrin of Collier and even though Rhoads lamented that "within many of the reservations a large part of the best agricultural land has been sold or fee patented."[25] Between 1930 and 1932, Rhoads issued 503 fee patents totaling 66,418 acres.[26]

Whereas, at the commencement of his administration Rhoads favored increased tribal authority over property and resources, in 1930 he broke with Collier after Collier favored greater control of tribal property than Rhoads was willing to consider. Congress did not act on, and Rhoads did not advocate for, increased tribal control over property. Nor did Congress end land severalty and the concomitant sale of land. Collier denounced Rhoads for not doing more to protect resources and encourage tribal control over such resources, further straining their relationship.[27]

To his credit, Rhoads tethered land policies to natural resource conservation. In 1930, for instance, he reorganized grazing regulations and directed the Indian Forestry Division to evaluate the health of tribal ranges and devise a "systematic grazing plan" defining the most practicable number of grazing units, carrying capacity of the range, and most suitable stock for reservation rangelands.[28] Such conservation was tied to restoration of native grasses, checking erosion, and overall protection of natural resources. In 1930, the Senate Committee on Indian Affairs reported favorably on a bill to create Colville Indian Forest and Klamath Indian Forest. A year later, another bill called for the creation of Warm Springs Indian Forest and Yakima Indian Forest. Neither bill was enacted into law, but they underscored the means by which Rhoads sought to protect tribal natural resources and implement range management.[29] He also organized the Division of Agricultural Extension and Industry, with agents working with tribes to develop programs to increase agricultural productivity, improve the quantity and quality of food and fiber crops, implement weed control and prevention, and upgrade farm management and soil productivity via crop rotation.[30]

As for the court of Indian claims that Rhoads asked Congress to consider, the commissioner and Secretary Wilbur found little congressional support, notwithstanding the Meriam Report's advocacy for such a forum.[31] While Wilbur sent a proposal to the House Committee on the Judiciary, which reported a bill to the full House, it died when the Justice Department and Bureau of the Budget opposed it as too costly and the matter lay dormant until after World War II.[32] And as for turning over irrigation projects to the Reclamation Service, neither Congress nor Rhoads after 1930 supported the transfer. While the Report of the Advisors on Irrigation recommended such an action for seven of the largest Indian irrigation projects, including Gila River (San Carlos Project), Flathead, Yakima, Fort Hall, Crow, Uintah, and Wind River, the matter ended when Representative Louis C. Cramton (R-MI) inserted a proviso into the appropriation act in 1930 precluding such transfers.[33]

Rhoades reorganized the Indian Office in 1931, creating five divisions under two subdepartments, one under an assistant commissioner of human relations and the other under an assistant commissioner of property. Human relations included the health, education, and agricultural extension and industry divisions, while property included the forestry and irrigation divisions.[34] The reorganization was both practical and philosophical, as it freed the commissioner's office of many of the day-to-day decisions, enabling it to focus on policy matters. More significant, was the philosophical change by which the Indian Office for the first time considered people distinct from property, a nuance that was the first step in repealing wardship while retaining trusteeship.

The commissioner also made substantive changes in health and education policy, implementing a number of "Recommendations for Immediate Action" enumerated by the Meriam Report.[35] "The cost of Indian education and care of health obviously must exceed that of similar services amongst the white population," Rhoads explained in his inaugural report.[36] In part, this was because "practically no two groups of Indians are alike, either in inheritance or present environment, and the Indian Service must meet the situation as it applies to the Indians."[37] To address concerns in healthcare, Rhoads advocated "close cooperative health activities" with state and local jurisdictions, including the Association of State and Provincial Health Authorities of North America and the National Institutes of Health.[38]

The Indian Office further cooperated with the U.S. Public Health Service and secured funds to more accurately collect and report vital statistics and morbidity data.[39] Rhoads stressed the need and secured appropriations from Congress to construct new hospitals, noting that live births in government hospitals increased from 595 in 1928 to 1,888 in 1932.[40] Corresponding with hospital utilization was an increase in the number of medical staff, including nurses. "The eradication of [disease] will not be brought about until a well-organized and funded nursing service has been instituted," Rhoads explained. He encouraged closer cooperation with the Public Health Service to secure competent medical officers, field directors, sanitary engineers, physicians, and other medical professionals who devoted themselves to understanding the causes and transmission of disease.[41] Using the recommendations of the Meriam Report, Rhoads convinced Congress to increase medical appropriations each year, with the budget rising from $2,993,600 in 1930 to $4,227,500 in 1932.[42]

The transformation of educational policy was equally aggressive, with Rhoads following a recommendation of the Meriam Report to do away with the uniform course of study that emphasized Anglo values without considering tribal culture. Filling off-reservation boarding schools with young children was discouraged, with these children enrolled in day schools instead.[43] The Indian Office also encouraged Native students to adapt to both the dominant culture and their tribal culture, with Rhoads calling for the elimination of federal schools for those tribes having access to public schools. Otherwise, boarding schools focused on the upper grades, with Rhoads reducing "non-educational institutional work" to that "necessary" for school operations.[44] By 1931, more than forty-three thousand students were in public schools and Rhoads began talk of abandoning government schools altogether.

In a remarkably progressive step, and another encouraged by the Meriam Report, the Indian Office advocated that "Indians themselves should be consulted regarding . . . plans for [the] education of their children." To do so would enable them to "work themselves free from dependence and take an interest in their own educational affairs."[45] Local input into educational planning was for the first time policy, with school curriculum modified to include tribal heritage and culture.[46] In March 1929, Congress repealed the limit on per-pupil expenditures, giving the Indian Office "hope that reasonably liberal appropriations sufficient for the operation of efficient institutions may be hereafter secured."[47] Qualifications for teachers were increased and Rhoads issued policy directing elementary school teachers to use curriculum tied to the "environmental experience of children." The Indian Office also added to the curriculum physical education, fine arts, music education, and play time.[48]

All of the educational adjustments made by Rhoads called attention to a "change in point of view."[49] While Rhoads was committed to change, it was his director of Indian Education, W. Carson Ryan—one of the principle researchers for the Meriam Report—who was the driving force in reducing the number of boarding schools, increasing the availability of day schools, decentralizing education, adopting state curriculum, improving vocational training, providing job placement and career guidance, and establishing funds for higher education. With Rhoads's support, Ryan closed three boarding schools in 1931 (Mekusukey, Fort Bidwell, and Fort Mojave) and two more in 1932 (Segar and Tulalip); he also converted four boarding facilities into day schools (Pima, Lac du Flambeau, Fort Yuma, and Hoopa Valley).[50] In 1931, the Indian Office assumed responsibility for Alaska Native educational services.[51]

Rhoads, like his predecessors, was eventually besieged with criticism—especially from Collier, who believed the commissioner did not do enough to promote arts and crafts and economic development, and failed to protect civil liberties and advance self-government.[52] Collier was especially rancorous over Rhoads's failure to end land severalty and was particularly vitriolic in his perception that the commissioner did not work hard enough to establish an Indian court of claims or enable tribes to incorporate for business purposes.[53] When Democrats took control of the House after the 1930 midterm election, the House Committee on Indian Affairs backed Collier's reforms and Rhoads found himself more frequently on the outside looking in as members of Congress turned against him. His final months in office were filled with vitriol, as liberal reformers lost faith in him. After the election of Franklin D. Roosevelt as president in 1932, reformers such as Franz Boaz recommended the president-elect not reappoint Rhoads. The commissioner, Boaz wrote, must understand that administrative measures would never transform Native people into white Americans. The Rhoads-Scattergood era came to a close when Rhoads resigned effective April 20, 1933.

COMMISSIONER JOHN COLLIER

In January 1933, John Collier, executive-secretary of the American Indian Defense Association, advised President-elect Roosevelt to end land severalty, extend credit to American Indians who were unable to secure it due to the trust status of their land, discontinue boarding schools and replace them with day schools, and solicit the involvement of other state and federal agencies in Indian affairs.[54] As for head of the Indian Office, Collier promoted a politically strong candidate, while the Indian Rights Association favored the continuation of the Rhoads-Scattergood administration, and Senator Joseph T. Robinson (D-AR)—chairman of the Senate Committee on Indian Affairs—favored his brother-in-law and former assistant commissioner Edgar Meritt. The conservative Board of Indian Commissioners supported a man with Indian Service experience rather than a "party man."[55]

Collier met with Lewis Meriam and Nathan Margold, a New York City attorney, with each agreeing that should Roosevelt support one of them as commissioner, the others would fall in line behind the nominee. The All Pueblo Council, meanwhile, adopted a resolution on January 12, 1933, addressed to the president-elect supporting Collier.[56] In late January, some six hundred national educators, physicians, social workers, church leaders, and reformers sent a petition to Roosevelt counseling the president-elect to take immediate action to save the Indians from complete political, economic, and cultural disintegration caused by the General Allotment Act, regarding Roosevelt's administration as "a last chance for the Indian."[57]

Roosevelt grasped the urgency of attenuating policy and turned to Columbia University law professor Raymond Moley, who in turn collaborated with Felix Frankfurter, dean of Harvard Law School, for assistance in vetting candidates for commissioner of Indian affairs. Meriam, Collier, and Margold met with Moley and resolved that a final decision on the commissionership should await the appointment by Roosevelt of a secretary of the interior. When Roosevelt selected Harold Ickes as secretary, the decision was made. Ickes forwarded Collier's nomination to the Senate and refused to consider anyone else until the Senate voted on him. "All the winds of patronage" opposed Collier, including Robinson and Elmer Thomas (D-OK), a fellow member of the Senate Committee on Indian Affairs.[58] Roosevelt then invited Ickes and Robinson to the White House on April 11, where he asked Robinson to withdraw his support for Meritt. Collier was cleared for Senate confirmation on April 21 after Ickes exclaimed: "No one exceeds him in knowledge of

Indian matters or his sympathy with the point of view of the Indians themselves. I want someone in that office who is the advocate of the Indians[,] who will respect their customs and have a sympathetic point of view with reference to their culture."[59] Ickes appointed William Zimmerman Jr. assistant commissioner, Nathan Margold Interior solicitor, and Felix Cohen assistant solicitor.[60]

John Collier was perhaps the most qualified—and controversial—commissioner of Indian affairs to date, taking office April 21, 1933. The Indian Office that he had long criticized was now his to direct and he brought about an immediate change in policy and administration, with Zimmerman describing endless meetings in the Indian Office, at Collier's apartment, and on Sunday mornings at Potomac Park.[61] Collier, with the support of Roosevelt and Ickes, convinced Congress to enact into law a good deal of his vision for Indian affairs, and that which he could not convince Congress to accept legislatively, he accomplished administratively. At his request, Roosevelt abolished the Board of Indian Commissioners in May 1933 and in its place, Collier turned to social scientists to restore tribal culture and self-government.

In his first annual report, issued just months after taking office, Collier outlined four challenges confronting the Indian Office. The first was "the allotment system [that] has enormously cut down the Indian landholdings and has rendered many areas, still owned by Indians, practically unavailable for Indian use."[62] He then outlined an end to land severalty, restoration of unallotted lands to tribal ownership, and the purchase of land for landless Natives. A second problem was in educational philosophy. "The redistribution of educational opportunity for Indians, out of the concentrated boarding school, reaching the few, and into the day school, reaching the many, must be continued and accelerated."[63] Day schools, Collier asserted, were to be converted into community centers that influenced everyone, adults and children. A third difficulty was employment and the need to increase the "use of Indians in their own official and unofficial service." For Indian Office positions, Collier advocated adjusting civil service regulations to encourage broader "Indian self-service, a stead[y] widening [of] tribal and local participation by Indians in the management of their own properties and with administration of their own services."[64] To accomplish these goals, Collier's fourth challenge was to reorganize the department and vest authority "in the Indians themselves."[65]

The commissioner concluded his first report with a statement entitled "Reorienting Indian Land Policy." Continuing his lament of severalty, the commissioner observed, "It is only recently that we have come to fully realize the magnitude of the disaster which the allotment law of 1887 has wrought upon the Indians."[66] While theoretically intended to civilize Native people, and premised on the naïve assumption "that the way to make the Indian a responsible citizen was to forcibly give him private property and extinguish his concern in community property," the law instead was "an instrument to deprive the Indians of their lands." Two-thirds of the Native land base in 1887 (130 million acres reduced to forty-eight million) had been alienated, sold, or opened to homesteading by 1933. The remaining acres were fractionated into dozens and, at times, hundreds of heirs, which, combined with the sale of surplus land, resulted in great difficulty in managing grazing and forest lands or cultivating arable lands. This administrative reality pauperized Natives. As to reorienting land policy, Collier sought reversal of severalty, the purchase of land for the estimated ninety thousand homeless Native people, the reestablishment of tribal ownership of land, the utilization of tribal resources by the Indians themselves, and the cessation of non-Indian exploitation of natural resources. In short, land severalty "had destroyed the economic integrity of the Indian estate and deprived the Indians of normal economic and human activity." In a reflection of Collier's social-work philosophy, he advocated communal ownership and tribal incorporation.[67]

On August 14, 1933, Ickes implemented the first strands of Collier's land policy by supporting his administrative order prohibiting the sale of any allotment, inherited or original, but not before 16,416 acres of original and 22,500 acres of inherited land were sold—the last land sales outside of a few fee-patented parcels sold by tribal members of non-Indian Reorganization Act tribes.[68] In 1933 (1,216 allotments totaling 152,486 acres) and 1934 (48 allotments totaling 1,421 acres) the Indian Office issued its final allotments, which included the exchange of 500 ten-acre allotments on the Gila River Indian Reservation.[69] The same administrative order precluded the issuance of any fee patents, effectively ending further land loss.[70] Collier cancelled 401 fee patents in 1934 and, in 1936, placed 2,454 fee acres back into trust. President Roosevelt extended the trust period on all allotments set to expire in 1933 and 1934.[71]

The crown jewel of Collier's administration was the passage by Congress of the Wheeler-Howard Act, more commonly known as the Indian Reorganization Act.[72] While Collier originally sought to establish self-governing political communities, mandate collective land ownership, and institute special courts of Indian offenses, many American Indians were unwilling to accept such changes. In a series of ten congresses held throughout Indian Country, Collier heard concerns and support from tribal nations.[73] While tribes favored protection of their land, provisions for communal land ownership, absence of a claims forum, silence regarding treaty rights, and limited tribal resource (e.g., water) protection concerned many Native people.[74]

Due to Collier's autonomous political communities, self-determination, cultural pluralism, and reversal of assimilation policies, neither the House nor the Senate Committees on Indian Affairs initially supported the bill.[75] When President Roosevelt pressed Collier to compromise, he offered a series of amendments, the most significant of which were removing mandatory communal land ownership, restricting the authority of tribal governments, eliminating the transfer of all mineral rights to the tribes, allowing tribes to vote on acceptance of the act's provisions, and ensuring that tribal claims were unaffected by the bill.[76] The House and Senate agreed to the amended bill and on June 18, 1934, the Indian Reorganization Act became law.

The Indian Reorganization Act repealed the General Allotment Act, ending land severalty and the sale of land, except that which was sold to the tribe. It restored to tribal ownership all unentered surplus land, provided annual appropriations to purchase land for landless Natives, and included provisions to consolidate lands into viable economic units. As important, the act enabled tribes to organize governments with written constitutions and to adopt corporate charters for economic development. Collier described the act as not only ending "the long, painful, futile effort to speed up the normal rate of Indian assimilation . . . but also endeavor[ing] to provide the means, statutory and financial, to repair as far as possible, the incalculable damage done by the allotment policy and its corollary."[77]

From Collier's perspective, the act would restore the economic and cultural well-being of Native people. The former would be fostered by annual appropriations to purchase land, consolidation of checkerboarded reservations, extension of restrictions against alienation, a revolving credit fund of $10 million, a prohibition on the sale of restricted land, and the ability for Natives to leave or devise their trust or restricted land to any tribal member or the tribe itself.[78] The latter would be fostered by self-government and the reorganization of tribal life. "Through 50 years of 'individualization,'" Collier wrote, "coupled with an ever increasing amount of arbitrary supervision over the affairs of individuals and tribes so long as these individuals and tribes had any assets left, the Indians have been robbed of their initiative, their spirit has been broken, their health undermined, and their Native pride ground into the dust." But economic renewal would not occur unless there was a corresponding effort to rebuild the tribes, and since tribes once managed their own affairs, Collier was confident they could learn to do it again.[79]

The Indian Reorganization Act was a decisive shift in federal policy. But Collier admitted that to accomplish the goal of self-government would require "the active cooperation of the Indians, the utmost of intelligent and wholly sympathetic effort by the Indian Service," and the "assistance of many other governmental and State agencies," including Congress.[80] Because of opposition from Senator Elmer Thomas, the act did not apply to any tribe in Oklahoma. A legislative oversight also excluded Alaska Natives from the act's tribal incorporation provisions.[81] In 1936, Congress extended the provisions of the act to Oklahoma tribes with the passage of the Oklahoma Indian Welfare Act and expanded all of the act's provisions to Alaska Natives with the Alaska Reorganization Act.[82]

The Indian Reorganization Act was permissive, not mandatory, and between October 1934 and June 1935, the Indian Office supported 258 tribal elections on the acceptance (181 tribes) or rejection (77 tribes) of the provisions of the act.[83] The Confederated Tribes of Salish-Kootenai of the Flathead Reservation were the first to adopt a constitution under the act, followed by the Rocky Boy's, Lower Brule, and Fort Belknap Reservations.[84] By 1939, 93 tribes adopted constitutions, excluding 7 Alaska Native villages that organized and drafted constitutions and by-laws.[85]

For tribes accepting its provisions, the act was forthright: "Hereafter no land of any Indian reservation, created or set apart by treaty or agreement with the Indians, Act of Congress, Executive order, purchase, or otherwise, shall be allotted in severalty to any Indian." The federal trust and restrictions on the land were extended "until otherwise directed by Congress." Unsold surplus land was restored to tribal ownership, and Congress authorized appropriations of $2 million annually to purchase land for landless Indians. But the act was more than protection or restoration of land; it concentrated on efficient development, utilization, and conservation of tribal natural resources, with a $10 million revolving credit fund established to assist chartered tribes in engaging in private economic development.[86]

Collier's Indian Office also reinforced tribal sovereignty within the framework of limited self-government espoused by Chief Justice John Marshall in the early nineteenth-century Cherokee Nation cases. "Each tribe should have the right to exercise all of its inherent powers," Collier stated.[87] To this end, solicitor Nathan Margold instructed attorney Felix Cohen to analyze and assemble federal laws and treaties affecting tribal nations. Cohen and his colleague, Theodore Haas, accumulated forty-six volumes of laws and treaties. In 1939, Cohen was promoted to special assistant to the Attorney General and directed an "Indian Law Survey," resulting in the 1942 publication of the *Handbook of Federal–Indian Law*. His handbook focused on all aspects of federal-Indian law and emphasized the inherent authorities and rights of tribal nations, following Collier's assertion that tribes possessed "all powers of a sovereign State except those which have been specifically taken away from it either by treaty or act of Congress."[88]

Indian Office attorneys drafted many of the constitutions and bylaws of the tribes voting to accept the Indian Reorganization Act, allowing only limited tribal autonomy. Adoption of constitutions remained subject to secretarial approval, meaning many constitutions were modeled on the United States Constitution, rather than on tribal customs, and all included a list of tribal actions requiring secretarial approval. A number of tribes—Eastern Cherokee, Menominee, Red Lake Chippewa, and Standing Rock Sioux—adopted the act but operated under existing constitutions.[89] Fourteen tribes rejected the act but had constitutions in place, including the Colville, Hoopa Valley, Fort Peck, Fort Totten, Grande-Ronde, Klamath, Agua Caliente, Navajo, Seneca (Allegheny), Nez Perce, Sisseton-Wahpeton, Chehalis, Turtle Mountain, and Wind River Reservations.[90]

While acceptance of the act proved to be beneficial to tribes, it ushered in challenges that were hinted at in the Meriam Report when it noted that some Natives "favored abolition of wardship" while others were "more attached to their lands and homes."[91] Blood quantum created discordance between groups, and with the establishment of tribal governments, this intertribal factionalism "burst forth rather vociferously."[92] While not new, chartered government pointed to deep divisions among some tribes, fueling the assertion of the critics that self-government was a failure.

Collier unapologetically reoriented policy based on "organization and a fuller use of land."[93] If land matters were not solved, he hyperbolized, Natives would "go down to extinction."[94] Consequently, his singular objective was to modify policy by providing opportunities for people "to secure a livelihood through the use of reservation resources."[95] This guiding principle found expression in the strands of land acquisition and consolidation, extension of credit, soil and resource conservation, and education.

The Indian Office used the Pueblo Land Consolidation Act to purchase land for the New Mexico Pueblos.[96] Collier also consolidated checkerboarded reservations, such as Fort Mohave, where non-trust land was exchanged with trust land to create viable economic farming units.[97] While the Indian Reorganization Act authorized $10 million for land purchases, by 1940 Congress had appropriated less than $4 million, limiting the effectiveness of the program.[98] Nonetheless, using existing authorities and new legislation approved by Congress in 1934, Collier added nearly 1,000,000 acres to the Navajo Reservation.[99] Twelve tribes expended $177,000 of their own funds in 1945 to buy back 63,000 acres, with the Southern Ute spending $83,000 to purchase 40,546 acres, the largest single purchase outside of the Navajo. Ten additional tribes requested permission to use $250,000 of their own funds to purchase fractionated heirship lands.[100] In 1939, the Indian Office restored 631,887 acres of surplus land to the Wind River Reservation.[101] The Interior

Table 7.4. Changes in Acres Grazed by Select Indian Tribes, 1934–1936

Tribe	1934 Tribal Acres Grazed	1936 Tribal Acres Grazed	Percentage Change
Blackfeet	44,926	324,531	622%
Crow	62,343	142,334	128%
Fort Belknap	177,788	285,250	60%
Fort Berthold	173,102	285,325	65%
Fort Hall	80,000	171,900	115%
Fort Peck	80,550	102,510	27%
Klamath	502,411	544,306	8%
San Carlos	1,088,330	1,422,519	31%
Wind River	244,138	536,531	120%
Standing Rock	75,231	110,568	47%
Yakima	190,050	310,269	63%
Total	2,718,869	4,236,043	56%

Source: *Annual Report of the Commissioner of Indian Affairs*, 1937, 213.

Department also established reservations in Alaska, including Akutan (72,000 acres), Karluk (32,000 acres), Venetie (1,408,000 acres), Shishmaref (3,000 acres), and Wales (21,000 acres). Proposals for sixteen additional reservations in Alaska totaled 3,729,420 acres.[102]

Using nearly $100 million in New Deal funding (mostly Civilian Conservation Corps-Indian Division appropriations), Collier hired tens of thousands of American Indians to improve grazing and forest lands, and construct fire lookouts, access trails, roadside clearings, and fire breaks. To stem erosion, CCC-Indian Division funding enabled tribes to construct check dams, fences, and reservoirs, as well as to implement rodent control measures and remove noxious plants.[103] To improve range conditions, the department deployed new management objectives, eliminated undesirable stock, and reduced animal units grazing on tribal lands.[104] Collier singled out three reservations for stock reduction: Navajo, Hopi, and Papago. He also established cooperative relationships with the USDA Soil Conservation Service to improve soil conditions for agricultural lands, with the first efforts focused in the Southwest on the Gila River, Hualapai, Havasupai, Jicarilla, and Uintah-Ouray Reservations.[105]

As non-Indian leases expired, tribes increased their acres under grazing ventures by 56 percent, as shown in Table 7.4. Putting tribal lands to use was a principle goal of Collier's, chiefly due to allotted land being so fractionated.[106] The "tangled and complicated" ownership status of allotted trust land tended to lead the Indian Office to lease such land to non-Indians or allow it to lie fallow, with the Indian Office admitting for the first time in 1937 that the legal and administrative challenges of fractionated lands caused Native people and the Indian Office alike to "throw up their hands in despair."[107] A number of tribes, including the Rosebud Sioux via its Tribal Land Enterprise, used their corporate status to purchase fractionated interests.[108] The Indian Office in 1938 also secured passage by Congress of the Omnibus Leasing Act, which authorized tribes, with secretarial approval, to lease tribal lands for oil and gas mining purposes.[109]

Table 7.5. Indian Hospital Utilization Rates and Congressional Appropriations, 1929–1933

Year	Patients	Hospital Days	Percent Utilization	Medical Appropriations
1929	37,511	677,241	59.5%	$1,440,000
1930	38,536	768,160	56.9%	$2,993,000
1931	40,189	869,625	62.5%	$3,426,000
1932	45,086	1,003,311	68.8%	$4,227,500
1933	50,376	1,077,948	72.4%	$3,213,000

Source: *Annual Report of the Commissioner of Indian Affairs*, 1933, 84.

Collier championed a second legislative act in 1934: the Johnson-O'Malley Act.[110] The Indian Office also advocated state and local involvement for educational, medical, and social services, with Collier positing that: "Through many administrations the Office of Indian Affairs monopolized the Indians. What services it could not render them were not rendered at all."[111] While the Indian Office developed cooperative relationships with the Public Health Service, the Department of Agriculture's Soil Conservation Service, the Forest Service, and others, these were federal agencies. And while the department contracted with local public schools since the 1890s, such services were largely confined to education.

After release of the Meriam Report, a number of states—including California, Washington, Wisconsin, and Minnesota—exhibited a strong interest in increasing services to Natives, especially those that had public health implications. Minnesota, for instance, expressed a willingness to admit and treat tubercular patients at the state sanitarium at Ah-Gwah-Ching, and multiple California counties exhibited interest in providing similar services.[112] The impetus for state involvement—with federal subsidies—was also driven by Collier's attempt to end the monopoly of the Indian Service by engaging states in social services, particularly in areas where Natives were largely integrated or resided in areas where states could readily provide such services.[113] Collier made explicit that the Johnson-O'Malley Act was not predicated on state assumption of services for tribes that were still tribal in nature.

Utilizing state and local services was aided by increased Native hospital and medical service demands at a time of plateauing or decreasing appropriations, as illustrated in Table 7.5. With the passage of the Johnson-O'Malley Act, the Indian Office executed contracts for medical services with the state of North Carolina to organize a health district for the Eastern Cherokee and with the state of Florida to provide public health nursing among the Seminole.[114] Two years later, Congress amended the Johnson-O'Malley Act to include contracts with subdivisions of the states and territories, including universities, colleges, private corporations, agencies or institutions for the education, medical, agricultural assistance, and social welfare of the Indians.[115]

The Indian Office devoted no small effort to addressing the twin scourges of trachoma and tuberculosis. Decreasing medical appropriations were partially offset by 217 detailed medical professionals from the Public Health Service, with the overextension of nurses challenging the delivery of services. In 1934, sixty-seven nurses were hired even as seventy-one severed employment due to being overworked and underpaid.[116] Collier worked to train more Native nurses and also sought outside medical assistance, soliciting expertise from the University of Pennsylvania's Phipps Institute (tuberculosis), Columbia University (trachoma), Yale University (rheumatism), and Harvard University (venereal disease). Indian Office physicians led by Dr. Fred Loe conducted research at the Rosebud and Fort Apache Reservations between 1937 and 1941, demonstrating that sulfanilamide was an effective treatment for trachoma.[117] By 1943, the Native incidence rate dropped from 30 to 5 percent.[118] As for tuberculosis, the development of the Bacillus Calmette Guerin (BCG) vaccine provided relief to thousands of Indians.[119]

The Johnson-O'Malley Act also made it possible for the Indian Office to streamline contracts for educational services that heretofore had been provided through more than a thousand contracts with local school districts. California (1934) and Washington (1935) led the way by largely assuming educational services from the federal government, with Minnesota (1937) and Arizona (1938) following suit. In Washington, all government schools were turned over to the state.[120] Collier's educational philosophy was summed up in his conviction that tribal life had value, so it was not surprising that he focused policy on community schools.[121] He continued the closure of boarding schools initiated by Rhoads, shuttering or converting into day schools ten in his first year in office, with boarding school attendance declining from twenty-two thousand to thirteen thousand between 1932 and 1934.[122] The Indian Office revised its regulations allowing children to attend such schools only if they could not find suitable facilities near them, were homeless, or had no other access to educational services.[123]

As part of his effort to decrease the federal footprint, Collier reduced the capacity of the industrial boarding schools, with Sherman reduced from 1,000 to 650 students; Phoenix from 725 to 500; Haskell from 900 to 600; Albuquerque from 850 to 650; and Chilocco from 900 to 650. Attenuating capacity was "an essential first step that had to be taken before reconstruction of the Indian educational program in terms of basic Indian needs could go forward."[124] In place of boarding facilities, the Indian Office constructed scores of day schools using New Deal funding (Public Works Administration), with thirty-seven day schools constructed on the Navajo Reservation by 1937. By 1940, the Indian Office had constructed eighty new day schools.[125] Collier assigned social workers to each of the schools to aid in the "economic rehabilitation" and "organization of Indians for self-maintenance and self-direction," adding to his social engineering.[126] Willard Beatty, Director of Indian Education, modified the school curriculum, implemented cross-cultural education, and hired and trained more Native teachers.[127] "Ultimately, and the sooner the better, Indians should be the teachers and the local administrators of the schools," Collier waxed, particularly in the day schools.[128] To this end, the department expedited teacher training for Natives to return to the schools from which they had graduated and provided federal loans to those attending vocational or trade schools.

Collier further encouraged Congress to enact into law the Indian Arts and Crafts Act, which promoted and protected tribal artisans by certifying genuine Native arts and crafts, aiding them in marketing and licensing their products, stimulating quality production by organizing artisans, and helping them develop business relations.[129] Ickes directed the National Park Service to sell only genuine Indian arts and crafts. While Congress failed to act on a religious freedom bill, it did approve of an act repealing twelve sections of the U.S. Code that restricted civil liberties in Indian Country.[130] In the absence of freedom of conscience legislation, Collier issued two circulars in 1934 requiring all employees and school staff to provide the "fullest constitutional liberty" in all matters affecting religion, conscience, and culture. A second circular issued twelve days later mandated all employees at day and boarding schools to cease interference "with Indian religious life or expansion" and prohibited compulsory religious worship.[131]

Collier made cancellation of reimbursable debts central to his natural resource policy and, with the advent of World War II, the Indian Office encouraged increased agricultural production, with Collier advocating $50 million in irrigation investments.[132] He also made employment in the Indian Office a staple of his administration, with the Indian Reorganization Act providing for Indian preference to qualified candidates. Of the 5,463 employees in 1935, 2,037 were Natives (37 percent).[133] To ensure preference, the Indian Reorganization Act defined as Indian "all persons of Indian descent who are members of any recognized Indian tribe now under federal jurisdiction; and all persons who are descendants of such members who were, on June 1, 1934, residing within the present boundaries of any Indian reservation." The act, moreover, defined as a Native anyone "of one-half or more Indian blood," and for the first time classified Alaska Natives legally as "Indians."[134] By 1944, nearly two-thirds of Indian Office employees were American Indians or Alaska Natives.[135]

With the onset of the war, tens of thousands of Native people left their reservations to join the military, the war effort, or wartime industries.[136] In 1941, Collier devoted the first nine pages of his annual report to Natives and war defense preparation.[137] In the years prior to the commencement of American involvement in the war, Collier explained that most government school graduates returned to their reservation rather than pursing a vocational or industrial pursuit, driving policy in the early years of his administration to make available "every possible opportunity to secure a livelihood through the use of reservation resources." This aspect of policy manifested itself in land acquisition and consolidation, credit, soil conservation, natural resources development, and "other activities designed to conserve, enlarge, and properly use the natural resources of the Indians."[138] By 1942, over 7,500 men served in the armed forces and, by 1944, there were 21,756 in the armed services.[139] Of the 75,000 Natives participating in the CCC-Indian Division, roughly 9 percent (6,500) served in the military, with thousands more leaving the reservations to gain employment in wartime industries.[140]

Collier believed the "great exodus of Indians" was due to additional employment opportunities, resulting in many Native people continuing "to work away from the reservations." If postwar economic conditions did not enable them to remain employed, Collier noted in 1943, Indian Office technical experts would assist tribes in "intensif[ing] their plans for the fullest use of reservation resources."[141] Between 1939 and 1942, tribal growers increased their agricultural production by 150,000 acres to meet wartime exigencies, with more land going into production each year.[142] Against the wishes of the tribes involved, the Indian Office and the War Relocation Authority agreed in 1942 to establish relocation camps for Japanese evacuees on the Colorado River and Gila River Reservations, with the goal of encouraging Japanese agricultural production to stimulate Native production.[143]

By the late 1930s, Collier faced growing opposition, with Montana senator Burton Wheeler threatening to repeal the Indian Reorganization Act he had just a few years earlier sponsored. Wheeler and the critics argued Collier used the "same old tactics of controlling Indian councils."[144] The American Indian Federation went so far as to accuse Collier of being a communist for his support of ending allotment and restoring communal tribal control over reservation lands. The Navajo Tribe castigated Collier for his support of the unpopular stock reduction program.[145] Collier's Indian Office now included eighty-nine field offices governed by sixty-four superintendents, with the central office consisting of seventeen divisions and nine assistants to the commissioner. Congress, once supportive of the commissioner, now opposed him, with many politicians concluding there was no more self-government in 1944 than there had been ten years earlier. Some, such as Oklahoma's Elmer Thomas, called for an immediate "[r]elease [of] Indian property from Federal trust" and abolition of the Indian Office.[146] Moreover, an increasingly conservative Congress opposed Collier's education policy. The goal of education, a House investigating committee chaired by Representative Karl E. Mundt (R-SD) reported, "should be to make the Indian child a better American rather than to equip him simply to be a better Indian."[147]

Collier's loss of influence was in part attributed to the relocation of the Indian Office to Chicago during the war to make way for wartime activities in Washington, D.C. Outside the sphere of influence and with growing opposition to his leadership—including Representative Jed Johnson (D-OK) who, as chairman of the House Appropriations Subcommittee on Interior Appropriations, announced Indian Office funding would be reduced in 1946 if Collier remained as commissioner. Collier submitted his resignation on January 10, 1945, informing President Roosevelt that relocation to Chicago and decreased appropriations resulted in "insurmountable difficulties."[148] Roosevelt accepted Collier's resignation on January 22, and he left office on March 5, having markedly redirected Indian affairs.

COMMISSIONER WILLIAM A. BROPHY

Between 1943 and 1944, Congress shifted the strands of policy from self-governance. In a report supplementing its 1943 sentiments at the end of its fifteen-year investigation of Indian affairs, the Senate altered its position away from self-governance to withdrawal of federal trusteeship. When Collier resigned, the Senate initiated hearings on his replacement, William A. Brophy. In hearings held in late February 1945, the Senate Committee on Indian Affairs sought answers to two questions. First, was Brophy, as Collier's choice to head the Indian Office, committed to furthering Collier's policies? And second, would Brophy enforce the policies enumerated by Congress? Brophy publically accepted the policies set down by Congress, agreeing to implement, not make, policy.[149]

Born in New York, Brophy was an attorney from New Mexico who had worked on Pueblo land issues between 1934 and 1942, believing protection of tribal rights was fundamentally a federal responsibility. His selection as commissioner was not without controversy, including concerns from the New Mexico Pueblos stemming in large measure from his wife, Sophie Aberle, whose actions as superintendent of the United Pueblo Agency were at times contrary to the wishes of the Pueblo tribes.[150] The Pueblos were further concerned that Brophy might restore paternalistic policies that would set back tribal affairs.[151] Some in Congress, such as Representative George Schwabe (R-OK), argued it was time for an American Indian to serve as commissioner of Indian affairs.[152] Nonetheless, on March 6, 1945, William A. Brophy was confirmed as commissioner and took office.

Brophy was not cut from the same cloth as Collier and, while he worked to stem the growing sentiment of termination and withdrawal of federal services, he accepted the policy as a long-range goal and labored to ensure that tribes were ready when it was deployed. In his first annual report he outlined his primary objective: aid Native people in becoming economically independent.[153] Native lands, he noted, "were insufficient in quantity and quality to enable the Indian owners to derive from them a livelihood comparable to that of their rural white neighbors."[154] Poverty was due to land severalty and the alienation of "their best lands," and they lacked the "experience, equipment, and capital" necessary to make productive use of their remaining lands. If the goal was for the United States to withdraw as trustee and eliminate federal services, the only means by which tribal nations could provide for themselves was "through the development of [their] resources to maximize productivity." The execution of this policy strand had to be accomplished without "throwing an undue burden on States and counties."[155]

More fundamentally, Brophy argued, the United States had an obligation to assist Native people to develop their resources, raise their standard of living, improve their health, and prepare for the withdrawal of federal services and responsibility. Developing resources included improving the breed of livestock, increasing irrigated and dry-land agriculture, making use of timber resources, and maximizing mineral lands—and all without the tribes simply providing raw goods and seeing others enriched at their expense.

Brophy believed that it would be an injustice for Congress to simply exercise its plenary authority—and it would be economically disastrous to tribes to capriciously withdraw services. Aided by Assistant Commissioner William Zimmerman, Brophy outlined a process by which the United States might withdraw as trustee of land and resources, recommending the Indian Office analyze the status of each tribe and determine which were largely integrated, as measured by adoption of "white habits and acceptance of the Indians by the white community." Then the Indian Office would need to determine the economic condition of the tribes and consider the reasonableness of the Natives making a living off their resources. Moreover, the department would need to consider the willingness of the tribes to accept federal withdrawal; and it was critical to understand the ability and secure the affirmation of the states and local counties to provide such services.[156] It was immaterial if this process was not the most prudent, Brophy explained, since Congress had already resolved to throw the Indians "upon their own resources" and remove restrictions on the land "regardless of their readiness for such a move."[157]

In the interim, the commissioner continued the land acquisition and consolidation policy. In 1945, the Indian Office restored 157,000 acres of opened surplus lands to the Red Lake

Chippewa in northern Minnesota and added an additional 12,767 acres of unentered opened land to the Wind River Shoshoni in Wyoming.[158] In addition, tribes continued purchasing land using their own funds, with the Rosebud Sioux purchasing and restoring 21,000 acres of allotted and inherited land to tribal ownership. Allottees on the Cheyenne River Sioux Reservation turned over 521 allotments and 246 undivided heirship allotments to the tribal government in exchange for land assignments.[159] In 1946, 236,790 acres of land opened for homesteading within the Uintah-Ouray Reservation was restored to the Ute Tribe. By the end of that same year, the Cheyenne River Sioux conveyed nearly 300,000 acres—including 336 full allotments and 325 partial allotments totaling 120,000 acres in 1946 alone—to tribal ownership.[160]

Paradoxically, the Indian Office issued two hundred fee patents for thirty-five thousand acres in 1946 and twenty thousand acres of fee lands were sold, in part, Brophy noted, because some Natives desired to sell their land due to postwar land-value inflation.[161] The following year, forty-six bills were introduced into Congress directing the secretary of the interior to sell submarginal lands that the Collier administration had purchased on behalf of the tribes. Moreover, four bills called for the removal of all restrictions on Indian land, and, in the closing hours of the seventy-ninth Congress, nine bills were introduced to emancipate select tribes, including all Native people in New York and California, by liquidating tribal land and assets and distributing them per capita.[162]

Congress was aided by twenty-five thousand returned war veterans who stimulated progress by serving in tribal leadership and providing an infusion of progressive thinking.[163] These veterans—especially in Arizona and New Mexico, states that proscribed suffrage—objected to denial of civil rights.[164] The war, Brophy explained, brought new opportunities and raised the standard of living for many Natives.[165] The commissioner surmised there could be a postwar drift off reservations, with new opportunities developing for Natives. While some tribes readily adapted—such as the Prairie Pottawatomie—Brophy acknowledged there was and could be "no fixed pattern" of migration and integration in the postwar world.[166]

Brophy was quite progressive in his commitment to addressing social and resource issues on a tribe-by-tribe basis rather than applying a one-size-fits-all policy that historically governed Indian affairs. The most important matter of 1947 was the consideration by Congress of a Navajo-Hopi rehabilitation bill, "the first time that a plan for a specific Indian area has reached the stage of Congressional consideration."[167] Acting Commissioner Zimmerman, who took over for Brophy in June 1948 and finalized that year's annual report, explained the importance of the bill was to "determine whether our national Indian policy in the future is to be based on division of the total problem of human adjustment and resource utilization into parcels of a size that can be measured and dealt with on a time schedule."[168]

The concept of enacting policies specific to tribal nations was novel, although the Meriam Report had advocated such a framework twenty years earlier when it noted "the most fundamental step that can be taken is to work out for each jurisdiction [the advancement of] the economic and social conditions of the Indians with due regard to the economic resources of that jurisdiction."[169] The Indian Office considered this framework in 1936, when Collier instituted the

Technical Cooperation-BIA in conjunction with the USDA Soil Conservation Service to conduct soil analyses of tribal lands.[170] But this was unofficial policy and Congress did not consider it as a national policy until 1948.

In April of that same year, Brophy issued instructions to field staff to proceed with a limited number of tribal jurisdictions to begin planning discrete activities. Select tribes were divided into three categories, with the first for those who had progressed "in the use of their resources and [in] adapting themselves to capitalistic society." This included the Klamath Tribe and most of the tribes in California and Minnesota. A second category was for tribes in "an intermediate state" of resource development and included the Standing Rock Sioux and the Three Affiliated Tribes of Fort Berthold as two examples. A third category was for tribes "in need of major rehabilitation," such as the Papago and Turtle Mountain Chippewa.[171] The overall policy was resource development, a strand driven by the belief that such utilization could not be "attacked as a mass problem" as it was "too unwieldy and [had] too many coordinate elements of time and materials." The Indian Office had to particularize the challenges facing each tribe.[172]

The crown jewel for Brophy was the passage by Congress of the Indian Claims Commission in 1946.[173] Brophy proposed reforming how claims against the United States would be handled and in the fall of 1945 his ideas caught the attention of the House of Representatives and it entertained H.R. 237, which purported to establish a "Congressional committee to study the claims of Indian tribes."[174] The bill floundered and not until Representative Henry M. Jackson (D-WA) introduced a proposal in October for an Indian Claims Commission did reform gain traction.[175] Brophy supported the Jackson bill, believing that compensation tribes might receive from judgments against the United States would free them from federal dependency as they invested the money in land and resource development. Not until July 1946, however, did the Senate support the bill, and only after Joseph O'Mahoney (D-WY) submitted a report to the Senate Committee on Indian Affairs outlining the details of how the commission would work. O'Mahoney recommended that a commission made up of three men appointed by the president, with the advice and consent of the Senate, should have the power to call witnesses and engage in fact-finding measures. Tribes would have five years to submit claims and the commission would have an additional five years to complete the study and make awards.[176]

On August 13, 1946, President Truman signed into law the Indian Claims Commission Act. He was "glad to sign [his] name to a measure which removes a lingering discrimination against our first Americans and gives them the same opportunities that our laws extend to all other American citizens."[177] The Indian Claims Commission was a reform encouraging assimilation of Natives and was premised on the assumption that spending money today would save it in the future. Like other reforms, the Meriam Report had recommended such a commission to remove impediments to the ultimate assimilation of Native people. The act was a de facto precursor to terminating the federal-Indian relationship.[178]

Brophy did not always agree with Collier's handling of business, specifically opposing Collier's bureaucratic structure, and determined to simplify departmental administration. To deploy this policy objective, Congress authorized the reorganization of the Indian Office, creating five regional offices in Portland, Minneapolis, Phoenix, Oklahoma City, and Billings.[179] It also enacted legislation empowering the secretary of the interior to delegate authorities and duties to the commissioner and regional offices.[180] Secretary Julius A. Krug, on September 9, 1946, delegated to Brophy final authority on matters of health and welfare, finances, education, land and minerals, irrigation, forestry, and grazing. Five days later, Brophy in turn delegated these same authorities to regional staff or agency superintendents, subject to a right of appeal to the commissioner or secretary.[181]

Brophy further discharged responsibilities and simplified administration through a series of memorandum in 1947. On May 26, he authorized tribal corporations and enterprises to transfer their financial accounts from federal agencies to local banks, and Secretary Krug delegated to the commissioner authority to approve of tribal ordinances and resolutions. On June 15, the Indian Office authorized local superintendents to close out all individual Indian money accounts having less than $100 and, if the individual was capable of managing his own money, for accounts up to $500. On July 1, Krug amended long-standing practices by authorizing Natives to negotiate their own farming and grazing leases with payment made directly to the landowner.[182]

The remainder of Brophy's administration focused on improving infrastructure, although without much success. In 1946, he sought $50 million in capital improvements for 18,000 miles of roads in Indian Country in order to complete an efficient transportation system.[183] He further requested $93 million for irrigation facilities to serve 1,650,000 acres of irrigable tribal land.[184] Where appropriate, he also advocated development of the timber industry beyond the Menominee, Navajo, Chippewa, and Apache Tribes.[185] Equipping Native people with the necessary tools to make full use of their natural resources was instrumental if Congress were to terminate the federal trust relationship.

Before severing this relationship, Brophy encouraged all efforts to improve healthcare. In line with his policy of tribal-specific activities, he invited the American Medical Association to establish volunteer medical teams to visit the Navajo Tribe and Alaska Natives, where the tuberculosis incidence rates remained high. Such teams could better diagnose health maladies so that the Indian Medical Service might better understand the complexities of the issues and seek the fiscal and human resources needed to address the issues on a tribal-specific basis.[186]

Brophy also continued the community school model, viewing such institutions as "the heart of the community." At community schools, the entire tribe might learn, shaping economic and social life.[187] Despite the advancements of the previous two decades, there remained an educational crisis in Navajo country, where twenty thousand children lacked educational facilities. While the Papago Tribe also faced a shortage of facilities, the Navajo situation was acute, with the Navajo Tribal Council demanding the United States fulfill its treaty obligation to provide a school and teacher for every thirty children.[188]

In the days before Brophy left office, he lamented the policy being pursued by Congress of freeing Native land from its trust status. "Every advance made in the last 15 years is threatened," he argued to no avail.[189] As Congress progressed with terminating the federal trust and withdrawing services, the commissioner reminded the president that the United States had a legal obligation to protect Native property rights. Removing land from trust would remove the last important treaty guarantee and would be economically and socially disruptive.[190] But Brophy contracted pneumonia and tuberculosis while touring Alaska Native communities early in 1947 and had limited involvement and influence from that time forward, with the responsibility for leading the Indian Office falling to Assistant Commissioner William Zimmerman. Brophy never fully recovered and submitted his resignation to President Truman on December 31, 1947. Before leaving office, he urged Secretary Krug to continue the "policy of preserving Indian resources, of assuring the people the right to live ... in their own way." Brophy left office on June 3, 1948.[191]

Zimmerman served as acting commissioner for much of Brophy's final year and then remained for ten months after the commissioner left office. With Brophy ill, subordinates within the department supported the braids of rapid integration and termination. When Congress requested the Indian Office to draft a plan for termination, the responsibility devolved to Zimmerman, who testified before the Senate Civil Service Committee on February 8, 1947, identifying a process for withdrawing federal services. The "Zimmerman Plan," as it came to be known, identified specific tribes and their perceived readiness for withdrawal of federal supervision, with Zimmerman classifying tribes into three groups: those for which federal services could be ended immediately; those requiring a ten-year transition period; and those needing more than ten years for withdrawal of services.

The withdrawal of federal support was also advanced by former president Herbert Hoover, who chaired the "Hoover Commission on the Organization of the Executive Branch of the Government." The commission advocated assimilation as the "dominant goal of public policy."[192] The only questions the commission contemplated were: "What kind of assimilation and how fast?"[193] Nothing short of complete integration of the Natives was acceptable, with all social programs to be transferred to the states. Tribal self-government had become a strand in the braid of withdrawing federal services and trust responsibilities, and integrating Natives and giving them control over their own land.[194] In May 1948, Zimmerman deployed a comprehensive mechanism culminating in the "eventual discharge of the Federal government's obligation, legal and moral, and otherwise, and the discontinuance of Federal supervision and control."[195]

CONCLUSION

Throughout Zimmerman's tenure as acting commissioner, the Indian Office worked closely with Congress to establish a process that culminated in withdrawal of federal services and trusteeship. The national legislature was one step closer to a dramatic shift in federal policy, with the postwar years marked by significant budget cuts. By 1948, the Indian Office was "defending a failing position" and was impotent to stop the march towards termination. The economic boom in the late 1940s resulted in pressure on Congress to remove restrictions on Native property, with the Indian Office providing "an almost ideal experimental laboratory for cost-cutting and decentralization of government."[196]

Zimmerman's role as acting commissioner ended on March 10, 1949, when President Truman nominated John R. Nichols—a member of the Hoover Commission—as commissioner of Indian affairs. The Indian New Deal was at an end, and with it came a lapse in self-government. Federal-Indian policy paradoxically had shifted from self-government as a means of restoration and economic development to a vehicle of ending federal support and responsibility for Indian affairs. The Hoover Commission Report, much like the Meriam Report twenty years earlier, signaled another generational shift in policy. President Truman's Fair Deal and an increasingly conservative Congress indicated change was imminent.

8

"MEN, MONEY, AND MANAGEMENT"

Termination and Relocation, 1948–1961

With the end of World War II, a wave of nationalism swept the country, curtailing tribal self-government. While William Brophy stemmed the tide of terminating the federal trust relationship, he was powerless to stop it. By 1949 the congressional-led policy strands of termination and relocation gained important allies. While assimilation and the end of the legal relationship with tribal nations were long-standing policy goals, the passage of the Indian Citizenship Act in 1924 removed—for some politicians anyway—the remaining obstacles to terminating the federal-Indian relationship. While several states, including Arizona and New Mexico, denied suffrage to Native people, state supreme court decisions in 1948 and 1949 brought down this barrier, as well.[1] By 1949 all Natives were citizens of the United States and the state in which they resided and termination commenced. Between 1949 and 1961, three men served as commissioner of Indian affairs and advanced termination: John Nichols (1949–1950), Dillon Myer (1950–1953), and Glenn Emmons (1953–1961).

COMMISSIONER JOHN R. NICHOLS

President Truman nominated John Ralph Nichols to replace Brophy as commissioner on March 10, 1949.[2] As with Brophy before him, Nichols's nomination was met with opposition, both in Congress and across Indian Country. Senator William Langer (R-ND) of the Committee on Indian Affairs was especially critical of Nichols, stating that during Brophy's confirmation hearing three years earlier he had been promised that the next commissioner would "have some Indian blood in him."[3] Nichols took office in April 1949, despite having not been confirmed by

Table 8.1. Heads of the Indian Office and Major Policies, 1949–1961

Name	Title	Years of Service	Main Policies
John R. Nichols (D)	Commissioner	1.2 years (1949–1950)	Termination, economic rehabilitation of tribal economies, education, and develop and manage resources
Dillon S. Myer (D)	Commissioner	2.9 years (1950–1953)	Rapid termination, transfer BIA services to state and local agencies, public schools, decentralize BIA headquarters, IIM accounts freed from federal oversight, joint use hospitals, relocation
Glenn L. Emmons (R)	Commissioner	7.5 years (1953–1961)	HCR 108, termination acts, Pub. L. No. 280, Pub L. No. 277 (repeal liquor prohibition), McCarran Amendment, Indian Health Transfer Act, relocation, adoption to non-Indians, economic development

the Senate, and he immediately announced plans for termination.[4] When Assistant Secretary Bill Warne met with the Association of American Indian Affairs, he explained that Indian Country needed less traditional leaders who would follow the government's plan for them. "What we need most is knowledge which will enable us to awaken in our Indian fellow citizens a desire to move away from the past of their fathers to the future we have arranged for every youngster."[5] A month later, Nichols addressed the same forum, explaining that one day tribal designations and treaty rights would be a vestige of the past.[6]

Nichols had served as one of four men to draft the Hoover Commission's report on Indian affairs, concluding that integration was the only braid the federal government could adopt. In his only annual report, he quoted extensively from the Hoover Report, writing: "It is not the intention of the Federal Government to continue in the role of trustee of the Indians' property." "The role," he reasoned, "was not assumed arbitrarily but devolved upon the United States out of historic antecedents."[7] Quoting from Thomas Jefferson a century and a half earlier, Nichols summed up his views: "The ultimate point of rest and happiness for the [Indians] is to let our settlements and theirs meet and blend together, to intermix and become one people."[8]

From Nichols's perspective, the federal trust responsibility evolved out of specific treaty obligations "in which the tribe requested protection for its members and its property." Such a policy, "if pursued without regard to the welfare of the persons protected, can defeat its purpose."[9] The goal was to develop Native resources and property to their fullest and then encourage Native people "to accept responsibility for management." This was the vehicle by which the federal government, "within a reasonable time, [may] withdraw entirely from its historic role and turn over its trusteeship to a trained and responsible Indian people."[10]

Nichols suggested an expenditure of $150 million was necessary to fit Natives "into the economic and social structure of the country."[11] A federal investment in resource development was essential if tribal citizens were to make "full use of their soil and water resources on a sustained yield basis."[12] Past expenditures were not based on "any long-term plans for the orderly solving of the problem," Nichols argued, but were "sporadic, discontinuous, and generally insufficient."[13] What was needed to solve the challenge was "men, money, and management," which would facilitate the braid of "complete integration" on a gradual and carefully planned basis of self-sufficiency.[14]

Congress, Nichols surmised, had only recently been apprised of the depth of need, and on December 19, 1947, Congress directed the department to submit recommendations for a long-term program for Navajo and Hopi rehabilitation. This admonition resulted in an appropriation of $88,570,000 over ten years to prepare the two tribes for release from federal administration. A similar $24,000,000 plan for the Papago Tribe in southern Arizona was solicited, followed by a series of bills introduced into Congress to rehabilitate the Standing Rock ($10,000,000), Sisseton-Wahpeton ($1,000,000), Fort Berthold ($5,500,000), Chippewa-Cree and Rocky Boys ($3,510,000), Devil's Lake ($2,000,000), and Blackfeet ($2,000,000) Reservations.[15] When tribes were ready for emancipation, Nichols encouraged Secretary Oscar Chapman to release them from supervision, with the Stockbridge-Munsee and the Saginaw Chippewa immediately exempt from most vestiges of federal superintendence.[16]

Nichols did not support releasing land from federal oversight, arguing for a discontinuance of issuing fee patents and removing of restrictions.[17] Moreover, he requested $25 million from Congress to acquire land for resale to Natives "on a long-term payment basis." He then restored 818,000 acres to the Colville Reservation and facilitated the trust status of 609,713 acres in New Mexico for the Pueblo tribes and the Cañoncito Navajo.[18] Nonetheless, the Indian Office issued 871 fee patents totaling 146,655 acres, authorized the sale of more than 10,000 acres, and lifted restrictions on 75,000 acres among the Five Tribes in Oklahoma.[19]

Nichols's educational policy was unchanged from Brophy's, although he lamented the 19,300 children without schools, 15,000 of whom were Navajo.[20] In order to make productive use of land and resources, Natives had to be educated. Education was the fulcrum of any plan for rehabilitation and termination.[21] The commissioner focused on assisting tribes to develop their resources and become self-sufficient, which in turn would prepare them for termination. This sentiment governed what limited influence Nichols had on federal policy before President Truman, on March 22, 1950, unexpectedly announced that Dillion S. Myer would replace Nichols. A surprised Nichols submitted his resignation a day later and was reassigned as a special assistant to the secretary of the interior to supervise the transfer of Pacific trust possessions from the Navy to the Interior Department, formally leaving the bureau May 4.

COMMISSIONER DILLON S. MYER

With Truman's surprise nomination of Dillon Seymour Myer as commissioner, the president manifested his intention to rapidly end the federal-Indian relationship under his Fair Deal.[22] Myer accepted the nomination on the condition that the president support increased appropriations so that the bureau could prepare Indian Country for a drastic change—getting the Indian Office "out of business as quickly as possible." He also demanded a free hand in administering the department.[23] Prior to his nomination as head of the newly renamed Bureau of Indian Affairs, Myer had served as director of the War Relocation Authority (1942–1946), where he executed the government's policy of Japanese internment. Interior Secretary Oscar Chapman supported Myer, believing his work of enforcing Japanese relocation and internment qualified him for the work of commissioner of Indian affairs.

Myer was sworn in on May 5, 1950, and immediately replaced the upper management of the bureau, bringing in H. Rex Lee from the War Relocation Authority (WRA) to serve as assistant commissioner, replacing William Zimmerman with Erwin J. Utz of the WRA, supplanting chief counsel Theodore Haas with Edwin E. Ferguson of the WRA, and making Lewis A. Sigler assistant counsel. He also made a clean sweep of key staff positions at the central office and at the area offices.[24] Willard Beatty, longtime director of education, and Joseph C. McCaskill, of the Indian Arts and Crafts Board, both resigned, as did numerous agency superintendents. Former Commissioner John Collier and Interior Secretary Harold Ickes opposed Myer's nomination, with the latter convinced the commissioner ruthlessly replaced top level bureaucrats who disagreed with his harsh termination mindset.[25]

Forthwith, Myer articulated the goal of the Indian Office as "the step-by-step transfer of Bureau functions to the Indians themselves or to appropriate agencies of local, State or Federal Government."[26] He supported the Bosone resolution (House Joint Resolution 490), which had been introduced into the House by Reva Beck Bosone (R-UT) to immediately force Natives to become "free, unrestricted Americans." Senator Arthur Watkins (R-UT) opposed spending money for yet another study, arguing it would delay termination. Nonetheless, Myer found allies in Watkins and Senator Patrick A. McCarran (R-NV), who spent years trying to protect the rights of non-Indian squatters on land owned by the Pyramid Lake Paiute. He immediately pursued termination, gathering data on the readiness of tribes.[27]

To implement the termination strand, Myer worked to rapidly transfer students from government schools to public schools and expanded state and local responsibilities for healthcare. He also negotiated the transfer of civil and criminal jurisdiction over tribal lands to the states, and he prepared for use by Congress a process for how tribes might negotiate with the bureau for the step-by-step liquidation of the federal trust relationship, finding additional allies in the Eighty-Third Congress.[28]

The new commissioner was committed to terminating the federal-Indian relationship as swiftly as possible. Even though he acknowledged that any proposal resulting in "exploiting Indian groups by the precipitate withdrawal of guarantees protecting property rights, or the termination of Federal services in advance of others being made available, would be disastrous," he inaugurated a policy of issuing one-year trust extensions rather than the usual twenty-five-year extensions. In 1952, he proposed to reestablish the forced patent system to hasten federal withdrawal.[29] Officially, Myer stated that not until the Natives were "moved to accept their status alongside their non-Indian neighbors" would federal withdrawal occur.[30] The reality was incongruent.

In 1951, Myer commenced the process of Natives standing alongside non-Indians when he highlighted the initial appropriation of $8,645,520 in the ten-year Navajo-Hopi rehabilitation program that focused on school construction, soil and water conservation, range management, road construction, irrigation expansion, development of employment opportunities, and the relocation of willing Navajos and Hopis to the Colorado River Indian Reservation or to off-reservation employment centers.[31] The latter goal was critical, Myer surmised, since the Navajo Reservation could support only thirty-five thousand of its sixty-five thousand inhabitants, with returning war veterans exacerbating economic conditions.[32]

Concurrently, Myer initiated rehabilitation studies of other tribes in the Southwest, including the Apache, Pima, and Hualapai, intending to improve resource utilization and development in advance of termination. In 1951, he announced a major reorganization of the bureau's administrative structure, further decentralizing headquarters by delegating to the area offices authority for most policy implementation, including removal of restrictions, issuance of fee patents, and sale of land.[33] At the same time, he restricted the authority of field jurisdictions that were nearest the tribes and filled area office administrative positions with political cronies, who then issued 316 fee patents (50,350 acres) and authorized the sale of 41,048 acres of land, this coming after the bureau approved 605 fee patents (96,555 acres) and 60 land sales (7,177 acres) in 1950, with the sale of land to non-Indians continuing at a swift rate.[34] In 1952, the bureau approved of another 333 fee patents (61,283 acres) and authorized the sale of 496 allotments (61,312 acres), with the numbers increasing to 623 fee patents and 1,721 allotments sold the following year.[35] The steady increase in land transactions was such that Myer requested additional resources in order to meet the demands of non-Indians and "the high prices being paid."[36] In another step towards emancipation, Myer freed 80,000 individual Indian money accounts of all oversight.[37]

To initiate an efficient withdrawal of services, Myer established the Division of Program to outline policies and procedures and to formulate specific measures for federal withdrawal.[38] From his perspective, the bureau served as a consultant to the tribes by compiling "all the relevant factual data," including resources, treaty obligations, and an appraisal of existing tribal organization.[39] Within a year, the bureau developed plans for a survey of Indian Country, including demographics, claims against the United States, treaty rights, pace of progress, potential impediments, and a list of tribes that were "presently able to manage their own affairs without further supervision."[40] To fulfill the request of Congress, Myer developed three alternatives by which termination might commence: (1) issuance of fee patents, (2) sale of land with a fee patent issued to the purchaser, or (3) full removal of all restrictions preventing alienation of the land. Any of the three would "serve to remove the trusteeship of the Government."[41]

He also identified five categories of tribes for which withdrawal of supervision might occur. The first included those tribes or groups of Natives whom he believed desired independence from federal guardianship. A second encapsulated tribes with requisite financial assets who were already funding the major share of their own services, such as the Osage and Menominee. A third category included the Missouri River Basin tribes facing flood control and/or irrigation project impacts. A fourth included tribes such as the Sac and Fox in Iowa or the tribes in Michigan and Kansas that were remote from existing agencies and receiving limited federal services. The final group encompassed tribes such as the Ute, Red Lake Chippewa, and various Apache bands that needed time to adjust to any change in policy.[42]

By 1952, Myer declared that nearly every phase of the bureau targeted termination.[43] Federal schools no longer encouraged tribalism but assimilation, teaching not just the three R's but the "daily cultural expressions of . . . rural non-Indian children."[44] High schools focused on preparing teens to make "the best use of the resources of their Indian land" and teaching them the "mechanical and industrial skills necessary to obtain employment away from the reservation."[45] The bureau also negotiated new Johnson-O'Malley contracts and initiated a pilot adult education program for the Navajo that would provide basic literacy and enable unskilled Navajos to gain employment off reservation.[46] "It is obvious," Myer explained, "that all of the Indians cannot continue to live on livestock operations and that the solution lies in developing livelihoods for them in other lines of endeavor off the reservations."[47]

Myer argued that Native children, "by virtue of their citizenship in a state or residence in a state and district," were "entitled to the same free public education as rendered to any other citizen without any legal obligation resting on the Federal Government to pay tuition for this service."[48] Myer then accelerated transferring responsibility for education to public schools or, in areas where government and public schools were in close proximity, he merged the schools.[49] The bureau transferred twenty-five schools to local districts in 1952–1953, with nearly 53,000 Native children enrolled in public schools, 21,800 at no expense to the federal government. No bureau schools operated in Idaho, Minnesota, Washington, or Wisconsin after 1952.[50]

In concert with the goal of integrating Native services with non-Indians, the bureau secured congressional approval to construct a joint county-Indian hospital in Bernalillo, New Mexico.[51] Under this first joint hospital venture, Myer sought to transfer all Indian hospitals and medical services to state and local governments—without the consent of the tribes.[52] While there were no transfers in 1952, Congress authorized such conveyances contingent on tribal consent. Pub. L. No. 291 enabled Myer to transfer government hospitals to local jurisdictions and permitted the admittance of non-Indian patients in Indian hospitals in areas where no other facilities were available.[53] Myer, however, did not support tribal consent and drafted a series of bills eliminating concurrence for tribes in California and Oregon, although Congress refused to consider them.[54] He then announced that the bureau would not "operate health facilities when other similar facilities are available to the . . . Indians without segregation."[55] He closed the Fort Berthold hospital after determining there were other facilities available to serve the Three Affiliated Tribes.[56] He also negotiated thirty contracts with state and local public health and preventive service agencies and, a year later, he transferred the Hayward (Wisconsin) Indian hospital to a local management group, closed three additional facilities, and transferred all patients to community hospitals.[57] In 1953, Myer established a Public Health Services section within the bureau to work on the transfer of all public health services to state and local agencies.[58]

In another effort to encourage self-sufficiency, the bureau expanded its relationship with the USDA Soil Conservation Service to improve soil productivity, securing $13,118,770 in funding in 1951. Myer reported that for every dollar spent on the seventeen reservations where the bureau engaged in soil conservation, the return was $27.15.[59] He continued to advocate the development potential of Native lands, believing that growth had to proceed "at a more rapid rate" than the nation at large in order "for the Indians to play their proper role in America's expanding economy."[60] While laudable as a stand-alone policy strand, the commissioner sought to reduce the Indians' "demands on the national production for relief or other assistance" and viewed economic expansion as a necessary step in terminating tribes.[61] In tandem, Myer sought an orderly transfer of transportation routes in Indian Country to county jurisdiction but only after first improving the roads to local standards. Over one thousand miles of roads were transferred to the counties in 1952.[62]

Another objective of the bureau was to confer on state and local governments' civil and criminal jurisdiction over Indian Country, thereby eliminating bureau law enforcement. In 1950, Myer supported H.R. 1537 to establish state jurisdiction over reservations where it appeared desirable and when the Indians had called for a referendum on the matter.[63] If a tribal vote was affirmative, state jurisdiction took effect immediately; if the vote was negative, the tribe had one year in which to set up a code of Indian offenses, including adequate tribal enforcement.[64] Other bills were introduced conferring criminal jurisdiction over Indian Country in Arizona, Nebraska, and California. A House bill to repeal the federal liquor ban in Indian Country was drafted but failed to be introduced.[65]

Myer negotiated with a number of tribes and states regarding the transfer of civil and criminal jurisdiction, including Minnesota, Wisconsin, Nebraska, California, Oregon, and Washington. None of the bills was enacted but all continued the trajectory of divesting the federal government of its Indian responsibilities.[66] Similar bills were introduced in the first session of the Eighty-Third Congress seeking to confer state jurisdiction over Indian Country in California, Minnesota, Oregon, Wisconsin, and Nevada. As a first step in assisting "the Indians in becoming accustomed to the laws of the state," Myer encouraged tribes to adopt state statutes as tribal ordinances and to contract with county judges and sheriffs to serve as judicial and law enforcement officers.[67]

By February 1952, Myer defined the process by which tribes might sever their federal relationship, agreeing to recommend legislation terminating the trust relationship for any tribe that believed the bureau was "a handicap to its advancement." Rather than mitigate the deficiency and work with the tribes, Myer chose a single alternative: termination. If a tribe wished to modify its existing trust relationship in order to enhance control over its own affairs, and if it was willing to discuss the details of a partial termination, Myer agreed to assign the requisite staff to work with the tribe. If it desired to assume some of the bureau's responsibilities without terminating the trust relationship, Myer agreed to develop the appropriate agreement, identifying it as a first step in withdrawal.[68]

On July 1, 1952, the House of Representatives asked Myer to prepare a report enumerating which tribes could be immediately terminated and how the bureau would prepare itself for abolition.[69] Born in the Bosone resolution, the House Committee on Interior and Insular Affairs—absent the Senate Committee on Indian Affairs—forged ahead with termination, directing the bureau to investigate the process of terminating the federal-Indian relationship. Myer relied on the Zimmerman plan and then sent a letter to all bureau personnel informing them to prepare for withdrawal of services, agreeing to terminate the federal-Indian relationship by any means, whether it was full or partial. In a speech to the National Congress of American Indians, he informed tribal leaders that the bureau would do nothing for them that "others can do as well or better and as cheaply [or] which the Indians can do for themselves."[70] In the closing days of the Eighty-Second Congress—and again in the first session of the Eighty-Third Congress—termination bills for the California tribes, the tribes and bands in western Oregon, the Alabama-Coushatta Tribes in Texas, the Chitimacha Tribe of Louisiana, and the Prairie Island Band (Mdewakanton Sioux) in Minnesota, were introduced, but failed to gain traction, despite some tribal support.[71] Partial withdrawal of services for the California tribes was achieved when state and local agencies assumed all social and welfare responsibilities for Indians within the state.[72]

Complementing termination was a policy of relocating Native people from the reservations to urban centers, a matter Myer envisioned as tripling or quadrupling that of the WRA and Japanese internment.[73] The policy was informally initiated in 1948 after a devastating blizzard buried the Navajo and Hopi Reservations, resulting in a federal airlift of food and supplies to ward off starvation. That same year, the bureau initiated a job-placement program for the two tribes in Denver, Los Angeles, and Salt Lake City with the goal of finding off-reservation employment.[74]

In a 1950 study of sixteen reservations the bureau considered the most serious, Myer estimated the land and resources could support not more than 46 percent of the current population—and then only "at a minimum standard of subsistence."[75] The majority of the Natives would need to find their "livelihood off reservation," he stated, as the bureau expanded relocation to the Aberdeen, Billings, Minneapolis, Muskogee, and Portland area offices; a year later Alaska was added to the list.[76] More needed to be done, Myer stressed as he added placement offices in Phoenix and Chicago, in addition to the offices in Los Angeles, Denver, and Salt Lake City. More than twenty thousand placements were made that year, two-thirds of them Navajo and Hopi.[77]

Within a year of commencing the program, more than fifty-nine thousand placements had been made, with the bureau providing limited assistance for "operation relocation."[78] In 1953, additional relocation offices were added to encourage Natives in Arizona, California, Colorado, New Mexico, Oklahoma, and Utah to emigrate from the reservations.[79] Relocation to urban centers theoretically ended the connection of the individuals to their tribal communities and culture, and appeared to end all federal services to relocatees. In December 1952, Myer hired yet another former WRA official, Charles F. Miller, to head up the Branch of Training, Placement, and Relocation—a position Miller retained until he retired in 1962. Not until 1952 did the bureau acknowledge that relocation and employment were only two of the myriad social needs tethered to relocation. Only after the bureau estimated that one-third of the relocatees returned to the reservations, did it begin providing transitional services, including transportation and three weeks subsistence. Eventually, the bureau provided housing support, community and social services assistance, and access to medical and educational programs.[80]

Having surrounded himself with WRA employees, Myer aggressively promoted relocation, reaping a chorus of criticism from within and without Indian Country. In 1956, Dorothy Van de Mark, writing in *Harper's Magazine*, pointed to the challenges of relocation. "The plan consists primarily of inducing as many Indians as possible to leave the reservations." But it did not solve the problems, as relocatees still faced poverty and ill-health. "Dump[ing them] into urban centers," simply shifted the problem to urban centers.[81]

With the 1952 presidential election, former Commissioner John Collier sent both Adlai Stevenson, the Democratic nominee, and Dwight D. Eisenhower, the Republican nominee, a statement entitled "On Why Dillon S. Myer should not be Reappointed as Commissioner of Indian Affairs." Myer's "implacable commitment, subordinating all else, to a program of 'Relocation and withdrawal,'" was equally hostile to his "authoritative, racist and stereotyped administration" of the War Relocation Authority.[82] A year later, Collier wrote to President-elect Eisenhower seeking the removal of Myer and the restoration of tribal rights.[83] Harold Ickes went so far as to call Myer a blundering "Hitler and Mussolini rolled into one."[84] Felix Cohen described the imprudence of terminating tribes by differentiating *trusteeship*, which was a restriction of Native property based on law and treaties, and *wardship*, which was a restriction on the person.[85] Wardship was antiquated, Cohen explained, while trusteeship was a continuing obligation to protect property.

Myer also frustrated the efforts of tribes filing claims with the Indian Claims Commission prior to the deadline of August 13, 1951, by rejecting over half of the tribal attorney contracts using an obscure 1872 law that prohibited noncitizen Indians and tribes from hiring counsel without bureau approval. On November 9, 1950, he issued a memorandum that subjected tribes to minute and detailed controls over attorney contracts.[86] He also worked to block a bill in Congress that would give tribes additional time to file claims and hire attorneys.[87] Moreover, he refused to turn over information from the files of the Indian Office to the tribes or their attorneys. In 1951–52 every opinion on an Indian Claims Commission inquiry was adverse to the tribes.[88]

With Eisenhower's election, Indian Country breathed a collective sigh of relief. Taos Pueblo governor Juan de Jesus Romero requested Eisenhower act in the best interests of the tribes when considering a new commissioner.[89] Women's groups across the nation reminded Eisenhower that the commissioner of Indian affairs held the power of tribal advancement or regression, and that the president was obligated to consult with the tribes in naming a commissioner.[90] The president asked for and received Myer's resignation on March 19, 1953, after several of Myer's top deputies resigned. The president did not, however, shift course on policy, striving to create an America of one people. He did, however, honor his commitment to consult with tribes on a commissioner, sending assistant Secretary of the Interior Orme Lewis to confer with scores of tribal leaders and solicit their advice on the selection of the next commissioner. In the interim, W. Barton Greenwood served as acting commissioner between March 20 and July 28.[91]

COMMISSIONER GLENN L. EMMONS

President Eisenhower initially considered New Mexico's Alva Simpson for commissioner but Simpson withdrew after conferring with state leaders.[92] In Simpson's stead, the president turned to fifty-eight-year-old Alabama native Glenn L. Emmons, a New Mexico banker who was familiar with Navajo relocation efforts, a matter that had gained national attention. Emmons was named commissioner on July 28, 1953, and took office on August 10, just days after the Senate approved House Concurrent Resolution (H.C.R) 108, which established as congressional goals subjecting Indians "to the same laws and entitled to the same privileges and responsibilities" as other Americans; ending their status "as wards of the United States;" and granting them "all of the rights and prerogatives pertaining to American citizenship."[93]

Despite soliciting input from Indian Country in the selection of a new commissioner, Eisenhower proceeded with termination and emancipating tribal people from federal supervision. Emmons cooperated with a Congress engrossed with integration and supported a series of termination bills his first year in office. In fall of 1953, the president directed Emmons to meet with tribes and tribal groups where he learned the principle needs were better educational, medical, and economic opportunities.[94] Outside the withdrawal of federal services, Emmons elevated these three matters as his priorities.

H.C.R 108 set the tempo for Emmons's eight years in office, specifically declaring the congressional intent to free Natives from federal supervision and control, enumerating as a priority all Indians in California, Florida, New York, and Texas, as well as the Flathead, Klamath, Menominee, Pottawatomie (KN and NB), and Turtle Mountain Chippewa Tribes. Once these tribes were terminated, all bureau services within the specified states and for the enumerated tribes would be abolished. The secretary of the interior immediately began examining all legislation and treaties impacting the affected tribes and reported to Congress in January 1954, with his assessment of tribal readiness for withdrawal of services and support as summarized in Table 8.2.[95]

Emmons consulted with the tribes as part of his tour of Indian Country and, while not included in H.C.R 108, he added to the termination list the tribes and bands of Western Oregon, presenting to Congress a full report at the start of the 1954 legislative session.[96] In addition, he proposed bills to terminate the small bands and rancherias in Nevada and Utah, as well as the mixed-blood Ute from the Uintah-Ouray Reservation.[97] Congress held hearings on each of termination bills (except those related to the New York Indians) in 1954, with one—Pub. L. No. 399 calling for the termination of the Menominee Tribe—becoming law on June 17.[98]

Menominee termination closed the tribal roll as of June 17, with no child born subsequent to that date eligible for enrollment. A per capita payment of $1,500 was paid to each enrolled member from a summary judgment of Menominee claims against the United States.[99] The tribe had until December 31, 1959, to prepare a plan for distributing tribal assets and managing tribal property, with the responsibilities of the United States ending on December 31, 1958. The tribe faced the option of selling its property and distributing assets but if it failed to identify a preferred option, the secretary of the interior would transfer the land to a trustee "for liquidation purposes."[100] The Menominee chose to turn the reservation into Menominee County and retain communal ownership.[101]

Two weeks after passage of H.C.R 108, Congress enacted a series of termination-related bills calculated to end the distinction of Indians from the rest of the citizenry. Pub. L. No. 83-280 conferred civil and criminal jurisdiction over delineated tribal lands in California (all), Oregon (except Warm Springs), Nebraska (all), Minnesota (except Red Lake), and Wisconsin (except Menominee).[102] Congress authorized other states to assume jurisdiction by amending their constitutions or state statutes. The act relieved the bureau of law enforcement responsibilities within the reservations, although it coordinated with each state to ease the transition toward assumption of jurisdiction.[103]

Members of Congress and the bureau persistently lobbied the president to sign into law Pub. L. No. 280. And while the original bill did not provide for the assumption of jurisdiction by other states, Congress amended it before final passage, much to the chagrin of tribal leaders since it did not include tribal consent. The tribes petitioned President Eisenhower to veto the bill, but he signed it into law, believing it was "an important step in granting complete political equality to the Indians."[104] A year later, Pub. L. No. 280 was amended to encompass the Menominee Reservation and to grant the state of Nevada authority to amend its constitution and assume jurisdiction.[105] Nevada, in turn, authorized the several counties to opt out of assuming jurisdiction, with two-thirds declining.[106] In 1958, Alaska was granted jurisdiction over Native lands as well.[107]

While Congress considered an amendment stipulating tribal consent, Emmons opposed it and recommended consultation instead, although Congress failed to adopt either option.[108] In 1957, South Dakota and Washington acted to assume jurisdiction, although the former prefaced such assumption on county action and only after negotiating a contract with the Bureau of Indian Affairs for reimbursement of costs. South Dakota tribes opposed state assumption and retained the right to hold a referendum on whether or not to accept state jurisdiction.[109] The state of Washington required a tribal petition before assuming jurisdiction, with the Muckleshoot and Skokomish Tribes requesting such jurisdiction in 1957, and eight additional tribes falling under state jurisdiction the following year.[110]

The impact of Pub. L. No. 280 on tribes was substantial, as tribal judicial authority and law enforcement on the affected reservations ended. State jurisdiction displaced tribal authority and some states, such as Minnesota, used the law as a license to tax tribal members, something Congress did not authorize. As a result, most states authorized to assume jurisdiction provided little if any police protection. States such as Minnesota, Washington, Oregon, and Wisconsin insisted on asserting authority over hunting and fishing rights, a matter that would not be fully resolved for another twenty years.[111] The act, however, retained concurrent tribal jurisdiction in those states in which Congress granted state civil and criminal jurisdiction.

On the same day Congress enacted Pub. L. No. 280, it approved two other bills, including Pub. L. No. 277, which repealed federal prohibitions on the sale of alcoholic beverages to Natives outside of Indian Country and legalized the introduction of alcohol in Indian Country by recognizing a tribal right to determine whether or not to allow such beverages within the reservation.[112] Within the first year, nineteen tribes utilized the local option to legalize alcohol, with the number increasing to thirty-one by 1958.[113] A second bill, Pub. L. No. 281, repealed the federal restriction on the sale, purchase, or possession by Natives of personal property such as livestock, guns, and agricultural implements that could be sold, purchased, or possessed by non-Indians.[114]

Table 8.2. The Readiness of Tribes for Termination, 1954

Tribe	Yes/No	Tribe	Yes/No
Blackfeet	Yes*	Fort McDowell	No
California tribes	Yes	Salt River	Yes#
Cherokee (NC)	No	Gila River	No
Catawba	Yes	Ak Chin	No
Cheyenne River	No	Pine Ridge	No
Choctaw (MS)	No	Pipestone	?
Hualapai	No	Red Lake	No
Yavapai	Yes#	Rosebud	No
Havasupai	No	Yankton	Yes#
Camp Verde	No	San Carlos	No
Fort Mohave	No	Seminole (FL)	No
Cocopah	Yes	Sisseton-Wahpeton	Yes
Colorado River	No	Absentee Shawnee	No
Colville	Yes#	Alabama-Coushatta	Yes*
Spokane	Yes	Caddo	Yes
Fond du Lac	Yes	Cheyenne-Arapaho	No
Grand Portage	Yes#	Citizen Potawatomie	Yes
Leech Lake	Yes#	Fort Sill Apache	Yes
White Earth	Yes#	Iowa (KN-NB)	Yes
Nett Lake	Yes#	Kaw	Yes
Mille Lac	Yes	Kickapoo (KN)	Yes
Southern Ute	No	Kickapoo (OK)	No
Ute Mountain	No	Kiowa-Comanche-Apache	No
Crow	No	Otoe-Missouria	No
Crow Creek	No	Pawnee	Yes*
Lower Brule	No	Ponca (OK)	No
Five Tribes	No	Prairie Potawatomie	No
Eastern Shawnee	Yes#	Sac & Fox (KN-NB)	Yes
Ottawa	Yes	Sac & Fox (OK)	Yes*
Quapaw	Yes*	Tonkawa	Yes
Seneca-Cayuga	Yes#	Wichita	Yes*
Wyandotte	Yes#	Standing Rock	No
Flathead	Yes	Turtle Mountain	Yes
Fort Apache	No	Fort Totten	Yes#
Fort Belknap	Yes	Uintah-Ouray	No
Rocky Boy's	No	Shivwits	No
Fort Berthold	Yes	Koosharem	No
Fort Hall	Yes+	Indian Peaks	Yes#
Fort Peck	Yes*	Kaibab	No
Bad River	No	Kanosh	No
Bay Mills	Yes	Umatilla	Yes#
Forest Potawatomie	No	Acoma	No
Hannahville	Yes	Cochiti	No
Keweenaw Bay	Yes	Isleta	No
Lac Courte Oreilles	No	Jemez	No
Lac du Flambeau	Yes#	Laguna	No
Oneida (WI)	Yes	Nambe	No

Table 8.2. The Readiness of Tribes for Termination, 1954 (*cont'd*)

Tribe	Yes/No	Tribe	Yes/No
Red Cliff	Yes	Picuris	No
Sac & Fox (IA)	No	Pojoaque	No
Saginaw Chippewa	Yes	Sandia	No
St. Croix	Yes	San Felipe	No
Mole Lake	Yes#	San Idlefonso	No
Stockbridge-Munsee	Yes	San Juan	No
Winnebago (WI)	Yes#	Santa Anna	No
Hopi	No	Santa Clara	No
Jicarilla	No	Santa Domingo	No
Klamath	?	Taos	No
Menominee	Yes	Tesuque	No
Mescalero	No	Zia	No
Navajo	No	Zuni	No
Battle Mountain	Yes	Cañoncito	No
Carson County	Yes	Alamo	No
Duck Valley	Yes	Ramah	No
Elko	Yes	Warm Springs	No
Ely	Yes	Chehalis	Yes
Fallon Colony	No	Hoh	Yes
Fallon	Yes	Lower Elwaha	Yes
Fort McDermitt	Yes	Lummi	Yes#
Goshute	No	Makah	Yes
Las Vegas	Yes	Muckleshoot	Yes
Lovelock Colony	No	Nisqually	Yes
Moapa	Yes	Ozette	Yes
Pyramid Lake	Yes	Port Gamble	Yes
Reno-Sparks	Yes	Port Madison	Yes
Ruby Valley	Yes	Public Domain	Yes
Skull Valley	Yes	Puyallup	Yes
South Fork	Yes	Quileute	Yes
Summit Lake	Yes	Quinault	Yes
Walker River	Yes	Shoalwater	Yes
Washoe	No	Skokomish	Yes
Winnemucca Colony	Yes	Squaxon Island	Yes
Yerington Colony	No	Swinomish	Yes#
Yomba	Yes	Tulalip	Yes
Northern Cheyenne	No	Wind River	Yes
Kalispel	No	Omaha	Yes
Kootenai	No	Ponca	Yes
Nez Perce	Yes	Santee Sioux	Yes
Coeur d'Alene	Yes	Winnebago	Yes
Osage	?	Yakima	No
Papago	No		

* Except for a minority
# Conditionally
+ Gradually
Source: H.R. 2680 (1954).

The prohibition dated to the 1834 Nonintercourse Act and was intended to protect Indians and non-Indians from "uncivilized Indians."[115]

Congress also appended a short but significant provision to the 1953 appropriation act for the departments of Justice, Commerce, State, and Judiciary. Commonly referred to as the McCarran Amendment, after its primary sponsor, Senator Patrick McCarran (R-NV), the act waived the sovereign immunity of the United States and bound the federal government to any suit involving adjudication of federal water rights.[116] Federal water rights were now adjudicated in state forums, with the U.S. Supreme Court subsequently determining that the amendment joined the United States to state adjudication proceedings where any federal reserved rights were involved. Since Indian water rights were considered a reserved right, they, too, went into state courts.[117]

Two years later, Congress further narrowed the scope of the bureau's responsibilities by enacting into law the Indian Health Transfer Act—which authorized the transfer of the Indian Medical Service out of the Bureau of Indian Affairs and into the Public Health Service—reducing, Emmons stated, the bureau's "responsibilities to more manageable proportions."[118] The effective date of the transfer was July 1, 1955, and it represented the largest single reduction of bureau responsibilities while also shifting thirty-six hundred employees and $40 million in property (fifty-six hospitals, twenty-one clinics, and thirteen school infirmaries) into the Public Health Service and the newly named Division of Indian Health.[119] The transfer reflected a goal dating back thirty-five years, with the current endeavor commencing in 1949 when William P. Shepherd of the Metropolitan Insurance Company initiated a sustained effort to effect the transfer, both as a means of improving medical care and eliminating Native-only services.[120] After 1955, Emmons no longer referenced healthcare or medical services other than to state in 1956 that "with the responsibility for Indian health activities transferring to the United States Public Health Service, the Bureau of Indian Affairs [was] plac[ing] increasing emphasis" on education and economic development.[121]

Emmons refined the termination process, emphasizing consultation with—but not consent of—the tribes. To enforce economy and efficiency, he adopted three procedures, including preparing draft bills for internal departmental consideration with area office and agency input; implementing area office and agency consultation with tribes, as well as state and county governments; and drafting legislation for submission to Congress through departmental channels.[122] In 1955, he further perfected the process, noting the bureau was assisting the tribes in preparing "for the eventual cutoff of Federal trusteeship."[123] With termination acts representing "pioneer approaches" to the federal-Indian relationship, Emmons acknowledged there were differences of opinion regarding interpretation of the processes and procedures, although he was confident these disagreements could be "resolved by conferences of interested parties," thereby keeping termination on schedule.[124]

The Menominee Tribe was the first to be terminated, but it would not be the last. Between August 13 and September 1, 1954, Congress approved five additional terminations bills, beginning with the Klamath Tribes (Klamath, Modoc, and Yahooskin Band of Snake Indians) on August 13.[125] The tribal roll was closed, and all adults were given the option of taking a pro rata share of tribal assets (including property after it was "converted into cash," which totaled $90

Table 8.3. Tribes Terminated from Federal Supervision, 1954–1962

Tribe	State	Acres	Population	Date of Act	Effective Date
Menominee	WI	233,881	3,270	1954	1961
Klamath	OR	862,662	2,133	1954	1961
61 Bands	OR	3,158	2,081	1954	1956
Alabama/Coushatta	TX	3,200	450	1954	1955
Mixed Blood Ute	UT	311,430	490	1954	1961
Southern Paiute	UT	42,839	232	1954	1957
Lower Lake	CA	—	—	1956	1956
Wyandotte	OK	94	1,157	1956	1959
Peoria	OK	0	640	1956	1959
Ottawa	OK	0	630	1956	1959
Coyote Valley	CA	—	—	1957	1957
41 Rancherias	CA	4,315	1,107	1958	1961–1970
Catawba	SC	3,388	631	1959	1962
Ponca	NB	834	442	1962	1966

million) or retaining ownership in common with a local trustee.[126] The act had no bearing on tribal fishing rights retained by treaty, and water rights were protected for fifteen years, after which time they would be subject to state prior appropriation laws.[127] The effective date of withdrawal of federal services and trusteeship was August 13, 1958, although challenges in implementing the act extended the date to August 13, 1961.[128]

Klamath termination was followed by the end of federal services and supervision over sixty-one tribes and bands in western Oregon, with the original effective date of August 13, 1956, also extended to 1961.[129] Ten days later, the Alabama-Coushatta Tribes in Texas were terminated, effective July 1, 1955, although tribal members remained "eligible for admission, on the same terms that apply to other Indians, to hospitals and schools maintained by the United States."[130] Unlike other termination acts, Alabama-Coushatta lands transferred to the state of Texas to be held in trust. Three days later, Congress terminated the Ute Tribe of the Uintah-Ouray Reservation in eastern Utah, with tribal assets divided between the "full-bloods" and "mixed-bloods," with the latter then terminated in 1961.[131] On September 1, Congress terminated the Shivwits, Kanosh, Koosharem, and Indian Peaks bands of the Southern Paiute Indian Tribe, with an effective date of 1957.[132] In August 1956, the Wyandotte Tribe of Oklahoma was terminated, followed by the Peoria Tribe and the Ottawa Tribe, with each given three years to prepare for final withdrawal of federal services.[133] On August 18, 1958, forty-one rancherias and reservations in California were terminated, with effective dates between 1961 and 1970, and on September 21, 1959, the Catawba Tribe of South Carolina was terminated.[134] Two rancherias in California were effectively terminated under acts conveying tribal property to county (Lower Lake Rancheria) or secretary of the army (Coyote Valley Indian Rancheria) jurisdiction.[135] Table 8.3 lists the tribes that were terminated and their effective dates.

Although Emmons supported termination, congressional action to continue the policy waned after the 1956 election, when Democratic victories changed the composition of congressional committees and as national opposition increased. For the 118 tribes and bands that were terminated, their status fundamentally changed as their land was sold, the federal trust ended with state jurisdiction and judicial authority, and federal services withdrawn. Although some of the acts expressly extinguished tribal sovereignty, all terminated tribes were divested of their self-governing ability, and in many cases the land over which they exercised sovereignty was gone.[136]

In the midst of the termination fervor, the Arizona and New Mexico state supreme courts ruled that state laws had no application to Natives on their reservations, although the Arizona court held that the state could tax nontrust property.[137] The Navajo Tribe immediately sought a writ of certiorari to the U.S. Supreme Court, where in 1959 the court ruled in *Williams v. Lee* that Navajo jurisdiction over tribal members' debt to non-Indian merchants within the reservation was exclusive. Absent clear "governing acts of Congress," tribes retained the authority to "make and enforce their own laws and be ruled by them." To allow state jurisdiction "would undermine the authority of the tribal courts."[138] Notwithstanding termination, the basic legal doctrine outlined in the 1830s Cherokee Nation cases, while weakened, remained inviolate.[139]

The rehabilitation of the Navajo-Hopi Reservations continued under Emmons, with the bureau commencing irrigation feasibility studies for the San Juan-Shiprock project and nearing completion of the Hogback and Red Lake projects. The bureau installed fifty-one groundwater wells for range stock, constructed hundreds of miles of paved and gravel-surfaced roads and, in conjunction with the Indian Health Service, constructed new hospitals in Tuba City (seventy-five beds), Shiprock (seventy-five beds) and Gallup (two hundred beds).[140] The bureau also constructed a 536-student school in Kayenta and added thirty-seven trailer schools, although the latter were incongruous with the long-term educational needs of Navajo children. Federal Impact Aid funds enabled eleven new public schools to be constructed on reservation.[141] By 1957, over 27,000 Navajo children were in school, leading Emmons to adopt a Navajo-specific educational policy that provided bureau schools on reservation for children in elementary school; public schools for children in grades 7 to 12; vocational training in off-reservation boarding schools for high school-aged students; and state schools for mentally and physically challenged children, with high school graduates encouraged to pursue advanced training off reservation.[142]

Emmons was so pleased with the state of Navajo education that he set his sights on the Mississippi Choctaw and Alaska Natives, two other jurisdictions lacking facilities, for educational improvements.[143] By the mid-1950s, more than 113,000 children were in school, with the bureau using Johnson-O'Malley contracts with twenty state and territorial governments to provide assistance for 36,000 of these children.[144] Using Impact Aid and School Facilities Construction funding, the bureau constructed multiple public schools in Arizona, New Mexico, Colorado, and Montana.[145]

Emmons expanded the pilot adult education program to the Seminole (Florida), Papago (Arizona), Turtle Mountain Chippewa (North Dakota), Rosebud Sioux (South Dakota), and Fort Hall (Idaho) Reservations, with the goal of making adult Natives more attractive in the job market.[146] In 1956, with Emmons's support, Congress approved of the Indian Vocational Training Act, which provided funds for adult education but tied such services to relocation, making education an integral part of relocation.[147]

Table 8.4. Relocated Indians, 1954–1960

Year	Relocatees	Families	Individuals
1954	2,163	1,649	514
1955	3,461	2,656	805
1956	5,316	4,211	732
1957	6,964	5,420	1,544
1958	5,728	4,331	1,397
1959	N/R	N/R	N/R
1960	3,674	1,876	1,798

Source: *Annual Reports of the Commissioner of Indian Affairs*, 1954–1960.

Relocation complemented termination, with Emmons modifying Myer's policy by selecting for relocation Natives "of good character, in reasonably good health, and show[ing] evidence that they want to live permanently away from the home area." If they met these requirements, the bureau paid travel expenses (one-way) for the individual and his family to a relocation center.[148] In 1954, the bureau assisted 2,163 Natives in relocating, most of whom chose Los Angeles or Chicago, with 54 percent coming from the northern plains and 46 percent from the Southwest.[149] The primary reason for relocation, Emmons told the Daughters of the American Revolution, was simply "too many people and not enough land."[150] Between 1954 and 1960, the bureau assisted over 27,000 persons in relocating from the reservations, as shown in Table 8.4. Emmons reported that there remained "a marked and active interest in relocation," but that funds to assist relocatees were lacking, resulting in a "sizeable backlog" of applicants.[151]

In the midst of relocation, the Association on American Indian Affairs in 1956 issued another scathing report on relocation. While recognizing the need for off-reservation employment opportunities, the association disapproved of a policy that was forced on Natives due to the bureau's failure to assist tribes in developing alternative on-reservation economic opportunities.[152] While the bureau claimed the recidivism rate was one-quarter to one-third, the association suggested it was 60 percent to 90 percent. If the strand were to continue, the association implored the bureau to relocate Native people to cities near their home reservation, a consideration that was integrated into the program in the 1960s.

Child welfare also was an integral part of termination. While not a new policy strand, in the 1950s the bureau targeted the placement of children in non-Indian agencies and homes. Emmons reported in 1958 that some state courts had rejected jurisdiction over child protection, adoption, and custody.[153] "This hindered or prevented the provision of adoptive care," Emmons argued, as he contracted with the Child Welfare League of America to find "good adoptive homes" for children.[154] The bureau also continued to work with states to establish jurisdiction over children in Indian Country, with Emmons writing in 1960 that "the instability of many families on reservations remains a serious problem, [with] the number of dependent and neglected children coming to the attention of bureau social workers increase[ing]."[155] As a result of the Child Welfare League, the adoption of Native children by non-Indians increased as public and private agencies stimulated demand.[156]

Table 8.5. Land Removed from Federal Trust, 1954–1960

Year	Parcels removed from Trust	Acres
1954	3,200	500,000
1955	2,594	521,771
1956	2,526	265,033
1957	8,065	325,314
1958	8,523	335,896
1959	N/R	N/R
1960	2,137	701,805
Total	27,045	2,649,819

Source: *Annual Reports of the Commissioner of Indian Affairs, 1954–1960.*

In tandem with termination and relocation, the bureau expedited the braid of land alienation by issuing fee patents and removing restrictions on the sale of allotted land, with nearly 2,650,000 acres released from federal trust between 1954 and 1960, as shown in Table 8.5. Moreover, Emmons announced in 1954 that "Indians may now use their chief asset, trust or restricted land, as security for loans," with Congress authorizing execution of mortgages on trust and restricted land.[157] Under the authority of the long-term leasing act, Congress lifted statutory prohibitions on the leasing of land for more than five years.[158] In 1958, Emmons modified the policy on the sale of trust land, notifying tribes of the potential sale and then giving the tribe the option of negotiating for or bidding on the land. In instances where multiple Natives owned fractionated interests in the land, any one owner was given the opportunity to purchase the land at the bureau's appraised value or at an agreed upon price.[159]

Emmons also continued developing irrigation projects, believing that the "determination of water rights and the construction of adequate and proper irrigation facilities for all irrigable land on Indian reservations" remained a federal responsibility. Moreover, such projects were "necessary prior to termination of the Federal trusteeship" in order for Natives to take their place on an equal footing with the rest of the citizenry.[160] The commissioner also advocated—and Congress funded—further construction of roads in Indian Country, with the Federal Highway Administration providing $10 million for road construction in Indian Country each year between 1955 and 1957.[161]

Outside of education, economic development remained the staple of Emmons's administration and, on April 12, 1956, he sent a memorandum to all tribes and agencies encouraging tribes "to work out and adopt programs for their own social and economic betterment."[162] He then met with most western tribes in the summer and fall of 1956 to promote economic development, confident a "grassroots effort at the reservation level would take root and lead to opportunities for self-improvement and community development."[163] In 1957, the Department of Interior issued new loan regulations for tribes to attract industry to the reservations, enabling them to borrow money against their trust funds. The bureau hosted hundreds of meetings across the West, inviting state and local officials to participate in addressing common challenges to economic development.[164]

Table 8.6. Credit Extended to Indians, 1953–1956

Calendar Year	Non-BIA Loans	Tribal Loans	Revolving Loans	Reimbursable Loans	Livestock Loans
1953	$27,665,000	$9,704,611	$10,190,941	$988,007	$1,834,415
1954	$33,960,000	$9,669,468	$9,505,193	$841,568	$1,433,575
1955	$55,725,000	$17,300,578	$8,311,374	$498,299	$1,039,445
1956	$59,425,000	$21,216,542	$7,715,612	$314,040	$715,105

Source: *Annual Report of the Commissioner of Indian Affairs*, 1957, 263–64.

Non-bureau loans to Natives totaled $59,425,000 by 1956, with Indian credit totaling nearly $90 million in 1956, as shown in Table 8.6.[165]

The primary source of credit came from tribal funds and the federal revolving loan program, although Emmons after 1957 phased out reimbursable and livestock loans.[166] To further advance economic development, Emmons advocated industrial development on or near reservations to promote economic opportunities. In 1956, the bureau established ten facilities in Indian Country, including a furniture factory in Gallup, New Mexico, and two facilities near Cherokee, North Carolina—one a leather goods plant. Of the additional new facilities, two were in Arizona (Navajo and Pima), three were in South Dakota (Sioux) and one each in Montana (Northern Cheyenne) and Washington (Yakima).[167]

Emmons proved creative in constructing economic opportunities for tribes and, in 1957, was awarded the Department of the Interior's Distinguished Service Award for promoting the health, education, and economic potential of Indian Country.[168] He enhanced economic development across Indian Country, with the Seminole Tribe (Florida) honoring him in 1959 and recommending him for a second Distinguished Service Award. His efforts paid dividends as Congress in June 1959 introduced legislation promoting further development of economic activities in Indian Country via a program called "Operation Bootstrap."[169]

Federal policy regarding American Indians floundered during the final years of the Eisenhower administration, with Natives and many non-Indians confused and confounded. Appropriations for the Bureau of Indian Affairs reached a record $109,410,000 in 1957, 25 percent higher than the previous year. Termination had proven to be expensive and, with the start of an economic recession in fall of 1957, support declined. Public scrutiny was rekindled and, as the civil rights era blossomed, Americans began listening to tribal concerns. Termination was becoming a liability and, while it remained the primary strand of policy, economic development was becoming the fulcrum of federal activity. In November 1957, the *Christian Century* condemned the bureau and Congress for mishandling Indian affairs and ignoring tribal concerns, harshly critiquing H.C.R 108 as another policy braid to sever land from the Indians.[170]

As the 1960 presidential election approached, Indian affairs again found their way into the campaign. Frank George, a Nez Perce from Idaho, addressed the Democratic Platform Committee in spring of 1960, denouncing termination. "The fact remains that the Indian Bureau field personnel and the Washington staff devote considerable time in planting ideas in the minds of the general public and even of tribal governing bodies that the solution to the problems of American Indians is the termination of Federal trusteeship." What was needed was for tribes to maximize their assets, secure credit, and establish a joint federal-tribal process for dealing with property and treaty rights.[171]

On December 22, 1960, the Department of Interior announced a five-year extension on all expiring trust patents and restrictions, an action that implicitly repudiated termination. With the election of Democrat John F. Kennedy, in November 1960, Emmons elected to resign, submitting his resignation on December 23, 1960, and remaining in office until January 7, 1961, when John O. Crow assumed the mantle of acting commissioner of Indian affairs.[172]

The blame for termination fell upon Congress for advocating a policy that Native people were unprepared for and did not fully comprehend. Senators Arthur Watkins (R-UT) and Patrick McCarran (R-NV), as well as the Senate Committee on Indian Affairs, shouldered much of the blame for the failed policy.[173] Armed with rhetoric and a determination to impose their will on the tribes, Watkins and McCarran, abetted by Myer and others, orchestrated a seismic shift in policy, exhibiting a myopic perspective of Indian affairs in the process.

In the waning years of Emmons's administration, the Commission on the Rights, Liberties, and Responsibilities of the American Indians spoke for many when it critiqued federal policy and the impact of termination. Headed by O. Meredith Wilson and former Commissioner of Indian affairs William A. Brophy, the commission issued a series of stinging reports in 1958 and 1959 that enlightened the public and policymakers alike.[174] It began its final report with a novel statement: "The Indian himself should be the focus of all public policy affecting him." Tribal consent to termination, the commission stated, was largely passive, suggesting "a surrender to what seem[ed] unavoidable."[175] Treaties guaranteed self-government, which was fundamental to the legal intercourse between the United States and indigenous tribes but was also an "essential means for Indians to collaborate with the federal government." Terminating tribal governments would dissolve both the tribal social adhesion and the ability of tribes to interact with the United States. Strengthening tribal governments, however, was "the best means of meeting the problems of the modern world," with the democratic process mandating that tribes "determine for themselves whether their governments satisfactorily meet their needs."[176]

It was self-evident that Native prospects for economic advancement were intimately intertwined with those of the national and local economies. The solution to the "Indian problem" could not occur in isolation from mainstream America, and the economic goals of the tribes could only be found in "the development of their community and individual resources," not unlike rural America.[177] Termination was not the solution. It was a time for a new strand in the braids of policy.

CONCLUSION

The policy of termination, advanced by Myer and the Eighty-Third Congress, resulted in confusion and further confiscation of Native land, as shown by Table 8.7. On September 18, 1958,

Table 8.7. Indian Land Losses, 1948–1957, by Area Offices

Area Office	1948–1952	1953–1957	Total (acres)
Aberdeen	291,300	333,800	625,100
Anadarko	107,710	154,540	262,250
Billings	184,310	897,954	1,082,264
Gallup	5,500	1,080	6,580
Minneapolis	2,155	117,798	119,953
Muscogee	112,549	202,015	314,953
Phoenix	943	1,319	2,262
Portland	15,606	25,834	71,910
Sacramento	84,691	25,834	110,525
Total	804,764	1,790,650	2,595,414

Source: Indian Land Transactions, Eighty-Fifth Cong., 2nd Sess., Committee on Interior and Insular Affairs, U.S. Senate, 45.

Secretary of the Interior Fred Seaton announced in Flagstaff, Arizona, that no Indian tribe would be terminated unless it "clearly demonstrated ... that it understands the plan [and] concurs in and supports the plan proposed."[178] "It would be incredible, even criminal," Seaton acknowledged, "to send any Indian tribe out into the mainstream" unless it was fully prepared. A year later, Seaton added that providing Natives with opportunities for personal development and growth was the overriding objective of the bureau, with Emmons directed to focus all "resources and energy more sharply than ever before on a multifaceted program geared towards the ultimate attainment of this objective."[179]

Termination interrupted the movement toward self-determination, but it did not end it. While President Eisenhower enforced the policy, tribal leaders objected to its unilateral application. In 1961, President Kennedy pledged a policy of respect for treaty rights. Modifications to the federal-Indian relationship would occur only if tribal nations consented. Despite such assurances from the president, Congress did not repudiate termination until 1968, when it adopted a corollary policy of improving tribal economies so that Indians might help themselves.

9

"AWAKENING THE NATIONAL CONSCIENCE"

The Call for Self-Determination, 1961–1980

By 1960, indigenous Americans exhibited a phobia of the federal government, supposing every action and policy was termination in disguise. They remained wary of governmental actions throughout the decade, but at the same time took advantage of the Civil Rights era to voice tribal concerns.[1] Vine Deloria Jr., executive director of the National Congress of American Indians between 1964 and 1967, suggested that when Indians objected to termination in the 1950s, "no one had listened."[2] Termination "evaporated," Deloria later explained, "because not enough advocates could be found in Congress to make it an important issue."[3] As Native people began to make their voices heard in the voting booth, termination became politically hazardous.[4]

Presidential candidate John F. Kennedy pledged that, if elected, he would institute a policy of respect for tribes and treaty rights, assuring Natives that any change in the federal-Indian relationship would occur only with their consent. In place of termination, both President Kennedy and his successor, Lyndon B. Johnson, supported tribal involvement in policy development and implementation, making socioeconomic policy strands the core of their strategy. Throughout the decade, Congress and the president worked together to advance a policy fixed on economic development.

Between 1961 and 1981, there were six commissioners of Indian affairs, beginning with Philleo Nash, who served from 1961 until 1966. Nash was followed by Robert L. Bennett (1966–1969); Louis R. Bruce (1969–1973); Morris Thompson (1973–1976); Benjamin Reifel (1976–1977); and Raymond Butler (1977). In 1977, the head of the Bureau of Indian Affairs was elevated to an assistant secretary for Indian affairs, reporting directly to the secretary of the interior, with Forrest Gerard (1977–1980) the first to hold the title, followed by Thomas V. Fredericks (1980–1981). William Hallet (1979–1981) was the last individual to be nominated and confirmed as commissioner of Indian

Table 9.1. Heads of the Indian Office and Major Policies, 1961–1981

Name	Title	Years of Service	Main Policies
Philleo Nash (D)	Commissioner	4.5 years (1961–1966)	Native participation in program development, economic self-sufficiency, war on poverty programs, housing, Indian adoption
Robert L. Bennett (D) (Oneida)	Commissioner	3 years (1966–1969)	Native voice, community schools, tribes set own priorities, self-determination, lift federal paternalism, National Council on Indian Opportunity, Indian Civil Rights Act
Louis R. Bruce (R) (Mohawk/Sioux)	Commissioner	3.4 years (1969–1973)	Reorganize the BIA, Native decision-making, reaffirmed federal trust relationship, restoration of Blue Lake, Indian Education Act, Alaska Native Claims Settlement Act
Morris Thompson (R) (Athabaskan)	Commissioner	3 years (1973–1976)	Menominee restoration, Indian Financing Act, Indian Self-Determination Act, Indian Healthcare Improvement Act, Student Bill of Rights
Ben Reifel (R) (Sioux)	Commissioner	2 months (1976–1977)	none
Forrest Gerard (D) (Blackfeet)	Assistant Secretary	2.3 years (1977–1980)	Tribal recognition process, American Indian Religious Freedom Act, Indian Child Welfare Act, water and land claims
William Hallett (D) (Red Lake Chippewa)	Commissioner	1.3 years (1979–1981)	
Thomas Fredericks (D) (Mandan-Hidatsa)	Assistant Secretary	1 year (1980–1981)	Affirmative action in BIA, Indian-owned contracting

affairs. Nash drafted the last annual report in 1964, and between 1965 and 1969 the commissioner of Indian affairs prepared a simple *Annual Progress Report*. After 1969, the Bureau of Indian Affairs no longer prepared an annual report for the president, Congress, or secretary of the interior.

President Kennedy initiated a shift in policy, pledging a ten-point plan of economic development and renewal for Indian Country.[5] Kennedy nominated Congressman Stewart L. Udall (D-AZ) as his secretary of the interior, with the Senate confirming Udall on January 21, 1961. In his confirmation hearing, the new secretary committed to a policy of economic development designed to lift the standard of living in Indian Country.[6] Udall, who had strong sentiments as to what should be done in Indian Country, delayed for seven months the nomination of a commissioner of Indian affairs, awaiting the recommendations of the President's Task Force on Indian Affairs.[7] In the interim, Udall appointed veteran bureau administrator John O. Crow, a member of the Cherokee Nation, to serve as acting commissioner.[8]

For a time, Udall considered being his own commissioner of Indian affairs, having deep convictions on tribal affairs and a commitment to Kennedy's pledge to not modify "treaty or contractual relationships without the consent of the tribes concerned."[9] He pledged a policy strand of developing the human and natural resources of Indian Country.[10] At the request of the president, Udall assembled a Task Force on Indian Affairs and charged it with three goals: "Maximum Indian economic self-sufficiency; full participation of the Indians in American life; [and] equal citizenship privileges and responsibilities."[11] Headed by W. W. Keeler, principal chief of the Cherokee Nation and president of Phillips Petroleum Company, the task force included Philleo Nash, former lieutenant governor of Wisconsin and professor of anthropology; William Zimmerman, one-time assistant commissioner of Indian affairs; James E. Officer, professor of anthropology at the University of Arizona; and John Crow, acting commissioner of Indian affairs. The task force was given ninety days to advise Udall as to how the government could more effectively discharge its statutory obligations to the tribes.[12]

In the meantime, the Commission on Rights, Liberties, and Responsibilities of the American Indian issued another in a series of reports, recommending that the United States refrain from terminating tribes, enumerating ten reasons for maintaining the federal-Indian relationship.[13] In May, Congress approved of and President Kennedy signed into law the Area Redevelopment Act, fulfilling the first pledge the president made to the Indians, with the act providing services and assistance to mitigate pockets of poverty.[14] Congress, which had approved of a similar bill only to have it vetoed by President Eisenhower months earlier, established a policy of developing the resources of Indian Country to enable tribal citizens to help themselves. One month later, anthropologist Sol Tax, with support from the National Congress of American Indians, organized a conference in Chicago that drew 460 Natives from 90 tribes for a week of discussions. This resulted in a "Declaration of Indian Purpose," which recommended increased Native participation in federal programs, abandonment of termination and revocation of H.C.R 108, reorganization of the Bureau of Indian Affairs to allow for local control, and "establishment upon Indian reservations of industries and other activities which will provide employment."[15] Indian participation in program development was prerequisite. The committee presented Kennedy with a special bound copy of the report, and the president noted there was "still a good deal of unfinished business" to conduct in Indian Country.[16]

By July, the Task Force on Indian Affairs released its report, urging the federal government to shift from "termination of Federal supervision and benefits to spurring the development of Indian-owned resources."[17] The task force recommended protecting the civil rights of Native people and withdrawing federal services "from Indians with substantial incomes and superior educational experience, who are as competent as most non-Indians to look after their own affairs." Moreover, the task force suggested that if termination were to proceed, it should include a piecemeal transfer of bureau responsibilities to the states, but only upon a negotiated agreement with the tribes involved.[18] While not a formal repudiation of termination, the task force's report (drafted by governmental leaders) coincided with the Chicago Declaration (drafted by tribal leaders), indicating that an era of new cooperation was imminent.[19]

COMMISSIONER PHILLEO NASH

On July 31, 1961, Kennedy nominated Philleo Nash as his commissioner of Indian affairs. A former board member of the Association on American Indian Affairs, Nash joined the Kennedy administration in January to serve on the President's Task Force on Indian Affairs. Confirmation hearings held in August indicated Nash had only the tacit support of the Senate Committee on Interior and Insular Affairs. He was pressed by the committee regarding his views of termination and the role of the bureau, with chairman Clinton P. Anderson (D-NM) declaring the task force report was "unrealistic and retrogressive."[20] Despite antagonizing the committee with his candor, Nash was confirmed by the Senate and took office on September 26, 1961.[21]

Nash stressed economic self-sufficiency and encouraged industrial development on or near tribal lands, seeking to enhance tourism and recreation. In the process, he shifted the focus of the bureau from custodial care to economic development.[22] There were two prevailing theories regarding the role of the Bureau of Indian Affairs, Nash explained. "One held that the reservation system, with attendant trusteeship and the existence of the Bureau of Indian Affairs, with its program of property management and human betterment," restrained Native people. The other supported the idea that the "protection of property and the provision of special services" by the bureau was all that stood between the Natives and "ultimate poverty, destitution and dependency."[23] The former, while accurate, often strangled tribal development and advancement. The latter also was accurate, demonstrating the love-hate relationship between tribes and the bureau.

Life in Indian Country could be much improved, the commissioner observed, if the bureau strategically directed economic development and matched it with specific reservation resources. Contrary to popular opinion, poverty and distress were not a result of any inherent deficiency of Indian Country, neither were they the result of tribalism.[24] An escape from poverty required patience, but it also demanded "respect for a way of life that is different from ours." The key was the raising of capital—private and public—constructing a modern transportation system, and creating incentives to attract businesses to Indian Country. Without these, economic development would have little hope of success.[25]

Development in Indian Country faced challenges, and Nash admitted he was unsure how Natives as a whole might respond. Nonetheless, he committed to a multistrand process of growth, beginning with the bureau hiring experts from the fields of economics and social sciences. In conjunction with the Natives themselves, Nash directed the bureau to assist tribes in developing comprehensive plans on a reservation-by-reservation basis. And to ensure that the tribal organizational structure was compatible with economic development, Nash worked with tribes to streamline and modernize the process of developing resources and business ventures by amending constitutions and bylaws.[26] This was no small task, as most tribal economies were agrarian and the transition to a commercial, industrial, or recreational economy required changes in posture, processes, priorities, and policy.

The status quo was not an option for Nash. In 1961, he used an Accelerated Public Works Program to put Indians to work. Within two years, he secured appropriations of $12 million and created fifty-seven hundred jobs on eighty-eight reservations in eighteen states that included road construction, improving tribal timber stands, building community centers, and conserving soil.[27] At Laguna Pueblo, an electronics plant created two hundred jobs.[28] Nash also used force account work to create additional public works jobs by using tribal labor to construct, repair, and maintain governmental facilities, with 2,847 employed in such work.[29] In 1963, he initiated twenty-six feasibility studies to explore economic development on reservations, with a total of eighty-one studies completed within two years.[30]

Feasibility studies considered the universe of tribal resources but focused on industrial development, light manufacturing, and tourism/recreation. By mid-decade, seventy-six commercial and industrial enterprises operated in Indian Country, employing more than three thousand people, 80 percent of whom were Native. Tourism and recreational endeavors, such as resorts, winter sports venues, and summer cottages, rapidly expanded and provided seasonal employment.[31] The latter endeavors had the potential to transform "some of the most desirable" mountain and desert scenery in the West into "major recreational resources" for the tribes.[32] Nash estimated that the timber industry provided an additional five thousand jobs, with tribal forest production surpassing one billion board feet harvested annually.[33] Some 57,523 leases of Native land netted $55,989,000 in payments, but created only a limited number of jobs and ran counter to the goal of providing Native employment opportunities.[34] While not focused on the agricultural sector, Nash lamented the fact that the bureau had yet to complete a single Indian irrigation project.[35]

To encourage development, Nash reorganized the bureau and established a Division of Economic Development that rested on two pillars. The first was "proper management of land, timber, water, range, livestock, minerals, and other resources" and the second was resource development by which such assets could be employed for maximum productivity.[36] Using an array of War on Poverty programs, including Economic Opportunity Act funding, Nash established Job Corps for employment and training; Youth Corps to encourage at-risk students to remain in school; Head Start for prekindergarten education; and Community Action Programs for adult education, preemployment training, and manpower availability to build capacity for long-term sustainability.[37] He envisioned each of these strands positively stimulating development in Indian Country. To underscore the potential of the anticipated renewal, Nash visited every tribal and Alaska Native community during his tenure in office.

But resource development in Indian Country would be successful only if Native people received an education commensurate with the need. Nash argued that improved educational opportunity was essential to realize the goal of "maximum Indian economic self-sufficiency."[38] The bureau in 1963 did move a step closer to its goal of every child in school when it completed thirty-eight facilities accommodating five thousand additional students. Nash also opened the Institute of American Indian Arts in the old Santa Fe Indian School to encourage and promote fine arts; and he converted Haskell Indian School into Haskell Junior College. As important, he established summer school and incorporated English as a Second Language into bureau schools to foster achievement.[39]

Nash's goal was to provide an education for every child and eliminate overcrowded and unsafe schools. While 48,000 children were enrolled in bureau schools, it did not attain its goal of 90 percent enrollment until 1965. By then, more than 82,300 children were in public schools, including all children in California, Idaho, Minnesota, Nebraska, Washington, and Wisconsin.[40] To meet the needs of the industrial and manufacturing plants being constructed across Indian Country,

Nash doubled vocational training. Congress appropriated $7.5 million to train more than 22,000 Indians.[41] But Nash also retained Hildegard Thompson as director of Indian education. A holdover from the Eisenhower administration, Thompson was committed to "continuity rather than innovation," limiting the overall level of change in philosophy.[42]

Kennedy made improved housing in Indian Country another of his priorities and, in 1961—twenty-two years after passage of the Public Housing Act—he made applicable to Indian Country the provisions of the Public Housing Administration.[43] While the Kennedy task force identified inadequate housing as a concern, it was Nash who championed the application of the Public Housing Administration to Indian Country. As a result, tribal nations for the first time established housing authorities, with eighty in place by 1966.[44] To make public housing responsive to tribal needs, the Bureau of Indian Affairs and the Public Housing Administration executed a memorandum of agreement under which tribes committed land and labor via a mutual aid program. The Public Housing Administration provided fiscal resources to construct homes, a process Nash described as analogous to an "old fashion barn-raising."[45] While a start, adequate housing remained an elusive goal.

Nash believed that economic development would be hindered if social needs stemming from poverty and discrimination were left unaddressed. To remedy these issues, he retained additional social workers, with more than twelve thousand Natives receiving monthly counseling by mid-decade. The bureau also provided monthly financial assistance to more than twenty thousand tribal people, demonstrating the depth of socioeconomic distress. Nash also continued the Indian Adoption Project, placing forty-five children into adoptive homes in 1965, bringing to 189 the total number of adoptions since 1959.[46]

While encouraging economic development and providing a host of social resources, the real challenge in Indian Country was securing capital, a need that nearly overwhelmed tribes.[47] Nash sought to finance development by encouraging tribes to devote their Indian Claims Commission (ICC) judgments to long-term development, rather than distributing them per capita.[48] In 1965, the ICC awarded nearly $60 million in judgments, the largest of which was a $29.1 million award to California tribes for Congress's failure to ratify the 1851–1852 treaties that resulted in the confiscation of their land and resources. Table 9.2 lists the 1965 judgments.

Nash committed to implementing the recommendations of the Kennedy task force, defining the purpose of the Bureau of Indian Affairs in strictly economic terms. He remained resolute in promoting the long-term goals of stabilizing and then improving tribal economic and political structures and developing tribal business capacity.[49] Such stabilization became more acute as tribes became eligible for federal grants and programs, navigated the federal bureaucracy to secure funds, and gained judgments from the Indian Claims Commission. There was no reason for poverty in a nation of abundance, Nash argued, when all that was needed was "the awakening of the national conscience."[50]

By mid-decade, there was a palpable rise in expectation throughout Indian Country. For the first time, federal policy encouraged tribal participation in programs established for their benefit. With the 1964 Economic Opportunity Act, President Johnson placed Indian welfare at the

Table 9.2. Indian Claims Commission Judgments Awarded in 1965

Tribal Nation	Award
Chemehuevi	$996,834.81
Oneida (Emigrant Party)	$1,313,472.65
California Tribes	$29,100,000.00
Iowa Tribe	$1,372,267.50
Iowa Tribe	$633,193.77
Miami Tribe (Indiana/Oklahoma)	$773,131.25
Ottawa Tribe	$406,188.19
Southern Paiute	$7,253,169.19
Pottawatomie, Ottawa, Chippewa	$2,094,573.02
Sac and Fox	$1,096,533.42
Sac and Fox	$965,560.39
Sac and Fox	$1,789,201.45
Sac and Fox (Missouri)	$192,000.00
Seminole Tribe	$63,680.00
Shoshone (Wind River)	$120,000.00
Confederated Ute Tribes	$7,908,586.16
Ute (Uncompahgre)	$300,000.00
Yakima Tribe	$61,991.40
Yakima & Confederated Colville	$3,446,700.00
Total	$59,887,057.20

Source: *Annual Report of the Commissioner of Indian Affairs*, 1965, 9.

front of the War on Poverty. But Udall sought more radical change—the "best, boldest and most imaginative thinking"—than the slower, long-term approach adopted by Nash.[51] When Senator Henry Jackson (D-WA)—who advocated termination of the Colville tribes, which was opposed by Nash—became chairman of the Committee on Interior and Insular Affairs, Nash's days were numbered. By 1965, both the House and Senate Interior and Insular Affairs committees opposed the commissioner. "The gains made so far have not yet wiped out all Indian unemployment," Nash lamented in his final report, "nor raised the average level of Indian income above the poverty line, nor eliminated substandard housing, nor brought equal educational opportunity."[52] He recognized time was a requisite for change, a fact Udall refused to accept. While reestablishing trust with tribal nations, Nash was forced to resign on March 9, 1966. "The whole government will be better served with different leadership," he wrote in his letter of resignation to President Johnson, as "much remains to be done."[53] Nash left office March 15, 1966.

COMMISSIONER ROBERT L. BENNETT

President Johnson nominated Robert Lafollette Bennett, a member of the Oneida Tribe of Wisconsin, to replace Nash. Bennett became the second American Indian after Ely Parker (Seneca) in 1869—both from the Iroquois Confederacy—to hold the title of commissioner of Indian affairs.

Bennett joined the Indian Office in 1933 after completing law school and worked his way up the organization, before Udall picked him as commissioner.[54] He assumed the mantle of leadership on April 27, 1966.[55] When President Johnson administered the oath of office, he charged Bennett to be "progressive, venturesome, and farsighted." If he did, the president pledged, "the full power of the institution of the Presidency of the United States" would support him.[56]

Bennett vowed to bring Native people "to the forefront of the national conscience," arguing that tribal voices had for too long "been like whispers." It was time for them to be "raised in one chorus," Bennett added, as the federal-Indian relationship was at a crossroad.[57] In an address before the National Congress of American Indians in Oklahoma City, Bennett urged tribal leaders to unify their voice to shape policies, programs, and laws. Tribes were in a position to increase their contact and relationship with federal agencies, and the time was at hand for them once again to negotiate as political equals with the United States and for the bureau to reduce "its day-to-day involvement" in their affairs.[58] Udall was more vocal, noting that as long as the tribes were content "to make the Bureau a scapegoat," change would be dilatory. Progress was found in "boldness and taking risks, not timidity."[59]

At the same time, Udall was under pressure by senators Henry Jackson (D-WA), Clinton Anderson (D-NM), and Frank Church (D-ID) to support a full-fledged termination policy. Indeed, as part of Bennett's confirmation hearing, the Senate requested of Bennett a report describing how he would handle the problems of Indian Country. The Senate Committee on Interior and Insular Affairs argued that if tribes had been prepared to "go their own way more than a decade ago," they would now be prepared to do it alone. Bennett replied that, until Congress changed its political relationship with tribes, it should "meet its responsibilities to them . . . of maximum social and economic development."[60] When Udall met with the National Congress of American Indians in Santa Fe in the spring of 1966, he sought to bargain his way out of termination, promising that if the tribal delegates supported termination of the Agua Caliente Band of Mission Indians, he would work to stay termination altogether. The tribal leaders refused to surrender and left Santa Fe victorious, with termination halted.[61]

Bennett was committed to the goal of tribes setting their own priorities, seeking to turn the bureau into a consulting and professional agency. When the Senate Subcommittee on Interior and Insular Affairs inquired as to the policy of the United States with respect to termination, Bennett was forthright: the tribes "will have to help us define [the role]." He covenanted with tribal leaders to foster tribal decision-making, accelerate and improve public school opportunities for Native children, and assist tribes in expanding industrial and recreational/tourism opportunities.[62] Whether Indians resettled in urban centers where there were better educational and economic opportunities, or remained on their reservations, was a personal choice. Bennett directed the bureau to make greater use of its authority to contract with tribes to operate and manage programs under the 1908 Buy Indian Act.

In the 1968 appropriation hearings, Bennett informed the Senate Subcommittee on Appropriations that he was working to develop tribal capacity to assume "full responsibility for managing their own property and income," and that he was seeking to transfer "management responsibilities from the Federal trustee to Indians and Indian tribes."[63] Paternalism "must be a thing of the past," Bennett stated, as it was time for a policy of self-determination.[64] President Johnson supported Bennett's vision in a March 1968 message to Congress when he called for "a goal that ends the debate about 'termination' . . . and stresses self-determination."[65]

Bennett heeded the voice of Indian Country and worked to eliminate the "stifling effects" of federal domination. In an address to the Governors' Interstate Indian Council in Reno, Nevada, he reminded state executive leaders that "civil rights remain theoretical as long as economic exclusion continues."[66] The most significant obstacle to development was keeping tribes "in isolation from, rather than in relationship with . . . the total community." If state and local governments corroborated with tribes, Bennett stressed, state economies would be strengthened, as well. It was no longer practical for federal, state, local, and tribal governments to work in isolation.[67]

The commissioner continued the poverty programs initiated by Nash but faced a Native citizenry concerned with termination, with tribes continuing to view policies and agencies suspiciously when federal officials discussed turning over management to them. When Congress considered the Indian Resources Development Act in 1967, it proposed to lessen regulatory oversight to increase self-sufficiency through federal loan guarantees and insurance. It also considered federal charters that would enable tribes to form corporations and issue tax-exempt bonds but included a provision that required tribes to mortgage trust land.[68] Tribal opposition to the mortgage provision doomed the bill and it failed to gain passage.

At Udall's request, Bennett reorganized the bureau, but not before hosting tribal leaders in a series of nine regional meetings, soliciting their input on increasing self-government, attracting capital to Indian Country, and fostering economic endeavors.[69] With the reorganization, Bennett established the position of assistant commissioner for Indian education, adding stature to educational matters. Between 1966 and 1968, funding for government schools under the Elementary and Secondary Education Act increased from $5 million to $9 million. Vocational funding increased to $25 million by 1968, with 28,900 adults enrolled.[70] But the most significant change was Bennett's support for locally controlled schools and the active participation of Native people in "all phases of community life."[71]

Using Economic Opportunity Act (EOA) funding, a group of Navajo leaders converted Rough Rock Day School into the first tribally controlled school: Rough Rock Demonstration School. While the bureau offered the use of its school at Lukachukai, federal civil service laws required that the school retain its teaching staff. To bypass civil service, the Navajo chartered DINE, Inc. (Demonstration in Navajo Education), under Arizona law in 1966 to receive direct funding from EOA. The bureau then turned over to DINE a brand-new school at Rough Rock, with DINE hiring the teachers and administering the school. DINE received $636,000 in bureau and Office of Economic Opportunity funding for school year 1966–1967, successfully demonstrating the vitality of tribally controlled schools.[72] A year later, the Gila River Indian Community followed suit when it converted Blackwater Day School into Blackwater Community School.[73]

To facilitate local control over education and build capacity in self-government, Bennett established a sixteen-member National Indian Education Advisory Committee and created the first guidelines for transferring bureau schools to tribal control.[74] Using bureau and Head Start funding, Bennett launched kindergarten classes in thirty-four bureau schools in 1968, the same year that the Navajo Tribe established Navajo Community College, the first tribally controlled institution of higher learning in the nation.

By 1968, the scene was set for a major policy announcement. In a special address to Congress, President Johnson asked for $500 million in educational, job training, economic development, and healthcare funding for Indian Country. "Our goal must be a standard of living for Indians equal to that of the country as a whole," Johnson stated. Natives had to be afforded "an opportunity to remain in their homeland, if they choose, without surrendering their dignity, and an opportunity to move to the towns and cities of America, if they choose, equipped with skills to live in equality and dignity."[75]

To give substance to his request, Johnson established the National Council on Indian Opportunity to promote Indian affairs and tribal involvement. Chaired by Vice President Hubert H. Humphrey, the council included the heads of six federal cabinets: Interior (Stewart Udall); Agriculture (Orville Freeman); Commerce (Cyrus R. Smith); Labor (W. Willard Wirtz); Health, Education, and Welfare (Wilbur R. Cohen); Housing and Urban Development (Robert C. Weaver); and the Office of Economic Opportunity (Bertrand M. Harding). Five Indian and one Alaska Native leaders were also appointed, including Wendell Chino (president of the National Congress of American Indians and chairman of the Mescalero Apache Tribe); Cato Valandra (president of the Rosebud Sioux Tribe); Roger Jourdain (chairman of the Red Lake Chippewa); Raymond Nakai (chairman of the Navajo Tribe); La Donna Harris (Comanche); and William Hensley (Alaska Native and member of the Alaska state legislature).[76]

Outside of building infrastructure to support self-government, Bennett fostered economic development, periodically releasing for public consumption success stories from Indian Country. In August 1966, for instance, he lauded the Hopi Tribe for its success in negotiating a $1.5 million contract using tribal resources for a garment factory in Winslow, Arizona. The plant was projected to employ eight hundred people in the border town and create additional jobs at on-reservation feeder sites.[77] Using Office of Economic Opportunity Act funds, Bennett launched the Selected Indian Reservation Program in 1968 to speed the process of on-reservation development and stimulate tribal economies.[78] In the Southwest, seventeen tribes formed the Indian Development District of Arizona for mutual planning and economic development supporting tribal and nontribal interaction.[79] The Gila River Indian Community pioneered the work by collaborating with neighboring towns to develop the Chandler Lone Butte and Coolidge Blackwater industrial parks.[80] By 1968, federal funding for Indian programs was dispersed throughout the federal agencies, with 56 percent of the funds coming through the Bureau of Indian Affairs, as shown in Table 9.3.

Tribes were reticent to embrace self-governing programs, with the National Congress of American Indians and tribal leaders advocating official repudiation of termination. This reticence stemmed in part from the social policies initiated by Nash, including the Indian Adoption Project, which by 1968 had arranged for the adoption of 608 Indian children.[81] On April 11, 1968,

Table 9.3. Federal Funding for American Indians, 1968

Federal Agency	Funding
Small Business Administration	$380,000
Labor	$1,845,000
Housing and Urban Development	$2,573,000
Interior (non-BIA)	$2,813,000
Agriculture	$12,124,000
Commerce	$18,542,000
Health, Education and Welfare	$21,672,000
Office of Economic Opportunity	$35,203,000
Indian Health Service	$103,552,000
Bureau of Indian Affairs	$249,719,000
Total	$448,423,000

Source: *Annual Report of the Commissioner of Indian Affairs, 1968*, 15.

Congress granted tribes a partial victory when it approved of the Indian Civil Rights Act, which amended Pub. L. No. 280 by mandating tribal consent before any state assumed civil or criminal jurisdiction over reservations.[82] Title I of the act extended basic civil rights to all Native peoples in Indian Country, limiting the power of tribal governments through the extension of the due process and equal protection clauses of the U.S. Constitution.

Congress had considered civil protections for Indians as early as 1961, when the Senate held hearings on the "Constitutional Rights of the American Indian."[83] In 1965, a federal appellate court upheld a tribal member's right to sue for a writ of habeas corpus against a tribal court.[84] While the court held the matter applicable only to the Fort Belknap Reservation—by virtue of the fact that the tribal government was organized under the Indian Reorganization Act and, therefore, was an extension of a federal agency—tribes across the country were stunned. Senator Sam Ervin (D-NC) and the Senate Judiciary Committee then advanced a bill protecting the civil rights of all American Indians in Indian Country. While extending most of the Bill of Rights to tribal people in Indian Country, the Indian Civil Rights Act did not include a first amendment establishment clause (in deference to tribes such as the theocratic Pueblos) and did not include a right to counsel unless at a defendant's own expense.[85] The civil rights guaranteed are listed in Table 9.4.

COMMISSIONER LOUIS R. BRUCE

In the end, Bennett struggled to overcome tribal concerns with termination and, with the election of Richard M. Nixon as president in November 1968, he resigned effective May 31, 1969. Nixon's presidency was greeted with concern, as many Native leaders had fresh in their minds the termination mindset of the previous Republican president. Tribal leaders, Vine Deloria Jr. later recalled, "waited for the axe to fall," but in the end "were pleasantly surprised" with the policies of the Nixon administration.[86] But while the president committed to filling the commissionership with an

Table 9.4. Indian Civil Rights Protections

1968 Act	U.S. Constitution Provision
Free Speech	First Amendment
Free Exercise	First Amendment
Free Press	First Amendment
Right to Assemble and Petition	First Amendment
Unreasonable Searches and Seizures	Fourth Amendment
Double Jeopardy	Fifth Amendment
Self-Incrimination	Fifth Amendment
Just Compensation	Fifth Amendment
Due Process	Fifth Amendment
Speedy and Public Trial	Sixth Amendment
Right to Confront and Cross-Examine Witnesses	Sixth Amendment
Right to Counsel (own expense)	Sixth Amendment
Trial by Jury (criminal only)	Sixth Amendment
No Excessive Bail	Eighth Amendment
Equal Protection of the Law	Fourteenth Amendment
No Ex Post Facto Law	Article 1 §9
No Bill of Attainder	Article 1 §9

Source: Adapted from Deloria, *American Indians, American Justice*, 129.

indigenous leader, he discovered most qualified candidates were Democrats. After a seven-month search, Secretary of the Interior Walter J. Hickel found a man for the position: Louis Rook Bruce, a Mohawk-Sioux who was born on the Onondaga Reservation in central New York. An enrolled Oglala Sioux, Bruce had been one of the founders of the National Congress of American Indians, where he served as Executive Director, and had organized the first National Indian Conference on Housing in 1961. He assumed office on August 8, 1969, just three months before the occupation of Alcatraz Island.[87]

While an American Indian, Bruce was neither a prominent leader nor did he come from within the hierarchy of the bureau.[88] He surrounded himself with young Native activists and advocated self-determination despite the inertia of the federal government. Hickel supported an increased voice for tribes, directing Bruce to restructure the bureau to make it fully responsive to the Indians.[89] Bruce dismantled some of the bureaucratic restrictions that interfered with self-determination and set out to "assist Indians to develop themselves and their resources to the maximum."[90] In his first policy address, given to the National Congress of American Indians on October 9, 1969, Bruce pledged to "develop a climate of understanding" that would permit "full development" of the tribes "without the threat of termination."[91] Hickel informed tribal leaders that he supported Bruce and was committed to improving the "relationship that exists between Government, the Indians, and the land."[92]

Bruce reorganized the bureau, seeking to make it responsive to the needs of Indian Country by supporting tribal involvement. He targeted a redefinition of education (pre-K to adulthood), tribal government, community services, and tribal control.[93] Hickel then named Morris Thompson, an Athabascan from Alaska, as special advisor on Indian affairs and established an advisory committee in the secretary's office made up of tribal leaders.[94] Working with Bruce, he abolished agency superintendents and replaced them with field administrators, with Bruce eliminating the deputy director and six assistant commissioners in the central office and replacing them with two associate commissioners of his own choosing.[95]

Hickel and Bruce concurred on the direction they sought to bend the strands of policy, with the former explaining it was "time to stop thinking merely of 'economic development,'" with the latter adding that the Great Society was "just not our thing."[96] Now was the time for Native leaders to define the policies that would govern them in the future, with Native decision-making the only means of improving tribal economies and self-governance.[97] "I want non-Indians to stop telling us what is wrong, what to do, and how it should be done," the commissioner shared with western Oklahoma tribal leaders, as he pledged Indian direction would henceforth be "the standard operating procedure" for the bureau.[98]

Bruce advised President Nixon in defining a new direction in policy and, on July 8, 1970, the president outlined his vision in an address to Congress in which he described why "the time has come to break decisively with the past and to create the conditions for a new era in which the Indian future is determined by Indian acts and Indian decisions." Federal policy oscillated between termination and paternalism, with both equally harmful. It was time for a policy of self-determination "without the threat of eventual termination."[99]

Nixon then outlined nine specific policy considerations:

- Rejection of termination with a new concurrent resolution expressly denouncing and repealing H.C.R 108
- Legislation empowering tribes or tribal groups to "take over the control and operation" of bureau or Indian Health Service programs "whenever the tribal council or ... governing group voted to do so," with the United States providing technical assistance to ensure tribes were equipped to administer such programs
- Restoration of Blue Lake and forty-eight thousand acres of land to Taos Pueblo
- Enabling tribes to control the education of their children, with Johnson-O'Malley funds going directly to the tribes
- Encouraging economic development via an Indian financing bill that would authorize ninety-nine-year leases and increase from $25 to $75 million the revolving loan fund
- Increasing funding for healthcare
- Assisting urban Indians, with an express recognition of the bureau's obligation to provide services
- Creation of an Indian Trust Council to provide independent legal representation for tribal natural resources
- Establishment of an assistant secretary for Indian and Territorial Affairs

By fall 1970, Bruce deployed his policy priorities, beginning with the transformation of the bureau from a management to a service agency. He reaffirmed the trust status of Indian land,

Table 9.5. Buy Indian Act Contracting, Fall 1971

Number of Contracts	Dollar Value
32	< $5,000
14	$5,000–$9,999
16	$10,000–$19,999
22	$20,000–$99,999
4	> $100,000
93	$26,602.53 (average)

Source: U.S. Department of the Interior, Indian Affairs, "Statement on Indian Affairs by Secretary Rogers C. B. Morton," October 4, 1971.

pledged assistance and training for tribes to assume control over federal programs—if they chose—and incorporated protection of tribal natural resources by establishing an Indian Water Rights Office with representatives from the solicitor's office, the bureau, and the U.S. Geological Survey. That same fall, Congress restored sacred Blue Lake and forty-eight thousand acres of land to Taos Pueblo.[100]

In 1970, Zuni Pueblo became the first tribe to contract with the United States for administering all bureau functions within the Zuni Reservation and, a year later, the Miccosukee Tribe in Florida followed suite.[101] The bureau also approved of 724 Buy Indian Act contracts with tribes and tribal groups by the summer of 1971, and approved an additional 93 contracts that fall, each averaging $26,602, as shown in Table 9.5. The single largest contract was with the Ute Tribe for $424,502 for fabrication of dormitory furniture for the Intermountain Boarding School.[102]

To facilitate tribal capacity, Bruce offered a Tribal Affairs Management Program, with the bureau initiating training in 1972 for tribes to plan and manage their own development programs and administer day-to-day governmental functions.[103] He utilized the Reservation Acceleration Program to enable tribes to negotiate changes in local bureau budgets to support tribal priorities, an early effort to make the bureau amenable to local needs.[104] Bruce also worked with the newly established National Tribal Chairmen's Association to solicit input on policy and continued coordinating with the National Congress of American Indians to delineate policy strands.

Changes in educational policy highlighted Bruce's tenure, with a Senate Subcommittee on Indian Education issuing a report in the fall of 1969 entitled "Indian Education: A National Tragedy—A National Challenge." Education had become "a stain" on the national conscience, reflecting a continuing story of despair, frustration, and hopelessness. There were "children who want to learn but are not taught [and] adults who try to read but have no one to teach them."[105] The Native drop-out rate was double the national average, fewer than 18 percent of Native youth went to college (national rate was 50 percent), and a per capita expenditure for school books and supplies was just 45 percent of the national average.[106]

The report (colloquially known as the "Kennedy Report" after Senator Robert Kennedy, who initiated the study, and Edward Kennedy, who completed it) recommended the president establish a White House Conference on Indian Affairs and elevate the commissioner of Indian affairs to an assistant secretary of the interior level to increase the visibility of Indian affairs and provide direct access to the secretary. Reminiscent of the 1928 Meriam Report, the Kennedy Report pointed to "the low quality of virtually every aspect of schooling available to Indian children," with all aspects of education of a "shocking quality."[107] Not surprisingly, the "coercive assimilation" policy had a "strong negative influence on national attitudes," "disastrous effects" on the education of children, and fostered an "intolerance of tribal communities." An expectation of failure had proven to be a self-fulfilling prophecy. In short, American Indians had "little, if any, influence or control in the education of their children," whether in public or bureau schools.[108]

The report helped give rise to a renewed call for maximum Indian participation "in the development of exemplary educational programs." To support such programs, the subcommittee recommended educational set-asides for tribal schools and an Indian Education Act that would consolidate all educational programs and authorities. More than thirty pages of recommendations covered pre-K to adult education.

The report buttressed President Nixon's call for self-determination, especially in the field of education. In 1972, Congress approved the Indian Education Act, providing a 5 percent set-aside for tribally controlled schools; authorizing grants for tribes, institutions, and organizations to develop and implement programs to improve educational opportunities for children; and promoting adult education. All federal programs for Indian education, including Impact Aid, were now consolidated.[109] While the act did not address the matter of self-determination—calling instead for tribal input into, not control of, grants for education and teacher training—it was a start. Two years later, the act was amended to increase the tribal set-aside to 10 percent and provide preference to Indians in awarding of grants.[110] By 1973, there were thirteen tribally controlled schools.[111]

Congress also addressed the matter of Alaska Native aboriginal rights with the passage of the Alaska Native Claims Settlement Act (ANCSA) in 1971. Driven by oil companies desiring to extract minerals from Alaska, the act extinguished all aboriginal claims within the state in exchange for forty million acres of land set aside in fee for Alaska Natives.[112] The United States compensated Alaska Natives $962.5 million for land they might have lost and then opened the state to the exploration and development of mineral resources. The ANCSA recognized 225 Alaska Native village corporations and set up twelve regional corporations to hold and manage Native land and resources. Individual Alaska Natives were issued one hundred shares of stock and enrolled in a village corporation, which could be organized as for-profit or not-for-profit. Alaska Natives also became shareholders in their regional corporations, which governed mineral development on a regional basis. While the villages received ownership of the land and surface features, the regional corporations retained the subsurface minerals and were set up to oversee the several villages. The act proved important in that it not only settled the issue of land ownership in Alaska but it also indicated that the United States was willing to enter into bilateral agreements with tribal nations to resolve complex land and policy issues, something that had not been done for more than sixty years.

Hickel supported Bruce's efforts to increase the tribal voice, but after the November 1969 takeover of Alcatraz Island by members of "Indians of All Tribes," a more militant voice emerged in Indian Country. By the following fall, President Nixon asked for Hickel's resignation. The Senate confirmed Rogers C. B. Morton as the new secretary of the interior in late January 1971. Morton was not as flexible as Hickel and forthwith promoted John O. Crow to the reestablished position of deputy director "to tighten [the bureau's] administrative management."[113] Crow was then given authority to administer all internal operations of the bureau.[114] In a further effort to tighten his grip, Morton eliminated the two assistant commissioners Bruce had established and reorganized thirteen subdepartments with department heads reporting to Bruce and Crow.[115]

Morton's appointment as secretary and Crow's selection as deputy commissioner initiated a power struggle within the Bureau of Indian Affairs, with Bruce supportive of younger activists and Crow supporting the establishment. The rise of the American Indian Movement and the urban Indian activists that occupied Alcatraz created tension at a time of great civil unrest in the United States. The year 1972 was one of incredulity in Indian Country, as a number of Natives were murdered and/or beaten without justice, leading a group of activists to assemble in Denver to plan a caravan to Washington, D.C.[116] In October 1972, these activists embarked on a Trail of Broken Treaties, stopping at reservations across the country. The caravan converged on Washington, D.C., during the final week of the 1972 presidential election, having prepared a list of twenty points regarding Indian status and the nature of the federal-Indian relationship to present to federal officials.

The twenty points centered on reopening the treaty process and demanding respect for existing treaties, including an acknowledgment of treaty rights to land and resources, such as hunting and fishing. The demonstrators demanded that all Natives be governed by the treaty relationship. While Crow sought to send the protestors home, Bruce remained open to meeting with them. On November 3, the activists took over and occupied and then ransacked the bureau offices in Washington, resulting in complete disorganization of Indian affairs and disregard for civil discourse.[117] Bruce personally met with the protestors in an unsuccessful attempt to bring the occupation to a close.

On December 8, Bruce announced his resignation, effective January 20, 1973.[118] On the same day, the bureau announced that its Washington, D.C., offices were repaired and the bureau was back in operation. By then, Morton had vested all "authority for administrative control" in Assistant Secretary of the Interior Richard S. Bodman.[119] One month later, the American Indian Movement occupied the Pine Ridge hamlet of Wounded Knee, South Dakota, drawing international attention to Indian affairs. Bruce, caught between an evolving policy of self-determination and militant activism, was forced from office along with a cadre of senior management officials.[120]

ASSISTANT TO THE SECRETARY MARVIN L. FRANKLIN

Morton did not immediately replace Bruce, instead appointing Marvin L. Franklin, an attorney, oil executive, and member of the Iowa Tribe, as assistant to the secretary for Indian affairs, on February 7, 1973.[121] Franklin was assigned responsibility for all bureau programs and functions, reporting directly to Morton. To his credit, the new assistant to the secretary did not sit passively, agreeing with Undersecretary John C. Whitaker that the federal government had "exhausted the limits of existing [Buy Indian Act] authority" to provide tribes with opportunities to achieve self-determination.[122]

To take self-government to the next level, the Nixon administration prepared a series of legislative proposals, including elevating the commissioner of Indian affairs to an assistant secretary of the interior position to increase the visibility of Indian affairs. While not a new concept, the administration proposed allowing tribes to assume control of bureau programs and enable federal civil servants to transfer with the programs while retaining their federal benefits. The administration also proposed guarantees for loans to make Indian Country more attractive to private lenders while at the same time raising the ceiling to $75 million for Indian financing. Nixon also proposed the creation of an Indian Trust Council to provide independent legal counsel for tribes to better protect natural resources. A separate bill would authorize tribes to enact laws governing trader licenses on the reservations and providing penalties for individuals allowing stock animals to trespass on trust or restricted land.[123]

Franklin outlined four objectives to lay the groundwork for the future of Indian affairs, including a constitutional amendment to "lay to rest once and forever the matter of termination." If self-government were to materialize, the United States could not take unilateral action without tribal involvement. Moreover, Franklin proposed a national banking system for Indian Country and an Indian Reservation Renewal Act that would provide $250 million annually for ten years to improve tribal economies.[124] He informed the National Congress of American Indians that unity was essential since the federal courts engaged in an "insidious encroachment" upon tribal property and rights each year.[125]

The assistant to the secretary lamented the continued lack of understanding of Native peoples on the part of the American public. This failure to understand tribes jeopardized tribal resources—human and natural—Franklin argued, since half of the Indians in the country were either non-federally recognized or urbanized and "unjustly separated from [their] base of services." Equal treatment for all Natives, Franklin explained, meant that urban and non-federally recognized tribes should also be eligible for federal services.[126]

COMMISSIONER MORRIS THOMPSON

By early fall, Nixon settled on a candidate to lead the bureau and, on October 30, 1973, he nominated thirty-four-year-old Morris Thompson, an Athabascan from Alaska, as commissioner of Indian affairs.[127] A civil engineer, Thompson had been active in the Alaska Native Claims Settlement Act and had served as an assistant to Secretary Hickel in 1969. He was confirmed by the Senate on November 28 and sworn in on December 4, 1973, stressing his optimism that the nation was coming to grips with a "new awareness of Indian needs" and that the climate was favorable for "truly meaningful progress."[128] Thompson was the first commissioner of Indian affairs to report directly to the secretary of the interior.[129]

Table 9.6. Lands Restored to Tribal Control by 1975

Reservation	Acres Restored
Fort Peck	85,000
Navajo	70,000
Bad River Chippewa	13,149
Blackfeet	9,037
Cheyenne River Sioux	3,739
Crow Creek Sioux	19,170
Lower Brule Sioux	13,300
Fort Totten	1,425
Fort Belknap	25,531
Lac Court Oreilles	13,185
L'Anse Chippewa	4,017
White Earth Chippewa	28,545
Pine Ridge Sioux	18,065
Rosebud Sioux	28,735
Fort Hall	8,712
Standing Rock Sioux	10,256
Cherokee Nation	18,750
Laguna Pueblo	520
Fort Mojave	3,500
Warm Springs	60,000
Total	434,636

Source: U.S. Department of the Interior, Indian Affairs, "New Legislation Adds Lands to Indian Reservations," October 31, 1975.

In his first address to tribal leaders, Thompson stated that if all of the Nixon legislative agenda was enacted into law, tribes would "be further ahead in self-determination than we have been in 150 years."[130] He immediately called the National Tribal Chairmen's Association and the National Congress of American Indians to Washington, D.C., for a two-day conference on the organization of the bureau, its recruitment efforts for management positions, and budgetary goals. He pledged effectiveness and efficiency in bureau operations and called for increased tribal involvement in determining priorities.[131]

While Congress had yet to formally repeal termination, it did agree with the Nixon administration on restoring the Menominee Tribe to federal status and, on December 22, 1973, the president signed into law the Menominee Restoration Act, a symbolic repeal of termination.[132] The act repealed the 1954 Menominee Termination Act and reinstated all of the rights and privileges to the Menominee Tribe under its federal treaties and statutes. On April 22, 1975, Menominee lands were formally restored to federal status, with Ada Deer, chair of the Menominee Restoration Committee and future assistant secretary for Indian affairs, describing the act as "the epitome of Indian Self-determination."[133] Thompson also worked to restore land to the tribes, reinstating over four hundred thousand acres by 1975, as shown in Table 9.6.

Another Nixon priority became law in 1974 when Congress approved of the Indian Financing Act, which provided capital to Indian Country on a reimbursable basis to develop and utilize tribal resources, with Title I establishing a $50 million revolving loan fund and Title II including a $20 million loan guaranty and insurance subsidy program.[134] But the most significant legislative enactment and the culmination of more than a decade of effort was the Indian Self-Determination and Educational Assistance Act of 1975, an act Thompson viewed as the commencement of a new era in the federal-Indian relationship. The Indian Self-Determination Act (Title I) was a watershed event in Indian Country, with the United States formalizing its obligation to respect and enhance self-government and its commitment to achieving "maximum" and "meaningful" tribal involvement for all federal programs in order to make them responsive and responsible to Native people by establishing a legal framework for contracting such control.[135]

Tribal reticence regarding the intent of the bill resulted in Congress enacting into law something less than the full takeover President Nixon originally sought. In the end, tribes agreed to a limited system by which they could contract with the Bureau of Indian Affairs and/or the Indian Health Service to assume control over portions of education, healthcare, and other programs serving them.[136] Congress committed to maintaining its "unique and continuing relationship with and responsibility to the Indian people" even while it put into place the mechanism for an "orderly transition from federal domination" to tribal control. As a corollary to self-determination, Congress enacted into law the Indian Healthcare Improvement Act to create a framework for bettering healthcare and providing the resources to accomplish it, and to create incentives for Natives to go into the field of medicine.[137]

Thompson also unveiled an Indian student bill of rights that guaranteed every child in a bureau or tribal contract school the right to an education free from unreasonable searches, guaranteeing reasonable privacy, with a safe and secure school environment, individual freedom of religion and cultural expression, free speech and expression, the right to peaceably assemble, petition for redress of grievances, and due process.[138] He also clarified that the Department of Health, Education and Welfare's financial aid package for Native college students was supplemental to, not in lieu of, other financial aid.[139] As a precursor to a religious freedom bill, Thompson issued protections for tribal members using federally protected bird feathers for ceremonial or cultural reasons.[140]

On November 3, 1976, Thompson resigned as commissioner, returning to Alaska where he became vice president of the Alcan Pipeline Company. He had assumed office at the nadir of the bureau, leading it out of the 1972 occupation of its Washington, D.C. offices and through the American Indian Movement of Wounded Knee occupation, during a time when there were few qualified Republican Natives willing to serve. Thompson transformed a department that fostered ideas of self-determination into one that played a policy-supporting, rather than a policy-making, role.

COMMISSIONER BEN REIFEL

President Gerald R. Ford, in a lame duck recess appointment, nominated Ben Reifel to replace Thompson. Reifel, a member of the Rosebud Sioux Tribe and a former Republican representative from South Dakota (1961–1971), was sworn in as commissioner on December 7, 1976.[141] At the age of seventy, he was the oldest man to serve as commissioner of Indian affairs. Reifel had little impact on policy, with newly elected President Jimmy Carter asking for and receiving his resignation on January 28, 1977.[142]

THE INTERLUDE

President Carter appointed Raymond Butler as acting commissioner on January 28 while he consulted with tribes on a replacement. Butler encouraged the president to set a consistent federal policy so tribes could improve their economic situation. The means of so doing were to protect tribal lands and natural resources, both of which were essential to the success of self-government.[143] Carter directed Interior Secretary Cecil D. Andrus to work with tribal leaders in compiling a list of potential nominees who would "be both an advocate of Indian causes and the administrator of a large, complex organization."[144]

In the interim, the Interior Department moved forward with the Maine Indian land claims based on a 1975 federal appellate court decision that concluded a federal trust relationship existed between the Passamaquoddy and Penobscot Tribes and the United States even though the latter had never federally recognized the tribes.[145] While unrecognized, the Passamaquoddy and Penobscot fit the definition of an Indian tribe and fell under the protection of the 1790 Trade and Nonintercourse Act. The 1794 Massachusetts treaty under which the tribes ceded their lands to the state (present-day Maine) was unconstitutional, the court opined, as the right to extinguish aboriginal title was "an attribute of sovereignty, which no state, but only the United States, can exercise."[146]

After Passamaquoddy, federal solicitor Leo Krulitz announced that Interior would support three additional tribal land claims, all in New York: the St. Regis Mohawk (10,500 acres), the Cayuga Tribe (64,000 acres), and the Oneida Nation (250,000 acres). All three Iroquoian tribes sought action to overturn New York state treaties resulting in the loss of their respective reservation lands. All three claims were premised on the protections of the 1790 Trade and Nonintercourse Act.[147] For similar reasons, the United States supported the Catawba Tribe, which sought to nullify the 1840 South Carolina state treaty resulting in the cession of their 140,000-acre reservation.[148]

Recognizing the adverse effect land claims would have on current landowners, Interior recommended solutions other than litigation, especially after the Narragansett Tribe in Rhode Island filed a claim for 3,900 acres lost to the state in 1880. The Rhode Island Indian Land Claims Settlement Act resolved the Narragansett Tribe's claims by recognizing 1,800 acres as Narragansett land in Charlestown in exchange for extinguishing all of their aboriginal claims.[149] The Narragansett settlement was the first of the Eastern Indian land claims and was instructive as it served as the prototype for resolving tribal land claims, following the precedent of the Alaska Native Claims Settlement Act in providing tribes with a bilateral process by which to settle claims and secure a land base.[150] But while the Carter Administration supported tribal land claims, it did not support the Shinnecock Tribe's claim to 3,150 acres on Long Island, New York, in large measure because the bureau could not determine whether the Shinnecock constituted an Indian tribe and there were serious questions as to whether the tribe ever fell under the protection of the Trade and Nonintercourse Act.[151]

Interior also advanced the defense of tribal natural resources—including water rights—arguing that "unless Indian tribes can fully utilize their natural resources, the opportunity to determine their own future will hold little promise."[152] To protect and enhance tribal development, the bureau advanced settlement of tribal water rights in the federal courts. After publishing regulations in 1977 governing the adoption of tribal water codes, Carter instructed federal agencies to begin quantifying and working to resolve Indian reserved water rights.[153] Secretary Andrus then requested the Justice Department to initiate legal action to protect the water rights on the Flathead, Blackfeet, Rocky Boy's, Fort Peck, and Fort Belknap Reservations (Crow and Northern Cheyenne water rights were already in litigation). The Montana state legislature then enacted a bill establishing a forum for all water rights, including Indian, in state courts.[154] Similar adjudication of western streams including water rights was undertaken on the Gila River in Arizona, the Walker and Truckee Rivers in Nevada, and elsewhere, with the president directing the bureau to develop a plan to resolve Indian water claims, emphasizing negotiated settlements.[155]

Another aspect of natural resources protection was the bureau's support of tribal hunting and fishing rights, particularly in the Pacific Northwest and in the Great Lakes. In the Northwest, the 1854–1855 treaties negotiated by Washington territorial governor Isaac Stevens expressly protected the tribal right "of taking fish, at all usual and accustomed grounds and stations . . . in common with all citizens."[156] The question was whether "in common" meant the tribes had a quantifiable right to fish and was this right exclusive or shared? There was also the matter of to what extent was the right protected and whether the state had jurisdiction over Indian fishing. The United States Supreme Court answered these questions emphatically in 1979 when it declared treaties guaranteed the tribes the right to take up to half of the fish.[157] Similar cases in the Great Lakes region recognized Chippewa rights to regulate off-reservation treaty-protected fishing as an exercise of tribal self-government.[158]

But while the courts upheld tribal hunting and fishing rights, it did not extend such recognition to include tribal criminal jurisdiction over non-Indians within Indian Country. When Mark Oliphant, a non-Indian living within the boundaries of the Port Madison Reservation in Washington State, was arrested for assaulting an officer and resisting arrest, he sued, arguing the tribe did not have criminal jurisdiction over him. In issuing its ruling, the Supreme Court opined in the *Oliphant* ruling that such jurisdiction was "inconsistent" with the dependent status of tribal nations and there were no principles in the jurisprudence of tribal jurisdiction to compel the court to "conclude that Indian tribes have inherent jurisdiction to try and punish non-Indians."[159]

By the spring of 1977, when James Joseph was sworn in as an undersecretary of the interior and assigned to oversee the Bureau of Indian Affairs, the bureau remained without a commissioner. Joseph announced that tribes and tribal organizations had nominated thirty-seven candidates for consideration and, by Memorial Day, he explained why Carter had yet to make a decision.[160]

"We have not wanted to sacrifice the opportunity for a broad input from Indian Country simply to get the selection done quickly." While the administration wanted a "new team fully capable of dealing with all the complexities of both the political landscape and Indian advocacy," tribes were concerned that Carter not only had not nominated a commissioner but also that he failed to issue a comprehensive policy statement.[161]

ASSISTANT SECRETARY FOR INDIAN AFFAIRS FORREST J. GERALD

On July 12, 1977, Carter nominated Forrest J. Gerard, a member of the Blackfeet Tribe, to replace Butler. The Senate confirmed Gerard on September 15, and he took office four days later as the first assistant secretary for Indian affairs.[162] Tribal governments had grown in scope and sophistication, Gerard explained in his first policy declaration to tribal leaders, even as he committed to making his administration one "of progress and achievement."[163] The president, having established an eleven-member task force, including representatives from the National Congress of American Indians and the National Tribal Chairmen's Association, reorganized the bureau, elevating the position of commissioner of Indian affairs to assistant secretary for Indian affairs. Although Secretary Andrus proposed adding several assistants, Gerard instead reinstituted the subordinate position of commissioner of Indian affairs. He appointed Martin E. Seneca Jr. to the position in October 1978, and appointed Sidney L. Mills, an Oglala Sioux, as acting deputy commissioner on July 30, 1979.[164] On September 28, 1979, President Carter nominated William E. Hallet, a member of the Red Lake Chippewa Tribe, as commissioner of Indian affairs; Hallet was confirmed on November 16 and assumed office on December 14, 1979.[165] He was the last commissioner of Indian affairs.

Throughout the later part of the decade, Gerard and the bureau utilized an antiquated process to recognize tribes, clearing the path for federal acknowledgment. Over the course of the federal-Indian relationship, some tribes or tribal groups were never acknowledged or did not engage in a government-to-government relationship with the United States. As Eastern land claims wound their way through the federal courts, these tribal groups demanded recognition. By June 1978, Gerard proposed the first regulations governing federal acknowledgment so tribes that had "maintained their political, ethnic, and cultural integrity" could be recognized.[166] Tribes "whose members and their ancestors existed in tribal relations since aboriginal times" and who had "retained some aspects of their aboriginal sovereignty" now had a process to seek federal recognition.[167] In 1978, the Pasqua Yaqui Tribe in Arizona was statutorily acknowledged as a federally recognized tribe under the process.[168] That same year, the Modoc, Wyandotte, Peoria, and Ottawa Tribes of Oklahoma were reinstated as federally recognized tribes, and two years later the Siletz Tribe and four Southern Paiute Bands were restored to federal status.[169] By 1979, forty tribal groups from twenty-one states petitioned for recognition, as shown in Table 9.7.

Two key elements of self-determination included recognition of American Indian religious freedom and tribal jurisdiction over the adoption and foster placement of Native children. After

Table 9.7. Tribes Seeking Federal Acknowledgment, 1978

Tribe	State	Tribe	State
Creek Nation	Alabama	Piscataway	Maryland
Poarch Creek	Alabama	Mashpee Wampanoag	Massachusetts
Tsimshian Tribe	Alaska	Grand Traverse Ottawa	Michigan
Antelope Valley	California	Huron-Pottawatomie	Michigan
Ione Band	California	Lac Vieux Desert	Michigan
Mono Lake	California	Little Shell Chippewa	Montana
Plumas County	California	Tiwa	New Mexico
Munsee-Delaware	Colorado	Shinnecock	New York
Eastern Pequot	Connecticut	Faircloth Indians	North Carolina
Mohegan Tribe	Connecticut	Hatteras Tuscarora	North Carolina
Nanticoke	Delaware	Little Shell Band	North Dakota
Creeks East	Florida	Edisto Tribe	South Carolina
Florida Creek	Florida	Coos Tribe	Oregon
Cherokee of Georgia	Georgia	Cowlitz Tribe	Washington
Lower Muscogee	Georgia	Duwamish Tribe	Washington
Southeast Cherokee	Georgia	Jamestown Clallam	Washington
Delaware Munsee	Kansas	Samish Tribe	Washington
Choctaw-Apache	Louisiana	Snohomish Tribe	Washington
Clifton Choctaw	Louisiana	Snoqualmie Tribe	Washington
Tunica-Biloxi Tribe	Louisiana	Steilacoom Tribe	Washington

Source: U.S. Department of the Interior, Indian Affairs, "Forty Indian Groups Petition for Federal Status as Tribes," December 27, 1978.

more than two centuries of subjecting Native people to civilizing policies and denying them access to traditional religious sites and the right to engage in cultural and religious practices, ceremonies, and traditions—including use of sacred objects, such as eagle feathers—Congress recognized Indian religious freedom with the American Indian Religious Freedom Act.[170] The act ensured that federal policies and procedures relating to tribal citizens were in compliance with the first amendment right to free exercise of religion.[171] Religious freedom was enhanced by the 1979 passage of the Archaeological Resources Protection Act, which prohibited destruction of archaeological sites without tribal consent.[172]

Congress also addressed the tribes' long-standing concern regarding the placement of children in non-Indian foster and adoptive homes. The Indian Child Welfare Act acknowledged the alarmingly high rate of Native families being broken up by the removal of children by nontribal agencies, especially as such adoptions escalated in the 1960s. The act included four provisions: defining state and tribal jurisdiction over the adoption process; authorizing state-tribal agreements over custodial proceedings; requiring full faith and credit of tribal placement proceedings; and providing for Indian preference (family, tribe, and other Indians) in the placement of children.[173]

By 1980, despite an infusion of federal resources and some positive changes, development still lagged in Indian Country, with Hallet observing that if the trend continued, "the goal of self-determination and self-sufficiency will eventually topple back onto the heap of good intentions."[174] Gerard observed Indian Country still lacked "some or all of the attributes necessary to support the economic enterprise functions."[175] For instance, Indian Country as a whole lacked an educated and trained work force, a sufficient transportation system, and adequate access to markets, each of which hindered development. Before leaving office, Gerard reminded tribes that the future was in their hands and that the children of the 1980s would "determine the future of Indian people." Just as policy changes in the 1970s emanated "from the unfinished agenda for racial and social justice in the 1960s," Gerard reminisced, "the generation of the 1980s will secure the benefits of the crucial Indian policy changes of the 1970s."[176]

ASSISTANT SECRETARY FOR INDIAN AFFAIRS THOMAS W. FREDERICKS

Gerard resigned as assistant secretary effected January 19, 1980, with Carter nominating Thomas W. Fredericks, a member of the Mandan-Hidatsa Tribe, on June 18, 1980.[177] In the lame duck days of the Carter administration, Hallet and Fredericks deployed a series of policy changes, including an affirmative action plan to recruit, employ, and promote Native women to mid- and senior-level management positions in the bureau.[178] Hallet also released a plan to generate more opportunities for Indian-owned businesses by modifying the definition of an Indian contractor from 100 percent Indian-owned to 51 percent.[179] In the final days of the Carter administration, Fredericks signed an interagency agreement to increase communication between the bureau and the U.S. Department of Education to improve education and increase the number of Native youth applying for federal educational assistance.[180] Fredericks and Hallet both resigned after Republican president Ronald Reagan was sworn into office in January 1981.

CONCLUSION

By 1980, the indigenous population in the United States had increased to 1,361,869, a considerable increase over the 237,196 enumerated eight decades earlier. By the dawn of the new decade, tribal nations were exercising more political authority than at any other time since the nineteenth century. The period between 1961 and 1980, therefore, proved to not only reverse the strands of termination and emphasize self-governance, but also resulted in a period of growth for tribes. With it was a strengthening of the government-to-government relationship and policies that were in some measure determined by the tribes themselves.

Tribes were also regaining their political voice and strengthening self-governance. But at the same time, some tribal intellectuals were asking what the future direction of self-determination was to be. Congress and the Bureau of Indian Affairs continued to encourage development of resources as an attribute of self-government. Self-determination, however—as some intellectuals defined the concept—differed from self-government. While the latter was economic development and resource exploitation, the former was social and cultural development. Self-determination was reflected in reservations as homelands predicated on responsible actions. If reservations were developed and the land was just another form of property, then self-government was the course to follow. If reservations were homelands, then the social reality of self-determination would look very different than self-government.

Self-government and self-determination were in fact two sides of the same coin; both pointed to the survival of tribal nations but represented different social realities.[181] Some tribal leaders argued that federal policy did not recognize the inherent nature of tribal existence. Oren Lyons, an Onondaga chief, expressed the sense of some when he stated tribes desired "to continue as separate nations," representing one side of the increasingly complex dichotomy of self-determination (cultural, spiritual, and social) and self-government (political).[182] Vine Deloria Jr., explained that too many Natives had forsaken self-determination for self-government, viewing themselves as nothing more than a needy minority. As a result of these complexities, Deloria predicted future federal policy would result in "smaller policy considerations" by the tribes and the United States, which would stabilize Indian affairs (and self-government) but do little in the way of self-determination.[183] How policy strands would be framed in the post-1980 political landscape would be reflected in either more self-government resulting from increased resource development (and movement towards integration), or self-government stemming from a core of self-determination (focused on tribalism and cultural renewal).

10

"A FEDERALIST PARTNERSHIP"

Indian Self-Determination, 1981–2017

Since 1981, when self-determination was in its infancy, the policy of self-government has expanded as tribal nations have reasserted their inherent sovereignty. The *sine qua non* was not whether self-government would continue but what shape it would take and whether it would facilitate self-determination. Would a collaborative federal policy strand encourage economic development that both strengthened self-government and enabled tribal nations to assert their economic and political authority in a manner that would rejuvenate tribal social and cultural sovereignty? Or, as Vine Deloria Jr. postulated, would tribes continue to see themselves as just another "needy minority"?

From the beginning of the Reagan administration, there have been eleven individuals confirmed as assistant secretary for Indian Affairs, beginning with Kenneth L. Smith, Wasco Tribe (1981–1984), and followed by Ross O. Swimmer, Cherokee Nation (1985–1989); Eddie F. Brown, Tohono O'odham-Yaqui (1989–1993); Ada E. Deer, Menominee Tribe (1993–1997); Kevin Gover, Pawnee Tribe (1997–2001); Neal A. McCaleb, Chickasaw Nation (2001–2002); David W. Anderson, Lac Courte Oreilles Chippewa (2004–2005); Carl J. Artman, Oneida Tribe (2007–2008); Larry Echo Hawk, Pawnee Tribe (2009–2012); Kevin K. Washburn, Chickasaw Nation (2012–2016); and Tara MacLean Sweeney, Inupiat, who was nominated by President Donald Trump in October 2017 and was confirmed by the Senate on June 28, 2018.

Over the past four decades, a handful of policy strands have governed the federal-Indian relationship. Beginning in 1975 as an outgrowth of self-government policies and a series of tribal resource claims, the United States engaged in a policy of trust reform reflected in a steady increase in the number of tribal groups seeking federal acknowledgment as indigenous tribes. This trust reform included tribal water settlements and an historic accounting claim in the *Cobell* case. Originating

Table 10.1. Heads of the Indian Office and Major Policies, 1981–2018

Name	Title	Years of Service	Main Policies
Kenneth L. Smith (R) (Wasco)	Assistant Secretary	3.8 years (1981–1984)	Self-reliance, budget reductions, federalism, Indian Land Consolidation Act
Ross O. Swimmer (R) (Cherokee)	Assistant Secretary	3.1 years (1985–1989)	Economic development, self-determination grants, Indian Gaming Regulatory Act
Eddie F. Brown (R) (Pasqua Yaqui)	Assistant Secretary	4 years (1989–1993)	Indian Self-Governance, trust reform, water settlements, Indian Graves Protection and Repatriation Act, education reform
Ada F. Deer (D) (Menominee)	Assistant Secretary	4.3 years (1993–1997)	Defended Indian Child Welfare Act, protect land-into-trust, opposed taxation of Indian Country, update federal acknowledgment, Office of Special Trustee
Kevin Gover (D) (Pawnee)	Assistant Secretary	3.2 years (1997–2001)	Government-to-government relationship, law and order reform
Neal A. McCaleb (R) (Chickasaw)	Assistant Secretary	1.5 years (2001–2002)	Economic development, trust reform, business-government model, No Child Left Behind to Indian Country, Cobell litigation
David W. Anderson (R) (Lac Courte Oreille)	Assistant Secretary	13 months (2004–2005)	Role model for Indian Country, economic development, Indian Land Consolidation Act expansion
Carl J. Artman (R) (Oneida)	Assistant Secretary	1.2 years (2007–2008)	Social, political and natural resources development, intertribal business agreements, new federal acknowledgment guidelines
Larry Echo Hawk (D) (Pawnee)	Assistant Secretary	3 years (2009–2012)	Tribal consultation, rescinded Indian Gaming Regulatory Act regulations, federal acknowledgment clarified, Tribal Law and Order Act, Cobell and other claims settlements
Kevin K. Washburn (D) (Chickasaw)	Assistant Secretary	4.2 years (2012–2016)	Implemented land buyback under Cobell, modified land-into-trust regulations, settled tribal accounting claims, Violence Against Women Act applied to Indian Country
Tara MacLain Sweeney (R) (Inupiat)	Assistant Secretary	(2017–)	

in the 1960s and continuing into the twenty-first century is the policy advancing economic development as a means of facilitating tribal independence and reducing federal expenditures for Indian affairs. The culmination of this policy was Indian gaming, which brought an infusion of much needed revenue and employment for some tribes. Moreover, Congress and each of the presidential administrations have—to varying degrees—strengthened the policy of self-determination and (beginning in the 1990s) self-governance as the vehicle of enhancing tribal sovereignty. And finally, in the midst of these policies, Congress reduced federal funds budgeted for tribal programs.

ASSISTANT SECRETARY FOR INDIAN AFFAIRS KENNETH L. SMITH

The election of Ronald Reagan as president in November 1980, initiated a series of policy modifications premised on limiting federal involvement in Indian affairs and encouraging self-government. Reagan nominated Kenneth L. Smith as assistant secretary for Indian affairs on April 1, 1981. A member of the Wasco Tribe from the Warms Springs Reservation in Oregon, Smith advanced Reagan's policy of self-reliance, suggesting that tribes had the primary responsibility for improving their social and economic status.[1] Smith argued that the proper role of the federal government was to foster an environment that would "enable tribal governments to move toward less dependency." He informed the National Tribal Chairmen's Association that he would "keep Indians in the mainstream" of society.[2] Smith took office April 28, 1981.

The Reagan administration significantly reduced the bureau's budget, with Smith declaring that federal funding was not always helpful as it fostered dependency.[3] In 1982, the president reduced the bureau's budget by more than 12 percent, with Smith eliminating seven of the twelve regional offices, maintaining only the Albuquerque, Anadarko, Aberdeen, Phoenix, and Portland offices. Two regional offices were reduced to program offices—Juneau and Navajo—and two were converted into field offices—Billings and Minneapolis. By 1983, Smith planned the transfer of all bureau schools for Alaska Natives to the state of Alaska, with further transfers planned.[4] He then announced the closures of all boarding schools except Chemawa (OR), Sherman (CA), and Riverside (OK).[5] As a result, some viewed the Reagan budgetary strand as termination via fiscal reductions.[6]

The hallmark of the Smith era was the Presidential Commission on Indian Reservation Economies that pointed to developing enhanced, private sector investment to reduce tribal dependence on the national government and lessen the federal presence in Indian Country.[7] After sixteen field hearings, a nine-man commission reported to the president and advocated shifting the federal-Indian relationship "beyond that of benign paternalism to that of a federalist partnership."[8] It was time to reorder the relationship between the United States and tribal nations, the Commission concluded, even as it outlined forty major challenges (2,320 specific obstacles) to economic development. Among the barriers were an overregulating and "incompetent" Bureau of Indian Affairs, trust constraints on the part of the federal government, jurisdictional disputes with local governments, and an unfavorable business climate and unskilled workforce in Indian Country.[9] To strengthen tribal autonomy required overcoming federal, tribal, state, and local barriers. The commission recommended replacing the bureau with an Indian Trust Services Administration.[10]

Reagan sought to create a positive economic environment that would encourage greater self-government and enhance the government-to-government relationship.[11] Joe De La Cruz, president of the National Congress of American Indians, agreed in concept with advancing the government-to-government relationship but expressed the sentiments of tribes that they should be the ones to take the initiative.[12] With the support of tribes, Congress approved legislation that treated tribes as states for tax purposes.[13] In an attempt to end the fractionation of allotted land, Congress also enacted into law the Indian Land Consolidation Act, authorizing tribes to purchase with federal dollars at fair market value any fractionated trust or restricted land interest from willing sellers.[14] Combined, tribal governments were strengthened and control over fractionated lands encouraged tribes to develop for economic purposes heretofore idle land.

The Reagan years also were a time of tribal litigation centering on natural resource rights, including water settlements. Smith and Interior Secretary James Watt negotiated settlements but emphasized there would be no support for negotiations that did not include all state and local parties and represent a fair and equitable settlement to all.[15] To execute the policy, Watt established an Interior Policy Advisory Group and a series of negotiating teams to quickly and equitably settle as many of the fifty outstanding water claims as possible.[16] By October 1982, the Southern Arizona Water Settlement Act (Papago Tribe) was finalized, providing the San Xavier District and the Schuk Toak District of the Papago Reservation with Central Arizona Project water.[17] Four other settlements neared completion, including the Fort Peck Assiniboine-Sioux Tribes, the Mission Indians (San Luis Rey), Yakima Tribe, and Pyramid Lake Paiute.[18] The Fort Peck settlement with the United States and the state of Montana—and the resulting Fort Peck water code—quickly became the model for Indian Country, sending a message to state and tribal leaders that they could work collaboratively within the federal framework to resolve complex and complicated water disputes.[19] The Fort Peck compact resulted in a reserved water right for the tribes of 1,050,472 acre-feet of annual diversions, with the Fort Peck tribes controlling the water on reservation trust lands and the state of Montana controlling nontribal growers pursuant to state law on fee lands within the reservation. The tribes also retained the right to market water within the reservation and to market water off reservation under specific guidelines.[20]

Smith also worked with tribal groups seeking federal recognition following the general principles outlined by Felix Cohen in 1942 based on a solicitor's memo from 1939 governing the Mole Lake Band of Chippewa in connection with the section 16 land-into-trust provisions of the Indian Reorganization Act. Under these principles, petitioning tribal groups had to singly or jointly demonstrate they (1) had a treaty relationship with the United States; (2) had been declared a tribe by act of Congress or executive order; (3) had been treated as having a communal right to land or funds; (4) were treated as a tribe by other indigenous tribes; and (5) exercised political authority over their members.[21]

In 1978, in response to tribal groups claiming federal protection and rights, the bureau adopted criteria that petitioners had to demonstrate in order to gain federal acknowledgment. Before the United States would recognize a petitioner's federal status, the petitioning group had to demonstrate a sense of solidarity; a common origin; that it exercised political authority over its members; that it presently or historically inhabited a specific geographic area; that it had never been terminated by Congress; and that its members were not members of another tribe.[22]

The Reagan administration considered seventeen petitions for federal recognition, granting six of them—Jamestown Clallam Tribe, Tunica-Biloxi Tribe, Death Valley Timba Sha Shoshone Band, Narragansett Tribe, Poarch Creek Band, and the Wampanoag Tribe of Gay Head.[23] Congress also legislatively acknowledged five tribal groups: Cow Creek Umpqua, Mashantucket Pequot, Confederated Coos Tribe, Lower Umpqua Tribe, and the Lac Vieux Desert Band of

Chippewa, each of which had previously been recognized as a tribe, having been signatories to at least one federal treaty.[24] All except the Lac Vieux Desert Chippewa were preceded by litigation, prompting Congress to act to avoid costly claims.

ASSISTANT SECRETARY FOR INDIAN AFFAIRS ROSS O. SWIMMER

Smith resigned effective December 7, 1984.[25] After a nine-month search, Reagan on September 26, 1985, nominated Ross Owen Swimmer, an attorney and former principal chief of the Cherokee Nation, as the fourth assistant secretary for Indian affairs.[26] Swimmer, cochair of the Presidential Commission on Indian Reservation Economies, was confirmed by the Senate on December 4, 1985, and took office immediately in the midst of additional budget cuts. Tribes expressed concern that the president might abolish the bureau, notwithstanding Interior Secretary Donald Hodel's assurances to the contrary. Swimmer informed tribal leaders that if they desired strong, effective governments, they needed to develop strong economies. Tribes could no longer be "islands surrounded by the rest of America," Swimmer stated, and they should no longer rely on automatic budget increases. New money would be available but only to tribes "willing to accept the challenge of economic, political, and social development."[27]

Swimmer believed that fundamental changes were necessary to fulfill the tribal goal of self-determination. Despite commissions seeking to solve the challenges facing Indian Country, the only consensus was the need for economic development and a desire of tribes to set their own goals. In the meantime, the bureau grew increasingly frustrated at the lack of progress, with Hodel informing the House Subcommittee on Interior and Related Agencies Appropriations that "almost every proposal to change the status quo" was "met with fear and resistance."[28] Swimmer concurred, noting that with the exception of national defense and healthcare, the bureau provided some form of every federal, state, and local governmental service to Native people. It could not realistically fulfill such expectations when there was no consensus among the tribes, Congress, or the president as to what the priorities should be.[29]

Swimmer supported the president's goal of reducing regulatory restrictions to enable tribes to develop their economies. He encouraged Congress to identify bureau functions related to trust resource management and then transfer them to other federal agencies better qualified to carry them out. He went so far as to reevaluate Indian preference, suggesting there were only so many qualified Natives, with the Bureau of Indian Affairs, Indian Health Service, tribal governments, and national Indian organizations "all competing to obtain the best of a very small workforce." To ameliorate the situation, Swimmer unsuccessfully advocated waivers of Indian preference at the federal level.[30]

As for non-trust assets, Swimmer advocated Congress authorize self-determination grants under which tribes would receive federal dollars with complete autonomy to determine which programs to fund. If tribes chose not to contract for such services, the bureau would continue to provide them, or tribes could contract for programs and subcontract back to the bureau to fulfill some or all of them. It was "time to give the tribes the responsibility they seek," Swimmer concluded, while at the same time redefining the concepts of self-determination and self-government.[31]

One aspect of economic development that tribes exploited was gaming. As early as 1969, the Oneida Indian Nation in New York sought to open a bingo hall on Oneida Territory as a way out of poverty. In the 1970s, the Seminole Tribe in Florida followed suit, opening a high stakes bingo facility only to see the state attempt to shut it down. The Seminole sued, with the Fifth Circuit Court of Appeals opining that Florida bingo laws were regulatory, not prohibitory, and, as such, unenforceable on the Seminole Reservation.[32]

The Fifth Circuit Court relied on a 1976 Supreme Court decision that clarified the breadth of state jurisdiction. When Itasca County, Minnesota, sought to tax the property of Helen and Russell Bryan—both members of the Leech Lake Band of Chippewa Indians—they sued, alleging the state did not have jurisdiction to tax personal property of Indians living on trust lands. While the district court and Minnesota Supreme Court ruled in favor of the state, the U.S. Supreme Court reversed the decision, interpreting Pub. L. No. 280 more narrowly. While some states—such as Minnesota—had civil and criminal jurisdiction over Indian Country, they did not have authority to tax trust land. Nowhere in the federal statute or legislative history of Pub. L. No. 280 had Congress granted states authority to subject reservation-based Indians to state taxation.[33]

The *Bryan* case opened the door for tribes to reassert sovereignty, leading to the *Seminole* ruling. As gaming expanded, the U.S. Supreme Court addressed its legality in a case originating on the Cabazon Indian Reservation in California—another Pub. L. No. 280 state. California also attempted to regulate tribal gaming, arguing it had jurisdiction under Pub. L. No. 280. In rendering its decision, the Supreme Court distinguished between "civil prohibitory" and "criminal prohibitory," arguing a state statute that was "criminal prohibitory" applied on reservations but statutes that were "civil prohibitory" did not. State gaming laws were civil prohibitory and, therefore, tribal gaming was not subject to California jurisdiction. The Cabazon Band of Mission Indians, as well as other tribes, was free to operate casinos outside of state jurisdiction.[34]

In the wake of the *Cabazon* decision, Congress enacted into law the Indian Gaming Regulatory Act (IGRA) to establish rules for the operation and regulation of tribal casinos, mandating gaming profits be directed to tribal governance activities.[35] The IGRA classified tribal gaming into three categories. Class I included traditional tribal or social gaming that was under exclusive tribal jurisdiction. Class II included bingo, poker, and other nonbanked games in which individuals competed against other players, but not the house. Class III included slot machines, blackjack, craps, roulette, and other games played against the house. Class II gaming was legal in Indian Country as long as it was legal within the state, and no tribal-state compact was required. Class III, however, required a compact to ensure protections were in place for state and local governments.[36]

Gaming had important impacts in Indian Country, the first of which was the development of tribal institutions to regulate gaming to preclude criminal infiltration. This included the National Indian Gaming Commission, which ensured compliance with federal law and provided oversight. The second was the development of a stronger tribal-state governmental relationship. With IGRA

Table 10.2. Land Acquisitions Approved by the Office of Indian Gaming, 1990–1999

Tribe	State	Acres	Date Approved	Category
Tunica-Biloxi	Louisiana	21.1	November 15, 1993	1
Coushatta	Louisiana	531.0	September 30, 1994	1
White Earth Chippewa	Minnesota	61.7	August 15, 1995	1
Wyandotte	Kansas	0.5	June 6, 1996	1
Saginaw Chippewa	Michigan	480.3	April 14, 1997	1
Cherokee	Oklahoma	15.7	September 24, 1993	2
Cherokee	Oklahoma	7.8	February 18, 1994	2
Sisseton-Wahpeton	North Dakota	143.1	September 30, 1994	2
Fort Sill Apache	Oklahoma	0.5	March 11, 1999	2
Forest Pottawatomie	Wisconsin	15.7	July 10, 1990	3
Kalispel	Washington	40.1	June 26, 1998	3
Grande Ronde	Oregon	5.6	March 5, 1990	4
Siletz	Oregon	11.0	December 4, 1994	4
Coquille	Oregon	20.0	February 1, 1995	4
Mohegan	Connecticut	240.0	September 28, 1995	4
Klamath	Oregon	42.3	May 14, 1997	4
Little River Ottawa	Michigan	152.8	September 24, 1998	4
Little Traverse Bay Ottawa	Michigan	5.0	August 27, 1999	4

Source: General Accounting Office. Indian Gaming Regulatory Act, October 1, 1999.

requiring state compacts, it was essential that tribal and state governments worked together, furthering the process of reducing barriers that benefit both governments today.

To ensure gaming did not expand to off-reservation lands tribes might acquire, Swimmer announced that the bureau would deny requests to take off-reservation land into trust if the purpose of such actions was for gaming. Land into trust that fit the "tribal homelands" concept remained unaffected.[37] The IGRA also established specific criteria for taking land into trust, with tribal requests needing to satisfy one of four categories: (1) the land had to be within or contiguous to a reservation as of October 17, 1988; (2) land that was once within a tribe's reservation or was contiguous to tribal land, in the case of Oklahoma; (3) land designated for gaming by the secretary of the interior after he determined it was in the best interests of the tribe and was not detrimental to local jurisdictions; and (4) land tribes acquired under a land claim settlement that was part of a terminated tribe's restoration to federal status, or instances where Congress gave federal recognition to a tribe and its reservation. Table 10.2 lists the approvals by the Office of Indian Gaming of land acquisitions for gaming purposes between 1990 and 1999.

ASSISTANT SECRETARY FOR INDIAN AFFAIRS EDDIE F. BROWN

Swimmer announced his resignation in November 1988, and left office on January 29, 1989, just days after George H. W. Bush took office as president.[38] Bush named William P. Ragsdale of the Cherokee Nation as acting head of the Bureau of Indian Affairs while he began a search for the next assistant secretary. On April 13, Bush nominated Eddie Frank Brown, an enrolled Pascua Yaqui (and Tohono O'odham) from Arizona, as assistant secretary for Indian affairs, with Brown confirmed by the Senate on June 21.[39] Brown held a doctorate in social work and was a former bureau employee and director of the Arizona Department of Economic Security before being nominated.

Brown emphasized education, economic development, trust reform, and self-governance, placing education at the top of his agenda.[40] Education became a priority after a Senate Special Committee on Investigation uncovered a pattern of sexual abuse in some bureau schools.[41] Brown initiated background checks and pledged his commitment to hire the best qualified staff to fill bureau schools, including the position of director of Indian education. To mitigate the "deplorable conditions" at many bureau schools, Brown—with Secretary of the Interior Manuel Lujan's support—proposed to move education into a separate Office of Indian Education, a move Congress blocked until Brown appointed a task force to evaluate how the bureau should be structured.[42] Not until August 2006 was the Office of Indian Education sequestered and renamed the Bureau of Indian Education with its own director. Lujan also accelerated funding for the $550 million backlog of repairs and maintenance of bureau facilities, although Congress remained reticent to appropriate the necessary funds.

To facilitate development, Lujan established a Working Group on Indian Water Rights to establish principles to guide settlements, linking such agreements with overall national water resource management and conservation. In 1991, he announced an agreement on the Animas La Plata Project that settled the claims of the Ute Mountain Ute and Southern Ute Tribes, while benefiting the Navajo Tribe and the states of Colorado, Utah, and New Mexico. While the Ute settlement had been authorized in 1988, it took three years to implement the agreement, apportion costs, and address environmental issues.[43] Interior also settled the Fort McDowell Yavapai Tribe (1990), Fort Hall Shoshone-Bannock Tribes (1990), Pyramid Lake Paiute (1990), Fallon Paiute Tribe (1990), Northern Cheyenne (1990), San Carlos Apache Tribe (partial 1992), and Jicarilla Apache (1992) water claims.

The driver of federal policy remained economic development, with Brown informing tribal leaders in Florida there was "no single magical formula that would solve unemployment and poverty." In a series of conferences held across the United States, Brown met with tribal leaders to address the challenge. Building on Swimmer's efforts before him, Brown approached the topic recognizing there was a role for tribal, federal, state, and local governments.[44] By July 1990, Lujan and Brown announced "a new chapter giving form and substance" to self-government. In a series of agreements with the Quinault Nation ($3.9 million), Lummi Tribe ($2.2 million), Jamestown Clallam Tribe ($687,000), Hoopa Valley Tribe ($2 million), Cherokee Nation ($6.1 million), and Mille Lac Band of Chippewa ($267,210), the bureau established pilot self-governance agreements enabling the six tribes to gain authority for budgeting and spending bureau funds. Annual funding agreements defined the scope of services and dollars associated with them, the first time tribal governments were afforded such latitude to bend programs to their unique needs.[45]

The Senate Select Committee on Indian Affairs urged Congress to consider a policy of entering into agreements that would enable tribal nations to direct their own affairs while at the same time negotiate federal support for tribal governments. In the process, the policy of New Federalism began to take shape.[46] Self-governance through voluntary agreements would enable tribes to assume responsibility for self-government, with federal assets and appropriations transferred in toto to the tribes under written compacts. The pilot project proved such a success that on October 25, 1994, Congress amended the Indian Self-Determination Act and authorized the Tribal Self-Governance Act.[47]

Congress explicitly recognized the inherent sovereignty of the tribes, even while lamenting how the federal bureaucracy had eroded and dominated tribal governments. Under self-governance, Congress authorized the secretary of the interior to select up to twenty tribes annually to participate and, using annual funding agreements, authorized tribes to "plan, conduct, consolidate, and administer programs, services, functions, and activities" then administered by the Department of the Interior, including, but not limited to, the Bureau of Indian Affairs.[48] Tribes could now assume control over other Interior programs, including the Bureau of Reclamation and the National Park Service, with the Gila River Indian Community becoming the first tribal nation to place an irrigation system under tribal self-governance when it executed a compact with Reclamation in 1995. Notwithstanding such latitude, the Tribal Self-Governance Act expressly prohibited the secretary from "waiving, modifying, or diminishing" his trust responsibilities.

In a move to protect self-determination over cultural patrimony, Congress enacted into law the Indian Graves Protection and Repatriation Act, one of the few Indian legislative enactments of the George H. W. Bush administration. The act enhanced tribal sovereignty over Native burial sites, the removal of human remains from federal lands, funerary objects, sacred objects, and other matters of cultural patrimony by mandating tribal consent and involvement.[49] All federal agencies and museums receiving federal funds that had possession of Native American human remains or associated funerary objects were required to complete an inventory within five years and repatriate them to culturally affiliated tribes for reburial.

Brown unsuccessfully sought to address the long-standing mismanagement of Indian trust funds, which totaled $2 billion, by deploying a strategic plan that included fifty action items.[50] For more than two centuries, the United States had deposited treaty or trust funds into accounts for tribes and/or individuals, losing track of or mismanaging the funds or misidentifying ownership interests in them for hundreds of thousands of Native people. By the 1990s, the problem had become acute, with Brown committing to resolve accounting discrepancies, improve the collection, investment, and distribution of funds, and ameliorate any deficiencies and "complexities" in the accounts.[51] The sheer magnitude of the matter would take decades to resolve.

Federal acknowledgment slowed during the Brown tenure, with only the San Juan Southern Paiute Tribe, which had been long encapsulated by the larger Navajo Tribe in northeastern Arizona, acknowledged. Congress also recognized the Aroostook Micmac Tribe by amending the Maine Indian Land Claims Settlement Act in 1991.[52] As important, the Department of the

Interior adopted additional regulations to clarify the existing acknowledgment process and expand its definitions to guide tribal groups seeking recognition.[53]

ASSISTANT SECRETARY FOR INDIAN AFFAIRS ADA E. DEER

With the election of Democrat Bill Clinton as president in November 1992, Brown resigned, agreeing to remain in office until the president nominated a replacement. On May 11, 1993, Clinton nominated Ada E. Deer as assistant secretary.[54] A former chair of the Menominee Tribe after leading the successful federal restoration of the tribe in 1975, Deer became the first woman to lead the Bureau of Indian Affairs. She was highly recommended by numerous tribes and tribal organizations after laboring more than twenty-five years with the Native American Rights Funds, Americans for Indian Opportunity, and the American Indian Graduate Program at the University of Wisconsin. She was unanimously confirmed by the Senate on July 16, 1993, and assumed office immediately.

Deer served at a time of further budget reductions by a Congress committed to its "Contract with America." In fall of 1995, the House Indian appropriations conferees reduced the bureau's central office budget 26 percent and area office budgets 28 percent, crippling the bureau and making it difficult to carry out its trust obligations. The Tribal Priority Allocation budget supporting basic governmental services (which tribes could move around to meet their priorities) was reduced by 15 percent, or $110 million.[55]

In 1995, Congress sought to weaken the Indian Child Welfare Act (ICWA) and tribal authority over adoption by defining members of a tribal nation as those who were on the active membership roll of a tribe, or those who were otherwise considered members. Tribal citizenship was effective from "the actual date of admission to membership" and was not retroactive so as to avoid any "arbitrary retroactive designation of individuals as members."[56] The following year the Pryce amendment was reintroduced, which sought to limit tribal sovereignty by amending the ICWA to grant non-Indian social service agencies authority to determine whether a biological parent retained sufficient "social, cultural, or political affiliation" with a tribe to warrant ICWA jurisdiction.[57] Deer countered that "this basic determination should rest with Indian tribal courts," as to do otherwise would strip such judicial forums of their fundamental authority.[58]

Tribal nations also faced a hostile judiciary. In 1990, the Lower Brule Sioux requested the Department of the Interior to take ninety-one acres of fee land into trust for purposes of economic development. The state of South Dakota and the city of Oacoma sued, believing they were deprived of property tax revenue and regulatory authority and that section 5 of the Indian Reorganization Act violated the federal nondelegation doctrine, which precludes Congress from delegating its legislative authority to the executive branch. While section 5 of the Indian Reorganization Act authorized the secretary "to acquire, through purchase, relinquishment, gift, exchange, or assignment, any interest in lands, water rights, or surface rights to land, within or without existing reservations, including trust or otherwise restricted allotments ... for the purpose of providing land for Indians," the Eighth Circuit Court ruled in favor of the state.[59]

The regulations governing land into trust dated to the Carter administration. In 1995, in response to South Dakota, the bureau revised its regulations, requiring public notification of intent to take land into trust and providing thirty days for any challenge. The regulations required the secretary to base his decision for taking land into trust on a number of factors, including (1) statutory authority for the acquisition, (2) tribal need for additional land, (3) purpose for which the land would be used, (4) amount of land a tribe already held in trust, (5) impact on state or local tax rolls, (6) potential for jurisdictional conflicts, (7) bureau preparation for the acquisition, (8) federal environmental compliance, (9) location of the land and distance from the reservation, and (10) tribal business plan describing the anticipated benefits of the acquisition.[60]

With these revisions, Deer requested the Justice Department to petition the Supreme Court for a *writ of certiorari* to vacate the appellate decision. The Supreme Court agreed to the writ, vacating the Eight Circuit Court's decision with instructions to vacate the district court's ruling and remand back to the secretary of the interior.[61] South Dakota, nonetheless, continued to litigate, with the district court rejecting its challenge. When the state appealed to the Eight Circuit Court on the same grounds, the court again rejected the state's argument; the U.S. Supreme Court also refused the state's petition for *certiorari*. South Dakota continued to resist land into trust, unsuccessfully litigating applications for the Yankton Sioux, Sisseton-Wahpeton Sioux, and Flandreau Sioux.[62] Had the state prevailed, nine million acres taken into trust for tribes since 1934 might have been susceptible to a clouded title, potentially subjecting tribes to state taxation, land-use policies, resource regulations (hunting and fishing), and law enforcement.

The House also considered subjecting tribes to taxation on gaming and other economic activities in Indian Country. Interior Secretary Bruce Babbitt and Assistant Secretary Deer strongly opposed the proposals, explaining that taxation of tribes was not only counter to the Indian Self-Determination Act but also foiled the federal trust responsibility. Moreover, taxation would contradict the intent of Congress in enacting into law the IGRA, which mandated gaming revenues be used to support economic development, self-sufficiency, and stable tribal governments. The federal government did not tax the several states, Deer noted in a letter to House Ways and Means Committee Chairman Bill Archer (R-TX), and it should not tax tribal governments, which were "struggling to overcome centuries of poverty."[63]

Deer also defended tribes and tribal groups against onerous federal acknowledgment criteria, which came under scrutiny during the Clinton administration as time-consuming—notwithstanding the fact that six of nine petitioners were granted federal recognition, including the Mohegan Tribe, Jena Band of Choctaw, Huron Band of Pottawatomie, Samish Tribe, Match-E-Be-Nash-She-Wish Band of Potawatomie, and the Snoqualmie Tribe. Interior, in 1994, revised the acknowledgment process largely based on criteria proposed by President Bush in 1991. These mandatory criteria are listed in Table 10.3.[64]

In 2000, the bureau released additional guidance on federal acknowledgment in an attempt to streamline the process and reduce the backlog of petitions by including a "reasonable likelihood" of the facts supporting a petitioner's case.[65] By the end of calendar year 2000, Congress recognized several tribal groups, including the Pokagon Pottawatomie, Little Traverse Odawa, the Little

Table 10.3. Federal Acknowledgment Criteria, 1994

Criteria	Code of Federal Regulations
a. Identify as an American Indian entity on a substantially continuous basis since 1900.	§ 83.7(a)
b. Comprise a distinct community and exist as a community from historical times until present.	§ 83.7(b)
c. Maintain political influence or authority over members as an autonomous entity from historical times until present.	§ 83.7(c)
d. Present governing documents, including membership criteria.	§ 83.7(d)
e. Members consist of individuals who descend from a historical tribe or from historical tribes that combined and functioned as a single autonomous political entity.	§ 83.7(e)
f. Membership composed principally of persons who are not members of any acknowledged North American Indian tribe.	§ 83.7(f)
g. Petitioner and its members are not the subject of Congressional legislation that has expressly terminated or forbidden the federal relationship.	§ 83.7(g)

Source: 25 C.F.R. § 83.7 (1994).

River Ottawa, Graton Rancheria, and the Loyal Shawnee, the latter of which was the last tribe to gain recognition via congressional act.[66] In 1994, the Interior Department administratively acknowledged the Ione Band of Miwok Indians of California.

ASSISTANT SECRETARY FOR INDIAN AFFAIRS KEVIN GOVER

Deer announced her resignation as assistant secretary on January 9, 1997, agreeing to remain in office until her successor was named.[67] Clinton nominated Kevin Gover in the summer of 1997, with the Senate confirming him on November 9; he was sworn in three days later. A member of the Pawnee Tribe, Gover worked with tribes to strengthen law enforcement and rebuild schools that were in disrepair. He defended tribes when the Senate proposed to waive sovereign immunity after a series of high-profile tribal corruption cases. Acknowledging that there were legal challenges between states and tribes, Gover argued for resolving such disputes "through the government-to-government" relationship, not via a unilateral waiving of sovereign immunity that was "reminiscent of the Termination Era."[68]

In a speech before the University of South Dakota School of Law, Gover urged tribes to restore their "warrior traditions" by redefining leadership as a "commitment and sacrifice that transcends all personal interests." Self-government was under attack, he stated—in part, not without cause—as some tribes and leaders, such as Peter McDonald of the Navajo Tribe, acted irresponsibly. It was important for tribes to exercise probity and guardedly use their authority so as not to lend credence to those critical of sovereign immunity.[69] On the 175th anniversary of the bureau, Gover apologized to American Indians and Alaska Natives for federal "ethnic cleansing and cultural annihilation" policies. Healing could begin only after the wrongs of the past were acknowledged and Natives replaced "anger with hope" and "allowed broken hearts to mend."[70]

To that end, Gover signed the first government-to-government consultation policy with tribal nations on December 13, 2000. An extension of the Indian Self-Determination Act, consultation included a federal pledge to advance self-government by involving tribes early on any federal action that might affect them, including regulations.[71] The policy not only encouraged greater self-government but also reflected interest in tribal concerns. At the 1998 National Congress of American Indians winter meeting, Gover requested a workgroup of tribal leaders to draft the policy. Two years later, he deployed it as a policy strand integral to self-government.

ASSISTANT SECRETARY FOR INDIAN AFFAIRS NEIL A. MCCALEB

Gover resigned January 3, 2001, and Interior Secretary Bruce Babbitt replaced him with acting Assistant Secretary Michael Anderson (Muscogee Creek), who remained through the end of the Clinton administration on January 20.[72] With the election of Republican George W. Bush, the search for the next assistant secretary began, with the president appointing James H. McDivitt as acting assistant secretary. On April 17, 2001, the president nominated Neil A. McCaleb of the Chickasaw Nation as the eighth assistant secretary for Indian affairs, with the Senate confirming him on June 29; he was sworn into office on July 4.[73] A professional engineer from Oklahoma, McCaleb served as Oklahoma director of transportation (1987–1995), oversaw construction and maintenance for the Oklahoma Transportation Authority (1995–2001), and served eight years in the Oklahoma state House. He was also a member of President Reagan's Commission on Indian Reservation Economies.[74]

Following his swearing in, McCaleb announced his immediate goal of making the bureau an "Indian service" to American Indians and Alaska Natives, deploying his first policy strands of economic development, education, public safety, and trust reform.[75] In an address before the National Congress of American Indians in Bismarck, North Dakota, he informed tribal leaders that they could "choose between poverty and prosperity" for their people, encouraging them to accept change and develop their economies. "If you keep doing what you've always done, then you're always going to get what you've always gotten," McCaleb exclaimed.[76]

To promote economic development, McCaleb pointed to the same three factors that long limited Indian Country: capital, access to markets, and a skilled workforce. But he also believed it was important for tribes to create a positive climate for job growth by establishing business and legal cultures that reduced risks to investors while at the same time improving economic and educational opportunities for tribal members. He endorsed the goal of creating one hundred thousand new jobs in Indian Country by 2008, notwithstanding the challenges of developing the infrastructure to support market-driven enterprises. Tribal gaming, McCaleb suggested, would provide a business-government model that could be expanded to other ventures, including renewable energy.[77]

To support economic development, the bureau hosted a National Summit on Emerging Tribal Economies that led to the creation of a national strategy to achieve the goal of one hundred thousand "sustainable, market driven" jobs by 2020.[78] To generate sustainable economies, McCaleb recognized that tribes needed access to markets, which required transportation networks enabling goods, services, and people to move to and from Indian Country, no small feat given the remote nature of most reservations.[79]

An educated populace was essential to a sustainable, market-drive economy, with a well-educated and skilled workforce "key to growth and sustaining growth." McCaleb and Interior Secretary Gale Norton set a series of goals under the No Child Left Behind Act that every child would read independently by the third grade, seven out of ten students would be proficient in reading and math, attendance in bureau and contract schools would be 90 percent or greater, and all students would demonstrate knowledge of their indigenous language and culture.[80] While presidential candidate George W. Bush pledged $920 million in school funding, President Bush's proposed budget included just $292.5 million for school construction and upgrades.[81] Two-thirds of tribal schools still lacked funds for expansion, replacement, and maintenance. To address this deficit, McCaleb encouraged Congress to afford tribal governments the same tax-exempt status as state and local governments so they might issue bonds for infrastructure.

A corollary to education was improving public safety, with McCaleb advocating privatization of bureau facilities to tribes and tribes leasing them back to the bureau to operate if they so chose. This had great potential if tribes issued tax free bonds to expand such facilities.[82] Public safety also required trained law enforcement officers to ensure a safe and stable environment to support development. Weak tribal courts and an overall lack of legal infrastructure adversely impacted Indian Country, with McCaleb calling on tribes to sequester their judicial from their executive functions. This, too, was an exercise of sovereignty, the assistant secretary stated, one that was central to nation-building.[83]

McCaleb acknowledged there was a "trust mess" at the bureau, including administration and accounting of tribal funds and resources. Before assuming office, he explained that no one should expect a "quick and immediate fix to problems that have been decades, if not more than a century, in the making."[84] When Congress established the Office of Special Trustee in 1994 to oversee trust funds, the Senate considered transferring all bureau trust responsibilities to the agency, a proposal McCaleb opposed, believing the bureau's day-to-day functions were so broad that to transfer basic trust functions to the Office of Special Trustee was equivalent to "the elimination of the BIA and its re-creation under another name."[85] While the 1984 Presidential Commission on Indian Reservation Economies—of which McCaleb was a member—concluded the bureau was "incompetent" to fulfil its trust obligations, including the management and investment of tribal funds and assets, neither Congress nor McCaleb supported such an extensive modification.[86] While Congress reorganized the bureau in 2002, it retained all of its trust responsibilities.

McCaleb was the conduit for tribal input on the reorganization, which was largely spurred by the lawsuit filed by Eloise Cobell, a banker and member of the Blackfeet Tribe. In 1996, Cobell filed a class action lawsuit against the U.S. Department of the Interior and the Department of Treasury for "mismanagement, ineptness, dishonesty, and delay" in withholding $150 billion in American Indian trust funds from the nineteenth century forward.[87] In September 2002, the U.S. District

Table 10.4. Federal Acknowledgment, 2002–2008

Tribal Group	State	Action	Year
Chinook Tribe	Washington	Denied	2002
Muwekma Ohlone Tribe	California	Denied	2002
Duwamish Tribe	Washington	Denied	2002
Cowlitz Tribe	Washington	Affirmed	2002
Snohomish Tribe	Washington	Denied	2004
Golden Hill Paugusett Tribe	Connecticut	Denied	2005
Eastern Pequot	Connecticut	Denied	2005
Paucatuck Pequot	Connecticut	Denied	2005
Schaghticoke Tribe	Connecticut	Denied	2005
Mashpee Wampanoag Tribe	Massachusetts	Affirmed	2007
Burt Lake Ottawa/Chippewa	Michigan	Denied	2007
St. Frances/Sokoki Abenaki	Vermont	Denied	2007
Steilacoom Tribe	Washington	Denied	2008
Webster/Dudley Band of Nipmuc	Massachusetts	Denied	2008
Hassanamisco Nipmuc Nation	Massachusetts	Denied	2008

Source: Petitions Resolved by Department of the Interior, Office of Federal Acknowledgment, 2017.

Court held McCaleb and Norton in contempt for failing to address in a timely manner how the bureau would administer trust funds and carry out an accounting of all trust assets.[88]

In November, Norton proposed stripping the bureau of all of its trust responsibilities, an overture McCaleb did not support, because tribes feared it was part of a larger effort to dismantle the agency.[89] Moreover, the transfer of trust obligations to the Office of the Special Trustee and increased tribal self-governance had legal ramifications, with the U.S. Supreme Court in 2003 ruling that the federal trust could be incompatible with tribal self-government. As tribes exercised more decision-making over their resources, the court hinted at diminishment of the federal trust, complicating an already delicate matter.[90]

Another aspect of trust reform was the federal acknowledgment process, which remained unchanged from the rule modification in 2000. While the Clinton administration proposed a moratorium on acknowledgment, the Senate—led by Daniel Inouye (D-HI) and Ben Nighthorse Campbell (R-CO)—opposed it. Federal recognition became one of the more controversial issues facing the administration, with the department affirming recognition for just two of fifteen tribal petitioners, as shown in Table 10.4.

On November 21, 2002, McCaleb unexpectedly resigned, citing the weight of the *Cobell* litigation and trust reform. He left office on December 31, with Norton appointing Aurene M. Martin, a member of the Bad River Band of Chippewa, as acting assistant secretary on January 6, 2003. Martin remained in the position until Bush, on September 12, 2003, nominated and the Senate on December 9, 2003, confirmed David W. Anderson as assistant secretary for Indian affairs. Anderson, a member of the Lac Courte Oreilles Band of Chippewa and the former chief executive of Lac Courte Oreilles Chippewa Enterprises, was more well known for his "Famous Dave's of America" family restaurants. He brought an impressive resume of economic development to the bureau, becoming the first assistant secretary to have founded three publicly traded companies on Wall Street, creating over eighteen thousand jobs in the process.[91]

ASSISTANT SECRETARY FOR INDIAN AFFAIRS DAVID W. ANDERSON

Anderson was sworn into office as the ninth assistant secretary on February 2, 2004.[92] His term was short—less than thirteen months—and his impact minimal. To a large degree, Anderson viewed himself as a role model for Indian Country, believing that if tribes approached governance "with a positive attitude" they could overcome obstacles and achieve economic success.[93] He believed that economic development was central to Indian Country, viewing gaming as simply a stepping stone to greater, sustainable development. Gaming would enable Native people to learn occupations and vocations that could be permanent and that would open doors to meaningful and fulfilling lives. Tribes could accomplish anything if they "took full responsibility for their own destinies."[94]

Not surprisingly, Anderson focused on economic development. In the spring of 2004, Special Trustee for American Indians Ross Swimmer and Anderson teamed up to reorganize the Office of the Assistant Secretary, the Bureau of Indian Affairs, and the Office of the Special Trustee to bolster their emphasis on development and self-governance. At the same time, he sought to increase accountability by adding one hundred new staff to improve fiduciary responsibilities at the field level. By late 2004, the Office of Special Trustee added forty-five trust officers and six regional administrators to superintend trust resources. Bush then issued an executive memorandum on the Government-to-Government Relationship with Tribal Governments that underscored the federal commitment.[95] Anderson was successful in increasing educational funding under No Child Left Behind and he oversaw the drafting of No Child Left Behind rules to govern bureau and tribal contract schools.[96]

Congress expanded the Indian Land Consolidation Act to additional tribes in 2004, with the Gila River Indian Community benefiting from the extension after the president increased its budget by $53.3 million to $75 million in 2005. Under the revamped program, tribes—using federal funds—purchased fractionated interests in trust or restricted land from willing sellers, some of whom owned undivided interests in allotments with denominators in the hundred thousands. By the end of 2003, tribes had purchased 42,075 fractionated parcels from 69,938 individual interests, with a goal of putting such lands to beneficial use.[97]

On January 31, 2005, Anderson announced his resignation, concluding that he could have a greater impact on Indian youth by focusing his time "on developing private sector economic opportunities for Indian entrepreneurs." When he left office on February 12, Norton tasked Associate Deputy Secretary Jim Cason with the role of acting assistant secretary, a role he retained for two years. In the meantime, Norton announced she would collaborate with tribal leaders in selecting the next assistant secretary.[98] Before leaving office, Anderson named W. Patrick Ragsdale

(Cherokee Nation) as director of the Bureau of Indian Affairs. A man of extensive experience, Ragsdale oversaw all day-to-day affairs of the bureau.[99]

ASSISTANT SECRETARY FOR INDIAN AFFAIRS CARL J. ARTMAN

Eighteen months later, President Bush nominated Carl J. Artman as assistant secretary on August 2, 2006, with the Senate confirming him on March 5, 2007.[100] A member of the Oneida Tribe of Wisconsin, Artman had served as chief legal counsel for the Oneida before joining Interior as solicitor in February 2006. He was sworn in on March 8, 2007, remaining as assistant secretary until May 23, 2008. Serving just fourteen months, Artman had limited impact on the strands of Indian policy, with *Cobell* the greatest challenge of his administration.

While Artman pledged to address the challenges of youth suicide, drug abuse, chronic unemployment, poor healthcare, inadequate educational facilities and curricula, crumbling infrastructure, and crime, the brevity of his tenure precluded any substantive change. The Great Recession that began in 2006 compounded matters. In his confirmation hearing, Artman stressed the need for tribes to develop their natural, political, and socioeconomic infrastructure, and he sought to provide "a fresh start and new commitments" to tribes, believing the success of one tribe was the best incubator for the success of others.[101]

As did Anderson before him, Artman stressed economic development. In May 2007 he convened tribal leaders to an economic summit in Phoenix to articulate policy recommendations. To his credit, the summit included tribal leaders, federal policymakers, Native entrepreneurs, tribal economic development professionals, and private sector leaders, the first time such a diverse gathering of leaders assembled. The summit addressed key issues including physical and legal infrastructure limitations in Indian Country, tribal access to capital and financing, and developing competitive business plans for national and international markets.[102] The prosperity of tribal nations, Secretary Dirk Kempthorne intimated, was dependent not on "federal aid and guidance" as much as it was on tribes making their own economic choices.[103] More than three hundred policy recommendations emerged from the summit, including increasing tribal construction capabilities, eliminating impediments to tax-exempt bond financing, and improving the management and development of tribal lands.

One tribal success was the development of an initiative that encouraged tribes to partner with other tribes to support economic activities. Pairing federally recognized producer tribes with Indian-owned businesses of purchaser tribes encouraged and supported incubator businesses and helped them gain experience in reaching outside markets. In February 2008, the Mashantucket Pequot Tribe and the Seminole Tribe of Florida partnered to promote intertribal business, with the Oneida Tribe, Cow Creek Umpqua Tribe, and Morongo Band of Mission Indians joining the consortium, which paired "resource rich, cash poor" tribes with Native-owned businesses struggling to access markets for their goods and services.[104]

The Bush administration also advanced new guidelines for federal acknowledgment in 2008 that were intended to expedite negative reviews and reduce the timeframe to demonstrate federal status, while also providing policy governing splinter groups seeking federal recognition.[105] The guidelines gave the Office of Federal Acknowledgment discretion to refuse to consider petitions from splinter groups, such as the United Houma Nation, which split into four distinct petitions. The revised policy modified criteria b, c, and e (shown in Table 10.3) by amending the date for continued contact from the early eighteenth century to March 4, 1789. The guidelines also structured the process to allow the Office of Federal Acknowledgment to deny a petition if it was clear that a petitioner would not meet any of the seven mandatory criteria.

In May 2008, Artman announced final regulations regarding section 20 of the Indian Gaming Regulatory Act, which prohibited land into trust for tribes seeking to conduct gaming activities on lands acquired after October 17, 1988. The culmination of a year-long effort to bring "predictability, stability, and accountability" to gaming, the amended regulations articulated a process for the Department of the Interior to bring land into trust, including granting the governor of the affected state one year's time to concur with a secretarial order. The two-part determination included exceptions for gaming if the secretary determined, after consultation with state and local leaders and neighboring tribes, that it would not be detrimental to surrounding communities and was in the best interest of the tribe.[106]

Artman resigned April 28 and left office on May 23, 2008. George T. Skibone (Osage Tribe), a career bureau employee, assumed leadership of the Office of the Assistant Secretary, the Bureau of Indian Affairs, and the Bureau of Indian Education, remaining acting assistant secretary through the end of the Bush administration. He represented the main challenge to Indian affairs during the Bush years, namely the assistant secretary's position was vacant four of eight years, resulting in an overall lack of policy direction and understanding of tribal affairs.[107]

ASSISTANT SECRETARY FOR INDIAN AFFAIRS LARRY J. ECHO HAWK

With the election of Democrat Barack Obama as president in November 2008, the search for the next assistant secretary began, with the president nominating Larry J. Echo Hawk (Pawnee Tribe) as the eleventh assistant secretary on April 9, 2009. A former Idaho attorney general (1990–1994) and state representative (1982–1986), Echo Hawk came from a distinguished family and was highly recommended by scores of tribal nations and organizations. On May 19, the Senate confirmed Echo Hawk as assistant secretary and he was sworn into office on May 22.[108]

The Great Recession that began during the Bush administration offered an immediate opportunity for the president to invest in Indian infrastructure. The passage of the American Recovery and Reinvestment Act (ARRA) authorized $787 billion for national infrastructure, with Ken Salazar, secretary of the interior, securing a nearly $2 billion investment for Indian Country.[109] The Interior Department provided $450 million in ARRA funding for tribal roads, schools, and detention centers, and $40 million for housing and workforce training. Another $510 million in

Native American Housing Block Grants (Housing and Urban Development), $310 million for Indian reservation roads (Federal Highway Administration), and $500 million in tribal infrastructure technology and health services (Health and Human Services), plus lesser amounts from other federal agencies rounded out the recovery program.

Echo Hawk advanced an ambitious agenda, stressing economic development while lamenting the 80 percent unemployment rate in some parts of Indian Country. He also praised the 670,000 jobs Indian gaming created, pledging to implement the Indian Gaming Regulatory Act in a "reasonable manner" while working with tribes to expand gaming and take land into trust.[110] He committed to amending the federal acknowledgment process that he believed was broken due to the length of time it took for petitioning tribes to go through the process. To further Obama's commitment to tribes, Echo Hawk enhanced consultation and, to combat violence against women and major crimes in general, he pledged to work with tribes to enhance public safety.[111] Along with Salazar, he resolved to settle the unending litigation related to trust resource management and water claims.

At the time Echo Hawk took office, there was uncertainty with the secretary taking land into trust for tribes that were not federally recognized in 1934, when the Indian Reorganization Act became law. The Supreme Court in 2009 ruled that it was unlawful for the secretary to take land into trust for tribes such as Narragansett if they were not federally recognized in 1934.[112] While Congress recognized the Narragansett land claims in the 1978 Rhode Island Indian Claim Settlement Act, the eighteen hundred acres of land the tribe secured was under state jurisdiction until 1983, when Interior federally recognized the Narragansett and took the land into trust.[113]

In 1991, the Narragansett purchased thirty-one acres of land and sought to place it into trust. The state of Rhode Island and the town of Charlestown objected on grounds that the tribe was not federally recognized at the time the IRA was adopted. The decision hinged on the meaning of the phrase "now under federal jurisdiction." While the Interior Department argued "now" meant at the time the tribe requested the secretary to take land into trust (1991), the state and town argued it was at the time of the act's approval (1934). The Supreme Court opined that the phrase unambiguously referred to tribes that were under federal jurisdiction at the time the act was approved and that the ordinary meaning of the term "now" was consistent with the meaning historically used by the court.[114]

In response to the court's ruling, Echo Hawk proposed to address the limitations of the department to take land into trust for tribes that did not enjoy a federal trust relationship in 1934. In 2010, the Senate considered an amendment to the IRA clarifying "now," fearing the court had eroded congressional intent and erected a barrier to achieving the purpose of the act of taking land into trust to encourage tribes to become economically self-sufficient. Moreover, the Senate concluded that the court had created two classes of tribes—those under federal jurisdiction in 1934 and those who were not.[115] In 2014, as part of the Gun Lake Trust Land Reaffirmation Act, the Senate expressly stated that land of the Match-E-Be-Nash-She-Wish Band of Pottawatomie was reservation land that could not be challenged under the court's recent ruling.[116] No definitive meaning of the word "now" has been codified by federal statute or court decree.

Echo Hawk also worked to rescind the 2008 regulations governing land into trust under the Indian Gaming Regulatory Act, calling the guidelines unnecessary and contrary to self-determination. After holding extensive consultation hearings with tribes, and after listening to their concerns, Echo Hawk rescinded the rules, arguing that existing IGRA regulations were sufficient to bring land into trust after an affirmative determination from Interior that such land for gaming was in the best interests of the tribe and the concurrence of the governor of the state in which the land was located.[117]

The assistant secretary next revised the guidelines of the Office of Federal Acknowledgment, seeking to clarify the review standards and definition of "reasonable likelihood" of success. The proposed guidelines would establish a process for tribes that were denied acknowledgment to repetition while also amending the timeframe for the assistant secretary to make a determination. Echo Hawk and his successor, Kevin Washburn, issued eight final decisions regarding federal acknowledgment. Denials were issued for the Juaneño Band of Mission Indians (1A and 1B) (June 2011), Central Band of Cherokee (July 2012), Brotherton Indian Nation (December 2012), Choctaw Nation of Florida (July 2013), and Tolowa Nation (February 2016). The Shinnecock Indian Nation (October 2010) and Pamunkey Indian Tribe (January 2016) were acknowledged, bringing the number of federally recognized tribes to 567.[118]

Echo Hawk courted improved relations with tribes, starting with Obama's commitment to consult with tribes on all matters affecting them. In his first year in office, the president issued a memorandum to all federal agencies requiring them to develop tribal consultation policies and designate a high level liaison to support not only a government-to-government relationship but also a nation-to-nation partnership.[119] Echo Hawk launched a comprehensive consultation policy developed in close cooperation with tribal nations, mandating consultation on all statutory or administrative actions, including rule-making, policy guidance, legislative proposals, grant funding formula changes, or operational activities that might impact tribes.[120] In line with these goals, Echo Hawk convened a conference with Salazar, tribal leaders, and tribal organizations to address a series of economic development, public safety, trust, and education reforms, beginning with organizational realignments, including elevating the line authority of the directors of the Bureau of Indian Affairs and Bureau of Indian Education to report directly to the assistant secretary.[121]

In partial fulfillment of the administration's pledge to improve public safety, Echo Hawk lobbied Congress to enact the Tribal Law and Order Act (TLOA) in 2010. Congress obliged and authorized the appointment of special assistant U.S. attorneys to prosecute tribal crimes in federal courts in an effort to address offenses that too often went unpunished due to lack of tribal resources. The TLOA empowered tribal courts to issue more stringent sentences and enabled tribal police officers to enforce federal law on tribal lands. Federal funds were available to improve drug trafficking prevention and to enhance recruitment of police officers.[122] The act also enabled tribes to access the National Crimes Information Center database and to retrocede jurisdiction to the federal government. Most importantly, the act increased tribal courts' sentencing authority from one to three years per offense and allowed judges to stack sentences for a maximum of nine years. For tribes accepting TLOA, their courts had to become courts of record and their judges were required to

Table 10.5. Crimes Considered for Enhanced Sentencing Under TLOA by Tribal Courts

- Murder
- Vehicular manslaughter
- Repeat driving under the influence
- Rape (spousal or other) and forcible sodomy, oral copulation, or penetration
- Assault with intent to commit rape
- Robbery
- Kidnapping
- Child molestation
- Human trafficking
- Repeat domestic violence
- Battery with a deadly or dangerous weapon
- Assault, battery, or threats to certain tribal employees or elders
- Financial abuse of elders
- Failure to register as a sex offender
- Manufacture or sale of hypnotic substances
- Desecration of graves

Source: National Tribal Judicial Center, 2015.

be licensed by any jurisdiction to practice law. Tribal laws had to be publicly available. The Tribal Judicial Institute encouraged tribes to consider enhanced sentencing for crimes listed in Table 10.5.

The most significant achievement of the Echo Hawk era was the settlement of the *Cobell* lawsuit. A priority of the Obama administration, a settlement of the fifteen-year-old claim was announced on December 8, 2010, providing a "fair" settlement for the plaintiffs and a "responsible" one for the United States. The agreement led to the disbursement of $1.4 billion to more than three hundred thousand individual Natives to compensate them for their historical accounting claims. A $2 billion fund was also established to assist tribes in buying back and consolidating fractionated interests in allotments. Congress approved of the settlement on November 30, 2010, and President Obama signed it into law on December 8.[123]

By fall of 2010, Echo Hawk announced the settlement of four tribal water claims totaling $1 billion. On November 19, 2010, Congress approved of omnibus legislation ratifying the White Mountain Apache water settlement that included funding for a rural water system to serve the reservation.[124] The Crow Tribe water settlement included funds for a safe drinking water system in addition to funds to rehabilitate the Crow Irrigation Project.[125] The Aamodt settlement ended forty-three years of Pueblo water rights litigation for Tesuque, Nambe, Pojoaque, and San Ildefonso pueblos.[126] The Taos Pueblo settlement added protections for sacred Blue Lake and made permanent a division of water in northern New Mexico.[127] In early 2012, Interior and the Justice Department announced the settlement of a $1 billion trust accounting and natural resources mismanagement claim filed by forty-one tribes. Resolved in fewer than twenty-four months, the settlement ended claims that dated back more than a century.[128]

Echo Hawk announced his resignation on April 9, 2012, leaving office on April 27, having accelerated land purchases (158,000 acres) for tribes, improved public safety (Tribal Law and

Order Act), concluded important tribal water settlements, proposed amendments to the federal acknowledgment process, and brought an end to the *Cobell* lawsuit.[129] Salazar appointed Donald "Del" Laverdure (Crow Tribe) as acting assistant secretary on April 27, where he remained until October 9, 2012.

THE INTERLUDE

The administration did not wait for a new assistant secretary to continue its historic policy changes. In July 2012, Congress amended the 1955 Indian leasing act to facilitate tribal self-government. The Helping Expedite and Advance Responsible Tribal Homeownership (HEARTH) Act enabled tribes, at their discretion, to develop and implement regulations for leasing tribal lands without secretarial approval if such leases were executed under regulations approved by the secretary. For tribes accepting responsibility under HEARTH, the time required for lease approval was reduced for business, agricultural, public, religious, educational, recreational, or residential purposes, facilitating homeownership and buttressing economic development.[130] The act had no effect on individually owned allotted lands.

With the passage of the HEARTH Act, tribes began the process of adopting, and the bureau approving, regulations enabling them to govern the leasing process on tribal lands, with the Graton Rancheria in California becoming the first to adopt such regulations, followed by Sandia Pueblo in 2013. Within two years, twelve tribes adopted and assumed control of tribal leasing, as shown in Table 10.6.

ASSISTANT SECRETARY FOR INDIAN AFFAIRS KEVIN WASHBURN

On August 2, 2012, Obama nominated Kevin Washburn (Chickasaw Nation) to be the twelfth assistant secretary, with the Senate unanimously confirming him on September 22.[131] He was sworn in and took office on October 9. Washburn was a former law school professor at the Universities of New Mexico, Arizona, and Minnesota, as well as Harvard University, and former counsel for the National Indian Gaming Association and assistant U.S. attorney for New Mexico. He was a widely published Indian law scholar, having written extensively on the Tribal Law and Order Act (drafting parts of it) and coediting the 2012 update of Felix Cohen's 1942 "Handbook of Federal-Indian Law."

Recognizing that self-governance was not the answer for every tribe, Washburn worked to ensure that tribes had the ability to choose whether to contract, compact, or maintain a direct-service relationship with the bureau. He believed the government-to-government relationship was strong because self-governance was at "its modern zenith."[132]

Washburn oversaw the implementation of the land buyback program under *Cobell*, with more than $730 million invested in Indian Country to purchase fractionated interests in allotted land

Table 10.6. Tribes Taking Control of Leasing Tribal Lands under the HEARTH Act

Tribe	State	Date Effective
Graton Rancheria	California	February 1, 2013
Sandia Pueblo	New Mexico	March 14, 2013
Pokagon Pottawatomie	Michigan	April 11, 2013
Ak Chin Indian Community	Arizona	November 10, 2013
Santa Rosa Band (Cahuilla)	California	November 10, 2013
Citizen Band Pottawatomie	Oklahoma	November 25, 2013
Kumeyaay Tribe	California	December 10, 2013
Kaw Tribe	Kansas	December 13, 2013
Dry Creek Rancheria	California	April 10, 2014
Jamestown Clallam	Washington	April 10, 2014
Mohegan Tribe	Connecticut	April 10, 2014
Wichita and Affiliated Tribes	Oklahoma	April 10, 2014

Source: U.S. Department of the Interior, Office of the Secretary, April 10, 2014.

in just the first three years. By the end of his tenure, Interior had acquired nearly 1.5 million acres and restored them to tribal ownership, launching the buyback in December 2012 using $1.9 billion from the *Cobell* settlement after the Supreme Court dismissed the final appeal on November 6, 2014.[133] The settlement included a ten-year window during which allottees could sell their fractional interests to the tribe at fair market value.[134] The purchase of highly fractionated parcels not only increased tribal control of such lands but also stimulated "economic development and promote[d] tribal sovereignty and self-determination." Among the largest payouts were a $298 million purchase of Crow allotments, $100 million in Pine Ridge Sioux allotments, and $100 million in purchases from the Gila River Indian Community and Northern Cheyenne Tribe.

In conjunction with the land buyback program, Washburn modified the land-into-trust policy by proposing changes to the regulations in 2013 after the Supreme Court a year earlier in the Match-E-Be-Nash-She-Wish Band of Pottawatomie case held that the Quiet Title Act (which allows a party to file suit if asserting a "right, title or interest" in real property that conflicts with U.S. claims) did not ban Administrative Procedures Act challenges to an Interior delineation to take land into trust for a tribe.[135] In so doing, the court eliminated the need for the thirty-day waiting period for interested parties to seek judicial review before the land was brought into trust. The proposed rule change established a "speak now or forever hold your peace" provision for the land-into-trust process, giving tribes greater certainty since challengers had to exhaust administrative procedures before seeking a judicial remedy.[136]

Interior Secretary Sally Jewell, working with Washburn, established a goal of taking 500,000 acres of land into trust for tribes by the end of her term, a goal she surpassed by more than 10 percent (570,799). This included the first land into trust for an Alaska Native tribe (1.08 acres for Craig Tribal Association); 321 acres for the Mashpee Wampanoag Tribe; 89,978 acres for Isleta Pueblo; and 71,000 acres for six Paiute tribes in Nevada. There were more than 2,260 land-into-trust applications approved.[137]

Continuing Obama's commitment to resolve tribal claims, Interior and the Navajo Tribe settled a historic accounting claim in 2014. One of eighty individual tribal trust management lawsuits resolved during the Obama administration, the Navajo claim at $554 million was the largest and resolved federal mismanagement and accounting of Navajo natural resources and funds dating back fifty years. The tribal claims settled during the Obama administration—absent *Cobell*—totaled nearly $3 billion.[138]

Washburn attempted to modify the federal acknowledgment process in 2013 to align the starting date for a petitioning tribal group with the 1934 Indian Reorganization Act. By May 2014, Interior had proposed two-fold regulations that would allow petitioners to use 1934 as the date to demonstrate tribal cohesion and political authority over its members (rather than 1789) and eliminate the petitioner's time for being recognized as a tribe by third parties from 1900 to the present.[139] The final rule was released in June 2015 but did not include the 1934 date for demonstrating tribal cohesion (criterion b) or political authority (criterion c), since many tribes feared that date would weaken the evidence for proving tribal cohesion and might redefine tribes as racial, rather than political, entities.[140] The rule change did, however, allow petitioners to use prior decisions that satisfied a particular criterion when re-petitioning and allowed greater public access to petitioning documents and expanded the distribution of notices to include local governments.[141] The rule defined historical as pre-1900 and adopted 1900 as the starting date of tribal cohesion and political influence, with petitioners having to prove descent from a historical tribe.

The crown jewel of Washburn's tenure was extension of the Violence against Women Act (VAWA) to Indian Country. While Congress had approved the VAWA in 1994, it did not address tribal jurisdiction over non-Indians committing domestic violence against Native women in Indian Country, where such women experienced violent crime at a rate double the national average. With the 1978 *Oliphant* decision restricting tribal jurisdiction over non-Indians, tribal courts were challenged in prosecuting non-Indians who committed domestic violence in Indian Country. Moreover, federal, state, and/or tribal courts had jurisdiction in Indian Country, depending on the location of the crime, the type of crime, the ethnicity of the perpetrator, and the ethnicity of the victim. The result was often such crimes went unprosecuted, as tribal courts had no recourse against non-Indian perpetrators.

The VAWA amended the Indian Civil Rights Act to authorize criminal jurisdiction for tribal courts over non-Indians who committed domestic violence, dating violence, or violated a protection order, even while state and federal courts retained concurrent jurisdiction over non-Indian defendants.[142] Tribal courts were not granted jurisdiction over non-Indian v. non-Indian domestic violence, although non-Indian women living or working in Indian Country, or the spouse or partner of a tribal member who resided on the reservation, are under VAWA protection.

The VAWA was a partial repeal of the *Oliphant* limitation and, after March 7, 2015, tribes exercised jurisdiction over domestic violence after amending their tribal codes. Tribal courts now provide due process, including a right to counsel. In addition, in conjunction with the Tribal Law and Order Act, tribal judges must have minimal judicial training and be licensed by any jurisdiction in the United States. Tribal criminal codes must be publicly available, including the rules of evidence and criminal procedures, and tribal courts must become courts of records.[143] While originally applicable only in Indian Country and the Metlakatla Indian Tribe and Annette Island Reserve in Alaska, Congress in 2014 repealed § 910 of the act to extend its provisions to all Natives in Alaska.[144]

Washburn executed a policy that intentionally reaffirmed the federal government's political relationship with tribal nations, one constructed on the foundation of the U.S. Constitution, treaties, federal statutes, executive orders, and federal court rulings. In 2014, Jewell underscored this relationship with Departmental Order 3335, which outlined seven guiding principles of the federal-Indian relationship, including respecting tribal sovereignty and the tribal right to "make important decisions about their own best interests." Concurrently, these principles underscored that trust and restricted lands and other trust resources remained under federal protection.[145] To add significance, the administration established an annual White House Tribal Nations Conference that focused on assisting tribes to "build a foundation for a successfully and culturally vibrant future."[146] The president also reestablished a government-to-government relationship with Native Hawaiians, something that had not occurred since 1893, when U.S. interests initiated the overthrow of the Kingdom of Hawaii.[147]

On December 10, 2015, Washburn announced his resignation and decision to return to the University of New Mexico School of Law, with Jewell appointing Principle Deputy Assistant Secretary Lawrence Roberts (Oneida) as acting assistant secretary.[148] Washburn left office on January 1, 2016, with Roberts remaining as acting assistant secretary through the end of the Obama administration. With the election of Donald Trump as president in November 2016, the search for the next assistant secretary began. After Trump nominated—and the Senate confirmed—Ryan Zinke as interior secretary, Zinke appointed Michael S. Black (Oglala Sioux) to serve in an acting capacity until the administration nominated the next assistant secretary.

ASSISTANT SECRETARY FOR INDIAN AFFAIRS TARA MACLEAN SWEENEY

On October 17, 2017, Trump nominated Tara MacLean Sweeney (Inupiat) as the first Alaska Native woman to serve as assistant secretary of the interior. An acclaimed businesswoman with the Arctic Slope Regional Corporation, Sweeney pledged to develop "strong organizational relationships" with tribes, Alaska Native villages, and Native Hawaiian organizations in order to devise "innovative solutions" for improving tribal communities.[149] Her nomination was sent to the Senate for confirmation on October 24 and she was confirmed June 29, 2018.

CONCLUSION

Since 1981, the strands of Indian policy have emphasized self-government and economic development. When McCaleb in 2002 urged tribes to choose prosperity over poverty, he unwittingly underscored the full intent of federal policy. Self-government was associated with economic development, which in turn was tethered to development of tribal natural resources. At the same time, economic development facilitated self-government, enabling tribes to provide for their people.

Tribal gaming has had the single greatest economic impact in Indian Country since indigenous tribes were sequestered on reservations. Gaming brings a much-needed infusion of revenue and employment into Indian Country. It is responsible for more than 670,000 jobs, which are improving the quality of life in Indian Country, providing for a more-educated citizenry, and providing meaningful opportunities that are enabling tribes to develop their economic portfolios. But deep pockets of poverty remain, especially those tribes that are far removed from transportation routes and the market place, with South Dakota tribes among the most poverty stricken in America.[150]

In recent decades the dichotomy of political philosophy underscoring Indian policy has become more pronounced. The Republican administrations of Ronald Reagan, George H. W. Bush, and George W. Bush reflected a philosophical framework of enabling tribes to engage in the fullest extent of self-government by reducing federal control and involvement. Unfortunately, this message has been interpreted as reminiscent of termination. Reagan, for instance, believed he was empowering tribes by reducing their reliance on the federal government. These administrations sought to reduce federal regulatory oversight as a means of encouraging natural resource development to support self-government and reduce the federal footprint in Indian Country. Tribal nations have viewed this political framework with great reticence.

The Democratic administrations of Bill Clinton and Barrack Obama, on the other hand, adopted a more guarded approach, encouraging economic development but with a greater level of federal support. To this end, these administrations strengthened tribal infrastructure (economic, political, and jurisdictional) even while the federal government stood as a supporting partner and encouraged land acquisition and development of tribal economies. The difference was largely philosophical and calls attention to the chasm between modern Republicans and Democrats and the influence and direction of policy as emphasized or executed by the assistant secretary for Indian affairs.

A parallel policy strand of the past four decades is trust reform, with *Cobell* simply the largest and most costly. While water settlements were generally bipartisan (to get through Congress), successful implementation of such accords characterized policy considerations in the post 1981 landscape, with more than $10 billion expended on mitigating trust resource mismanagement, accounting suits, and water claims. Reform was also reflected in an increased number of tribal groups seeking federal acknowledgment, with recognition typically followed by gaming as a means of economic independence. While just 35 percent of tribal petitions for federal acknowledgment have been successful, those that were, have enjoyed success by engaging in economic development or gaming. This includes the highly successful Pequot and Mohegan tribal gaming operations in Connecticut, but also the Grand Traverse Ottawa-Chippewa and Tunica-Biloxi Tribes. Land into trust was a corollary to federal acknowledgment, with both an integral part of the nation-building efforts.

Finally, recent decades witnessed self-governance (as opposed to self-determination) as an official policy strand of the United States. Instead of simply contracting for federal services under the tradition Pub. L. No. 638 contracting process, tribes have compacted for these services, enabling them to plan, conduct, direct, and administer responsibilities for implementing such services. The result of such self-governance compacts has been the development of infrastructure in much of Indian Country that is enabling tribes to increasingly become sophisticated governmental entities that are meeting the needs of tribal citizens. To this end, recent decades have reflected a federalist partnership.

11

"A MOST ANONYMOUS POSITION"

Federal Indian Policy and the Bureau of Indian Affairs, 1824–2017

One of the more complicated positions in the federal bureaucracy—one born in the bowels of the War Department—is the commissioner of Indian affairs. The head of the Indian Office (the Bureau of Indian Affairs since 1947) is "one of the most important yet anonymous in the federal bureaucracy," having "rarely satisfied either the Indians or the American public."[1] For two centuries the commissioners and the assistant secretaries have been responsible for executing the strands that gave flesh to the philosophical braids of federal Indian policy as directed by the president and/or the Congress. The forty-three commissioners and thirteen assistant secretaries directly or indirectly influenced and executed this macro-policy, which fits the prevailing political winds of Congress or the president, while at the same time directing the implementation of those policies at a micro-level.[2]

The overarching goal of federal-Indian policy executed and enforced by the commissioner or assistant secretary has long been the social and political integration of Native people, extinguishment of their aboriginal title, and the ultimate abolition of Indian Country. This goal has been represented by two main braids of policy. The first is exhibited in several linear strands, including policies of civilization, Christianization, assimilation, termination, and integration of Native people, although historically this meant Indians were marginalized on the social and economic periphery of the nation. The second braid is reflected in gaining access to tribal land and its resources, as demonstrated in the linear strands of treaty and/or agreement making, which facilitate land cessions, land alienation initiated by the General Allotment Act, sale of original and inherited lands, the issuance of fee patents and the removal of trust restrictions, and termination. Into these two braids—integration and land alienation—all policy strands are woven.

With the advent of the American Revolution, the United States appointed special commissioners to negotiate treaties of amity with the tribes, primarily to gain their neutrality during the war with Great Britain. During the next dozen years, Congress appointed additional commissioners to negotiate with the tribes for the cession of their land. Concurrently, Congress established two superintendents of trade to execute policy strands governing access to tribal resources. To ensure stability in its political intercourse with the tribes, the United States licensed traders under the authority of the Nonintercourse Act that clothed the federal government with the authority to negotiate for the purchase of tribal land. The vehicle for such transfers was duly executed and ratified treaties, with such instruments representing the "moments when the natural [Native] world *became* private property of the United States."[3]

Employing another strand of policy, Congress, in 1806, established the office of the superintendent of Indian trade within the War Department to oversee government trading houses along the frontier, with such facilities placating tribes with trade goods while also fostering dependency and promoting civilization. While two men—John Shee (1806–1807) and John Mason (1807–1816)—held the position prior to Thomas McKenney, it was McKenney who formalized the office. In 1816, McKenney became superintendent of Indian trade, remaining a strong advocate for civilization and agrarianism for nearly fifteen years, proving to be a forceful leader who dedicated his efforts on persuading Congress to adopt the Civilization Act as an early strand of integration.

When Congress abolished government trading houses in 1822, it left a void in the administration of Indian affairs. In 1824, Secretary of War John C. Calhoun administratively established an Indian Office, in part to carry out the Civilization Act and in part to administer the burgeoning day-to-day administration of Indian affairs. As the first chief clerk of the Indian Office, McKenney drafted the inaugural annual report in 1824, describing the breadth to which the Indian Office was bathed in executing diplomatic, trade, civilization, and land strands. These reports, as well as those written after Congress statutorily established the Indian Office in 1832, reflected various policy strands established by Congress and/or the president, including land acquisition, diplomacy, managing annuities, engaging in trade and intercourse, education, encouraging civilization, and enforcing the emigration of the tribes. The first person to hold the title of commissioner of Indian affairs was Elbert Herring, an efficacious man who executed and enforced policy.

The inaugural reports recognized indigenous nations as, in the words of Chief Justice John Marshall, "distinct political communities"[4] with unique rights as "domestic dependent nations,"[5] a recognition that was peculiar in the history of international diplomacy. Because the framers of the U.S. Constitution recognized this distinct political relationship, the federal government was the only constitutionally sanctioned government empowered to deal with indigenous nations. Indian affairs were a national concern and responsibility, with state governments precluded as a matter of law from joining in the relationship unless Congress specifically authorized their involvement. To reflect this, Congress in 1834 reorganized the Indian Office and codified all laws and treaties governing the federal-Indian relationship.

In the early nineteenth century, federal policy vacillated between two contrasting braids: integration and extermination. The former was a cardinal braid in policy predating the founding of the United States and was reflected in the strands of civilization, Christianization, emigration, reservations, severalty, citizenship, reorganization, and self-government. Each of these strands at its core was constructed on a philosophical foundation of social and political integration of Natives. The latter braid never represented official federal policy, notwithstanding the sentiments of those few people on the successive waves of the frontier who waged wars of extermination. The braid of cultural and political extermination, however, has long been a fixture of U.S. policy, reflecting a braid that both salved the national conscience of what to do with Native people and justified the national annexation of indigenous land.

In the post-emigration period, federal policymakers modified the strand—but not the braid—of integration. With emigration completed, and the matter of Indian affairs supposedly settled for generations to come, the Indian Office and Congress believed that time was required for a successful integration of Natives. It had taken two hundred years for the frontier to reach the Mississippi River and it would likely take another two centuries to settle the arid West. By the late 1840s, the Mexican Cession, annexation of Texas, and resolution of the Oregon Territory boundary unleashed a race across the continent, with most tribal nations overrun and surrounded, particularly the emigrant tribes living along the Kansas frontier.

In response, Congress in 1849 established the Department of the Interior and placed the Indian Office in the new executive department, representing a notable shift in the strands of policy. While the relationship between the United States and tribal nations remained political, the nation considered Indian affairs a domestic matter, commencing the process of enervating the tribes and methodically reducing them to a state of dependency. Commissioner Luke Lea evinced this status by focusing on the braid of land alienation via the strands of consolidation, reducing tribal land holdings, and renewing efforts to transform Natives into yeoman farmers.

Beginning with the Civil War and continuing into the 1880s, the Indian Office enforced a transformative braid predicated on peace and truncated reservations. After Commissioner Nathaniel Taylor lost credibility when peace on the frontier collapsed immediately after the Civil War, Pennsylvania Quakers found fertile ground in President Grant's quest for peace. Grant's Peace Policy—enforced by the first indigenous commissioner, Ely Parker (Seneca)—further sequestered tribes on diminished reserved tracts that were deemed necessary to spare Natives from extinction. Parker emphasized the braid of integration through the strands of agrarianism and further consolidation of the tribes and reduction of their land by relocating them into Indian Territory.

Postbellum policy strands ushered in the unilateral cessation of treaty making by the United States as tribes capitulated before an overwhelming federal presence and successive waves of immigrants settling the interior plains and far West. A strand of confining Native people to their reservations until such time as they were sufficiently civilized governed the period of commissioners Francis Walker, Edward P. Smith, and John Smith. American industrialism rapidly expanded and harvested the abundance of natural resources, gobbling up the landscape, and further threatening tribal existence. While land severalty surfaced in a series of treaties negotiated by Commissioner George Manypenny along the Kansas frontier in the 1850s, by the early 1880s a strand of general severalty took shape, even as the Indian Office expanded federally controlled education to foster cultural change among the Natives by turning them into yeoman farmers.

These strands were driven by a new generation of humanitarians who feared the industrial age would swallow the tribes and leave them destitute and landless, a concern not without merit. The remedy to this coming destruction was to assign each individual a parcel of property upon which he could build a home and earn a living by cultivating the soil, thereby grafting Natives into the American social contract of private property and individual free labor. This modified strand intended to convert Natives into landowning citizens and then leave them to find their way in modern industrial America.

The last decades of the nineteenth century unleashed an ardent effort to assimilate indigenous people, dissolve tribal governments, and gain access to additional land. To "save the Indian," commissioners Hiram Price, John Atkins, John Oberly, Thomas Morgan, Daniel Browning, and William Jones labored to achieve and then enforce the crown jewel of nineteenth-century land policy: the General Allotment Act. This strand of severalty facilitated the braid of land alienation, demonstrating that the United States had achieved complete hegemony over Indian affairs. Over the next half century, severalty unshackled a continental juggernaut that subsided only after the loss of 100 million acres of tribal land.

With the introduction by Congress of severalty as a strand in the braid of land alienation, agreements and congressional legislation forced the cession and sale of so-called surplus land to homesteaders, introducing hundreds of thousands of non-Indians into and surrounding Indian Country, and facilitating a strand of emulation that was part of the larger braid of integration. Surrounding Natives with industrious, Christianized non-Indians was assumed to be acculturative, even if the influences didn't always match the promise. In line with this, new strands of jurisprudence exhibited in the Courts of Indian Offenses and federal criminal jurisdiction over major crimes opened the door for outside law enforcement in Indian Country, with the Supreme Court methodically upholding the constitutionality of federal criminal jurisdiction and legalizing the strand of wardship.

A wave of industrial boarding schools followed throughout the West, with Oberly, Morgan, and Jones proving to be capable executors of the twin braids of integration and land alienation. The focus of integration was off-reservation boarding schools that were used to bathe students in all attributes of civilization and then send them back into Indian Country as ambassadors of civilized life. To ensure no Native digressed, Morgan, Browning, and Jones forbade them from participating in the Wild West shows that were so prevalent at the turn of the century.

These linear strands were intended to rapidly progress towards fulfillment of the targeted braid of integration as exemplified by federal citizenship with all of its rights and responsibilities. In theory, once a Native became a citizen, he was a full-fledged American and no longer a tribal citizen with any rights as such. As allottees became citizens, the Indian Office no longer considered them to be tribal citizens and removed them from the enumeration of the tribes. At the same time, Morgan pressed the transfer of children into public schools and, by the 1890s, thousands of allottees were U.S. citizens, including Native women married to white men. Jones bookended the years on either side of the turn of the twentieth century by prohibiting tribal cultural events, facial paint, long hair, and ceremonial expressions. He withheld rations and annuities from those unwilling to work. The culmination of these strands in the braid of integration was the judicial pronouncement in the *Lone Wolf v. Hitchcock* case by which the Supreme Court uncovered a hidden plenary authority in Congress. This plenary power enabled Congress to act in Indian affairs with near impunity. The alienation of land escalated in proportion to the authority exerted by the Indian Office. Governmental paternalism was a *fait accompli*.

After the turn of the twentieth century, Commissioner Francis Leupp introduced a new twist to the braid of integration when he advanced the strand of carrying civilization to the Indians (on-reservation boarding and day schools) rather than carrying Indians to civilization (off-reservation boarding schools). This shifted the focus of integration from off reservation to on reservation. While Leupp introduced the U.S. Department of Agriculture, the Reclamation Service, the Public Health Service, and sundry other federal agencies to Indian Country to aid in integration, his successor Robert Valentine commuted annuities, integrated some Indian schools, and socially engineered land severalty to hasten the day of integration.

In the initial decades of the new century, land alienation accelerated, especially under Cato Sells's competency commissions and Charles Burke's sale of original and inherited allotments. Concurrently, there was a sharp increase in the leasing of Native land, surpassing 4.5 million acres, with both strands facilitating the braid of land alienation. Bureau schools were closed or transferred to local jurisdictions and additional students were moved into public schools, strengthening the braid of integration and culminating in Indian citizenship in 1924. This period was the nadir of American Indians, with fewer than two hundred fifty thousand remaining. Strands encompassing medical care were in their infancy, even as tuberculosis and trachoma became the twin nemeses of Indian Country.

By the late 1920s, a series of studies that included the Meriam Report and the Preston-Engel Report, described what many Native people and another generation of reformers understood all too well. Taken as a whole, nearly all strands of federal policy had failed Natives. Educational achievement and healthcare were abysmal and tribal social structures were in disarray. Irrigation projects designed to facilitate tribal growers instead benefited non-Indians who homesteaded on opened Native lands or acquired alienated allotments. Law-and-order was in shambles. The braid of integration through land ownership was assumed to have had some mystical power of assimilation while at the same time transforming Natives into yeoman farmers. In reality, severalty accelerated land alienation, facilitated leasing, and pressured Natives to develop their natural resources or stand aside while others did it on their behalf.

Shifting political philosophies initiated a new phase of policy and ushered in a modified strand in the braid of integration. Between 1929 and 1948, just three men served as commissioner of Indian affairs, with Charles Rhoads and John Collier deploying and executing a strand of self-government. The Rhoads administration introduced a more secular and liberal-minded generation of progressive reformers who influenced the braids of policy, including Collier who was one of the bureau's harshest critics prior to 1933 while advocating a radical transformation of the braids of land alienation and integration. Between 1933 and 1945, Collier led the movement to restore tribalism, including reacquiring land, encouraging arts and crafts, emphasizing cultural pluralism, and supporting self-government. He successfully encouraged President Roosevelt to abolish the Board of Indian Commissioners and replace it with social scientists. The engine by which the modified braid of integration would progress was economic development, with the Indian Reorganization Act enabling tribes to reestablish governments, charter businesses, and develop their natural resources.

The premise of all policy strands up to the 1930s focused on the braids of integration and land alienation, with little effort to support tribes in developing economic enterprises. These strands instead focused on the abolition of tribal government and the opening of land to settlement and development. After 1934, integration and self-government became two sides of the same coin, with self-government intended to foster tribal control and encourage modernization of tribalism. The publication of the *Handbook of Federal-Indian Law* under Collier's watch was the first attempt to codify the rights and authorities of tribes. While Collier closed numerous boarding schools and constructed scores of day schools, the underlying intent remained integration via acculturating forces and access to tribal resources.

Immediately after World War II, President Truman thought to reduce the size of the federal government and reign in spending, reintroducing the overt braids of integration and land alienation. As part of the reorganization of the Executive Branch, the president adopted policy targeting the rapid integration of Native people and termination of the federal-Indian relationship, releasing Native land of all of its federal trust protection. Self-government was simply a step in the withdrawal of federal services. While Commissioner William Brophy fended off the inevitable for a time, he was powerless to stop the trajectory of executive and legislative policy. To prepare tribes for termination, he advocated tribal-specific legislation to address unique tribal challenges and secured congressional enactment of legislation addressing tribal claims against the United States. In 1953, Congress formalized its strand of termination with the enactment of H.C.R. 108, which detailed the congressional intent to unilaterally withdraw from the 178-year-old federal-Indian relationship.

Between the late 1940s and the early 1960s, termination propelled tribal affairs, with the United States unilaterally terminating its political relationship with scores of tribes, in the process discharging itself from all federal trust responsibilities and obligations. Congress transferred the Division of Indian Health to the Public Health Service, conferred on select states civil and criminal jurisdiction over Indian Country, and sent water disputes into state judicial forums. Forced fee patents and removal of tribal land from federal trust accelerated alienation, with the strand of relocation encouraging Natives to leave their reservations and integrate into urban centers throughout the country. As the bureau withdrew federal services, Commissioner Dillon Myer (and to a lesser extent, Glenn Emmons) undertook every effort to sever the political relationship with tribes and integrate Natives once and for all, including setting into place a strand encouraging the adoption of Native children by non-Indian families.

By the early 1960s, it was apparent that the strands of termination and relocation were less than successful. Tribal governments proved resilient, with the administration of President Kennedy recognizing they were an essential vehicle by which the United States dealt with tribal nations. Tribal governments were now considered essential to this political relationship, as well as to the social cohesion of the tribes for whom the United States had treaty and trust obligations. The most appropriate manner by which tribes could meet the challenges of the modern world was for the United States to strengthen tribal government, not weaken it. This would encourage Natives to adjust to modern life, but support them at the same time through economic development. Persistent poverty, poor health, substandard housing, inadequate educational opportunities, and lack of socioeconomic well-being would not dissipate by simply terminating tribes. What they needed was for the Bureau of Indian Affairs to cease controlling and start supporting them. Philleo Nash initiated this shift from custodial care to supporting tribes by adopting a strand that encouraged tribes to develop their economies in a culturally relevant manner. In the process, the braid of integration was rebranded into one of consumerism driven by self-government.

Indigenous Americans then called for a policy of self-government without termination. While on the fringes of the Civil Rights movement, tribal intellectuals and youth used the social unrest of the 1960s and 1970s, including the occupation of Alcatraz, the Trail of Broken Treaties, and the takeover of Wounded Knee, to voice tribal concerns. During the next two decades, a rebranding of the strand of integration occurred with relative ease, bearing fruit in the late twentieth century as Indian gaming rooted and began to raise the standard of living in parts of Indian Country. Self-government within the framework of federalism expanded, signaling the day when self-determination might be realized.

With self-government the rallying cry, every presidential administration since the 1960s influenced the strand of economic development. By the 1970s, tribes were regularly using the Buy Indian Act to contract for select federal services to build capacity in Indian Country or employing a War on Poverty program to establish the first tribally controlled schools. But these funding mechanisms had limitations or represented soft money. President Nixon—to the surprise of Indian Country—then proposed a strand of self-government that culminated in the passage of the Alaska Native Claims Settlement Act (ANCSA), the Indian Education Act, and the Indian Self-Determination and Educational Assistance Act. The former reopened bilateral negotiations for tribal people to settle complex resource disputes, while the latter supported their desire to control the programs established for their benefit.

For the first time, tribes could contract to assume Bureau of Indian Affairs and Indian Health Service programs. Despite concerns that the Indian Self-Determination Act was a masqueraded version of termination, self-government proved highly successful and reached nearly all tribal nations. The political atmosphere of the 1960s encouraged tribes to file land claim suits that blossomed into a new strand of resolving tribal claims in order to enable them to engage in nation-building and plan for a better future. A reduction of federal expenditures in Indian Country was no small parallel objective. In time, this strand encouraged water and resource settlements that followed the pattern of the ANCSA. In 1977, to demonstrate that Indian affairs were a priority,

Congress elevated the position of commissioner of Indian affairs to that of assistant secretary for Indian Affairs, who reported directly to the secretary of the interior. Congress buttressed tribal rights with a religious freedom act and a child welfare act. While the two main braids of integration and land alienation remained entrenched, the strands supporting them were less unsavory as the United States deferred to the tribes themselves in how policy was shaped. The post-1980 world was not entirely defined by the strand of self-government but was influenced by tribal calls for a new strand of self-determination to be woven into self-government.

Since the election of Ronald Reagan as president, the strands of policy have been driven by disparate political philosophies. While the United States has been committed to the policy of self-government, each administration since has reflected the national dichotomy of partisan politics. While the past forty years have witnessed an outgrowth in the strand of economic development, culminating in the statutory enactment of the Indian Gaming Regulatory Act as a means of improving tribal socioeconomic status, the philosophical framework of each administration reflects how the substrands of economic development (i.e., land into trust, federal acknowledgment, water settlements, etc.) are enforced or executed. Tribal resource claims, including the *Cobell* accounting claim, have emboldened tribes. Consequently, scores of tribal groups have sought federal acknowledgment, a distinction that is no small matter since federal services, trust protection, and gaming are only available to federally acknowledged tribes.

The Republican administrations of Ronald Reagan, George H. W. Bush, and George W. Bush executed a policy of self-government intent on reducing federal control and involvement in Indian affairs under the theory that curtailing federal oversight and support would enable tribes to engage in true self-government. The primary focus of this philosophy has been job creation and economic development. For assistant secretaries Kenneth Smith and Russ Swimmer, this was reflected in budgetary reductions, further development, and increased federalism. For Eddie Brown, it was increased attention to education (No Child Left Behind Act) and pilot self-governance compacts, with the Tribal Self-Governance Act giving shape to this emerging strand of federalism.

The Democratic administrations of Bill Clinton and Barack Obama, on the other hand, adopted strands supportive of tribes while they reconstructed critical governmental infrastructure. For assistant secretaries Ada Deer and Kevin Gover, these strands resulted in consultation that involved tribes in all policy matters before any legislation became law. Deer and Gover amended the federal acknowledgment process to provide greater transparency and revised Indian Child Welfare Act policies to protect tribal human resources. With assistant secretaries Larry Echo Hawk and Kevin Washburn, tribes were invited to the table to consult on matters affecting them. The Tribal Law and Order Act and the extension to Indian Country of the Violence against Women Act further empowered tribal governments and improved public safety, both of which were central to enabling tribes to build capacity and infrastructure. The settlement of more than four dozen tribal claims (exceeding $5 billion) and the reacquisition by tribes of over 1.5 million acres of land, intentionally reaffirmed the political and trust relationship between tribes and the United States.

The political dichotomy of recent decades is unlikely to ameliorate any time soon and represents the main challenge facing tribes in their quest to be self-governing and self-determining.

Policy strands encouraging self-government with too much federal involvement works against tribes by fostering dependency. While healthy tribal economies are essential to the twenty-first century, overemphasizing economic development that is not compatible with tribal values can be regressive and foster greater consumerism—and integration. If economic development is the fulcrum of policy to the detriment of tribal cultural values, then it, too, is integrative. If the intent of economic development is to ultimately eliminate the federal trust responsibility and the government-to-government relationship, then it, too, will facilitate the alienation of tribal land and resources. The goal of federal policy, then, must be to balance self-government and all of the policy strands surrounding it, to enable tribes to be self-determining in the fullest sense, including cultural, social, political, economic, and spiritual development.

The history of federal-Indian policy is a complex braid of treaties, acts of Congress, executive orders, court interpretations, and tribal actions. The circumstances and application of policy strands influencing these actions is unique to each tribe. Since tribal nations reside within the geographic boundaries of the United States and are subject to the (at times capricious) plenary power of Congress, they will continue to face the ebb and flow of governing political philosophies at the federal (and tribal) level. Unique manifestations further influence these policy strands and governing braids. Two-and-a-half centuries of political intercourse between the tribes and the United States reflects a simple axiom: the federal government has rarely remained committed to a specific policy strand for more than a generation, with wide pendulum swings occurring about every other generation.

Since 1824, the head of the Indian Office has shaped and influenced federal policy. Each commissioner or assistant secretary brought his or her thoughts on federal policy to the office, with these thoughts as much intellectual as political. While most commissioners were political appointees with little regard for or knowledge of Native people or federal policies, some came to the office with a breadth of experience. Since 1966, every head of the department has been an enrolled member of a federally recognized tribe, with some bringing a great knowledge of policy and philosophy. Each has represented Indian Country and fostered an increased tribal voice in the midst of a most politically charged topic. The key for tribal nations in the future is to ensure that they retain not only a seat at the table of decision-making, but that they also shape the political relationship into one that supports and enhances their unique and inherent sovereign authority.

NOTES

PREFACE

1. Vine Deloria Jr., *Custer Died for Your Sins: An Indian Manifesto* (New York: MacMillan, 1969), 125–26.
2. Ibid., 135, 145.
3. Martin Case, *The Relentless Business of Treaties: How Indigenous Land Became U.S. Property* (St. Paul, MN: Minnesota Historical Society Press, 2018), 3–4.
4. Ibid., 7.
5. John Locke, *The Second Treatise of Government: An Essay Concerning the True, Original, Extent and End of Civil Government*, ed. Thomas P. Pearson (New Jersey: Prentice Hall, 1997), chap. 5, sec. 26, 17.
6. Ibid., chap. 5, sec. 27, 17.
7. *Seventeenth Annual Report of the Board of Indian Commissioners*, Appendix E, 3rd Annual Meeting of the Lake Mohonk Conference (Washington, D.C.: Government Printing Office, 1886), 90.

CHAPTER 1

1. See, for instance, eighteenth-century jurist Emmerich de Vattel, *The Law of Nations, or Principles of the Law of Nations, Applied to the Conduct and Affairs of Nations and Sovereigns* (Philadelphia: T & J. W. Johnson and Company Press, 1883). For a sixteenth-century Spanish theologian treatise, see Bartolomé de Las Casas, *In Defense of the Indians*, trans. and ed. Stafford Poole (DeKalb: Northern Illinois Press, 1974).
2. Robert A. Williams, *The American Indian in Western Legal Thought: The Discourse of Conquest* (New York: Oxford University Press, 1990). Vine Deloria Jr. and Clifford M. Lytle, *American Indians, American Justice* (Austin: University of Texas Press, 1983).
3. See Cass County, Minnesota, v. Leech Lake Chippewa Band of Indians, 524 U.S. 103 (1998). See also Connecticut ex rel Blumenthal v. U.S. Department of Interior, 228 F.3d 83 (2d Cir. 2000).
4. Shivwits Band of Paiute Indians v. Utah, 428 F.3d 966 (10th Cir. 2005); South Dakota v. U.S. Department of Interior, 487 F.3d 548 (8th Cir. 2007).
5. An Act to regulate gaming on Indian lands, 102 Stat. 2467 (October 17, 1988) (hereafter Indian Gaming Regulatory Act).
6. See [no author or title] *Minnesota Daily*, October 8, 1998, www.mndaily.com. See also Laura J. Smith, "Native American Trust Land Transfers in Minnesota," *CURA Reporter* 34, no. 2 (Spring 2004).
7. United States v. Winans, 198 U.S. 371 (1905). The court argued that the 1859 Yakima treaty "was not a grant of rights to the Indians, but a grant of rights from them—a reservation of those not granted."
8. Vine Deloria Jr., *Behind the Trail of Broken Treaties: An Indian Declaration of Independence* (Austin: University of Texas Press, 1985), 135.
9. Johnson v. M'Intosh, 21 U.S. 543 (1823).

10. Felix S. Cohen, *Handbook of Federal-Indian Law* (Charlottesville, VA: Michie, 1982), 241–42.
11. Sac and Fox Treaty with the United States, November 3, 1804, 7 Stat. 84.
12. Worcester v. Georgia, 31 U.S. 515 (1832).
13. Cherokee Nation v. Georgia, 30 U.S. 1 (1831).
14. See An Act to provide for the punishment of crimes and offenses committed within the Indian boundaries, 3 Stat. 383 (March 3, 1817). This act concerned offenses committed by non-Indians against Indians, but did not include Indian-Indian acts in Indian Country, which remained under tribal jurisdiction. The nonintercourse acts and numerous treaties included provisions governing (and limiting) tribal criminal jurisdiction. See An Act to regulate trade and intercourse with the Indian tribes, 1 Stat. 137 (July 22, 1790); An Act to regulate trade and intercourse with the Indian tribes, 1 Stat. 329 (March 1, 1793); An Act to regulate trade and intercourse with the Indian tribes and to preserve peace on the frontiers, 1 Stat. 469 (May 19, 1796); An Act to regulate trade and intercourse with the Indian tribes, and to preserve peace on the frontiers, 1 Stat. 743 (March 3, 1799); and An Act to regulate trade and intercourse with the Indian tribes, and to preserve peace on the frontiers, 2 Stat. 139 (March 30, 1802). Under the nonintercourse acts, the victim had to be Indian in order for tribal jurisdiction to prevail. Examples of treaty limitations include the Delaware Treaty of September 18, 1778 (7 Stat. 13) and the Choctaw Treaty of January 3, 1786 (7 Stat. 21).
15. An Act to amend an act, entitled An Act to divide the state of Arkansas into two judicial districts, approved March the third, eighteen hundred and fifty-one, 10 Stat. 269 (March 27, 1854) (hereafter General Crimes Act); An Act making appropriations for the current and contingent expenses of the Indian Department, and for fulfilling treaty stipulations with various Indian tribes, for the year ending June thirtieth, eighteen hundred and eighty-six, and for other purposes," 23 Stat. 385, § 9 (March 3, 1885) (hereafter Major Crimes Act); and An Act to protect the harbor defenses and fortifications constructed or used by the United States from malicious injury, and for other purposes, 30 Stat. 717 (July 7, 1898) (hereafter the Assimilative Crimes Act). The former act exempted Indians if the crime was in Indian Country and had "been punished by the local law of the tribe," while the Major Crimes Act enumerated seven criminal acts as federal jurisdiction, a number that has increased to fourteen today. The Assimilative Crimes Act allowed Congress to apply state statutes in federal enclaves such as Indian Country if no definitive federal statute governed. An Act to provide for the preparation and presentation to Congress of the revision of the laws of the United States relating to post-roads, and a code relating to military offenses, and the revision of treaties with the Indian tribes now in force, 17 Stat. 570 (March 3, 1873); and An Act providing for the publication of the revised statutes and the laws of the United States—published as An Act to revise and consolidate the statutes of the United States, in force on the first day of December, anno domini one-thousand eight hundred and seventy-three, 18 Stat. 113 (June 20, 1874); § 2145 and § 2126 of the 18 U.S.C., further limited tribal jurisdiction.
16. Deloria and Lytle, *American Indians, American Justice*, 171–72.
17. *Indian Reservations: A State and Federal Handbook*, comp. the Confederation of American Indians (Jefferson, NC: McFarland and Company, 1986); Veronica E. Tiller, *Federal and State Indian Reservations and Indian Trust Areas* (U.S. Department of Commerce, 1974); and Veronica E. Tiller *American Indian Reservations and Trust Areas* (Albuquerque, NM: Tiller Research, 1996). In Alaska there are 44,970,873 acres owned by Alaska Native Corporations, established under the principles of the Alaska Native Claims Settlement Act. These lands are held in fee by Alaska Natives.
18. David H. Getches, Charles F. Wilkinson, and Robert A. Williams, *Cases and Materials on Federal-Indian Law* (St. Paul: West Publishing, 1993), 6.
19. Cohen, *Handbook of Federal-Indian Law*, 1.
20. United States v. Holliday, 70 U.S. 407 (1866). See also The Kansas Indians, 72 U.S. 737 (1867).

21. U.S. Const. art. I, § 8, cl. 3. This federal authority is limited to circumstances where tribes are a "distinct people with an existing tribal organization." United States v. Forty-three Gallons of Whiskey, 93 U.S. 188 (1876).
22. See Chippewa Indians v. United States, 307 U.S. 1 (1939). The federal courts give deference to Congress and the president in such recognition, deeming it a political matter. In *The Kansas Indians,* the court's only requirement was that the tribe have ancestors who lived in the United States before European settlement and that the Indians be a "people distinct from others." The Kansas Indians, 72 U.S. at 757.
23. 18 U.S.C. § 1151 (2018).
24. An Act to confer jurisdiction on the states of California, Minnesota, Nebraska, Oregon and Wisconsin, with respect to criminal offenses and civil causes of action committed on or arising in Indian reservations within such states, and for other purposes, 67 Stat. 588 (August 15, 1953). In the 1953 act, any state could assume jurisdiction over Indian Country within its borders by amending its constitution or by state statute. In 1968, Congress enacted the Indian Civil Rights Act and required tribal consent before any state assumed jurisdiction. See An Act to prescribe penalties for certain acts of violence or intimidation, and for other purposes, 82 Stat. 77 (April 11, 1968) (hereafter the American Indian Civil Rights Act).
25. An Act to amend the law with regards to civil and criminal jurisdiction over Indian Country in Alaska, 72 Stat. 545 (August 8, 1958).
26. 18 U.S.C. § 1151(a).
27. 18 U.S.C. § 1151(b).
28. 18 U.S.C. § 1151(c). See also Donnelly v. United States, 228 U.S. 243 (1913).
29. Delaware Treaty with the United States, September 17, 1778, 7 Stat. 13. The territory of the Delaware Tribe had been described and bounded by several treaties made with the British prior to 1778.
30. Delaware Treaty with the United States, October 3, 1818, 7 Stat. 188.
31. Choctaw Treaty with the United States, September 27, 1830, 7 Stat. 335.
32. Cherokee Treaty of December 29, 1835, 7 Stat. 478; Creek Treaty of February 14, 1833, 7 Stat. 417; Chickasaw Treaty of October 20, 1832, 7 Stat. 381.
33. Wea Treaty with the United States, October 2, 1818, 7 Stat. 186.
34. An Act making appropriations for the current and contingent expenses of the Indian Department, and for fulfilling treaty stipulations with various Indian tribes, and for other purposes, 11 Stat. 388 (February 28, 1859).
35. An Act to conserve and develop Indian land and resources; to extend to Indians the right to form business and other organizations; to establish a credit system for Indians; to grant certain rights of home rule to Indians; to provide for vocational education for Indians; and for other purposes, 48 Stat. 984, § 5 (June 18, 1934) (hereafter Indian Reorganization Act).
36. United States v. Jackson, 280 U.S. 183 (1930). The significant qualifier is the land must be held in federal trust or in a restricted status.
37. Executive Order of June 14, 1879, in Charles Kappler, *Indian Laws and Treaties,* vol. 1 (Washington, D.C.: Government Printing Office, 1906), 806.
38. When Congress prohibited the president from establishing any more executive order reservations, it reserved sole authority to withdraw public lands on behalf of a tribal nation. See 18 U.S.C. § 150.
39. This is true unless Congress clearly and expressly "disestablishes" non-Indian-owned land from the reservation. This has frequently been contested in the federal courts. See Solem vs. Bartlett, 465 U.S. 463 (1984), which dealt with the issue on the Cheyenne River Sioux Reservation. The issue arises on reservations that have been allotted, with either the allotments being sold or the "surplus" lands having been opened for non-Indian settlement.
40. United States v. Sandoval, 231 U.S. 28 (1913).

41. An Act making appropriations for the current and contingent expenses of the Indian Department, and for fulfilling treaty stipulations with various Indian tribes, for the year ending June 30, 1876, and for other purposes, 18 Stat. 420 (March 3, 1875).
42. An Act making Appropriations for the current and contingent expenses of the Indian Department, and for fulfilling treaty stipulations with various Indian tribes, for the year ending June 30, 1885, and for other purposes, 23 Stat. 96 (July 4, 1884).
43. Examples include the Lumbee Tribe of North Carolina (notwithstanding partial recognition in 1956), the Cornplanter Reservation in New York, and the Coharie Reservation in North Carolina.
44. Nonrecognized tribes are not under the Major Crimes Act and do not enjoy the federal trust benefit. As individuals, these tribal members may be eligible for federal services under the Indian Education Act of 1972, An Act to amend the Higher Education Act of 1965, the Vocational Education Act of 1963, the General Education Provisions Act, the Elementary and Secondary Education Act of 1965, Public Law 874, 81st Congress, and related Acts, and for other purposes, Title IV, 86 Stat. 334 (June 23, 1972) and the Indian Healthcare Improvement Act of 1976, An Act to implement the Federal responsibility for the care and education of the Indian people by improving the services and facilities of Federal Indian health programs and encouraging maximum participation of Indians in such programs, and for other purposes, 90 Stat. 1400 (September 30, 1976), as amended. These individuals must meet the definition of "Indian," usually defined as at least one-quarter Indian blood.
45. Upstate Citizens for Equality (UCE) was organized in 1997 to oppose the Oneida Indian Nation's geographic and political expansion. It opened a chapter in western New York to oppose the Cayuga Nation's land claims, as well. UCE has set its sights on the end of the federal reservation system. "We're basically interested in equality of all citizens," UCE states. "We are against Indian sovereignty. We think it's detrimental to the Indians as well as us." Reservations, according to UCE, are the "last vestige of legal segregation in the United States." See www.upstate-citizens.org.
46. See "Native American Rights—Hunting and Fishing Rights," http://law.jrank.org/pages/8750/Native-American-Rights-Hunting-Fishing-Rights.html#ixzz3p3FQWoOP. The most intense opposition to Indian fishing and hunting rights has been in the Pacific Northwest, where tribes have fought to defend their right to fish in their traditional locations, unhindered by state regulations. The battle has also been fought in Michigan and Wisconsin.
47. See Grant Foreman, *Indian Removal: The Emigration of the Five Civilized Tribes of Indians* (Norman: University of Oklahoma Press, 1932).
48. The original Indian territory included parts of Oklahoma, Kansas, Nebraska, and the Dakotas. Indian Territory as a unique territory included just present-day Oklahoma. In 1907, Congress attached Indian Territory to Oklahoma Territory creating the state of Oklahoma.
49. Angie Debo, *A History of the Indians of the United States* (Norman: University of Oklahoma Press, 1970), 296–98, 305–6.
50. See Donald J. Berthrong, "Legacies of the Dawes Act: Bureaucrats and Land Thieves at the Cheyenne and Arapaho Agencies of Oklahoma," *Arizona and the West* 21, no. 4 (Winter 1979): 335–54. Some tribal nations were landless except for a few parcels of trust land still under federal protection. See also Angie Debo, *And Still the Waters Run: The Betrayal of the Five Civilized Tribes* (Norman: University of Oklahoma Press, 1980).
51. Cheyenne-Arapaho Tribes v. Oklahoma, 618 F.2d 665 (10th Cir. 1980). Restricted lands have titles with restrictions against alienation.
52. Mineral rights are reserved to the Osage for all former Osage Reservation lands in accordance with the 1906 act of dissolution. See An Act for the division of the lands and funds of the Osage Indians of Oklahoma Territory, and for other purposes, 34 Stat. 539 (June 28, 1906). The mineral rights beneath the former Osage Reservation—whether the surface land is Indian or non-Indian owned—are reserved by the Osage Tribe with royalties distributed to holders of Osage headrights.

53. The Annette Island Reserve was created by the An Act to repeal timber-culture laws, and for other purposes, 26 Stat. 1095, at 1101 (March 3, 1891). The executive order reserves were Copper Center, Fort Yukon, Kobuk River, Klukwan, Tyonek, Chilkat Fishing Reserve, Yendistucky, Norton Bay (Elim), Akiah, Mountain Village, and Tatitlek. Hydaburg and Klawock were established as reservations but were later reduced to school reserves of less than two acres. After Congress prohibited the creation of executive order reservations in 1919, the president continued to withdraw land for "public purposes," such as reindeer herding, education, and fishing.
54. An Act to provide civil government for Alaska, 23 Stat. 24 (May 17, 1884).
55. Tee Hit Ton Indians v. United States, 348 U.S. 272 (1955).
56. An Act to provide for the admission of the state of Alaska into the Union, 72 Stat. 339 (July 7, 1958).
57. An Act to provide for the settlement of certain land claims of Alaska Natives, and for other purposes, 85 Stat. 688 (December 18, 1971).
58. Another two million acres was reserved for individual allotments that an Alaska Native could select under § 1613(h) of the ANCSA.
59. See § 1611(c) of the ANCSA.
60. Regardless of whether the land is considered Indian Country, all Alaska Native lands are under state criminal and civil jurisdiction.
61. Donald L. Fixico, *Termination and Relocation: Federal Indian Policy 1945–1960* (Albuquerque: University New Mexico Press, 1986), 21–28.
62. Indians, H.C.R. 108, 83rd Cong. 67 Stat. B132 (1953).
63. David H. DeJong, *Plagues, Politics, and Policy: A Chronicle of the Indian Health Service, 1955–2008* (Lanham, MD: Lexington Press, 2011), 32–36.
64. Cohen, *Handbook of Federal-Indian Law*, 813.
65. Menominee Tribe v. United States, 391 U.S. 404 (1968).
66. An Act to repeal the Act terminating Federal supervision over the property and members of the Menominee Indian Tribe of Wisconsin; to reinstate the Menominee Indian tribe of Wisconsin as a federally recognized sovereign Indian Tribe; and to restore to the Menominee Indian Tribe of Wisconsin those Federal services furnished to American Indians because of their status as American Indians; and for other purposes, 87 Stat. 770 (December 22, 1973).
67. Joint Council of the Passamaquoddy and Penobscot Tribes v. Morton, 528 F.2d 370 (1st Cir. 1975).
68. See United States v. John, 437 U.S. 634 (1978). See also Eastern Band of Cherokee Indians v. North Carolina Wildlife Resources Commission, 588 F.2d 75 (4th Cir. 1978) for matters related to the Eastern Cherokee.
69. See 25 Code of Federal Regulations § 83.
70. Mashpee Tribe v. The Town of Mashpee, 447 F. Supp. 940 (D. Mass. 1978) and Mashpee Tribe v. New Seabury Corp, 592 F.2d 575 (1st Cir. 1979). The federal acknowledgment process had not yet been put into place at the time of legal action. See also Mashpee Tribe v. Watt, 542 F. Supp. 797 (D. Mass 1982), *aff'd*, 707 F.2d 23 (1st Cir. 1983), cert. denied 464 U.S. 1020 (1983).
71. Federal acknowledgment granted February 15, 2007, by the assistant secretary for Indian affairs, "Summary Under the Criteria and Evidence for Final Determination for Federal Acknowledgment of the Mashpee Wampanoag Indian Tribal Council, Inc."
72. Getches, *Cases and Materials on Federal-Indian Law*, 394.
73. An Act to extend Federal recognition to the Chickahominy Indian Tribe, the Chickahominy Indian Tribe—Eastern Division, the Upper Mattaponi Tribe, the Rappahannock Tribe, Inc., the Monacan Indian Nation, and the Nansemond Indian Tribe, 132 Stat. 40 (January 29, 2018).
74. An Act to codify and enact into law Title 3 of the United States Code, entitled The President, § 1151, 62 Stat. 757 (June 25, 1948).
75. DeCoteau v. District County Court, 420 U.S. 425 (1975); and Moe v. Confederated Salish Kootenai Tribes, 425 U.S. 463 (1976).

CHAPTER 2

1. John C. Fitzpatrick, ed. *Journals of the Continental Congress, 1774–1789*, 34 vols. (Washington, D.C.: Government Printing Office, 1904–1937), 2:174–77.
2. "Conference with the Six Nations at German Flats," September 1, 1775, in *Documents Relative to the Colonial History of the State of New York Procured in Holland, England, and France by John P. Brodhead*, ed. E. B. O'Callaghan, vol. 8 (Albany, NY: Weed, Parsons, 1857), 605.
3. "Treaty with the Shawnee, Mingo, Ottawa, Delaware, and Wyandot," October 19, 1775, in *Early American Indian Documents: American Revolution*, ed. Colin Gordon Calloway, vol. 18 (Washington, D.C.: University Publishers of America, 1994), 98.
4. "Treaty with the Cherokee Nation at Pittsburg," July 22, 1779, Ibid., 187.
5. Case, *The Relentless Business of Treaties*, 166. Case examines the twenty-three hundred men that signed treaties, in the process identifying five means of securing tribal land: speculators, traders, industrialists, politicians, and bureaucrats.
6. *Journals of the Continental Congress, 1774–1789*, 4:674–89.
7. *Journals of the Continental Congress, 1774–1789*, 9:844–45.
8. Francis Paul Prucha, *The Great Father: The United States Government and the American Indians* (Lincoln: University of Nebraska Press, 1984), 5–28.
9. *Journals of the Continental Congress, 1774–1789*, 33:340–41.
10. U.S. Const. art. 1, § 8, para. 3, in Max Farrand, ed., *The Records of the Federal Convention of 1787*, ed. Max Farrand, vol. 1 (New Haven: Yale University Press, 1911), 316.
11. *Journals of the Continental Congress, 1774–1789*, 31:491.
12. Ibid., 493.
13. An Act for establishing the salaries of the executive offices of government, with their assistants and clerks, 1 Stat. 67 (September 11, 1789), referred to the "superintendent of Indian Affairs in the northern department" and the first trade and intercourse act in 1790 referenced the "superintendent of the department." Similar language related to the southern department is found in the 1790 act establishing "the power, duties, and emoluments of Superintendent of Indian Affairs for the Southern Department." See An Act for the government of the territory of the United States, south of the river Ohio, 1 Stat. 123 (May 26, 1790).
14. An Act to regulate trade and intercourse with the Indian tribes, 1 Stat. 137 (July 22, 1790).
15. Ibid. Section 1 spelled out the bond requirements for traders, with section 2 allowing the superintendents to recall for cause any license. Section 4 governed land purchases from the tribes and applied to all parties, persons, or states regardless of any "right of pre-emption."
16. Ibid., section 5.
17. An Act to regulate trade and intercourse with the Indian tribes, section 9, 1 Stat. 329 (March 1, 1793).
18. An Act to regulate trade and intercourse with the Indian tribes, and to preserve peace on the frontier, 1 stat 469 (May 17, 1796); An Act to regulate trade and intercourse with the Indian tribes, and to preserve peace on the frontier, 1 stat 743 (March 3, 1799); An Act to regulate trade and intercourse with the Indian tribes, and to preserve peace on the frontier, 2 Stat. 139 (March 30, 1802).
19. An Act to regulate trade and intercourse with the Indian tribes, and to preserve peace on the frontier, 2 Stat. 139 (March 30, 1802), section 13. For a complete analysis of the nonintercourse acts, see Francis Paul Prucha, *American Indian Policy in the Formative Years: The Indian Trade and Intercourse Acts, 1790–1834* (Lincoln: University of Nebraska Press, 1954).
20. An Act for establishing trading houses with the Indian tribes, 2 Stat. 402 (April 21, 1806).
21. An Act establishing Trading Houses with the Indian Tribes, 1 Stat. 452 (April 18, 1796).
22. Quoted in Case, *The Relentless Business of Treaties*, 40–41.
23. Prucha, *American Indian Policy in the Formative Years*, 84–93.

24. See "President Thomas Jefferson to Congress," January 18, 1803, in *A Compilation of the Messages and Papers of the Presidents*, ed. James Richardson, (Washington D.C.: Government Printing Office, 1896–1897), 1:352.
25. The closure of the trading houses came via An Act to abolish the United States' trading establishments with the Indian tribes, 3 Stat. 679 (May 6, 1822). The licensing requirements as an extension of the Nonintercourse Act came via An Act to amend an act entitled An Act to regulate trade and intercourse with the Indian tribes, and to preserve peace on the frontier, approved thirtieth March, one thousand eight hundred and two, 3 Stat. 682 (May 6, 1822).
26. Herman J. Viola, "Thomas L. McKenney, 1824–30," in *The Commissioners of Indian Affairs, 1824–1977*, ed. Robert M. Kvasnicka and Herman J. Viola (Lincoln: University of Nebraska Press, 1979), 1–7.
27. Letter of the Superintendency of Indian Affairs, March 20, 1826, H.R. Doc. No. 146, 19th Cong., 1st Sess., Congressional Serial Set 138, 69.
28. "Report of Thomas L. McKenney, Office of Indian Affairs, Department of War, dated November 1, 1828, to the Honorable P. B. Porter, Secretary of War," *Annual Report of the Commissioner of Indian Affairs* (hereafter *ARCIA*) (Washington D.C.: Government Printing Office, 1828), 79.
29. Report on Indian Affairs, February 9, 1829, H.R. Doc. No. 117, 20th Cong., 2nd Sess., Congressional Serial Set 186.
30. House Committee of Indian Affairs, *American State Papers: Indian Affairs*, vol. 2, 14th Cong., 1st Sess. (Washington, D.C.: Gales and Seaton, 1834), 151.
31. An Act making provision for the civilization of the Indian tribes adjoining the frontier settlements, 3 Stat. 516 (March 3, 1819).
32. Report of the Civilization of Indian Tribes, House Committee on Indian Affairs, H.R. Doc. No. 91, 15th Cong., 2nd Sess., Congressional Serial Set 20, vol. 6, 1–3.
33. Case, *The Relentless Business of Treaties*, 102. Case demonstrates that one-third of the twenty-three hundred men signing treaties were related by blood or family. These connections were multigenerational.
34. Report on Creating a Home Department, March 29, 1830, S. Doc. No. 30, 21st Cong., 1st Sess., Congressional Serial Set 193.
35. An Act to provide for the appointment of a commissioner of Indian affairs, 4 Stat. 564 (July 9, 1832). This act made permanent the position of commissioner of Indian affairs. The commissioner now served at the discretion of the president, even though he was subject to the secretary of war.
36. "Letter of Peter B. Porter, Secretary of War, to President John Q. Adams," November 24, 1826, *ARCIA, 1828*, 22.
37. Herman J. Viola, *Thomas L. McKenney: Architect of America's Early Indian Policy, 1816–1830* (Chicago: Swallow Press, 1974).
38. "Instructions of Secretary of War John H. Eaton to Generals William Carroll and John Coffee," May 30, 1829, *ARCIA, 1829*, 178.
39. "President Adams Message of December 2, 1828, State of the Union Message," Richardson, *Compilation of the Messages and Papers of the President*, 1:287.
40. The Cherokee Constitution is reprinted in H.R. Doc. 91, 23rd Cong., 2nd Sess., Congressional Serial Set 273, 10–19.
41. Foreman, *Indian Removal*, 229–36.
42. Ronald N. Satz, *American Indian Policy in the Jacksonian Era* (Lincoln: University of Nebraska Press, 1974), 12–13.
43. "Message of December 8, 1829," in Richardson, *Compilation of the Messages and Papers of the Presidents*, 2:456–59. *ARCIA, 1830*, 2–3.
44. Quoted in Richard N. Ellis, *General Pope and U.S. Indian Policy* (Albuquerque: University of New Mexico Press, 1975), 37.
45. *ARCIA, 1830*, 3.

46. *Register of Debates in Congress*, 21st Cong., 1st Sess. (Washington, D.C.: Gales and Seaton, 1830), 6, 305ff and 580ff (February 24, 1830, in the House and April 6, 1830, in the Senate).
47. An Act to provide for an exchange of lands with the Indians residing in any of the states or territories and for their removal west of the river Mississippi, 4 Stat. 411 (May 28, 1830).
48. R. David Edmunds, "Samuel S. Hamilton, 1830–31," in Kvasnicka and Viola, *Commissioners of Indian Affairs*, 9–10. Hamilton began signing documents as chief clerk immediately after McKenney's dismissal. See Satz, *American Indian Policy in the Jacksonian Era*, 171n15.
49. "Samuel Hamilton to Secretary of War John Eaton," November 26, 1830, in *ARCIA, 1830*, 160–63. See also "Report of Elbert Herring, Superintendent of Indian Affairs, to Lewis Cass, Secretary of War," November 19, 1831, in *ARCIA, 1831*, 174–75.
50. Satz, *American Indian Policy in the Jacksonian Era*, 156. Hamilton returned to his role as clerk but then died suddenly in 1832.
51. Satz, "Elbert Herring, 1831–36," in Kvasnicka and Viola, *Commissioners of Indian Affairs*, 13–16.
52. *ARCIA, 1833*, 184.
53. *ARCIA, 1832*, 160.
54. Satz, *American Indian Policy in the Jacksonian Era*, 255–56.
55. *ARCIA, 1833*, 135. Treaties of removal were executed with the Shawnee, Delaware, Kaskaskia, Peoria, Kickapoo, Piankeshaw, Wea, Winnebago, Apalachicola, Chippewa, Pottawatomie, Ottawa, and Quapaw. *ARCIA, 1833*, 133–36.
56. An Act to provide for the appointment of a commissioner of Indian affairs, and for other purposes, 4 Stat. 564 (July 9, 1832).
57. An Act to provide for the appointment of three commissioners to treat with the Indians, and for other purposes, 4 Stat. 595 (July 14, 1832).
58. An Act to provide for the organization of the department of Indian affairs, 4 Stat. 735 (June 30, 1834).
59. An Act to regulate trade and intercourse with the Indian tribes, and to preserve peace on the frontiers, 4 Stat. 729 (June 30, 1834).
60. *ARCIA, 1833*, 258–66.
61. Satz, *American Indian Policy in the Jacksonian Era*, 157.
62. Satz, "Carey Allen Harris, 1836–38," in Kvasnicka and Viola, *Commissioners of Indian Affairs*, 17–22.
63. *ARCIA, 1836*, 30. If the value of the land (32,381,000 acres) assigned to the emigrating Indians is added, the cost of removal of the tribes totaled $67,458,318 (47).
64. *ARCIA, 1837*, 4–6.
65. Ibid., 90–133. President Jackson approved of the regulations between November 11, 1836, and June 18, 1837. See *Office Copy of the Laws, Regulations, etc., of the Indian Bureau, 1850* (Washington, D.C.: Gideon, 1850), 15–78.
66. Satz, "Carey Allen Harris," 17–18.
67. Satz, *American Indian Policy in the Jacksonian Era*, 157–58.
68. *ARCIA, 1838*, 440.
69. *ARCIA, 1840*, 233.
70. Ibid.
71. *ARCIA, 1841*, 230–31.
72. *ARCIA, 1842*, 370–72.
73. Satz, *American Indian Policy in the Jacksonian Era*, 224–25.
74. Foreman, *Indian Removal*, 229–314.
75. *ARCIA, 1840*, 229.
76. Ibid., 249–50.
77. Under the terms of the Winnebago Treaty of November 1, 1837 (7 Stat. 544), the tribe agreed to emigrate. But the treaty was not authorized by the Winnebago as a whole, and resulted in a permanent split in the tribe. One faction negotiated the treaty and emigrated to the Neutral Grounds

(present-day Nebraska) while the other faction remained in scattered areas of Wisconsin. See also William T. Hagan, *American Indians* (Chicago: University of Chicago Press, 1993), 91–93.

78. Treaty with the Chippewa of Saginaw, January 23, 1838, 7 Stat. 565 (emphasis added).
79. An Act to appropriate the proceeds of the sales of the public lands, and to grant pre-emption rights, 5 Stat. 553 (September 4, 1841). Under the act, 160 acres could be secured at not less than $1.25 per acre.
80. *ARCIA, 1843*, 267–68 and 305–6. Any lands unsold as of September 1, 1846, were to be sold for not less than seventy-five cents per acre.
81. United States v. Rogers, 45 U.S. 567 at 572 (1846).
82. Case, *The Relentless Business of Treaties*, 63.
83. *ARCIA, 1938*, 450.
84. *ARCIA, 1839*, 343.
85. *ARCIA, 1843*, 272.
86. An Act to provide for the organization of the department of Indian affairs, 4 Stat. 735 (June 30, 1834), § 11.
87. *ARCIA, 1840*, 241.
88. *ARCIA, 1841*, 238.
89. Robert A. Trennert, "William Medill, 1845–49," in Kvasnicka and Viola, *Commissioners of Indian Affairs*, 29.
90. Satz, *American Indian Policy in the Jacksonian Era*, 163.
91. An Act to amend an act entitled An Act to provide for the better organization of the Department of Indian Affairs, and an act entitled An Act to regulate trade and intercourse with the Indian tribes, and to preserve peace on the frontier, 9 Stat. 203 (March 3, 1847).
92. Ibid.
93. *ARCIA, 1848*, 400. Notwithstanding such changes in law, traders who did not want to give up the lucrative trade continued to persuade the Indians to resist emigration. See *ARCIA, 1847*, 4.
94. *ARCIA, 1847*, 6.
95. Treaty with the Chippewa, Ottawa, and Pottawatomie Tribes, June 5, 1846, 9 Stat. 853.
96. *ARCIA, 1850*, 13. Ewing, as secretary, made almost all policy decisions for the department.
97. Ibid.
98. *ARCIA, 1845*, 455.
99. Ibid., 454. Lena Clara Koch, "The Federal Indian Policy in Texas, 1845–1860," *Southwestern History Quarterly* 28, no. 3 (January 1925): 223–34.
100. *ARCIA, 1846*, 16.
101. Case, *The Relentless Business of Treaties*, 100.
102. See "Letter of Thomas Ewing, Secretary of the Interior, and G. W. Crawford, Secretary of War, to Samuel Spencer, Sub-agent, Tampa Bay, Florida, and Brigadier General D. E Twiggs, U.S. Army, Tampa Bay, Florida," September 17, 1849, *ARCIA, 1849*, 26–27. The authority of Spencer was revoked on September 28, 1849. See *ARCIA, 1849*, 6.
103. *ARCIA, 1848*, 385.
104. Ibid., 386. Prucha, *The Great Father*, 340–41.
105. *ARCIA, 1848*, 390; *ARCIA, 1849*, 5.
106. An Act to regulate trade and intercourse with the Indian tribes, 1 Stat. 137 (July 22, 1790).
107. *United States v. Rogers*.

CHAPTER 3

1. *Annual Report of the Secretary of the Treasury, 1848* (Washington, D.C.: Government Printing Office, 1849), 36–37.

2. An Act to establish the Home Department, and to provide for the Treasury Department as assistant secretary of the treasury, and a Commissioner of the Customs, 9 Stat. 395 (March 3, 1849). See also Prucha, *The Great Father*, 319–23.
3. *ARCIA, 1849*, 7. Federal Nonintercourse Act regulations had yet to extend over the Mexican Cession territory of California and New Mexico.
4. Worcester v. Georgia, 31 U.S. 515 (1832) at 561–562.
5. Robert A. Trennert, "Orlando Brown, 1849–50," in Kvasnicka and Viola, *Commissioners of Indian Affairs*, 41–47.
6. Robert A. Trennert, *Alternative to Extinction: Federal Indian Policy and the Beginnings of the Reservation System, 1846–1851* (Philadelphia: Temple University Press, 1975).
7. *ARCIA, 1849*, 21.
8. Ibid., 22.
9. Ibid.
10. Ibid., 22–23.
11. Ibid., 18.
12. *ARCIA, 1850*, 10. Only three agents were approved for California. See An Act making appropriations for the current and contingent expenses of the Indian Department, and for fulfilling treaty stipulations with the various Indian tribes, for the year ending June 30, 1850, 9 Stat. 382 (March 3, 1849).
13. *ARCIA, 1849*, 21.
14. *ARCIA, 1850*, 23.
15. Trennert, "Luke Lea, 1850–53," in Kvasnicka and Viola, *Commissioners of Indian Affairs*, 49–55. Lea should not be confused with his uncle Luke Lea, who fought with Andrew Jackson during the Creek and Seminole wars and later served two terms in the House of Representatives (D-TN) before becoming an Indian agent.
16. Prucha, *The Great Father*, 324.
17. *ARCIA, 1852*, 3.
18. *ARCIA, 1851*, 3–4, and 12.
19. *ARCIA, 1850*, 3–4.
20. Treaty with the Menominee Tribe, October 18, 1848, 9 Stat. 952.
21. Treaty with the Menominee Tribe, May 12, 1854, 10 Stat. 1064. See also *ARCIA, 1851*, 5.
22. An Act making appropriations for the current and contingent expenses of the Indian Department, and for fulfilling treaty stipulations with the various Indian tribes, for the year ending June 30, 1852, 9 Stat. 574 at 586 (February 27, 1851).
23. Prucha, *The Great Father*, 381–92 (California), and 392–402 (Oregon).
24. David H. DeJong, *American Indian Treaties: A Guide to Ratified and Unratified Colonial, United States, State, Foreign, and Intertribal Treaties and Agreements, 1607–1911* (Salt Lake City: University of Utah Press, 2015), 39–40, and 167–76. Treaty with the Rogue River Tribes, September 10, 1853, 10 Stat. 1018; and Treaty with the Umpqua Tribes, September 19, 1853, 10 Stat. 1027.
25. *ARCIA, 1851*, 9–10.
26. Treaty of Fort Laramie, September 17, 1851, 11 Stat. 749.
27. *Annual Report of the Secretary of the Interior 1851* (Washington, D.C.: Government Printing Office, 1851), 502. S. Doc. No. 1, 32nd Cong., 1st Sess., Congressional Serial Set 612.
28. *ARCIA, 1852*, 11.
29. Case, *The Unrelenting Business of Treaties*, 138–39.
30. Prucha, *The Great Father*, 438.
31. *ARCIA, 1851*, 12.
32. Ibid. See also Case, *The Relentless Business of Treaties*, 39–92.
33. *ARCIA, 1851*, 12.
34. *ARCIA, 1852*, 10–12.

35. Prucha, *The Great Father*, 326.
36. Robert M. Kvasnicka, "George W. Manypenny, 1853–57," in Kvasnicka and Viola, *Commissioners of Indian Affairs*, 57–67. The Ohio congressional delegation recommended Manypenny to President Pierce for the assistant postmaster position; Pierce instead appointed him to the more prestigious position of commissioner of Indian affairs.
37. *ARCIA, 1854*, 10.
38. Ibid., 14–15. Funds to negotiate treaties were appropriated by Congress but were available too late in the season to procure the goods and gifts necessary to negotiation.
39. *ARCIA, 1855*, 18.
40. *ARCIA, 1858*, 9.
41. *ARCIA, 1855*, 14.
42. Case, *The Relentless Business of Treaties*, 139–40, 154. For the treaty, see Chippewa Treaty with the United States, September 30, 1854, 10 Stat. 1109.
43. *ARCIA, 1854*, 22–23.
44. *ARCIA, 1855*, 18.
45. *ARCIA, 1856*, 23.
46. Ibid.
47. *ARCIA, 1855*, 6.
48. *ARCIA, 1853*, 21.
49. Congressional authorization for the treaties is in An Act making appropriations for the current and contingent expenses of the Indian Department, and for fulfilling treaty stipulations with the various Indian tribes, for the year ending June 30, 1853, 10 Stat. 238 (March 3, 1853). An example of the annuity language can be seen in article 9 of the treaty with the Ioway Tribe. All tribal funds from earlier treaties, as well as funds from the sale of land under the 1854 treaty, and all annuities were to be "expended under the direction of the President for the erection of houses, breaking and fencing lands, purchasing stock, farming utensils, seeds, and such other articles as may be necessary for their comfort." Treaty with the Ioway Tribe, May 17, 1854, 10 Stat. 1069.
50. *ARCIA, 1854*, 5–6. In 1854, the Senate recommended the Indian Office negotiate treaties with the tribes in the Southwest, as well as in the Pacific Northwest. Between September 1853 and July 1855, the Indian Office negotiated seventeen treaties with tribes in Washington and Oregon, fifteen of which were ratified. In the Southwest, nine treaties were negotiated, but just one, the Kiowa, Comanche, and Apache, was ratified by the Senate.
51. DeJong, *American Indian Treaties*, 151–156, 176–77.
52. Robert M. Utley, *The Indian Frontier of the American West, 1846–1890* (Albuquerque: University of New Mexico Press, 1984), 61–62.
53. *ARCIA, 1854*, 16–17.
54. Ibid., 17
55. *ARCIA, 1853*, 370, for the report of Thomas Fitzpatrick, Indian agent for the Upper Platte and Arkansas Agency.
56. Deloria and Lytle, *American Indians, American Justice*, 166–68.
57. An Act to amend an act, entitled An Act to divide the state of Arkansas into two judicial districts, approved March the 3rd, eighteen hundred and fifty-one, 10 Stat. 269 (March 27, 1854).
58. Manypenny left sympathetic to the cause of American Indians. In his 1856 report (*ARCIA, 1856*, 22) he noted, "the history of the sufferings of the Indians has never been written; the story of his wrongs never been told." In 1880, he wrote *Our Indian Wards* (Cincinnati: R. Clarke, 1880), exposing these injustices.
59. During his tenure as governor of Kansas Territory, Colorado Territory was created and its capital city, Denver, was named for him.
60. *ARCIA, 1857*, 5.

61. Ibid., 7.
62. Donald Chaput, "James W. Denver, 1857, 1858–59," in Kvasnicka and Viola, *Commissioners of Indian Affairs*, 70.
63. *ARCIA, 1857*, 4.
64. *ARCIA, 1858*, 5.
65. Ibid., 6.
66. *ARCIA, 1857*, 9. See "Report of Sylvester Mowry, Lt. United States Army, to the Honorable J. W. Denver," November 10, 1857 (304). See also David H. DeJong, *Stealing the Gila: The Pima Agricultural Economy and Water Deprivation, 1848–1921* (Tucson: University of Arizona Press, 2009), 41–56.
67. "Report of Sylvester Mowry to A. B. Greenwood, Commissioner of Indian Affairs," in *ARCIA, 1859*, 355–56.
68. *Office Copy of the Laws, Regulations, etc., of the Indian Bureau, 1850* (Washington, D.C.: Gideon, 1850), 45–78.
69. Ibid., 28–29.
70. Ibid., 45–49, and 79–91.
71. Harry Kelsey, "Charles E. Mix, 1858," in Kvasnicka and Viola, *Commissioners of Indian Affairs*, 77–78.
72. Gary L. Roberts, "Alfred Burton Greenwood, 1859–1861," in Kvasnicka and Viola, *Commissioners of Indian Affairs*, 81. Greenwood was confirmed by the Senate on January 10, 1860.
73. *ARCIA, 1859*, 5.
74. Treaty with the Sauk and Fox Tribes, October 1, 1859, 15 Stat. 467; and Treaty with the Kansas Tribe, October 5, 1859, 12 Stat. 1111.
75. Donald J. Berthrong, *The Southern Cheyenne* (Norman: University of Oklahoma Press, 1979), 144–50. The resulting treaty was the February 18, 1861, Treaty of Fort Wise, 12 Stat. 59.
76. *ARCIA, 1859*, 385.
77. *ARCIA, 1860*, 17.
78. Trennert, *Alternative to Extinction*.
79. *ARCIA, 1859*, 22 and 25.
80. *ARCIA, 1858*, 9–13. Treaty with the Ponca Tribe, March 12, 1858, 12 Stat. 997.
81. *ARCIA, 1859*, 19. Case, *The Relentless Business of Treaties*, 141.
82. *Annual Report of the Secretary of the Interior, 1860*, 3. Between September 1857 and May 1860, the Indian Office negotiated eleven treaties resulting in the acquisition of 30,232,580 acres at a cost of $3,726,880 ($0.081 per acre). These treaties included the Pawnee; Seneca; Ponca; Yankton Sioux; Mdewakaton Sioux; Sisseton-Wahpeton Sioux; Winnebago; Chippewa-Munsee; Sauk and Fox of the Mississippi; Kansas; and Delaware. *ARCIA, 1860*, 12.
83. Roberts, "Alfred Burton Greenwood, 1859–61," in Kasvinicka and Viola, *Commissioners of Indian Affairs*, 86. Annie Heloise Abel, *The American Indians as Slaveholders and Secessionist* (Lincoln: University of Nebraska Press, 1992), 127–206.
84. *Congressional Globe*, 35th Cong., 2nd Sess., February 26, 1859, 1406–7.

CHAPTER 4

1. *ARCIA, 1861*, 3.
2. *ARCIA, 1865*, ii.
3. *Congressional Globe*, 41st Cong., 3rd Sess., February 22, 1871, 1499–1507, at 1501.
4. Cathleen D. Cahill, *Federal Fathers and Mothers: A Social History of the United States Indian Service, 1869–1933* (Chapel Hill: University of North Carolina Press, 2011), 15–17.

5. Between 1824 and 1860, the annual report averaged 175 pages; for the period 1861 to 1881 the average was 449 pages, or 2.5 times greater.
6. Harry Kelsey, "William P. Dole, 1861–65," in Kvasnicka and Viola, *Commissioners of Indian Affairs,* 89–98.
7. Prucha, *The Great Father,* 465–66.
8. Francis Paul Prucha, *American Indian Treaties: A History of a Political Anomaly* (Berkley: University of California Press, 1994), 243–45.
9. *ARCIA, 1861,* 17, 20; *ARCIA, 1863,* 15.
10. *ARCIA, 1862,* 36.
11. *ARCIA, 1861,* 20.
12. Ibid., 22–23. See Albert Hurtado, *Indian Survival on the California Frontier* (New Haven: Yale University Press, 1990).
13. *ARCIA, 1864,* 12.
14. *ARCIA, 1862,* 39–40.
15. *ARCIA, 1861,* 29.
16. *ARCIA, 1864,* 30–31. Debo, *A History of the Indians of the United States,* 176–77.
17. *ARCIA, 1862,* 24.
18. *ARCIA, 1863,* 25. Annie Abel, *The American Indian in the Civil War, 1862–1865* (Lincoln: University of Nebraska Press, 1992), 234–35.
19. *ARCIA, 1863,* 14–15.
20. *ARCIA, 1864,* 19. See also L. R. Bailey, *The Long Walk: A History of the Navajo Wars, 1846–1868* (Tucson: University of Arizona Press, 1988).
21. *ARCIA, 1863,* 3, 6.
22. Ibid., 7.
23. DeJong, *Stealing the Gila.*
24. *ARCIA, 1862,* 33–34.
25. *ARCIA, 1861,* 9.
26. DeJong, *American Indian Treaties,* 52–55, 192–94.
27. *ARCIA, 1864,* 33.
28. Able, *The American Indians as Slaveholder and Secessionist,* 127–206.
29. *ARCIA, 1862,* 41–43; *ARCIA, 1863,* 36.
30. *ARCIA, 1864,* 6.
31. See, for instance, Treaty with the Tabeguache Ute, October 7, 1863, 13 Stat. 673. Article 10 provided each family making a commitment to pursue agriculture with one head of cattle per year for five years, ten sheep per year for the first two years, and five sheep per year for the third through fifth years. Treaty with the Shoshone and Goship, October 12, 1863, 13 Stat. 681. Article 7 provided cattle for breeding.
32. See Ellis, *General Pope and U.S. Indian Policy,* 33–34.
33. "John Pope, Major General Commanding, to Honorable E. M. Stanton, Secretary of War, Washington, D.C.," Milwaukie, Wisconsin, February 6, 1864, in *ARCIA, 1864,* 426.
34. Ibid., 428.
35. Ibid., 6.
36. Ibid., 7.
37. "William Dole to Honorable J. P. Usher, Secretary of the Interior, Department of the Interior, Office of Indian Affairs, April 6, 1864," in *ARCIA, 1864,* 431.
38. Gary L. Roberts, "Dennis Nelson Cooley, 1865–66," in Kvasnicka and Viola, *Commissioners of Indian Affairs,* 99–108.
39. *ARCIA, 1865,* 5.
40. Ibid., 2–6.

41. Ibid.
42. *Congressional Globe*, 38th Cong., 2nd Sess., February 23, 1865, 1021–24.
43. *Congressional Globe*, 38th Cong., 2nd Sess., March 2, 1865, 1303–6. Reference is to the treaty clause.
44. Ibid., 1308–10.
45. *ARCIA, 1865*, iii.
46. Quoted in Annie Abel, *The American Indian and the End of the Confederacy, 1863–1866* (Lincoln: University of Nebraska Press, 1993), 219–26.
47. *ARCIA, 1865*, 34.
48. Unratified Treaty with the Cherokee, Choctaw, Chickasaw, Creek, Seminole, Seneca, Osage, Quapaw, and Shawnee, September 13, 1865, in DeJong, *American Indian Treaties*, 43, 181.
49. *ARCIA, 1865*, 34.
50. *ARCIA, 1866*, 8. Prucha, *The Great Father*, 434–36.
51. An Act for the admission of Kansas to the Union, 12 Stat. 126 (January 29, 1861).
52. *ARCIA, 1866*, 19.
53. See "James Harlan, Secretary, to the Honorable James Speed, Attorney General of the United States," February 6, 1866, Washington, D.C. and also "Speed to Harlan," March 9, 1866, both in Ibid., 304–5.
54. The Kansas Indians, 7 Wallace U.S. 737 at 744 (1866). See Treaty with the Shawnee Tribe, September 29, 1817, 7 Stat. 160.
55. Article 9 of the Treaty with the Shawnee Tribe, May 10, 1854, 10 Stat. 1053.
56. *The Kansas Indians*, 737.
57. The New York Indians, 7 Wallace U.S. 761 (1866).
58. S. Rep. No. 140, July 26, 1867, 40th Cong., 2nd Sess., Congressional Serial Set 1320. See also "Defense of Mr. Commissioner Bogy before the Committee of Indian Affairs of the House of Representatives," January 12, 1867, 39th Cong., 2nd Sess., (Washington, D.C.: Government Printing Office, 1867).
59. Case, *The Relentless Business of Treaties*, 105–6. See also William E. Unrau, "Politics, Bureaucracy, and the Bogus Administration of Indian Commissioner Lewis Vital Bogy, 1866–1867," *American Indian Law Review* 5, no. 1 (Summer 1977): 185–94.
60. William E. Unrau, "Lewis Vital Bogy, 1866–67," in Kvasnicka and Viola, *Commissioners of Indian Affairs*, 109–14.
61. Unrau, "Nathaniel Green Taylor, 1867–69," in Kvasnicka and Viola, *Commissioners of Indian Affairs*, 115–22.
62. *Condition of the Indian Tribes* (Washington, D.C.: Government Printing Office, 1867). See also S. Rep. No. 156, 39th Cong., 2nd Sess., Congressional Serial Set 1279. For the Fetterman report, see S. Doc. No. 13, 40th Cong., 1st Sess., Congressional Serial Set 1308.
63. *Condition of the Indian Tribes*, 3–10.
64. *ARCIA, 1867*, 3.
65. Stan Hoig, *The Sand Creek Massacre* (Norman: University of Oklahoma Press, 1961).
66. *ARCIA, 1867*, 4.
67. An Act to establish peace with certain hostile Indian tribes, 15 Stat. 17 (July 20, 1867). See also *Congressional Globe*, July 15, 1867, 40th Cong., 1st Sess., 667.
68. *Congressional Globe*, July 17, 1867, 40th Cong., 1st Sess., 681.
69. Ibid.
70. Prucha, *The Great Father*, 488–90.
71. Kiowa-Comanche Treaty of Medicine Lodge Creek, October 21, 1867, 15 Stat. 581; Kiowa, Comanche, and Apache Treaty of Medicine Lodge Creek, October 21, 1867, 15 Stat. 589; Southern Cheyenne and Arapaho Treaty of Medicine Lodge Creek, October 28, 1867, 15 Stat. 593. Major General (retired) Christopher C. Augur was an extra member of the commission and eventually replaced Sherman.

72. Sioux-Arapaho Treaty of Fort Laramie, April 29, 1868, 15 Stat. 635; Crow Treaty of Fort Laramie, May 7, 1868, 15 Stat. 649; Northern Cheyenne and Northern Arapaho Treaty of Fort Laramie, May 10, 1868, 15 Stat. 655.
73. Navajo Treaty, June 1, 1868, 15 Stat. 667; Ute Treaty, March 2, 1868, 15 Stat. 593; and Shoshone-Bannock Treaty, July 3, 1868, 15 Stat. 673.
74. "Report to the President by the Indian Peace Commission," January 7, 1868, in *ARCIA, 1868*, 43.
75. *ARCIA, 1867*, 5.
76. "Report to the President by the Indian Peace Commission," in *ARCIA, 1868*, 43.
77. *Congressional Globe*, January 29, 1867, 39th Cong., 2nd Sess., 843–44.
78. "Report to the President by the Indian Peace Commission," in *ARCIA, 1868*, 47.
79. Prucha, *The Great Father*, 551.
80. *ARCIA, 1868*, 8.
81. Ibid., 8–10.
82. Ibid., 10.
83. Ibid., 20.
84. Ibid., 6.
85. "Report to the President by the Indian Peace Commission," in Ibid., 43.
86. *ARCIA, 1867*, 5. The Peace Commission advanced the idea of two large reservations: Indian Territory and the Dakotas west of the Missouri River. See *ARCIA, 1868*, 46.
87. "William T. Sherman, Lt. General, to General E. D. Townsend, Assistant Adj. General, U.S. Military Telegraph, August 22, 1868," in *ARCIA, 1868*, 74.
88. Stan Hoig, *The Battle of the Washita* (Lincoln: University of Nebraska Press, 1976).
89. Cahill, *Federal Fathers and Mothers*, 18–19.
90. Henry G. Waltmann, "Ely S. Parker, 1869–71," in Kvasnicka and Viola, *Commissioners of Indian Affairs*, 123–33.
91. Report of Colonel Parker on Indian Affairs, January 30, 1867, H.R. Doc. No. 37, 39th Cong., 2nd Sess., Congressional Serial Set 1302, 1–11.
92. *ARCIA, 1869*, 3.
93. *ARCIA, 1870*, 10.
94. *ARCIA, 1869*, 5.
95. "Parker to Commission on Indian Affairs," May 26, 1869, in Ibid., 43.
96. Ibid., 6.
97. "Report of the Board of Indian Commissioners, Pittsburgh, Pennsylvania, November 23, 1869," in Ibid., 45. Treaty making was ended because of a political feud between the House of Representatives and the Senate. The House was left out of the treaty process (and was excluded according to the Constitution) and refused to appropriate funds for the peace treaties unless the Senate agreed to end treaty making. See DeJong, *American Indian Treaties*, 31–32, 43–45.
98. Case, *The Relentless Business of Treaties*, 51.
99. *ARCIA, 1869*, 4–6.
100. Ibid., 9.
101. "Report of the Hon. Vincent Colyer, U.S. Special Indian Commissioner, on the Indian tribes and their surroundings in Alaska Territory from Personal Observation and Inspection in 1869," in Ibid., 535–616.
102. *ARCIA, 1870*, 10.
103. *Annual Report of the Board of Indian Commissioners, 1869* (Washington: Government Printing Office, 1870), 3.
104. *Annual Report of the Secretary of the Interior, 1871*, 6.
105. H.R. Rep. No. 39, 41st Cong., 3rd Sess., Congressional Serial Set 1464, 11.
106. H. Craig Miner, "Francis A. Walker, 1871–73," in Kvasnicka and Viola, *Commissioners of Indian Affairs*, 135–40.

107. *ARCIA, 1871*, 4.
108. Ibid., 5.
109. Ibid., 6.
110. Editorial, *New York Times*, November 22, 1871.
111. "The Recent Change in the Indian Bureau," *The Nation*, August 17, 1871, 100.
112. *ARCIA, 1872*, 10.
113. Ibid., 5.
114. Ibid., 5–6.
115. Ibid., 12.
116. Ibid., 13.
117. Ibid., 9.
118. Ibid., 15.
119. Richard C. Crawford, "Edward Parmalee Smith, 1873–75," in Kvasnicka and Viola, *Commissioners of Indian Affairs*, 141–47.
120. *ARCIA, 1873*, 3.
121. Ibid., 4.
122. Ibid.
123. Ibid., 5
124. *ARCIA, 1874*, 6; *ARCIA, 1875*, 6. Prucha, *The Great Father*, 540.
125. *ARCIA, 1874*, 8.
126. *ARCIA, 1875*, 7–9.
127. Ibid., 11. DeJong, *American Indian Treaties*, 39–41.
128. *ARCIA, 1875*, 12, 22.
129. *ARCIA, 1873*, 9.
130. *ARCIA, 1874*, 15.
131. Ibid., 16
132. Ibid., 23–30.
133. *ARCIA, 1875*, 26–27.
134. *ARCIA, 1876*, iii.
135. Ibid., iv–vi.
136. Ibid., vi.
137. Ibid., vii–ix.
138. Ibid., ix–x.
139. *Congressional Globe*, 39th Cong., 1st Sess., May 30, 1866, 2890–97, at 2890 and 2893. As such, Indians were not considered "persons under the law" for purposes of congressional apportionment.
140. *Congressional Globe*, 41st Cong., 1st Sess., April 6, 1869, 560. S. Rep. No. 268, 41st Cong., 1st Sess., Congressional Serial Set 1443.
141. *ARCIA, 1876*, xii.
142. Ibid., xi–xii.
143. Edward E. Hill, "John Q. Smith, 1875–77," in Kvasnicka and Viola, *Commissioners of Indian Affairs*, 149–53.
144. Roy E. Meyer, "Ezra A. Hayt, 1877–80," in Kvasnicka and Viola, *Commissioners of Indian Affairs*, 155–66.
145. *ARCIA, 1877*, 2.
146. *ARCIA, 1878*, xlii. See also William T. Hagan, *Indian Police and Judges* (Lincoln: University of Nebraska Press, 1966), 40–43.
147. *ARCIA, 1878*, x.
148. *ARCIA, 1879*, vi.
149. Ibid., v.

150. *ARCIA, 1878,* iv.
151. Ibid., vi.
152. David Wallace Adams, *Education for Extinction: American Indians and the Boarding School Experience, 1875–1928* (Lawrence: University Press of Kansas, 1995), 38–46.
153. See Charles Eastman, *My People the Sioux* (Lincoln: University of Nebraska Press, 1975), 123–50. Eastman arrived at Carlisle Indian School in 1879. See also Luther Standing Bear, *My Indian Boyhood* (Lincoln: University of Nebraska Press, 1988). Both are first-person accounts.
154. See article seven of the Treaty of Medicine Lodge Creek with the Kiowa and Comanche Tribes, October 21, 1867, 15 Stat. 581.
155. *ARCIA, 1878,* xxvi–xxvii.
156. *ARCIA, 1879,* v, vi; *ARCIA, 1878,* xxlii; *ARCIA, 1877,* 4, 5.
157. *ARCIA, 1878,* iii.
158. Prucha, *The Great Father,* 552–53.
159. Transfer of the Indian Bureau, March 9, 1876, H.R. Rep. No. 354, 44th Cong., 1st Sess., Congressional Serial Set *1709*. See also Report of Transfer of the Indian Bureau, March 14, 1876, H.R. Rep. No. 240, 44th Cong., 1st Sess., Congressional Serial Set 1708.
160. United States ex. Rel. Standing Bear v. Crook, 25 F. 695 at 700 (C.C.D. Neb. 1879).
161. Report of the Ponca, U.S. Senate Select Committee on Indian Affairs, S. Rep. No. 670, 46th Cong., 2nd Sess., xiv (1880).
162. "Report of Special Commission to the Ponca," Washington, D.C., January 25, 1881, in *ARCIA, 1881,* 217–25. The commission recommended every Ponca man, woman, and child be allowed to secure a 160 acre allotment in either Indian Territory or Dakota Territory and that Congress appropriate $25,000 for agricultural implements, stock, seed, etc. The commission was made up of General George Crook, General Nelson Miles, William Stickney and Walter Allen, the latter of whom issued a dissenting report. See also Thomas Henry Tibbles, *Standing Bear and the Ponca Chiefs* (Lincoln: University of Nebraska Press, 1972), 134.
163. An Act making appropriations to supply deficiencies in the appropriations for the fiscal year ending June 30, 1881, and for prior years and for those certified as due by the accounting office of the Treasury, in accordance with section four of the Act of January 14, 1878, heretofore paid from permanent appropriations, and for other purposes, 21 Stat. 414 at 422 (March 3, 1881). See also Removal of the Ponca, February 2, 1881, S. Doc. No. 30, 46th Cong., 3rd Sess., Congressional Serial Set 1941.
164. *ARCIA, 1880,* iii and xiii.
165. Ibid., vi.
166. Ibid., xvi.
167. Cahill, *Federal Fathers and Mothers,* 67, notes the first matron was appointed by the Quaker Church in 1878.
168. Michael A. Goldman, "Roland E. Trowbridge, 1880–81," in Kvasnicka and Viola, *Commissioners of Indian Affairs,* 167–72.
169. Helen Hunt Jackson, *A Century of Dishonor* (New York: Harper, 1965), 9.
170. Ibid., 337.
171. Ibid., 31.

CHAPTER 5

1. Janet McDonnell, *The Dispossession of the American Indians, 1887–1934* (Bloomington: University of Indiana Press, 1991), 121.
2. Cahill, *Federal Fathers and Mothers,* 6. Cahill demonstrates how "at the micro-level" federal employees, male and female, executed policies of colonialism.

3. Floyd A. O'Neil, "Hiram Price, 1881–85," in Kvasnicka and Viola, *Commissioners of Indian Affairs*, 173–79.
4. *ARCIA, 1881*, iii–iv.
5. *ARCIA, 1883*, iii.
6. *ARCIA, 1882*, xi.
7. *ARCIA, 1881*, iv.
8. Ibid., v.
9. Ibid., xxii.
10. Ibid., xxv.
11. *ARCIA, 1882*, xliii.
12. William T. Hagan, *The Indian Rights Association: The Herbert Welsh Years, 1882–1904* (Tucson: University of Arizona Press, 1985), 9.
13. An Act to secure homesteads to actual settlers on the public domain, 12 Stat. 392 (May 20, 1862). An Act making appropriations for the current and contingent expenses of the Indian Department, and for fulfilling treaty stipulations with the various Indian tribes, for the year ending June 30, 1875, 18 Stat. 420 (March 3, 1875). The homesteading provisions were largely ineffective, as few Indians took advantage of them. See Francis Paul Prucha, *American Indian Policy in Crisis: Christian Reformers and the Indian, 1865–1900* (Norman: University of Oklahoma Press, 1976), 234.
14. *ARCIA, 1881*, xxv.
15. See Prucha, *The Great Father*, 865–67, for a further discussion of public domain allotments.
16. See Treaty with the Ottoes and Missourias, March 15, 1854, 10 Stat. 1038. See also Yakima Treaty of June 9, 1855, 12 Stat. 951.
17. *ARCIA, 1883*, xvi–xvii.
18. Richard J. Perry, *Apache Reservation: Indigenous People and the American State* (Austin: University of Texas Press, 1993), 151–52.
19. *ARCIA, 1882*, xlviii. The solicitor opinion of April 25, 1883, deemed neither the Indians nor the Indian Office had authority to lease land.
20. *ARCIA, 1881*, xxxiv.
21. *ARCIA, 1882*, vii.
22. *ARCIA, 1881*, xxxiv; *ARCIA, 1883*, xxx; Adams, *Education for Extinction*, 156–63.
23. *ARCIA, 1884*, xx.
24. *ARCIA, 1881*, xxxvii. Rhode Island expended, according to Price, $600,000 for forty-nine thousand students. The Indian Office expended $139,000 for about the same number of eligible students, excluding the Five Tribes. About 10 percent of the eligible Indian school-aged population was enrolled in school.
25. *ARCIA, 1883*, xl.
26. *ARCIA, 1882*, vi; and *ARCIA, 1883*, xl.
27. Cahill, *Federal Fathers and Mothers*, 63–82, esp. 66.
28. *ARCIA, 1884*, xxxvi.
29. *ARCIA, 1882*, xvi.
30. Prevention of Trespass on Indian Lands, March 29, 1888, H.R. Doc. No. 145, 47th Cong., 1st Sess., Congressional Serial Set 2030. *ARCIA, 18881*, xvii.
31. *ARCIA, 1881*, xix.
32. *ARCIA, 1883*, xiv. Hagan, *Indian Police and Judges*, 69–81.
33. *ARCIA, 1884*, xi.
34. *ARCIA, 1883*, x–xi.
35. Hagan, *The Indian Rights Association*, 44.
36. *ARCIA, 1881*, xvii.
37. *ARCIA, 1883*, iv.

38. Deloria, Jr. and Lytle, *American Indians, American Justice*, 169. Ex Parte Crow Dog, 109 U.S. 556 (1883).
39. Major Crimes Act, 23 Stat. 385 (March 3, 1885).
40. Hagan, *The Indian Rights Association*; Cahill, *Federal Fathers and Mothers*, 29.
41. Gregory C. Thompson, "John D. C. Atkins, 1885–88," in Kvasnicka and Viola, *Commissioners of Indian Affairs*, 181–88.
42. *ARCIA, 1885*, iii.
43. *ARCIA, 1887*, xxvi. Atkins and many of the reformers were influenced by Lewis Henry Morgan's *Ancient Society: Or Researches in the Lines of Human Progress from Savagery, through Barbarism to Civilization* (New York: Henry Holt, 1877). Morgan used an evolutionary lens to identify seven stages of human development.
44. Cited in Case, *The Relentless Business of Treaties*, 115.
45. *ARCIA, 1885*, xxiv–xxv.
46. Ibid., iv.
47. Ibid., v.
48. Allotment of Lands in Severalty to Indians, April 20, 1886, H.R. Rep. No. 1835, 49th Cong., 1st Sess., vol. 6, Congressional Serial Set 2440.
49. *ARCIA, 1887*, vi.
50. Ibid., viii–ix.
51. *ARCIA, 1888*, ix.
52. *ARCIA, 1887*, vi.
53. *ARCIA, 1886*, v.
54. Ibid., xi.
55. *ARCIA, 1887*, xi–xiii.
56. *ARCIA, 1886*, xiii.
57. *ARCIA, 1885*, xii.
58. *Congressional Globe*, February 22, 1871, 41st Cong., 3rd Sess., part 2, 1501.
59. *ARCIA, 1887*, xxxiv.
60. Ibid., liv.
61. Ibid., xlvi.
62. *ARCIA, 1886*, xli; *ARCIA, 1887*, li.
63. *ARCIA, 1887*, xxii. See also Hagan, *The Indian Rights Association*, 86.
64. *ARCIA, 1886*, xxiii. Adams, *Education for Extinction*, 137–41.
65. *ARCIA, 1887*, xvi.
66. *ARCIA, 1885*, xiii. See Adams, *Education for Extinction*, 289.
67. Elk v. Wilkins, 112 U.S. 94 (1884). The exception was if a treaty provision governed. See Wyandotte Treaty of January 31, 1855, 10 Stat. 1159. See also Seneca Treaty of June 23, 1867, 15 Stat. 513.
68. United States v. Joseph, 94 U.S. 614 (1877). In deciding the *Joseph* case, the court noted "we leave that question [citizenship] until it shall be made in some case where the rights of citizenship are necessarily involved." Under the Treaty of Guadalupe Hidalgo, residents in New Mexico were given the option of retaining Mexican citizenship or taking U.S. citizenship. No Pueblo Indians elected Mexican citizenship and were assumed to be U.S. citizens, even though they could not vote in New Mexico. After statehood in 1912, the U.S. Supreme Court in United States v. Sandoval, 231 U.S. 28 (1913) held that the Pueblo people were under federal supervision, although it did not issue an opinion on the matter of citizenship.
69. *ARCIA, 1887*, lxvii.
70. *ARCIA, 1888*, xvi.
71. Ibid., xviii.
72. Ibid., xix.

73. Ibid., xxiii.
74. Ibid., xv. See also Hagan, *The Indian Rights Association*, 99–109 for further discussion of the Bureau of Catholic Missions and influence of policy in the Harrison administration.
75. *ARCIA, 1888*, xvi. An Act making appropriations for the current and contingent expenses of the Indian Department, and for fulfilling treaty stipulations with various Indian tribes, for the year ending June 30, 1895, and for other purposes, 28 Stat. 286 at 311 (August 15, 1894).
76. *ARCIA, 1888*, xl.
77. United States v. George Cook, 86 U.S. 591 (1873). The U.S. Supreme Court opined that the case was governed by the 1823 *Johnson v. M'Intosh* decision and it affirmed that the United States was the owner of the fee, and that Indians could not alienate the land except to the United States. As timber was "part of the realty," it could not be sold absent federal authorization.
78. *ARCIA, 1888*, xlv–xlvi.
79. Ibid., xlvi.
80. Ibid., xl.
81. Ibid., lxxxv.
82. Ibid., lxxxvii. See also Prucha, *The Great Father*, 723–25, and 730–33.
83. *ARCIA, 1888*, xxxviii.
84. Ibid., lxxxix.
85. The Cherokee Nation v. Georgia, 30 U.S. 1 (1831) (emphasis added).
86. United States v. Kagama, 118 U.S. 375 (1886) (emphasis in original). The ruling did not apply to Indian Territory, which remained under its own judicial authority.
87. Hagan, *The Indian Rights Association*, 102–3.
88. Francis Paul Prucha, "Thomas Jefferson Morgan, 1889–93," in Kvasnicka and Viola, *Commissioners of Indian Affairs*, 193–203.
89. *ARCIA, 1889*, 4.
90. Ibid., 3–4.
91. *ARCIA, 1890*, vi.
92. Cahill, *Federal Fathers and Mothers*, 39–45.
93. *ARCIA, 1891*, 3–4.
94. Ibid., 4–9.
95. Ibid., 9–37; *ARCIA, 1892*, 31–37.
96. *ARCIA, 1891*, 36.
97. *ARCIA, 1892*, 37.
98. Prucha, *The Great Father*, 701.
99. *ARCIA, 1890*, clx.
100. Ibid., cxlvi–cxlviii.
101. *ARCIA, 1889*, 3.
102. *ARCIA, 1890*, xvi.
103. *ARCIA, 1889*, 8. Adams, *Education for Extinction*, 283–88.
104. *ARCIA, 1892*, 40–41; *ARCIA, 1891*, vi.
105. *ARCIA, 1892*, 46.
106. Ibid., 49, 56–57.
107. *ARCIA, 1889*, 17. An Act to amend and further extend the benefits of the act approved February 8, 1887, entitled An Act to provide for the allotment of land in severalty to Indians on various reservations, and to extend the protection of the laws of the United States over the Indians, and for other purposes, 26 Stat. 1891 (February 28, 1891).
108. *ARCIA, 1891*, 44.
109. Ibid., 46.
110. *ARCIA, 1892*, 66–70.

111. See An Act to amend sections 2139, 2140, and 2141 of the revised statutes touching the sale of intoxicants in the Indian Country, and for other purposes, 27 Stat. 260 (July 23, 1892). This legislation put reformers in a difficult position. As Indians were "civilized" and "became as white men," they remained subject to the law. The courts upheld this police authority of the Indian Office although for Indian allottees, the court held in *A Matter of Heff* (1905) that they were not subject to the statute once they became citizens. This decision was overturned in 1916. In 1919 prohibition became national law.
112. *ARCIA, 1890*, lviii.
113. *ARCIA, 1892*, 61.
114. L. G. Moses, "Performative Traditions in American Indian History," in *A Companion to American Indian History*, ed. Philip Deloria and Neal Salisbury (Maldin, MA: Blackwell Publishing, 2004), 193–208.
115. An Act to amend and further extend the benefits of the act approved February 8, 1887, entitled An Act to provide for the allotment of land in severalty to Indians on various reservations, and to extend the protection of the laws of the United States over the Indians, and for other purposes, 26 Stat. 1891 (February 28, 1891). Section 3 authorized the leasing of tribal lands with the approval of the governing council.
116. *ARCIA, 1890*, lv, ci.
117. *ARCIA, 1891*, 143–44.
118. *ARCIA, 1892*, 10.
119. Ibid., 27–31.
120. *ARCIA, 1889*, 113–14.
121. Editorial, *New York Times*, November 28, 1894, 13.
122. William T. Hagan, "Daniel M. Browning, 1893–97," in Kvasnicka and Viola, *Commissioners of Indian Affairs*, 205–9.
123. *ARCIA, 1896*, 1.
124. *ARCIA, 1893*, 59; *ARCIA, 1894*, 59.
125. An Act making appropriations for the current and contingent expenses of the Indian Department, and for fulfilling treaty stipulations with various Indian tribes, for the fiscal year ending June thirtieth, eighteen hundred and ninety-three, and for other purposes, 27 Stat. 120 (July 13, 1892).
126. *ARCIA, 1896*, 4–5.
127. *ARCIA, 1893*, 10.
128. Ibid., 11.
129. An Act making appropriations for the current and contingent expenses of the Indian Department, and for fulfilling treaty stipulations with various Indian tribes, for the year ending June 30, 1895, and for other purposes, 28 Stat. 286 at 311 (August 15, 1894).
130. *ARCIA, 1896*, 17. See also David H. DeJong, *Promises of the Past: A History of Indian Education in the United States* (Golden, CO: North American Press, 1993), 71–85, for further discussion.
131. *ARCIA, 1894*, 14.
132. *ARCIA, 1895*, 3.
133. *ARCIA, 1896*, 18.
134. *ARCIA, 1895*, 7.
135. Commissions were sent to the Wind River, Pyramid Lake, Puyallup, Siletz, Osage, Tonkawa, Pawnee, Turtle Mountain, Crow, Flathead, Fort Hall, Uintah, Yakima, Blackfeet, and Fort Belknap Reservations to negotiate agreements for land cessions. In 1894, the Dawes Commission was sent to negotiate with the Five Tribes for dissolution of their governments, land severalty, and sale of surplus lands.
136. *ARCIA, 1895*, 23.
137. *ARCIA, 1895*, 24; *ARCIA, 1896*, 29.

138. *ARCIA, 1893*, 26–27.
139. An Act making appropriations for the current and contingent expenses of the Indian Department, and for fulfilling treaty stipulations with various Indian tribes, for the year ending June 30, 1895, and for other purposes, 28 Stat. 286 at 305 (August 15, 1894).
140. *ARCIA, 1895*, 41.
141. Ibid., 37–41.
142. Prucha, *The Great Father*, 673.
143. *ARCIA, 1894*, 61–62.
144. *ARCIA, 1893*, 63.
145. *ARCIA, 1894*, 63–64.
146. Ibid., 64.
147. Eells v. Ross, 64 F. 417 (12th Cir. 1895).
148. *ARCIA, 1895*, 57; *ARCIA, 1896*, 55. See Sale of Intoxicants to Indians, February 7, 1895, H. Rep. No. 1781, 53rd Cong., 2nd Sess., Congressional Serial Set 3289, vol. 2, 1–2. Prohibition of Liquor Sales to Indians, December 11, 1895, S. Doc. No. 21, 54th Cong., 1st Sess., Congressional Serial Set 3347, vol. 1, 1–6. Sale of Liquor to Indians, April 10, 1896, H. Rep. No. 1209, 54th Cong., 1st Sess., Congressional Serial Set 3461, vol. 5, 1–13.
149. An Act in relation to marriage between white men and Indian women, 25 Stat. 392 (August 9, 1888).
150. *ARCIA, 1894*, 65.
151. Ibid., 65–66.
152. W. David Baird, "William A. Jones, 1897–1904," in Kvasnicka and Viola, *Commissioners of Indian Affairs*, 211–20.
153. *ARCIA, 1904*, 25–26.
154. *ARCIA, 1902*, 13–14.
155. *ARCIA, 1901*, 9–10. Adams, *Education for Extinction*, 292–93.
156. *ARCIA, 1897*, 60; *ARCIA, 1900*, 49; and *ARCIA, 1901*, 53.
157. *ARCIA, 1901*, 47–48.
158. *ARCIA, 1900*, 5.
159. Ibid., 6–7. Brule Agreement of September 23, 1876; Oglala Agreement of September 26, 1876; Lower Yanktonai Agreement of October 11, 1876; Hunkpapa Agreement of October 11, 1876; Blackfeet Agreement of October 11, 1876; Upper Yanktonai Agreement of October 11, 1876; Two Kettle Agreement of October 16, 1876; Blackfeet Sioux Agreement of October 16, 1876; Minniconjou Agreement of October 16, 1876; San Arcs Agreement of October 16, 1876; and Santee Agreement of October 27, 1876; 19 Stat. 254.
160. *ARCIA, 1900*, 4, 9.
161. *ARCIA, 1901*, 3–4.
162. *ARCIA, 1900*, 19.
163. Ibid., 11.
164. Ibid., 4, 11, and 41.
165. An Act to amend and further extend the benefits of the act approved February 8, 1887, entitled An Act to provide for the allotment of land in severalty to Indians on various reservations, and to extend the protection of the laws of the United States over the Indians, and for other purposes, 26 Stat. 1891 (February 28, 1891) authorized three-year farming and grazing leases and ten-year mineral leases. An Act making appropriations for the current and contingent expenses of the Indian Department, and for fulfilling treaty stipulations with various Indian tribes, for the year ending June 30, 1895, and for other purposes, 28 Stat. 286 (August 15, 1894) increased the farming and grazing leases to five years. An Act making appropriations for the current and contingent expenses of the Indian Department, and for fulfilling treaty stipulations with various Indian tribes,

for the year ending June 30, 1898, and for other purposes, 30 Stat. 62 (June 7, 1897) reduced the farming and grazing leases back to three years. An Act making appropriations for the current and contingent expenses of the Indian Department, and for fulfilling treaty stipulations with various Indian tribes, for the year ending June 30, 1899, and for other purposes, 31 Stat. 221 (May 31, 1900) increased the farming and grazing leases to five years.

166. *ARCIA, 1900*, 75–81.
167. Ibid., 12–13.
168. *ARCIA, 1903*, 56.
169. *ARCIA, 1901*, 2.
170. Ibid., 2.
171. Ibid., 9.
172. *ARCIA, 1898*, 10.
173. *ARCIA, 1902*, 29.
174. *ARCIA, 1903*, 3, 6.
175. *ARCIA, 1904*, 33–38. DeJong, *Promises of the Past*, 19–21.
176. *ARCIA, 1898*, 5, 7.
177. Ibid., 8.
178. *ARCIA, 1900*, 33–36.
179. Ibid., 33.
180. David H. DeJong, *If You Knew the Conditions: A Chronicle of the Indian Medical Service and American Indian Health Care, 1908–1955* (Lanham, MD: Lexington Press, 2008), 20–22.
181. An Act for the protection of the people of the Indian Territory, and for other purposes, 30 Stat. 495 (June 28, 1898).
182. Debo, *And Still the Waters Run*, 32–33. The Curtis Act did not apply to the Seminole Tribe, as it consented to an agreement in 1897.
183. *ARCIA, 1900*, 13.
184. An Act making appropriations for the current and contingent expenses of the Indian Department, and for fulfilling treaty stipulations with various Indian tribes, for the year ending June 30, 1895, and for other purposes, 28 Stat. 286 at 295 (August 15, 1894); and An Act making appropriations for the current and contingent expenses of the Indian Department, and for fulfilling treaty stipulations with various Indian tribes, for the year ending June 30, 1898, and for other purposes, 30 Stat. 72 (June 7, 1897).
185. An Act making appropriations for the current and contingent expenses of the Indian Department, and for fulfilling treaty stipulations with various Indian tribes, for the year ending June 30, 1901, and for other purposes, section 7, 31 Stat. 221 at 247 (April 30, 1901). *ARCIA, 1901*, 62–63.
186. *ARCIA, 1902*, 120, 139.
187. *ARCIA, 1904*, 102. See generally Debo, *And Still the Waters Run*.
188. *ARCIA, 1903*, 46; *ARCIA, 1904*, 62.
189. *ARCIA, 1904*, 62–63.
190. Ibid., 64–65. For a case study at the Cheyenne-Arapaho agencies in Oklahoma Territory, see Berthrong, "Legacies of the Dawes Act," 335–54.
191. *ARCIA, 1900*, 598.
192. *ARCIA, 1903*, 29.
193. *ARCIA, 1904*, 29.
194. Lone Wolf v. Hitchcock, 187 U.S. 553 (1903).
195. Treaty of Medicine Lodge Creek, October 21, 1867, 15 Stat. 581, article 12. See also Deloria, Jr. and Lytle, *American Indians, American Justice*, 43–44.
196. Cherokee Nation v. Hitchcock, 187 U.S. 294 (1902).
197. *ARCIA, 1903*, 3.

CHAPTER 6

1. Donald L. Parman, "Francis Ellington Leupp, 1905–09," in Kvasnicka and Viola, *Commissioners of Indian Affairs*, 221–32.
2. Hagan, *The Indian Rights Association*, 234–35.
3. *ARCIA, 1905*, 1.
4. Ibid., 2.
5. Ibid.
6. Ibid., 1.
7. Ibid., 43.
8. *ARCIA, 1907*, 21.
9. Adams, *Education for Extinction*, 308; *ARCIA, 1907*, 22.
10. *ARCIA, 1907*, 22.
11. *ARCIA, 1908*, 16.
12. *ARCIA, 1907*, 25.
13. Ibid., 27.
14. Theodore Roosevelt, *Theodore Roosevelt: An Autobiography* (New York: MacMillan, 1913), 399–400.
15. DeJong, *Promises of the Past*, 71–85.
16. *ARCIA, 1905*, 36, 39.
17. *ARCIA, 1906*, 52.
18. Reuben Quick Bear v. Leupp, Commissioner of Indian Affairs, 210 U.S. 40 at 82 (1908).
19. *ARCIA, 1905*, 3.
20. Wind River (33 Stat. 1016); Rosebud (34 Stat. 1230); Coeur d'Alene (34 Stat. 335); Blackfeet (34 Stat. 1035); Flathead (35 Stat. 448); Fort Peck (35 Stat. 558); and Spokane (35 Stat. 458).
21. A Matter of Heff, 197 U.S. 488 (1905).
22. An Act to amend section six of an act approved February 8, 1887, 34 Stat. 182 (May 8, 1906).
23. *ARCIA, 1907*, 68.
24. *ARCIA, 1912*, 64.
25. *ARCIA, 1907*, 67; *ARCIA, 1908*, 68.
26. William McKay et al. v. Agnes Kalyton, 204 U.S. 458 (1907); *ARCIA, 1907*, 69.
27. *ARCIA, 1906*, 30.
28. *ARCIA, 1907*, 31.
29. *ARCIA, 1908*, 71.
30. *ARCIA, 1906*, 80.
31. Leupp and his successor, Robert Valentine, argued Native people no longer held rights to water already claimed under prior appropriation laws. See DeJong, *Stealing the Gila*, 115.
32. *ARCIA, 1907*, 81.
33. *ARCIA, 1908*, 64.
34. *ARCIA, 1906*, 82.
35. Ibid., 83. An Act appropriating the receipts from the sale and disposal of public lands in certain states and territories to the construction of irrigation works for the reclamation of arid lands, 32 Stat. 388 (June 30, 1902).
36. *ARCIA, 1906*, 83.
37. Ibid., 84.
38. An Act making appropriations for the current and contingent expenses of the Indian Department, for filling treaty stipulations with various Indian tribes, and for other purposes for the fiscal year ending June 30, 1907, 34 Stat. 327 (June 21, 1906).
39. Winters v. United States, 207 U.S. 564 (1908).

40. Daniel McCool, *Command of the Water: Iron Triangles, Federal Water Development, and Indian Water* (Tucson: University of Arizona Press, 1994), 36–65.
41. *ARCIA, 1906*, 84.
42. *ARCIA, 1907*, 55.
43. Irrigation projects were funded for the Zuni, Pala, Crow, Navajo, Walker River, Tongue River, Pueblo, Uintah, Shoshoni, Yakima, Pima, Mescalero, San Carlos, Fort Peck, Fort Hall, Mission, Colorado River, and Fort Belknap Reservations.
44. *ARCIA, 1907*, 8.
45. Ibid., 9.
46. *ARCIA, 1906*, 64; *ARCIA, 1907*, 53.
47. *ARCIA, 1906*, 24.
48. An Act providing for allotment and distribution of Indian tribal funds, 34 Stat. 1221 (March 21, 1907).
49. *ARCIA, 1906*, 24.
50. *ARCIA, 1905*, 5.
51. *ARCIA, 1906*, 6.
52. *Annual Report of the Board of Indian Commissioners, 1905*, 10–11. See also Cahill, *Federal Fathers and Mothers*, 224–27.
53. Francis Leupp, *The Indian and His Problem* (New York: Scribner, 1910), 110–11.
54. *ARCIA, 1907*, 16–17. Most of the workers were Pima and Papago (1,100), but also included Hopi, Navajo, Mohave, Pueblo, Apache, and Blackfeet.
55. An Act making appropriations for the current and contingent expenses of the Indian Department, for filling treaty stipulations with various Indian tribes, and for other purposes for the fiscal year ending June 30, 1909, 35 Stat. 70 at 71 (April 30, 1908).
56. For instance, the 1863 Red Lake Chippewa treaty included article 7, which provided: "The laws of the United States now in force or that may hereafter be enacted, prohibiting the introduction and sale of spirituous liquors in the Indian Country, shall be in full force and effect throughout the country hereby ceded, until otherwise directed by Congress or the President of the United States." Red Lake and Pembina Chippewa Treaty, October 2, 1863, 13 Stat. 667.
57. *ARCIA, 1906*, 20–21.
58. Ibid., 103. Leupp based his actions on the following treaty provisions: Sisseton and Wahpeton Sioux Treaty, July 23, 1851, 10 Stat. 959 (article 5); Mdewakanton and Wahpeton Sioux Treaty, August 5, 1851, 10 Stat. 954 (article 6); Chippewa Treaty, September 30, 1854, 10 Stat. 1109 (Article 7); Winnebago Treaty, February 27, 1855, 10 Stat. 1172 (article 8); Red Lake and Pembina Treaty, October 2, 1863, 13 Stat. 667 (article 7); Yankton Agreement, August 15, 1894, 28 Stat. 314 (article 17); and Nez Perce Agreement, August 15, 1894, 28 Stat. 326 (article 9).
59. A Matter of Heff, 197 U.S. 488 (1905).
60. *ARCIA, 1906*, 39.
61. *ARCIA, 1909*, 1.
62. Leupp, *The Indian and His Problem*; and Francis Leupp, *In Red Man's Land: A Study of the American Indians* (New York: Fleming H. Revell, 1914).
63. *ARCIA, 1905*, 29–30; *ARCIA, 1906*, 35, 65.
64. Diane T. Putney, "Robert G. Valentine, 1909–12," in Kvasnicka and Viola, *Commissioners of Indian Affairs*, 233–42.
65. *ARCIA, 1909*, 2.
66. *ARCIA, 1910*, 9–10.
67. Ibid., 11.
68. *ARCIA, 1912*, 19–21.
69. "Contagious and Infectious Diseases among the Indians," S. Doc. No. 1038, 62nd Cong., 3rd Sess. (Washington, D.C.: Government Printing Office, 1913), 74, 77.

70. *ARCIA, 1909*, 3–4.
71. An Act making appropriations for the current and contingent expenses of the Indian Department, for filling treaty stipulations with various Indian tribes, and for other purposes for the fiscal year ending June 30, 1913, 37 Stat. 519 (August 24, 1912).
72. "Contagious and Infectious Diseases among the Indians," 77.
73. Ibid., 74. David H. DeJong, "Unless They Are Kept Alive: Federal-Indian Schools and Student Health, 1890–1917," *American Indian Quarterly* 31, no. 2 (Spring 2007): 256–82.
74. *ARCIA, 1910*, 12–13.
75. *ARCIA, 1911*, 34–35.
76. Perrin v. United States, 232 U.S. 478 (1913).
77. Hallowell v. United States, 221 U.S. 317 (1911).
78. *ARCIA, 1911*, 33.
79. *ARCIA, 1912*, 24.
80. *ARCIA, 1911*, 6.
81. An Act making appropriations for the current and contingent expenses of the Indian Department, for filling treaty stipulations with various Indian tribes, and for other purposes for the fiscal year ending June 30, 1909, 35 Stat. 70 (March 28, 1908).
82. See Prairie Pottawatomie Agreement, February 4, 1909, 36 Stat. 289; Sauk and Fox of Oklahoma Agreement, February 27, 1909, 36 Stat. 289; Pottawatomie of Kansas and Wisconsin Agreement, March 16, 1909, 36 Stat. 289; and Sauk and Fox of Iowa Agreement, May 28, 1909, 36 Stat. 289.
83. *ARCIA, 1912*, 7.
84. *ARCIA, 1911*, 19; *ARCIA, 1912*, 10.
85. *ARCIA, 1909*, 1.
86. Ibid., 7, 10.
87. *ARCIA, 1910*, 5.
88. *ARCIA, 1911*, 3.
89. *ARCIA, 1909*, 16.
90. Ibid.
91. *ARCIA, 1911*, 27.
92. *ARCIA, 1909*, 25; *ARCIA, 1911*, 27.
93. *ARCIA, 1912*, 12.
94. *ARCIA, 1910*, 28.
95. *ARCIA, 1909*, 37–38.
96. *ARCIA, 1912*, 5.
97. *ARCIA, 1911*, 24–25.
98. Ibid.
99. *ARCIA, 1912*, 89. There were 3,807 Indians unaccounted for in the severalty schedule.
100. Ibid., 114, 125, 134.
101. Ibid., 62, 63, 134.
102. *ARCIA, 1911*, 20–21.
103. *ARCIA, 1912*, 63.
104. Ibid., 51.
105. Ibid., 59.
106. An Act for the removal of restrictions from part of the lands of allottees of the Five Civilized Tribes, and for other purposes, 35 Stat. 312 (May 27, 1908). This act removed restrictions on the land for all members of the Five Tribes except certain tribal members with more than one-half Indian blood.
107. *ARCIA, 1912*, 8.

108. Choate v. Trapp, 224 U.S. 665 at 671 (1913). The court held that the Choctaw and Chickasaw allottees acquired rights under the Curtis Act that were protected by the Fifth Amendment to the United States Constitution, regardless of the intent of the Act of May 27, 1908 (35 Stat. 312).
109. Investigation of White Earth Reservation, Minnesota, sale of Chippewa timber land allotments, H.R. Rep. No. 1336, 62nd Cong., 3rd Sess., Congressional Serial Set 6338, vol. 2, 2146.
110. "Proceedings of the Lake Mohonk Conference of Friends of the Indian and other Dependent Peoples, 1912" (New York: Lake Mohonk Conference, 1912), 81–82.
111. *ARCIA, 1913*, 1.
112. Lawrence C. Kelly, "Cato Sells, 1913–21," in Kvasnicka and Viola, *Commissioners of Indian Affairs*, 243–50.
113. In 1912, Senator Robert L. Owen (D-OK) introduced a bill calling for immediate completion of severalty. See S. Doc. No. 6767, 62nd Cong., 2nd Sess. A year later, Senator Henry L. Meyer (D-MT) introduced another bill to "throw Indian reservations open to allotment and settlement." See *Congressional Record*, 64th Cong., 1st Sess., 2111–112.
114. *ARCIA, 1913*, 2.
115. See An Act to amend section six of an act approved February 8, 1887, 34 Stat. 182 (May 8, 1906); and An Act to authorize the sale and disposition of the surplus and unallotted lands in the Standing Rock Indian Reservation, in the states of South Dakota and North Dakota, and making appropriations and provision to carry the same into effect, 37 Stat. 675 (February 14, 1913).
116. *ARCIA, 1913*, 2.
117. Ibid., 5.
118. *ARCIA, 1914*, 45.
119. *ARCIA, 1917*, 4–5.
120. Ibid., 4.
121. *ARCIA, 1918*, 62.
122. Ibid., 22.
123. *ARCIA, 1919*, 7–8.
124. Ibid. 8.
125. An Act making appropriations for the current and contingent expenses of the Bureau of Indian Affairs, for filling treaty stipulations with various Indian tribes, and for other purposes for the fiscal year ending June 30, 1917, 39 Stat. 123 (May 18, 1916).
126. *ARCIA, 1920*, 172.
127. Frederick E. Hoxie, *A Final Promise: The Campaign to Assimilate the Indians, 1880–1920* (Cambridge: Cambridge University Press, 1989), 180–81.
128. *ARCIA, 1916*, 48. The allotments affected were on the Omaha, Santee, Sisseton, Grande Ronde, San Xavier, Ponca (NB), Eastern Shawnee, and Yankton Reservations. In addition, Sells extended the trust period on Indian homesteads and allotments on the public domain. In 1917, he extended the trust period for expiring trust patents on the Modoc, Absentee Shawnee, Citizen Pottawatomie, Cheyenne and Arapaho, Wyandotte, Sac and Fox of Oklahoma, Iowa, and the Oneida in Wisconsin. See *ARCIA, 1917*, 47.
129. *ARCIA, 1914*, 124. See also Prucha, *The Great Father*, 879–86.
130. *ARCIA, 1913*, 6–7.
131. *ARCIA, 1917*, 29.
132. *ARCIA, 1920*, 23.
133. *ARCIA, 1913*, 17–18.
134. Ibid., 4.
135. *ARCIA, 1914*, 41.
136. DeJong, *Stealing the Gila*, 130.
137. *ARCIA, 1914*, 37.

138. An Act making appropriations for the current and contingent expenses of the Bureau of Indian Affairs, for filling treaty stipulations with various Indian tribes, and for other purposes for the fiscal year ending June 30, 1915, 38 Stat. 582 (August 1, 1914). Prior to August 1, 1914, all tribal members paid for the irrigation projects regardless of whether they benefited from it. After that date, beneficiaries paid the cost from their share of tribal funds.
139. *ARCIA, 1916*, 163.
140. *ARCIA, 1917*, 35.
141. *ARCIA, 1919*, 37; *ARCIA, 1920*, 27.
142. *ARCIA, 1913*, 9; *ARCIA, 1915*, 24.
143. *ARCIA, 1914*, 16.
144. *ARCIA, 1915*, 7; *ARCIA, 1919*, 41; *ARCIA, 1921*, 12–13.
145. *ARCIA, 1914*, 48.
146. An Act for the removal of restrictions from part of the lands of allottees of the Five Civilized Tribes, and for other purposes, 35 Stat. 312 (May 27, 1908).
147. *ARCIA, 1920*, 173.
148. *ARCIA, 1888*, 370; *ARCIA, 1920*, 81–82.
149. *ARCIA, 1920*, 82.
150. Debo, *And Still the Waters Run.*
151. *ARCIA, 1914*, 52–55.
152. Debo, *And Still the Waters Run*, 311–12.
153. *ARCIA, 1920*, 31.
154. *ARCIA, 1919*, 50.
155. *ARCIA, 1914*, 5–7.
156. *ARCIA, 1920*, 13, 156.
157. *ARCIA, 1918*, 31; *ARCIA, 1920*, 26–27.
158. *ARCIA, 1918*, 36.
159. *ARCIA, 1917*, 12–14.
160. *ARCIA, 1919*, 26–27.
161. *ARCIA, 1915*, 8.
162. *ARCIA, 1916*, 9–10.
163. Cahill, *Federal Fathers and Mothers*, 82–89.
164. *ARCIA, 1915*, 17.
165. *ARCIA, 1916*, 4–5
166. Ibid., 5–8.
167. *ARCIA, 1918*, 21.
168. *ARCIA, 1915*, 15–16. See Mississippi Bands of Chippewa Indians Treaty, February 22, 1855, 10 Stat. 1165. Article 7 stated that federal acts governing the introduction, manufacturing, use of, and traffic in ardent spirits, wines, or other liquors "shall continue and be in force, within the entire boundaries of the country herein ceded to the United States, until otherwise provided by Congress."
169. United States v. Joseph, 94 U.S. 614 (1877).
170. United States v. Sandoval, 231 U.S. 28 (1913).
171. United States v. Nice, 241, U.S. 591 (1916).
172. *ARCIA, 1918*, 8–9.
173. *ARCIA, 1919*, 12.
174. Prucha, *The Great White Father*, 885.
175. Lawrence C. Kelly, *The Navajo Indians and Federal Indian Policy, 1900–1935* (Tucson: University of Arizona Press, 1968), 56. Wright was supported by Interior Secretary Albert Fall and his nomination was considered a *fait accompli* until his supporters in Oklahoma publicly announced his nomination, leading Harding to bypass Oklahoma and nominate Burke instead.

176. Lawrence C. Kelly, "Charles Henry Burke, 1921–29," in Kvasnicka and Viola, *Commissioners of Indian Affairs*, 251–61.
177. Ibid., 252–53.
178. *ARCIA, 1923*, 1.
179. *ARCIA, 1922*, 2.
180. Ibid., 3–5; *ARCIA, 1923*, 4. Treaty with the Navajo Nation, June 1, 1868, 15 Stat. 667.
181. An Act making appropriations for the current and contingent expenses of the Bureau of Indian Affairs, for filling treaty stipulations with various Indian tribes, and for other purposes for the fiscal year ending June 30, 1921, 41 Stat. 408 (February 14, 1920).
182. *ARCIA, 1925*, 6.
183. *ARCIA, 1926*, 6; *ARCIA, 1928*, 15.
184. *ARCIA, 1926*, 7.
185. Ibid.
186. *ARCIA, 1927*, 9–10.
187. An Act authorizing appropriations and expenditures for the administration of Indian affairs, and for other purposes, 42 Stat. 208 (November 1, 1921). The eight categories were: (1) conservation of health, (2) industrial assistance, (3) irrigation and water supplies, (4) general plant and projects, (5) specific employees of the Indian Office, (6) suppression of intoxicating liquors, (7) vehicles for official use, and (8) general and incidental expenses.
188. *ARCIA, 1927*, 1.
189. Ibid., 12.
190. *ARCIA, 1921*, 9–10.
191. Ibid., 9.
192. *ARCIA, 1922*, 8. "A Study of the Need for Public Health Nursing on Indian Reservations," in *A Survey of the Conditions of the Indians in the United States: Hearings before a Subcommittee of the Committee on Indian Affairs, United States Senate, Part 3* (Washington, D.C.: Government Printing Office, 1929), 933–1018.
193. *ARCIA, 1922*, 8; DeJong, *If You Knew the Conditions*, 36. Newberne's criticism of public health nurses is in "A Review of Miss Patterson's Report entitled 'A Study of the Need for Public Health Nursing on Indian Reservations,'" in *A Survey of the Conditions of the Indians in the United States*, 1005–17.
194. *ARCIA, 1924*, 1.
195. *ARCIA, 1925*, 3.
196. *ARCIA, 1922*, 11; *ARCIA, 1924*, 12; *ARCIA, 1925*, 8. Cahill, *Federal Fathers and Mothers*, 245.
197. *ARCIA, 1921*, 29–30.
198. Ibid., 23.
199. *Congressional Record*, 61:4664.
200. *ARCIA, 1922*, 15.
201. *ARCIA, 1921*, 21; *ARCIA, 1922*, 14; *ARCIA, 1923*, 8; *ARCIA, 1924*, 8; *ARCIA, 1925*, 10; *ARCIA, 1926*, 9; *ARCIA, 1927*, 12; *ARCIA, 1928*, 27. The reservations allotted during this time included Gila River, Salt River, Flathead, Blackfeet, Fort Berthold, Fort Peck, and nearly two dozen scattered California reservations and rancherias.
202. See *ARCIA, 1921*, 23 (Fond du Lac, Sycuan, Kickapoo {KN}, Agua Caliente, and Pala); *ARCIA, 1923*, 9 (Devil's Lake, Round Valley, and Santee); *ARCIA, 1924*, 9 (Hoopa Valley, Round Valley, Umatilla, Lake Traverse, and Kickapoo {OK}); *ARCIA, 1925*, 11 (Bois Forte, Deer Creek, Colville, Yakima, Omaha, Twenty-Nine Palms, and Cabazon); *ARCIA, 1926*, 9 (San Xavier, Cass Lake, Leech Lake, White Oak Point, Ponca, Fort Berthold, Iowa, Sac and Fox {OK}, Kiowa-Comanche-Apache, Wichita, Eastern Shawnee, Otoe, Grande Ronde, Yankton, Rosebud and Moses Band); *ARCIA, 1927*, 12 (Sac and Fox {KN}, White Earth, Sac and Fox, Winnebago, Cheyenne-Arapaho,

Modoc, Ottawa, Citizen Pottawatomie, Seneca, Absentee Shawnee, Wyandotte, Oneida {WI}, and Capitan Grande); *ARCIA, 1928*, 22 (Nez Perce, Prairie Pottawatomie, Devil's Lake, Tonkawa, Pawnee, and sixteen mission bands in California).

203. *ARCIA, 1928*, 23.
204. An Act to promote the mining of coal, phosphate, oil, oil shale, gas, and sodium on the public domain, 41 Stat. 437 (February 25, 1920) (hereafter the General Leasing Act); *ARCIA, 1922*, 23.
205. *ARCIA, 1925*, 18–19.
206. Supplemental to Circular No. 1665, "Indian Dancing," February 14, 1923. *ARCIA, 1923*, 21.
207. Kenneth R. Philp, *John Collier's Crusade for Indian Reform, 1920–1954* (Tucson: University of Arizona Press, 1977), 57–67.
208. The following are examples of citizenship qualifiers. World War I veterans: An Act granting citizenship to certain Indians, 41 Stat. 850 (June 4, 1919); Indian women married to white men: An Act in relation to marriage between white men and Indian women, 25 Stat. 392 (July 26, 1888); and Indian Territory: Indian Appropriation Act of 1890, section 43, 26 Stat. 99 (May 2, 1890). Treaties also conferred citizenship. See for instance: Treaty with the Seneca, Mixed Seneca and Shawnee, Quapaw, Peoria, Kaskaskia, Wea, Piankeshaw, Ottawa, and certain Wyandotte, February 23, 1867, 15 Stat. 513; Cherokee Treaty of July 8, 1817, 7 Stat. 156. There are numerous treaty provisions granting citizenship; there are also acts directed to specific tribes. The Stockbridge were granted citizenship under the Indian Appropriation Act of March 3, 1843, 5 Stat. 645 (March 3, 1845); and the Brotherton Indians were granted citizenship under the Indian Appropriation Act of March 3, 1839, 5 Stat. 349 (March 3, 1839).
209. An Act to authorize the secretary of the interior to issue certificates of citizenship to Indians, 43 Stat. 253 (June 2, 1924).
210. The Indian Citizenship Act granted federal—not state—citizenship. Although most states granted citizenship, Arizona and New Mexico held out until 1948, believing that Indians as "wards of the government" were prohibited from exercising citizenship rights and privileges.
211. *ARCIA, 1924*, 20.
212. *ARCIA, 1927*, 18–19. *Reservation Courts of Indian Offenses: Hearings before the Committee on Indian Affairs, House of Representatives*, 69th Cong., 1st Sess., on H.R. 7826 (February 13, 1926–May 25, 1926) (Washington, D.C.: Government Printing Office, 1926).
213. *ARCIA, 1923*, 16.
214. *Hearings on Department of the Interior Appropriation Bill, Fiscal Year 1933: U.S. Senate, Committee on Appropriations*, 72nd Cong., 1st Sess., 26 (1932). For instance, in 1922, Burke requested $13,089,863, with Congress granting him $9,817,702. In 1929, Burke requested $20,190,839 and was granted just $15,144,509.
215. *ARCIA, 1925*, 9. An Act to provide for the classification of civilian positions within the District of Columbia and in the field service, 67 Stat. 1488 (March 4, 1923).
216. *ARCIA, 1928*, 21.
217. Lewis Meriam, *The Problem of Indian Administration* (Baltimore: John Hopkins University Press, 1928).
218. Ibid., 7, 189.
219. *ARCIA, 1928*, 12.
220. Ibid., 12–13. Porter J. Preston and Charles A. Engel, *Report of Advisors on Irrigation on Indian Reservations, Volume 1* (Washington, D.C.: Government Printing Office, 1928), 2217.
221. *ARCIA, 1928*, 33–34.
222. *ARCIA, 1921*, 31; *ARCIA, 1924*, 23; *ARCIA, 1927*, 25. See also An Act to quiet title to lands within Pueblo land grants, and for other purposes, 43 Stat. 636 (June 7, 1924).
223. Department of the Interior, Office of Indian Affairs, "Land Tenure, Economic Statistics, and Population Trends" (Washington, D.C.: Government Printing Office, 1935), 7–8.

CHAPTER 7

1. Meriam, *The Problem of Indian Administration*, 86.
2. See, for instance, the John Collier-assisted articles written by Vera Connelly in *Good Housekeeping*: "Cry of a Broken People," February 1929, 30–31; "We Still Get Robbed," March 1929, 34–35; and "End of the Road," May 1929, 44–45.
3. John Collier, *From Every Zenith: A Memoir and Some Essays on Life and Thought* (Denver: Sage Books, 1963).
4. Lawrence C. Kelly, "Charles James Rhoads, 1929–33," in Kvasnicka and Viola, *Commissioners of Indian Affairs*, 263–71.
5. Edgar Eugene Robinson and Paul Carroll Edwards, eds., *The Memoirs of Ray Lyman Wilbur, 1875–1949* (Stanford: Stanford University Press, 1960), 479–80.
6. John Collier, *American Indian Life* (New York: American Indian Defense Association Bulletin, July 1930), 16:7.
7. *Congressional Record*, 71st Cong., 2nd Sess., December 4, 1929, Part 1, 1051–53.
8. Ibid. See also Collier, *American Indian Life*, Bulletin 16.
9. *ARCIA, 1929*, 15.
10. Ibid.
11. *ARCIA, 1930*, 22.
12. *ARCIA, 1931*, 18.
13. Ibid., 18–19.
14. *ARCIA, 1932*, 19–20. Indian fee landowners were no longer viewed as Indians for Indian Office purposes.
15. Non-Indian lands included non-Indian fee patented lands within reservations and non-Indian lands within joint works irrigation projects, such as the San Carlos Irrigation Project in Arizona.
16. An Act to cancel certain reimbursable charges against certain Indian lands within the Gila River Indian Reservation, Arizona, 46 Stat. 1519 (March 4, 1931); *ARCIA, 1931*, 31.
17. *ARCIA, 1931*, 31–32.
18. An Act to authorize the secretary of the interior to adjust reimbursable debt of Indians and tribes of Indians, 47 Stat. 564 (July 1, 1932).
19. Meriam, *The Problem of Indian Administration*, 508–15; *Report of Advisors on Irrigation*, 2219.
20. U.S. Congress, House of Representatives, Report of the Committee on Indian Affairs, H.R. Rep. No. 951, 72nd Cong., 1st Sess., 1 (1932).
21. Meriam, *The Problem of Indian Administration*, 7.
22. *ARCIA, 1930*, 2.
23. *ARCIA, 1932*, 28.
24. Allotments set to expire in 1929 on the following reservations were extended by the president: Prairie Pottawatomie, Iowa Tribe (KN and NB), Winnebago (NB), Siletz, Lower Brule, and Rosebud (*ARCIA, 1929*, 10); 1930: Nez Perce, Crow, Omaha, Seneca (OK), Devil's Lake, Rosebud, Yankton, Uintah, and White River Ute (*ARCIA, 1930*, 16); 1931: Klamath, Agua Caliente, Kickapoo, Pottawatomie (KN), Cass Lake, Leech Lake, Fond du Lac, White Oak Point, Winnibigoshish, Santee Sioux, Ponca, Cayuse, Umatilla, Walla-Walla, Cheyenne River, and Pine Ridge (*ARCIA, 1931*, 36); 1933: Pechanga, Sac and Fox (KN and NB), Grand Portage, White Earth, Winnibigoshish, Crow, Santee Sioux, Walker River, Devil's Lake, Standing Rock, Eastern Shawnee, Otoe-Missouria, Warm Springs, Cheyenne River, Crow Creek, Pine Ridge, Rosebud, Yakima, Quinault, and Wind River Shoshone (*ARCIA, 1932*, 30).
25. *ARCIA, 1930*, 17.
26. Ibid.; *ARCIA, 1931*, 37; *ARCIA, 1932*, 25.
27. Philp, *John Collier's Crusade*, 99–101.

28. *ARCIA, 1930,* 17.
29. *ARCIA, 1932,* 25.
30. Ibid., 16.
31. Meriam, *The Problem of Indian Administration,* 749.
32. H.R. Rep. No. 7963, 71st Cong., 2nd Sess.; *Congressional Record,* 72nd Cong., 1st Sess., 1139.
33. Philp, *John Collier's Crusade,* 96. *Report of the Advisors on Irrigation,* 2216. An Act making appropriations for the current and contingent expenses of the Indian Department, and for fulfilling treaty stipulations with the various Indian tribes, for the year ending June 30, 1930, 45 Stat. 1478 (March 2, 1929).
34. *ARCIA, 1931,* 3.
35. Meriam, *The Problem of Indian Administration,* 52–55.
36. *ARCIA, 1929,* 1.
37. *ARCIA, 1930,* 1.
38. *ARCIA, 1929,* 2.
39. *ARCIA, 1930,* 4.
40. *ARCIA, 1929,* 3; *ARCIA, 1930,* 5; *ARCIA, 1931,* 15; and *ARCIA, 1932,* 10–11.
41. *ARCIA, 1929,* 2–3.
42. *ARCIA, 1931,* 16; Meriam, *The Problem of Indian Administration,* 33.
43. Meriam, *The Problem of Indian Administration,* 33–35.
44. *ARCIA, 1930,* 11.
45. *ARCIA, 1931,* 9.
46. Ibid., 6–7.
47. *ARCIA, 1929,* 7. An Act making appropriations for the current and contingent expenses of the Indian Department, and for fulfilling treaty stipulations with the various Indian tribes, for the year ending June 30, 1930, 45 Stat. 1478 (March 2, 1929).
48. *ARCIA, 1930,* 9; *ARCIA, 1931,* 10.
49. ARCIA, 1931, 5.
50. *ARCIA, 1931,* 5; *ARCIA, 1932,* 4.
51. *ARCIA, 1931,* 12.
52. Prucha, *The Great Father,* 932–37.
53. *ARCIA, 1932,* 31. In his 1932 annual report, Rhoads mentioned the "Law and Order on Indian Reservations" study produced by the Brookings Institute but made no recommendations from it. The first fracture in the relationship between Collier and Rhoads came in late 1929 when President Hoover sent a message to Congress requesting $1.1 million in emergency appropriations for food and clothing for Indian children. The request would have increased the per pupil food allowance from twenty to thirty-seven cents per day and annual clothing allowance from twenty-two to forty-two dollars. Louis Cramton, chairman of the House Appropriation Subcommittee, refused the request in the name of economy. Rhoads and Scattergood appeared before the committee to no avail and ultimately accepted a 75 percent food and 80 percent clothing allowance reduction from what the president requested. Collier disagreed and lambasted the Indian Office. While the Senate increased the amount—and a Conference Committee agreed to a twenty-eight-cent food allowance and shifted the clothing allowance into equipment, livestock, and salaries—the damage was done. In 1931, the Indian appropriation act provided money equivalent to what the Meriam Report had requested for the food and clothing allowances. See Philp, *John Collier's Crusade,* 97–101.
54. Collier, *American Indian Life,* January 1933, 1–5.
55. Philp, *John Collier's Crusade,* 113.
56. Collier, *American Indian Life,* January 1933, 2.
57. Philp, *John Collier's Crusade,* 114.

58. *Congressional Record*, 73rd Cong., 1st Sess., April 21, 1933, Part 2, 2102–3.
59. Quoted in Prucha, *The Great Father*, 941.
60. Philp, *John Collier's Crusade*, 117.
61. Philp, "John Collier, 1933–45," in Kvasnicka and Viola, *Commissioners of Indian Affairs*, 273.
62. *ARCIA, 1933*, 68.
63. Ibid.
64. Ibid., 68–69.
65. Ibid., 69.
66. Ibid., 108.
67. Ibid., 109.
68. Ibid., 99–100; *ARCIA, 1936*, 193, *ARCIA, 1940*, 367.
69. *ARCIA, 1933*, 96; *ARCIA, 1934*, 99.
70. *ARCIA, 1933*, 100. An Act to amend section 1 of the act entitled An Act to provide for determining the heirs of the deceased Indians, and for the disposition and sale of allotments of deceased Indians, for the leasing of allotments, and for other purposes, 48 Stat. 647 (April 30, 1934), modified the rules governing the sale of Indian heirship lands such that if the purchaser defaulted, the Indian seller retained all prior payments.
71. *ARCIA, 1934*, 99; *ARCIA, 1936*, 206. After passage of the Indian Reorganization Act (IRA), the trust period was extended indefinitely for tribes accepting the Act's provisions. For tribes rejecting the IRA, the president, starting in 1937, extended the trust period for twenty-five years. In 1933, trust patents were extended ten years for those expiring on the Round Valley, Temecula, Sac and Fox (KN), Grand Portage, White Earth, Crow, Sac and Fox (NB), Santee, Devil's Lake, Standing Rock, Kiowa, Eastern Shawnee, Pine Ridge, Quinault, Yakima, and Wind River Reservations (*ARCIA, 1933*, 97). In 1935, extensions were issued for the Torres-Martinez, Crow, Klamath, Crow Creek, Colville, Spokane, and Yakima Reservations (*ARCIA, 1935*, 141). In 1936, all tribes in Oklahoma had trust patents extended for ten years, with all other allottees facing expiration of the trust having it extended to December 31, 1936 (*ARCIA, 1936*, 193). In 1937, all non-IRA tribal members had their trust patents extended for twenty-five years by order of the president on September 30, 1936 (*ARCIA, 1937*, 206). In 1938, all non-IRA tribal members with expiring trust patents had their trust extended for twenty-five years under the presidential order of September 30, 1937 (*ARCIA, 1938*, 214).
72. An Act to conserve and develop Indian land and resources; to extend to Indians the right to form business and other organizations; to establish a credit system for Indians; to grant certain rights of home rule to Indians; to provide for vocational education for Indians; and for other purposes, 48 Stat. 984 (June 18, 1934) (hereafter known as the "Indian Reorganization Act"). The bill's sponsors were Senators Burton Wheeler (D-MT) and Edgar Howard (D-NB).
73. Congresses were held as follows: Rapid City, SD, March 2–5, 1934; Chemawa, OR, March 8–9, 1934; Fort Defiance, AZ, March 12–13, 1934; Santo Domingo, NM, March 15, 1934; Phoenix, AZ, March 15–16, 1934; Riverside, CA, March 17–18, 1934; Anadarko, OK, March 20, 1934; Muscogee, OK, March 22–23, 1934; Miami, OK, March 24, 1934; and Hayward, WI, April 23–24, 1934.
74. See statements of Harry Sundust of the Gila River Indian Community (Maricopa Tribe) and Harvey Cawker, of the Gila River Indian Community (Pima), in "Report of Southern Arizona Indian Conference held at Phoenix, Arizona, March 15–16, 1934, for the purpose of explaining the Howard-Wheeler Bill to the assembled Indians" (Phoenix: Phoenix Indian School Print Shop, n.d.), 27–30.
75. *Readjustment of Indian Affairs: Hearings on H.R. 7902 before the House Committee on Indian Affairs*, 73rd Cong.,, 2nd Sess. (1934) (hereafter *Radjustment of Indian Affairs*); and *To Grant to Indians Living under Federal Tutelage the Freedom to Organize for Purposes of Local Self-Government and Economic Enterprise: Hearings on S. 2755 and S. 3645 before the Senate Committee on Indian Affairs*, 73rd Cong., 2nd Sess. (1934).

76. *Readjustment of Indian Affairs*, 1–14.
77. *ARCIA, 1934*, 79.
78. Ibid., 79–81. *Readjustment of Indian Affairs*, 15–29.
79. *ARCIA, 1934*, 82.
80. Ibid., 84.
81. *Congressional Record*, 73rd Cong., 1st Sess., June 12, 1934, (78) part 10, 11122–37.
82. An Act to promote the general welfare of the Indians of the state of Oklahoma, and for other purposes, 49 Stat. 1967 (June 26, 1936) (hereafter Oklahoma Indian Welfare Act). An Act to extend certain provisions of the act approved June 18, 1934, commonly known as the Wheeler-Howard Act, to the territory of Alaska to provide for the designation of Indian reservations in Alaska, and for other purposes, 49 Stat. 1250 (May 1, 1936) (hereafter Alaska Reorganization Act).
83. Indian Reorganization Act, section 18. The original act allowed twelve months' time for elections. The act of June 15, 1935, extended the period for elections by one additional year. The act required the participation of a minimum of 30 percent of eligible voters in order to be binding. Theodore H. Haas, *Ten Years of Tribal Government under the I.R.A.* (Washington, D.C.: United States Indian Service, 1947), 3.
84. Haas, *Ten Years of Tribal Government*, 3.
85. *ARCIA, 1939*, 25.
86. Indian Reorganization Act, sections 1, 2, 3, 5, and 10.
87. *ARCIA, 1940*, 364.
88. *ARCIA, 1942*, 245.
89. Haas, *Ten Years of Tribal Government*, 32.
90. Ibid., 34.
91. Meriam, *The Problem of Indian Administration*, 103–4.
92. *ARCIA, 1939*, 26.
93. *ARCIA, 1938*, 248.
94. *ARCIA, 1939*, 35.
95. *ARCIA, 1941*, 409.
96. An Act to quiet the title to lands within Pueblo land grants, and for other purposes, 43 Stat. 639 (June 6, 1924), as amended by An Act to authorize appropriations to pay in part the liabilities of the United States to the Indian Pueblos herein named, under the terms of the act of June 7, 1924, 48 Stat. 108 (May 31, 1933).
97. *ARCIA, 1934*, 96.
98. *ARCIA, 1940*, 451.
99. In 1928, the Navajo Tribe requested the use of $1.2 million of their own oil and gas royalties to purchase land in Arizona and New Mexico. Kelly, *The Navajo Indians and Federal-Indian Policy*, 121–31. See An Act making appropriations to supply deficiencies in certain appropriations for the fiscal year ending June 30, 1928, and prior fiscal years to provide supplemental appropriations for the fiscal year ending June 30, 1928 and June 30, 1929, and for other purposes, 45 Stat. 899 (May 24, 1928). In Arizona, Congress authorized the use of $481,879 of Navajo funds to purchase land within the state (An Act to define the exterior boundaries of the Navajo Indian Reservation in Arizona, and for other purposes, 48 Stat. 960 {June 14, 1934}). A second bill was to authorize $482,136 of Navajo funds to purchase land in New Mexico. While the Senate approved of a bill, the House of Representatives did not. For the Arizona purchase, see U.S. House of Representatives, Boundaries of the Navajo Reservation in Arizona, H.R. Rep. No. 1602, 73rd Cong., 2nd Sess. (1934). For the New Mexico discussion, see U.S. Senate, Committee on Indian Affairs, Define the Exterior Boundaries of the Navajo Indian Reservation in New Mexico and for other Purposes, S. Rep. No. 1074, 73rd Cong., 2nd Sess. (1934). Passage of the Taylor Grazing Act in 1934 (48 Stat. 1269) ended any boundary expansion in New Mexico since the Department of the Interior now

carefully regulated grazing on public domain lands and non-Indians were no longer willing to sell any of their land in New Mexico.

100. *ARCIA, 1945*, 234.
101. *ARCIA, 1935*, 141; *ARCIA, 1944*, 239. An Act to provide for the distribution of the judgement fund of the Shoshone Tribe of the Wind River Reservation in Wyoming, and for other purposes, 53 Stat. 1128 (July 27, 1939).
102. *ARCIA, 1944*, 239.
103. *ARCIA, 1933*, 70; *ARCIA, 1934*, 104; *ARCIA, 1936*, 189; Prucha, *The Great Father*, 946–47.
104. *ARCIA, 1934*, 104. Prucha, *The Great Father*, 964–66.
105. *ARCIA, 1936*, 188.
106. *Readjustment of Indian Affairs*, 15–29.
107. *ARCIA, 1940*, 369; *ARCIA, 1937*, 199.
108. *ARCIA, 1944*, 240.
109. An Act to regulate the leasing of certain Indian lands for mining purposes, 52 Stat. 347 (May 11, 1938). The act exempted the Crow, Papago, and Wind River Reservations, with the Osage, Choctaw, and Chickasaw lands in Oklahoma also exempt.
110. An Act authorizing the secretary of the interior to arrange with states or territories for the education, medical attention, relief of distress, and social wellbeing of Indians, and for other purposes, 48 Stat. 596 (April 16, 1934).
111. *ARCIA, 1935*, 119.
112. *ARCIA, 1933*, 83.
113. S. Rep. No. 511, 73rd Cong., 2nd Sess. (1934).
114. *ARCIA, 1934*, 93.
115. An Act to amend an act entitled An Act authorizing the secretary of the interior to arrange with states or territories for the education, medical attention, relief of distress, and social wellbeing of Indians, and for other purposes, 49 Stat. 1458 (June 4, 1936).
116. *ARCIA, 1934*, 94.
117. DeJong, *If You Knew the Conditions*, 96–98.
118. *ARCIA, 1943*, 281.
119. *ARCIA, 1940*, 382. DeJong, *If You Knew the Conditions*, 98–101.
120. *ARCIA, 1934*, 89.
121. *ARCIA, 1937*, 227; *ARCIA, 1933*, 72.
122. *ARCIA, 1934*, 84. Boarding school closures or transfers included: Mt. Pleasant (MI) transferred to the state of Michigan; Genoa (NB) transitioned into a local public school; Tohatchi (NM) converted into a day school, and Rapid City (SD), Hayward (WI), Fort Belknap (MT), Mescalero (NM), Browning (MT), Red Lake (MN), and Standing Rock (ND) closed.
123. *ARCIA, 1935*, 130.
124. *ARCIA, 1934*, 85.
125. Ibid., 86–87; *ARCIA, 1937*, 228; *ARCIA, 1940*, 389.
126. *ARCIA, 1936*, 171.
127. *ARCIA, 1935*, 128; *ARCIA, 1936*, 173; and *ARCIA, 1937*, 229.
128. *ARCIA, 1933*, 75.
129. *ARCIA, 1937*, 224. An Act to promote the development of Indian arts and crafts and to create a board to assist therein, and for other purposes, 49 Stat. 891 (August 27, 1934). See also Robert F. Schrader, *The Indian Arts and Crafts Board: An Aspect of New Deal Policy* (Albuquerque: University of New Mexico Press, 1983), 77–89.
130. An Act repealing certain sections of the revised Code of Laws of the United States relating to Indians, 48 Stat. 787 (May 21, 1934).
131. *ARCIA, 1934*, 90.

132. *ARCIA, 1940*, 377.
133. *ARCIA, 1935*, 122.
134. Indian Reorganization Act, section 19.
135. Philp, "John Collier, 1933–45," 277.
136. *ARCIA, 1944*, 237. See also Tom Holm, *Code Talkers and Warriors: Native Americans and World War II* (New York: Chelsea House, 2007).
137. *ARCIA, 1941*, 407–15.
138. Ibid., 409.
139. *ARCIA, 1942*, 238; *ARCIA, 1944*, 235.
140. *ARCIA, 1942*, 243.
141. *ARCIA, 1943*, 295.
142. Ibid., 275.
143. *ARCIA, 1942*, 233–35. There were twenty thousand Japanese interned on the Colorado River Indian Reservation and fifteen thousand on the Gila River Indian Reservation.
144. *Congressional Record*, 75th Cong., 1st Sess., June 26, 1937, (81), part 6, 6379–80.
145. Philp, *John Collier's Crusade*, 200, and 189–93.
146. U.S. Senate, Committee on Indian Affairs, Survey of conditions among the Indians of the United States, analysis of the statement of the Commissioner of Indian Affairs in justification of appropriations for 1944 and the liquidation of the Indian Bureau, S. Rep. No. 310, 78th Cong., 1st Sess., 8, 17 (June 11, 1943).
147. U.S. Congress, House of Representatives, The Report of the Select Committee to Investigate Indian Affairs, H.R. Rep. No. 2091, 78th Cong., 2nd Sess., 17– 18 (1944).
148. Philp, *John Collier's Crusade*, 211.
149. S. Lyman Tyler, "William A. Brophy, 1945–48," in Kvasnicka and Viola, *Commissioners of Indian Affairs*, 283–87.
150. Fixico, *Termination and Relocation*, 23.
151. "Indians Oppose Brophy Choice," *Albuquerque Tribune*, February 27, 1945.
152. Fixico, *Termination and Relocation*, 24.
153. *ARCIA, 1945*, 233.
154. *ARCIA, 1947*, 345.
155. Ibid., 346.
156. Ibid., 348–49.
157. Ibid., 349.
158. *ARCIA, 1945*, 234.
159. Ibid., 235.
160. *ARCIA, 1946*, 365.
161. *ARCIA, 1947*, 351.
162. Ibid. See also *Removal of Restrictions on Indian Property and for the Emancipation of the Indians: Hearings before the Committee on Indian Affairs on H.R. 3680, H.R. 3681, and H.R. 3710*, 79th Cong., 2nd Sess. (1946). *Removal of Restrictions on Property of the Indians who served in the Armed Forces: Hearings before the Committee on Indian Affairs on S. 93 and S. 1194*, 79th Cong., 2nd Sess. (1946).
163. *ARCIA, 1946*, 376.
164. Ibid., 381. In 1948, as a result of state court rulings, both Arizona and New Mexico recognized Indian suffrage.
165. Ibid., 351.
166. Ibid., 353.
167. *ARCIA, 1948*, 369.
168. Ibid.
169. Meriam, *The Problem of Indian Administration*, 472.

170. *ARCIA, 1948,* 370.
171. Ibid., 369.
172. Ibid., 389.
173. *ARCIA, 1945,* 244. In 1855, Congress created the U.S. Court of Claims to permit suits against the United States, although in 1863, after the Minnesota Sioux War, Congress barred tribes from suing the United States without specific jurisdictional acts (An Act to amend an act to establish a court for the investigation of claims against the United States, approved February 24, 1855, 12 Stat. 765 {March 3, 1863}). Such acts were difficult to attain and narrowly defined, resulting in numerous tribal complaints of unresolved claims. Between 1881 and 1950, there were 118 tribal claims in the court of claims but only 34 resulted in a positive judgment. See Nancy Oestreich Lurie, "The Indian Claims Commission Act," *Annuals of the American Academy of Political and Social Sciences* 311, no. 1 (May 1957), 57. In 1944, the court of claims issued a ruling in favor of California tribal nations, awarding $5,024,842 in "partial satisfaction" of claims arising out of the 1851–1852 unratified California treaties that ceded to the United States 75,000,000 acres and promised to reserve 8,619,000 acres as reservation lands. The treaties were never ratified and Congress acted in poor faith when the tribes received just 624,000 acres of poor, unproductive land. That same year, Menominee claims to 33,870 acres of swamplands within the reservation were settled, as well as the Sioux pony claims from 1876.
174. U.S. Congress, House, A Joint resolution establishing a joint congressional committee to make a study of claims of the Indian tribes against the United States, and to investigate the administration of Indian affairs, H.R. 237, 79th Cong., 1st Sess. (1945).
175. U.S. Congress, House, A House resolution to create an Indian Claims Commission, to provide for the powers, duties, and functions thereof, and for other purposes, H.R. 4497, 79th Cong., 1st Sess. (1945).
176. Joseph O'Mahoney, "Creating an Indian Claims Commission," in Fixico, *Termination and Relocation,* 27.
177. *Public Papers of the President of the United States, Harry S. Truman, 1946* (Washington, D.C.: Government Printing Office, 1965), 414. An Act to create an Indian Claims Commission, to provide for the power, duties, and functions thereof, and for other purposes, 60 Stat. 1050 (August 13, 1946).
178. *ARCIA, 1946,* 347. Meriam, *The Problem of Indian Administration,* 805–15.
179. The Meriam Report had strongly recommended "maximum decentralization" of authority down to the local offices. Meriam, *The Problem of Indian Administration,* 113.
180. *ARCIA, 1946,* 353.
181. *ARCIA, 1947,* 349–50.
182. Ibid., 349–51.
183. *ARCIA, 1946,* 242–43.
184. Ibid., 243.
185. *ARCIA, 1945,* 236.
186. *ARCIA, 1947,* 362.
187. *ARCIA, 1948,* 382.
188. *ARCIA, 1945,* 358. Navajo Treaty with the United States, June 1, 1868, 15 Stat. 667.
189. *ARCIA, 1948,* 380.
190. *ARCIA, 1947,* 345–48.
191. *ARCIA, 1948,* 392.
192. "Report of the Committee on Indian Affairs to the Commission on Organization of the Executive Branch of the Government," October 1948, 54. Charles J. Rhoads, John R. Nichols, Gilbert Darlington, and George A. Graham served as the principle researchers and authors of the Indian assessment.

193. Ibid., 55.
194. While the Zimmerman Plan was not originally a blueprint for termination, it became the de facto plan of termination, a policy that gained traction in 1950. On January 6, 1948, Assistant Secretary William E. Warne explained to Congress the goal of the Indian Office was to "work itself out of a job," in the process referring to Zimmerman's testimony of 1947 as the orderly plan for withdrawal of services. Quoted in Kvasnicka and Viola, *Commissioners of Indian Affairs*, 286.
195. Circular 36575, May 28, 1948, National Archives and Records Services, Record Group 75, Numbered Circular File.
196. Larry J. Hasse, "Termination and Assimilation: Federal-Indian Policy, 1943–1961" (PhD diss., Washington State University, 1974), 64–65, 92.

CHAPTER 8

1. For New Mexico, see Trujillo v. Garley, unreported (1949), in which the New Mexico Supreme Court ruled that the state's position of denying suffrage based on the Indians "not taxed" clause of the U.S. Constitution violated the Fourteenth and Fifteenth Amendments to the U.S. Constitution. For Arizona, see Harrison v. Laveen, 196 P.2d 456 (Ariz. 1948).
2. Truman originally offered the position to Dillon Myer in 1947, but he turned it down. After winning reelection in 1948, Truman again offered the commissionership to Myer, who again rejected it. In both instances, Myer declined because he did not want to leave his position at the Institute for Inter-American Affairs until its charter was adopted. See Richard Drinnon, *Keepers of Concentration Camps: Dillion S. Myer and American Racism* (Berkley: University of California Press, 1987), 166.
3. *Congressional Record* (95), 81st Cong., 1st Sess., March 23, 1949, 2929–30.
4. William J. Dennehy, "John R. Nichols, 1949–50," in Kvasnicka and Viola, *Commissioners of Indian Affairs*, 289–92.
5. *Congressional Record* (95), 81st Cong., 1st Sess., May 5, 1949, A2711–12.
6. "Indian Commissioner Sees Tribes Treated Like Other American Citizens, *New York Times*, May 5, 1949.
7. *ARCIA, 1949*, 338.
8. Ibid., 366.
9. Ibid., 338.
10. Ibid.
11. Ibid., 358.
12. Ibid., 347.
13. Ibid., 340.
14. *ARCIA, 1949*, 341; Report of the Committee on Indian Affairs to the Commission on Organization of the Executive Branch of the Government, October 1948 (Hoover Commission), 66.
15. *ARCIA, 1949*, 337.
16. Ibid., 339.
17. Ibid., 342.
18. Ibid., 343.
19. Ibid., 341.
20. Ibid., 353.
21. Ibid., 356.
22. Patricia K. Ourada, "Dillon Seymour Myer, 1950–53," in Kvasnicka and Viola, *Commissioners of Indian Affairs*, 293–99.
23. Drinnon, *Keepers of Concentration Camps*, 166–67.

24. Ibid., 168.
25. Harold Ickes, "The Indian Loses Again," *New Republic*, September 24, 1951, 16.
26. *ARCIA, 1951*, 353.
27. Drinnon, *Keepers of Concentration Camps*, 170–72. Prucha, *The Great Father*, 1031–33.
28. *ARCIA, 1952*, 393–94.
29. See H.R. 7490, H.R. 7491, and S. 3005, 82nd Cong., 2nd Sess., April 11, 1952. See also S. 3004, 82nd Cong., 2nd Sess., April 11, 1952.
30. *ARCIA, 1950*, 342–43.
31. An Act to promote the rehabilitation of the Navajo and Hopi Tribes of Indians and a better utilization of the resources of the Navajo and Hopi Indian Reservations, and for other purposes, 64 Stat. 44 (April 19, 1950). Funding was available as follows: $10 million for soil and water conservation; $9 million for irrigation; $500,000 for timber, coal and mineral studies; $1 million for industrial development; $3.5 million for off-reservation resettlement; $5.75 million for relocation to the Colorado River Indian Reservation; $20 million for roads; $250,000 for communications; $5 million for a revolving loan fund; $4.75 million for healthcare; $25 million for schools; $820,000 for housing; and $500,000 for community services. See *ARCIA, 1950*, 351.
32. *ARCIA, 1950*, 350.
33. *ARCIA, 1951*, 352; *ARCIA, 1952*, 369.
34. Felix S. Cohen, "The Erosion of Indian Rights, 1950–1953: A Case Study in Bureaucracy," *Yale Law Review* 62, no. 3 (1953): 382. See also *ARCIA, 1951*, 368–69.
35. *ARCIA, 1952*, 405; *ARCIA, 1953*, 32.
36. *ARCIA, 1953*, 32; *ARCIA, 1952*, 405.
37. *ARCIA, 1951*, 353.
38. *ARCIA, 1952*, 392–93.
39. Ibid., 393.
40. *ARCIA, 1953*, 26–27.
41. Ibid., 30.
42. *ARCIA, 1952*, 394.
43. Ibid., 389.
44. *ARCIA, 1950*, 347.
45. Ibid., 347–48.
46. *ARCIA, 1951*, 360–62. The Johnson-O'Malley states included Arizona, California, Idaho, Minnesota, Montana, Nebraska, Nevada, North Dakota, Oklahoma, Oregon, South Dakota, Texas, Washington, and Wisconsin.
47. *ARCIA, 1952*, 409.
48. *ARCIA, 1950*, 349.
49. *ARCIA, 1952*, 390.
50. Ibid., 399–400.
51. *ARCIA, 1950*, 340. An Act authorizing an appropriation for the construction, extension, and improvement of a county hospital at Albuquerque, New Mexico, to provide facilities for the treatment of Indians, 63 Stat. 1049 (October 31, 1949).
52. *House Subcommittee on Indian Affairs Hearings on H.R. 7491*, 82nd Cong., 1st Sess. (May 7, 1951).
53. *ARCIA, 1952*, 390. An Act to provide medical services for non-Indians in Indian hospitals, and for other purposes, 66 Stat. 35 (April 3, 1952). The act was repealed in 1954 with the Indian Health Transfer Act.
54. H.R. 7490, H.R. 7491, and S. 3005 (California), and S. 3004 (Oregon), 82nd Cong., 2nd Sess., April 11, 1952.
55. *ARCIA, 1952*, 395.
56. Ibid. DeJong, *If You Knew the Conditions*, 130–31.

57. Ibid., 396; *ARCIA*, 1953, 24, 34.
58. *ARCIA*, 1953, 35.
59. *ARCIA*, 1951, 371.
60. *ARCIA*, 1950, 355–56.
61. Ibid., 357.
62. *ARCIA*, 1952, 413.
63. *ARCIA*, 1950, 364.
64. Ibid., 365.
65. Ibid.
66. H.R. 3624 (California); H.R. 6695 (Oregon); H.R. 1551 (Wisconsin); and S. 1077 (Washington). *ARCIA*, 1952, 391, 419.
67. *ARCIA*, 1953, 41.
68. *ARCIA*, 1952, 393–94.
69. H. R. 698, *Congressional Record* (98), 82nd Cong., 2nd Sess., July 1, 1952, 8814.
70. Ourada, "Dillon Seymour Myer, 1950–53," 294–95.
71. *ARCIA*, 1953, 23.
72. Ibid., 23–24.
73. Drinnon, *Keeper of Concentration Camps*, 240.
74. Fixico, *Termination and Relocation*, 97.
75. *ARCIA*, 1951, 375.
76. Ibid.
77. Ibid., 376. In 1954, the Salt Lake City office moved to Oakland, California; in 1956 relocation offices were opened in St. Louis, San Francisco, and San Jose; and a year later new offices were opened in Cincinnati, Joliet, and Waukegan, Illinois.
78. *ARCIA*, 1952, 403.
79. Ibid., 402–4.
80. *ARCIA*, 1953, 40.
81. Dorothy Van de Mark, "The Raid on Reservations," *Harper's Magazine*, March 1956, 48–49.
82. Drinnon, *Keepers of Concentration Camps*, 244–45.
83. John Collier, "Letter to General Eisenhower," *Nation*, January 10, 1953, 29.
84. Harold L. Ickes, "Justice in a Deep Freeze," *New Republic*, May 21, 1951, 17.
85. Cohen, "The Erosion of Indian Rights," 348–90.
86. Ibid., 355–56; Drinnon, *Keepers of Concentration Camps*, 188–213.
87. *Hearings before the Subcommittee of Indian Affairs on H.R. 2896, H.R. 3203, and House Joint Resolution 210*, 82nd Cong., 1st Sess. (July 3, 1951).
88. Cohen, "The Erosion of Indian Rights 372.
89. Fixico, *Termination and Relocation*, 74.
90. Ibid., 74–75.
91. "Greenwood Acting Indian Commissioner," March 20, 1953, Department of the Interior Information Service. Greenwood penned the annual report for 1953.
92. Patricia K. Ourade, "Glenn L. Emmons, 1953–61," in Kvasnicka and Viola, *Commissioners of Indian Affairs*, 301; "Glenn L. Emmons Nominated for Indian Post," July 15, 1953, Department of the Interior Information Service.
93. Indians, H.C.R. 108, 67 Stat. B132 (August 1, 1953).
94. *ARCIA*, 1954, 229.
95. H.C.R. 108; *ARCIA*, 1954, 227.
96. *ARCIA*, 1954, 228.
97. Ibid. See U.S. Congress, House of Representatives, House Interior and Insular Affairs, 83rd Cong., 2nd Sess., "Termination of Federal supervision over certain tribes of Indians," Part 1,

Utah, H.R. 7674 and S. 2670, February 15, 1954; Part 2 Texas, H.R. 6282, H.R. 6547, and S. 2744, February 16, 1954; Part 3, Western Oregon, H.R. 7317 and S. 2746, February 17, 1954; Part 4, Klamath Indians, H.R. 7320 and S. 2745, February 23–24, 1954; Part 4A, Klamath Indians, H.R. 7320 and S. 2745, April 19, 1954; Part 5, California, H.R. 7322 and S. 2749, March 4–5, 1954; Part 6, Wisconsin, H.R. 2828, H.R. 7135, and S. 2813, March 10–12, 1954; Part 7, Montana, H.R. 7319 and S. 2750, February 25–27, 1954; Part 8, Florida, H.R. 7321 and S. 2747, March 1–2, 1954; Part 9, Washington, H.R. 7981, February 24, 1954; Part 10, Nevada, H.R. 7552, April 16, 1954; Part 11, Sac and Fox, etc., H.R. 7318 and S. 2743, February 18, 1954; and Part 12, North Dakota, H.R. 7316 and S. 2748, March 2–3, 1954.

98. An Act to provide for a per capita distribution of Menominee tribal funds and authorize the withdrawal of the Menominee Tribe from Federal jurisdiction, 68 Stat. 250 (June 17, 1954).
99. Menominee Tribe of Indians v. United States, 101 Ct. Cl. 10, 22 (1944).
100. *ARCIA, 1954*, 232.
101. Prucha, *The Great Father*, 1049–52.
102. An Act to confer jurisdiction on the states of California, Minnesota, Nebraska, Oregon, and Wisconsin, with respect to criminal offenses and civil causes of action committed on or arising in Indian reservations within such states, and for other purposes, 67 Stat. 588 (August 15, 1953). There were separate bills for each of the five states (plus one for Nevada) that were consolidated—absent Nevada—into a single bill.
103. *ARCIA, 1954*, 227, 243.
104. Ibid., 243; Fixico, *Termination and Relocation*, 111–12.
105. *ARCIA, 1955*, 247. An Act to amend title 18 and 28 of the United States Code, 68 Stat. 795 (August 24, 1954).
106. *ARCIA, 1955*, 215.
107. An Act to amend the law with respect to civil and criminal jurisdiction over Indian Country in Alaska, 72 Stat. 545 (August 24, 1958). See Fixico, *Termination and Relocation*, 111–33 for a discussion of Pub. L. No. 280.
108. *ARCIA, 1955*, 248; *ARCIA, 1956*, 215.
109. *ARCIA, 1957*, 253; *ARCIA, 1958*, 211.
110. *ARCIA, 1957*, 254; *ARCIA, 1958*, 211.
111. Deloria and Lytle, *American Indians, American Justice*, 175–77.
112. An Act to eliminate certain discriminatory legislation against Indians in the United States, 67 Stat. 586 (August 15, 1953). Indians—Discriminatory Legislation—Elimination, S. Rep. No. 722, July 29, 1953 (Washington, D.C.: Government Printing Office, 1953), 2399–2401.
113. *ARCIA, 1954*, 244; *ARCIA, 1955*, 248; *ARCIA, 1957*, 254.
114. An Act to terminate certain Federal restrictions upon Indians, 67 Stat. 590 (August 15, 1953).
115. Indians—Personal Property—Purchase and Sale, S. Rep. No. 793, July 30, 1953 (Washington, D.C.: Government Printing Office, 1953), 2414–17.
116. An Act making appropriations for the current and contingent expenses of the Departments of Justice, Commerce, State, and Judiciary, for the year ending June 30, 1953, Title II, 66 Stat. 549 (July 10, 1952).
117. United States v. District Court for Eagle County, 401 U.S. 520 (1971). Such water rights cases were still adjudicated according to federal law.
118. *ARCIA, 1954*, 229. An Act to transfer the maintenance and operation of hospital and health facilities for Indians to the Public Health Service, and for other purposes, 68 Stat. 674 (August 5, 1954). *ARCIA, 1955*, 231.
119. *ARCIA, 1955*, 231.
120. DeJong, *If You Knew the Conditions*, 133.
121. *ARCIA, 1956*, 199.

122. *ARCIA, 1954*, 231.
123. *ARCIA, 1955*, 237.
124. Ibid.
125. An Act to provide for the termination of Federal supervision over the property of the Klamath Tribe of Indians located in the state of Oregon and the individual members thereof, and for other purposes, 68 Stat. 718 (August 13, 1954) (hereafter Klamath Termination). *ARCIA, 1955*, 237–39.
126. Those accepting the pro rata share of tribal assets (77.78 percent or 1,659 Indians) each received $43,700 after more than 600,000 acres of tribal land was sold. For the 474 (22.22 percent) tribal members who chose to retain communal ownership, 145,000 acres of land were placed into a trust administered by the National Bank of Portland. *ARCIA 1959*, 232.
127. Klamath Termination, section 14.
128. *ARCIA, 1956*, 207; *ARCIA, 1960*, 190.
129. An Act to provide for the termination of Federal supervision over the property of certain tribes and bands of Indians in western Oregon and the individual members thereof, and for other purposes, 68 Stat. 724 (August 13, 1954). The following bands and tribes were terminated: Confederated Grande Ronde, Confederated Siletz, Alsea, Applegate Creek, Calapooya, Chaftan, Chempho, Chetco, Chetlessington, Chinook, Clackama, Clatskanie, Clatsop, Clowwewalla, Coos, Cow Creek, Euchees, Galic Creek, Grave, Joshua, Karok, Kathlamet, Kusotony, Kwatami, Lakmiut, Long Tom Creek, Lower Coquille, Lower Umpqua, Maddy, Mackanotin, Mary's River, Multnomah, Munsel Creek, Naltunnetunne, Nehalem, Nestucca, Northern Molalla, Port Orford, Pudding River, Rogue River, Salmon River, Santiam, Scoton, Shasta, Shasta Costa, Siletz, Siuslaw, Skiloot, Southern Molalla, Takelma, Tillamook, Tolowa, Tualatin, Tututui, Upper Coquilla, Upper Umpqua, Willamette Tumwater, Yamhill, Yaquina, and Yoncalla. *ARCIA, 1955*, 237–39.
130. *ARCIA, 1955*, 237–39. See section 2 of An Act to provide for the termination of Federal supervision over the property of the Alabama and Coushatta Tribes of Indians of Texas and the individual members thereof, and for other purposes, 68 Stat. 768 (August 23, 1954).
131. An Act to provide for the partition and distribution of the assets of the Ute Indian Tribe of the Uintah-Ouray Reservation in Utah between the mixed-blood and full-blood members thereof; and for the termination of Federal supervision over the property of the mixed-blood members of said tribe; and to provide a development program for the full-blood members of such tribes, and for other purposes, 68 Stat. 868 (August 27, 1954). Congress defined full blood as one-half Ute blood and a total Indian blood in excess of one-half. *ARCIA, 1955*, 237–39.
132. An Act to provide for the termination of Federal supervision over the property of certain tribes, bands, and colonies of Indians in the state of Utah and the individual members thereof, and for other purposes, 68 Stat. 1099 (September 1, 1954). *ARCIA, 1955*, 237–39.
133. An Act to provide for the termination of Federal supervision over the property of the Wyandotte Tribe of Oklahoma and the individual members thereof, and for other purposes, 70 Stat. 893 (August 1, 1956); An Act to provide for the termination of Federal supervision over the property of the Peoria Tribe of Oklahoma and the individual members thereof, and for other purposes, 70 Stat. 937 (August 2, 1956); An Act to provide for the termination of Federal supervision over the property of the Ottawa Tribe of Oklahoma and the individual members thereof, and for other purposes, 70 Stat. 963 (August 3, 1956).
134. An Act to provide for the distribution of the land and assets of certain Indian rancherias and reservations in California, and for other purposes, 72 Stat. 619 (August 18, 1956). *ARCIA, 1957*, 242–43. An Act to provide for the division of the tribal assets of the Catawba Indian Tribe of South Carolina among the members of the tribe, and for other purposes, 73 Stat. 592 (September 21, 1959).
135. An Act to authorize the conveyance to Lake County, California, of the Lower Lake Rancheria, and for other purposes, 70 Stat. 58 (March 29, 1956), as amended by 70 Stat. 595 (July 20, 1956). See

also An Act to authorize transfer of the Coyote Valley Indian Rancheria to the secretary of the army, and for other purposes, 71 Stat. 283 (July 10, 1957).

136. As Roberta Ulrich, *American Indian Nations from Termination to Restoration, 1953–2006* (Lincoln: University of Nebraska Press, 2011) notes, virtually all of the terminated tribes and bands were restored to federal status. See 143–235 for specific case studies and 247 for an overall listing of tribes.
137. *ARCIA, 1958*, 211.
138. Williams v. Lee, 358 U.S. 217 (1959).
139. Deloria and Lytle, *American Indians, American Justice*, 205.
140. *ARCIA, 1954*, 231; *ARCIA, 1957*, 239.
141. *ARCIA, 1955*, 233–34; *ARCIA, 1956*, 201; *ARCIA, 1957*, 237.
142. *ARCIA, 1956*, 201.
143. *ARCIA, 1957*, 237.
144. *ARCIA, 1955*, 242.
145. *ARCIA, 1956*, 210. In 1950, the School Facilities Construction Act (Pub. L. No. 81-815) authorized federal funds for school construction in areas impacted by federal activities. See An Act related to the construction of school facilities in areas affected by Federal activities, and for other purposes, 64 Stat. 967 (September 23, 1950). The same year Congress enacted the Federally Impacted Areas Act to provide funds for school operating budgets in federally impacted areas. See An Act to provide financial assistance for local educational agencies in areas affected by Federal activities, and for other purposes, 64 Stat. 1100 (September 30, 1950). In 1958, the acts were applied to Indian Country for use as general operating funds. See An Act to amend Public Laws 815 and 874, 81st Congress, to make permanent the programs providing financial assistance in the construction and operation of schools in areas affected by Federal activities, insofar as such programs relate to children of persons who reside and work on Federal property, to extend such programs until June 30, 1961, insofar as such programs relate to children, and to make certain changes in such laws, 72 Stat. 548 (August 12, 1958).
146. *ARCIA, 1957*, 249.
147. *ARCIA, 1958*, 203; *ARCIA, 1960*, 206. Fixico, *Termination and Relocation*, 139.
148. Glenn Emmons, "U.S. Aim: Give Indians a Chance," *Nation's Business*, July 1955, 42.
149. *ARCIA, 1954*, 242.
150. "Address by Glenn L. Emmons, Commissioner of Indian Affairs, before the 66th Continental Congress, National Society, Daughters of the American Revolution, Washington, D.C.," April 18, 1957, Department of the Interior Information Service, 3.
151. *ARCIA, 1955*, 247.
152. La Verne Madigan, *The American Indian Relocation Program* (New York: Association on American Indian Affairs, 1956), 10–11.
153. *ARCIA, 1958*, 209.
154. *ARCIA, 1959*, 238.
155. *ARCIA, 1960*, 203.
156. Ibid., 204.
157. *ARCIA, 1954*, 254. The secretary of the interior still retained authority to approve of such mortgages. *ARCIA, 1957*, 263.
158. An Act to authorize the leasing of restricted Indian lands for public, religious, educational, recreational, residential, business, and other purposes requiring the grant of long-term leases, 69 Stat. 539 (August 9, 1955).
159. "Emmons Issues Policy Statement on Sale of Individually Owned Indian Land," May 18, 1958, Department of the Interior Information Service, 2–3.
160. *ARCIA, 1955*, 252.

161. Ibid., 253; *ARCIA, 1956*, 223.
162. *ARCIA, 1957*, 241.
163. Ibid.
164. Ibid.
165. Ibid., 263.
166. Ibid., 264.
167. Ibid., 237. "Remarks by Commissioner of Indian Affairs Glenn L. Emmons at Woolaroc Ranch, Bartlesville, Oklahoma, Tuesday evening, October 29, 1957," Department of the Interior Information Services, 5.
168. "Glenn Emmons among 45 to Receive Award from Interior Department," *Washington Post*, April 26, 1957.
169. *Congressional Record* (105), 86th Cong., 1st Sess., June 12, 1959, 10714–116.
170. Lawrence E. Lindley, "Why Indians Need Land," *Christian Century*, November 6, 1957, 1316–18.
171. "Statement by Frank George, member of the Nationalities Division, Democratic National Committee, before the Democratic Platform Committee," Denver, Colorado, May 27, 1960, in Fixico, *Termination and Relocation*, 178.
172. Crow served as acting commissioner from January 7, 1961, to July 31, 1961. A member of the Cherokee Nation, Crow was also appointed by President Kennedy to an advisory board to make recommendations for a reorganization of the bureau and improve its policies and progress. See "John O. Crow Named Acting Commissioner of Indian Affairs and Member of Advisory Board on Indian Affairs," U.S. Department of Interior, Information Service, February 10, 1961.
173. Ourade, "Glenn L. Emmons, 1953–61," 306.
174. The final report was published in 1966 as William A. Brophy and Sophie A. Aberle, *The Indians: America's Unfinished Business, Report of the Commission on the Rights, Liberties, and Responsibilities of the American Indian* (Norman: University of Oklahoma Press, 1966). Members of the commission included Brophy and Aberle, as well as William Keeler, Karl N. Llewellyn, Soia Mentschikoff, Arthur Meier Schlesinger, Charles Arthur Sprague, and O. Meredith Wilson.
175. Ibid., 4.
176. Ibid., 39–41, 60.
177. Ibid., 113, 115.
178. *ARCIA, 1959*, 231.
179. Ibid; *ARCIA, 1960*, 189.

CHAPTER 9

1. American Indians did not share all of the goals of the Civil Rights movement. For instance, as a whole they did not desire to be integrated into the social and cultural fabric of the nation, seeking to retain their deeply held cultural values and beliefs. American Indians benefited from the Civil Rights movement, however, as cultural pluralism became more widely accepted, which in turn lent support for policy changes.
2. Vine Deloria Jr., *Of Utmost Good Faith* (New York: Bantam Books, 1972), 335.
3. Vine Deloria Jr., *American Indian Policy in the Twentieth Century* (Norman: University of Oklahoma Press, 1985), 251.
4. See statement by Representative Lee Metcalfe (D-MT), *Congressional Record* (104), 85th Cong., 2nd Sess., 1958, 6728. See also *Federal-Indian Policy: Hearings on S.C.R. 3, S. 331, and S. 809, before the Subcommittee on Indian Affairs of the Committee on Interior and Insular Affairs*, 85th Cong., 1st Sess., 267 (March 27, May 13 and 16, June 17, and July 1 and 22, 1957) (statement by Senator Richard Neuberger {D-OR}).

5. John F. Kennedy, "Letter on Indian Affairs from Senator John F. Kennedy to Mr. Oliver LaFarge, President, Association on American Indian Affairs," October 28, 1960, The American Presidency Project (hereafter "Kennedy to LaFarge").
6. *Hearings before the Committee on Interior and Insular Affairs, on the Nomination of Stewart L. Udall, to be Secretary of the Interior*, 87th Cong., 1st Sess., 15 (January 13, 1961).
7. *ARCIA, 1961*, 277.
8. "John O. Crow Named Acting Commissioner of Indian Affairs and Member of Advisory Board on Indian Affairs," February 10, 1961, Department of the Interior Information Services.
9. "Kennedy to LaFarge."
10. "Letter from Stewart Udall, Secretary of the Interior, to W. W. Keeler, dated Bartlesville, Oklahoma," February 8, 1961, Department of the Interior Information Services (hereafter "Udall to Keeler"), *ARCIA, 1961*, 277.
11. "Talk by Philleo Nash, Commissioner of Indian Affairs, before the Annual Meeting of the Association on American Indian Affairs, New York City," May 7, 1962, Department of Interior Press Release (hereafter "Nash New York City Address"), 1.
12. "Udall to Keeler."
13. Brophy and Aberle, *The Indian: America's Unfinished Business*, 39–42. The commission included O. Meredith Wilson (president of the University of Minnesota), W. W. Keeler (principal chief, Cherokee Nation), Arthur Schlesinger (Harvard historian), Karl N. Llewellyn (University of Chicago), and Charles A. Sprague (editor of the *Oregon Statesman*). The commission was directed first by Brophy then by his wife, Aberle.
14. An Act to establish an effective program to alleviate conditions of substantial and persistent unemployment and underemployment in certain economically distressed areas, 75 Stat. 48 (May 1, 1961). Indian reservations and Indian tribes were statutorily designated as eligible entities to receive funds and assistance.
15. "Declaration of Indian Purpose: The Voice of the American Indians. Proceedings of the American Indian Chicago Conference," (University of Chicago, June 13–20, 1961), 5–7.
16. *Public Papers of the Presidents of the United States: John F. Kennedy* (Washington, D.C.: Government Printing Office, 1964), 619.
17. "Report to the Secretary of the Interior by the Task Force on Indian Affairs," W. W. Keeler chairman, July 10, 1961.
18. Ibid., 27–33.
19. Margaret Connell Szasz, "Philleo Nash, 1961–66," in Kvasnicka and Viola, *Commissioners of Indian Affairs*, 312.
20. *Hearings before the Committee on Interior and Insular Affairs: on the Nomination for Commissioner of Indian Affairs*, 87th Cong., 1st Sess., 4 (August 14, 1961).
21. "Nash Sworn in as Commissioner of Indian Affairs," September 26, 1961, Department of the Interior News Release.
22. "Nash New York City Address," 1.
23. "Remarks by Philleo Nash, Commissioner of Indian Affairs, before the City Club of Portland, Portland, Oregon," July 26, 1963, Department of the Interior News Release (hereafter "Nash Portland Address"), 3.
24. "Address by Philleo Nash, Commissioner of Indian Affairs, Department of the Interior, at the Sunday Evening Forum, Tucson, Arizona," March 3, 1963, Department of the Interior News Release (hereafter "Nash Tucson Address"), 3–4.
25. "Nash Tucson Address," 4–5.
26. "Nash New York City Address," 5–6.
27. "Nash Portland Address," 6.
28. *ARCIA, 1963*, 15.

29. Ibid., 27–28.
30. *ARCIA, 1965*, 10.
31. Ibid., 12–13.
32. "Nash Portland Address," 9.
33. *ARCIA, 1965*, 13, 15.
34. Ibid., 18.
35. "Nash Portland Address," 8.
36. "Nash New York City Address," 2.
37. An Act to mobilize the human and financial resources of the nation to combat poverty in the United States, 78 Stat. 508 (August 20, 1964).
38. *ARCIA, 1963*, 16.
39. Ibid., 18–19.
40. *ARCIA, 1965*, 3.
41. "Nash Tucson Address," 7.
42. Szasz, "Philleo Nash 1961–66," 318.
43. An Act to assist in the provision of housing for moderate to low income families, to promote orderly urban development, to extend and amend laws relating to housing, urban renewal, and community facilities, and for other purposes, 75 Stat. 149 (June 30, 1961).
44. Task Force on Indian Affairs, 36–39; *ARCIA, 1965*, 6; "Nash Portland Address," 7.
45. "Nash Portland Address," 7.
46. *ARCIA, 1965*, 7.
47. "Nash Portland Address," 8.
48. "Nash New York City Address," 6; "Nash Portland Address," 10.
49. *ARCIA, 1963*, 45.
50. "Nash Portland Address," 10.
51. "Udall Calls for Ten-Year Plan for Reservation Indians," July 10, 1964, Department of the Interior News Release, 1.
52. *ARCIA, 1965*, 2.
53. "Resignation of Philleo Nash as Commissioner of Indian Affairs Announced," United States Department of the Interior News Release," March 10, 1966.
54. Richard N. Ellis, "Robert L. Bennett, 1966–69," in Kvasnicka and Viola, *Commissioners of Indian Affairs*, 325–31.
55. *ARCIA, 1966*, 2.
56. Ibid.
57. "Excerpts from Remarks by Robert L. Bennett, Commissioner of Indian Affairs, before the Indian Rights Association in Philadelphia, Pennsylvania," April 26, 1966, Department of the Interior News Release, 1 (hereafter "Bennett and the Indian Rights Association").
58. "Excerpts from Remarks by Robert L. Bennett, Commissioner of Indian Affairs, at the Annual Convention, National Congress of American Indians, Oklahoma City, Oklahoma," November 14, 1966, Department of the Interior News Release, 1.
59. "Bennett and the Indian Rights Association," 1.
60. "Nomination of Robert Lafollette Bennett to be Commissioner of Indian Affairs," S. Rep. No. 1, 89th Cong., 2nd Sess., April 8, 1966, 4.
61. Deloria, *Behind the Trail of Broken Treaties*, 28–31.
62. *ARCIA, 1966*, 4–5.
63. *Department of the Interior and Related Agencies Appropriations for Fiscal Year 1968: Hearing before a Subcommittee of the Committee on Appropriations*, 90th Cong., 1st Sess., part 1 679 (1967) (Washington, D.C.: Government Printing Office, 1967).
64. *ARCIA, 1968*, 5.

65. Lyndon Baines Johnson, "Special Message to the Congress on the Problems of the American Indians: The Forgotten Americans," March 6, 1968, *Public Papers of the Presidents of the United States: Lyndon B. Johnson* (Washington, D.C.: Government Printing Office, 1970), 335–44.
66. "Excerpts from Remarks of Commissioner of Indian Affairs Robert L. Bennett at the Governors' Interstate Indian Council, Reno, Nevada," October 18, 1967, Department of the Interior News Release, 1.
67. Ibid., 2–3.
68. Ibid., 5.
69. *ARCIA, 1966*, 5.
70. Ibid., 5 and 8; *ARCIA, 1968*, 7.
71. *ARCIA, 1966*, 9.
72. See DeJong, *Promises of the Past*, 228–29.
73. *ARCIA 1968*, 6.
74. Ibid.
75. Ibid., 4.
76. "National Council on Indian Opportunity to Meet on July 16," ca. July 1968, Department of the Interior News Release.
77. "Hopi Indians Sign Contract with BVD for $1.5 Million Plant in Winslow, Arizona," August 12, 1966, Department of the Interior News Release.
78. *ARCIA, 1968*, 12.
79. "Arizona Indians First in Country to Form Economic Planning Group under Economic Development Act," August 30, 1967, Department of the Interior News Release. *ARCIA, 1968*, 12.
80. *ARCIA, 1968*, 12.
81. "Indian Children Adopted during 1967 at Almost Double the 1966 Rate," March 24, 1968, Department of the Interior News Release; "89 Indian Children Placed for Adoption in 21 States during 1968," June 26, 1969, Department of the Interior News Release.
82. An Act to prescribe penalties for certain acts of violence or intimidation, and for other purposes, (Title IV Jurisdiction over Criminal and Civil Actions), 82 Stat. 73 at 77–80 (April 11, 1968) (hereafter Indian Civil Rights Act).
83. *Constitutional Rights of the American Indians: Hearings Pursuant to S. Res. 53, before the Subcommittee on Constitutional Rights of the Senate Committee on Judiciary*, 87th Cong., 1st Sess., pt. 1 (1961).
84. Colliflower vs. Garland, 342 F.2d 369 (9th Cir. 1965).
85. "Indian Civil Rights Act," Title II Rights of Indians, 82 Stat. 77–78.
86. Deloria, *Behind the Trail of Broken Treaties*, 36.
87. "Louis Bruce Nominated Commissioner of Indian Affairs," August 8, 1969, Department of the Interior News Release.
88. Joseph H. Cash, "Louis Rook Bruce, 1969–73," in Kvasnicka and Viola, *Commissioners of Indian Affairs*, 333–40.
89. "Remarks by Secretary of the Interior Walter J. Hickel," August 7, 1969, Department of the Interior News Release.
90. "Remarks of Commissioner of Indian Affairs Louis R. Bruce, Shiprock, New Mexico," September 6, 1969, Department of the Interior News Release, 2.
91. "Address by Commissioner of Indian Affairs Louis R. Bruce, at the 25th Anniversary Convention of the National Congress of American Indians, Albuquerque, New Mexico," October 9, 1969, Department of the Interior News Release (hereafter "Bruce-NCAI Address), 1.
92. "Remarks by Secretary of the Interior Walter J. Hickel before the National Congress of American Indians, Albuquerque, New Mexico," October 8, 1969, Department of the Interior News Release (hereafter "Hickel-NCAI Address"), 1.
93. "Bruce-NCAI Address," 3.

94. "Hickel-NCAI Address," 2.
95. "Executive Realignment Announced for BIA," January 9, 1970, Department of the Interior News Release.
96. "Hickel-NCAI Address," 3. "Remarks by Commissioner of Indian Affairs Louis R. Bruce before the Conference on Modern American Indians, Claremont Men's College, Claremont, California," February 27, 1970, Department of the Interior News Release, 2.
97. "The New BIA—The New Politics: Remarks by Commissioner of Indian Affairs Louis Rook Bruce at a Dinner Meeting of Western Oklahoma Indian Leaders, Oklahoma City, Oklahoma," October 24, 1969, Department of the Interior News Release, 2.
98. Ibid. 3.
99. Richard M. Nixon, "Special Message to the Congress on Indian Affairs," July 8, 1970, *Public Papers of the Presidents of the United States: Richard M. Nixon* (Washington, D.C.: Government Printing Office, 1971), 564–76.
100. An Act to amend section 4 of the act of May 31, 1933, 84 Stat. 1437 (December 15, 1970).
101. "Speech for NCAI Convention, Sarasota, Florida, Commissioner Bruce," October 20, 1972, Department of the Interior News Release, 3.
102. "Statement on Indian Affairs by Secretary of the Interior Rogers C. B. Morton," October 4, 1971, Department of the Interior News Release, 5–10.
103. "25 Tribes to Begin Management Program," February 1, 1972, Department of the Interior News Release.
104. "First 28 Indian Tribes Selected for Interior's Reservation Acceleration Program," March 19, 1972, Department of the Interior News Release, 1–2.
105. "Indian Education: A National Tragedy—A National Challenge," S. Rep. No. 91-501, Report of the Committee on Labor and Public Welfare, United States Senate, Made by its Special Subcommittee on Indian Education Pursuant to S. Res. 80, 91st Cong., 1st Sess. (Washington, D.C.: Government Printing Office, 1969), xi.
106. Ibid., xiii.
107. Ibid., xii.
108. Ibid., 52–53, and 101–2.
109. An Act to amend the Higher Education Act of 1965, the Vocational Education Act of 1963, the General Education Provision Act, the Elementary and Secondary Education Act of 1965, PL 874, 81st Congress and related acts, and for other purposes, 86 Stat. 235 (June 23, 1972), Title IV Indian Education Act at 334.
110. An Act to extend and amend the Elementary and Secondary Education Act of 1965, and for other purposes, 88 Stat. 585–87 (August 21, 1974).
111. "Speech of Marvin L. Franklin, Assistant Secretary to the Secretary of the Interior for Indian Affairs, at the Student Faculty Center, Oklahoma City University, Oklahoma Education Association Convention, Indian Education Division," October 19, 1973, Department of the Interior News Release, 5.
112. Another 2 million acres was reserved for individual allotments that Alaska Natives could select under §1613(h) of An Act to provide for the settlement of certain land claims of Alaska Natives, and for other purposes, 85 Stat. 688 (December 18, 1971).
113. "Morton Announces Organizational Changes in BIA," December 8, 1971, Department of the Interior News Release (hereafter "Morton's Organizational Changes").
114. "John O. Crow Appointed Deputy Commissioner of Indian Affairs," July 23, 1971, Department of the Interior News Release.
115. "Morton's Organizational Changes," 1–2.
116. Deloria, *Behind the Trail of Broken Treaties*, 45.
117. Ibid., 46–62.
118. "Resignation of BIA Commissioner Louis R. Bruce Announced," December 8, 1972, Department of the Interior News Release.

119. "Bureau of Indian Affairs Back in Full Operation," December 8, 1972, Department of the Interior News Release.
120. "Remarks of Marvin L. Franklin, Assistant to the Secretary of the Interior for Indian Affairs, Ponca City Chamber of Commerce," August 24, 1973, Department of the Interior News Release (hereafter "Franklin's Address").
121. "Marvin L. Franklin named Assistant to the Secretary for Indian Affairs," February 7, 1973, Department of the Interior News Release.
122. "Statement of the Honorable John C. Whitaker, Under Secretary of the Interior, Press Conference Re: Indian Affairs, Washington, D.C.," March 16, 1973, Department of the Interior News Release.
123. "Summary of President's Indian Legislative Proposals, Assistant Secretary for Indian Affairs," March 16, 1973, Department of the Interior News Release, 1–3.
124. "Franklin's Address," 3–4.
125. "Remarks by Marvin L. Franklin, Assistant Secretary to the Secretary of the Interior for Indian Affairs, at the NCAI 30th Annual Convention, Tulsa, Oklahoma," October 30, 1973, Department of the Interior News Release, 1.
126. Ibid. 3–6.
127. "Morton Lauds Nomination of Morris Thompson to be Commissioner of Indian Affairs," October 30, 1973, Department of the Interior News Release.
128. "Morris Thompson, Alaska Native, becomes 41st Commissioner of Indian Affairs," December 4, 1973, Department of the Interior News Release.
129. Michael T. Smith, "Morris Thompson, 1973–76," in Kvasnicka and Viola, *Commissioners of Indian Affairs*, 341–45.
130. "Morris Thompson, BIA Head, Addresses Indian Tribal Chairmen," December 7, 1973, Department of the Interior News Release.
131. "Commissioner of Indian Affairs Morris Thompson Consults with National Tribal Chairmen's Association, National Congress of American Indians, over Current BIA Goals," January 11, 1974, Department of the Interior News Release.
132. An Act to repeal the act terminating Federal supervision over the property and members of the Menominee Indian Tribe of Wisconsin; to reinstate the Menominee Indian Tribe of Wisconsin as a federally recognized sovereign Indian tribe; and to restore to the Menominee Tribe of Wisconsin those Federal services furnished to American Indians because of their status as American Indians; and for other purposes, 87 Stat. 770 (December 22, 1973).
133. "Menominee Land Restored to Reservation Status," April 22, 1975, Department of the Interior News Release.
134. An Act to provide for financing the economic development of Indians and Indian organizations, and for other purposes, 88 Stat. 77 (April 12, 1974).
135. An Act to provide maximum Indian participation in the government and education of the Indian people; to provide for the full participation of Indian tribes in programs and services conducted by the Federal Government for Indians and to encourage the development of human resources of the Indian people; to establish a program of assistance to upgrade Indian education; to support the right of Indian citizens to control their own educational activities; and for other purposes, 88 Stat. 2203 (January 4, 1975) (hereafter Indian Self-Determination Act).
136. See Indian Self Determination Act §102 for Interior (Bureau of Indian Affairs), and §103 for Health, Education, and Welfare (Indian Health Service) contracting provisions.
137. An Act to implement the Federal responsibility for the care and education of the Indian people by improving the services and facilities of Federal Indian health programs and encouraging maximum participation of Indians in such programs, and for other purposes, 90 Stat. 1400 (September 30, 1976).
138. "Indian Students Get Bill of Rights," September 12, 1974, Department of the Interior News Release.

139. "HEW Regulations Called 'Breakthrough' by Indian Commissioner," April 11, 1975, Department of the Interior News Release.
140. "Morton Issues Policy Statement on Indian use of Bird Feathers," February 5, 1975, Department of the Interior News Release.
141. "Ben Reifel Named Commissioner of Indian Affairs," December 7, 1976, Department of the Interior News Release.
142. Michael T. Smith, "Benjamin Reifel, 1976–77," in Kvasnicka and Viola, *Commissioners of Indian Affairs*, 347–48.
143. "President Carter Visits BIA Offices; Expresses Concern about Indian Affairs," February 22, 1977, Department of the Interior News Release.
144. "Interior Secretary Asks Tribal Leaders for Nominees for Indian Post," February 24, 1977, Department of the Interior News Release.
145. Joint Council of the Passamaquoddy and Penobscot Tribes v. Morton, 528 F.2d 370 (1st Cir. 1975).
146. Ibid. See also "Passamaquoddy, Penobscot, and Maliseet Treaty with Massachusetts," September 29, 1794, in *Documentary History of the State of Maine*, vol. 8 (Portland, ME: Maine Historical Society, 1902), 98.
147. Christopher Vecsey and William A. Starna, eds., *Iroquois Land Claims* (Syracuse: Syracuse University Press, 1988), 3–5.
148. "Interior Asks Justice Department to Begin Action in Support of Land Claims of Catawba Tribe in South Carolina," August 30, 1977, Department of the Interior News Release. "Catawba Treaty with South Carolina," March 1, 1840, in Vine Deloria Jr., and Raymond J. DeMallie, *Documents of American Indian Diplomacy: Treaties, Agreements, and Conventions, 1775–1979* (Norman: University of Oklahoma Press, 1999), 2:1103.
149. An Act to settle Indian land claims within the state of Rhode Island and Providence Plantations, and for other purposes, 92 Stat. 813 (September 30, 1978).
150. H.R. Rep. No. 1453, 95th Cong., 2nd Sess., 7–8.
151. "Interior Won't Ask Justice to Represent Shinnecock Indians in New York Land Claims," September 4, 1979, Department of the Interior News Release.
152. "Opportunity to Use Resources Essential for Indian Tribes, Solicitor Krulitz Declares," April 21, 1977, Department of the Interior News Release.
153. "President's Water Policy Message Sent to Congress," June 6, 1978, Department of the Interior News Release; "Regulations on Tribal Water Codes Published," March 25, 1977, Department of the Interior News Release.
154. "Andrus Says Water Rights Suits Necessary to Fulfill Trust Responsibilities," April 6, 1979, Department of the Interior News Release.
155. "Top Indian Affairs Official Rates Water Policy a Plus for Reservation Development," June 9, 1978, Department of the Interior News Release.
156. See, for instance, article 3 of the Treaty with the Nisqually, Puyallup, Steilacoom, Squawksin, S'Homamish, Steh-chass, T'Pecksin, Squiatle, and Sa-heh-wamish, December 26, 1854, 10 Stat. 1132.
157. United States v. Washington, 384 F. Supp. 312 (W.D. Wash. 1974); Washington v. Fishing Vessel Association, 443 U.S. 658 (1979).
158. United States v. Michigan, 471 F. Supp. 192 (W.D. Mich. 1979), based in part on the Chippewa of the Saginaw Treaty with the United States, January 14, 1837, 7 Stat. 528.
159. Oliphant v. Suquamish, 435 U.S. 191 (1978).
160. "Interior Secretary Neutral on Recommended Move of Indian Affairs from Department," April 1, 1977, Department of the Interior News Release.
161. "Under Secretary Joseph Says Indian Affairs Are Now a Major Interior Priority," May 26, 1977, Department of the Interior News Release; "Gerard Asks Indians for Unified Policy Statement," September 22, 1977, Department of the Interior News Release.

162. "Gerard Takes Oath as Assistant Secretary for Indian Affairs," October 14, 1977, Department of the Interior News Release.
163. "Gerard Asks Indians for Unified Policy Statement."
164. "Mills Appointed Acting BIA Head," July 24, 1979, Department of the Interior News Release.
165. "Hallet to Take Oath of Office as the 42nd Commissioner of the Bureau of Indian Affairs," December 6, 1979, Department of the Interior News Release.
166. "Proposed Regulations Governing Recognition of Indian Tribes are Published," June 5, 1978, Department of the Interior News Release.
167. "Regulations Governing Recognition of Indian Tribes are Published," August 30, 1978, Department of the Interior News Release.
168. An Act to provide for the extension of certain Federal benefits, services, and assistance to the Pascua Yaqui Indians of Arizona, and for other purposes, 92 Stat. 712 (September 18, 1978).
169. An Act to reinstate the Modoc, Wyandotte, Peoria, and Ottawa Indian Tribes of Oklahoma as federally supervised and recognized Indian tribes, 92 Stat. 246 (May 15, 1978). Siletz restoration is found in An Act to establish a reservation for the Confederated Tribes of Siletz Indians of Oregon, 87 Stat. 771 (November 18, 1977), as modified by An Act to establish a reservation for the Confederated Tribes of Siletz Indians of Oregon, 94 Stat. 1072 (September 4, 1980). The Southern Paiute were restored under An Act to restore to the Shivwits, Kanosh, Koosharem, and Indian Peaks Bands of Paiute Indians of Utah, and with respect to the Cedar City Band of Paiute Indians of Utah, to restore or confirm, the Federal trust relationship, to restore to members of such Bands those Federal services and benefits furnished to American Indian tribes by reason of such trust relationship, and for other purposes, 94 Stat. 317 (April 3, 1980).
170. Joint Resolution: American Indian Religious Freedom, 92 Stat. 469 (August 11, 1978).
171. H.R. Rep. No. 1308, 95th Cong., 2nd Sess., *United States Code and Administrative News* (Washington, D.C.: Government Printing Office, 1978), 1262.
172. An Act to protect archaeological resources on public lands and Indian lands, and for other purposes, 93 Stat. 721 (October 31, 1979).
173. An Act to establish standards for the placement of Indian children in foster or adoptive homes, to prevent the breakup of Indian families, and for other purposes, 92 Stat. 3069 (November 8, 1978).
174. *BIA Profile: The Bureau of Indian Affairs and American Indians* (Washington, D.C.: Government Printing Office, 1981), 6.
175. *Indian Economic Development Program: Oversight Hearings before the Committee on Interior and Insular Affairs, House of Representatives*, 96th Cong., 1st Sess., 115–26 (1979).
176. "Gerard Tells National Indian Education Conference Educating Indian Children is in Hands of Tribes," December 4, 1979, Department of the Interior News Release.
177. "Andrus Commends Nomination of Thomas W. Fredericks as Assistant Secretary of the Interior for Indian Affairs," June 18, 1980, Department of the Interior News Release.
178. "BIA Commissioner Issues Affirmative Action Policy for Indian Women," November 12, 1980, Department of the Interior News Release.
179. "Commissioner Hallet Initiates Plan to Benefit Minority and Indian Businesses," November 26, 1980, Department of the Interior News Release.
180. "Fredericks Signs Interagency Agreement to Bolster Indian Education," December 2, 1980, Department of the Interior News Release.
181. Vine Deloria Jr. and Clifford Lytle, *The Nations Within: The Past and Future of American Indian Sovereignty* (New York: Pantheon Books, 1984), 254–59.
182. Kenneth R. Philp, *Indian Self-Rule: First-Hand Accounts of Indian-White Relations from Roosevelt to Reagan* (Salt Lake City: Howe Brothers, 1986), 318.
183. Deloria, *American Indian Policy in the Twentieth Century*, 255–56.

CHAPTER 10

1. *Confirmation of Kenneth L. Smith: Hearing before the Committee on Indian Affairs*, 97th Cong., 1st Sess., 2 (April 28, 1981) (Washington, D.C.: Government Printing Office, 1981).
2. "Interior Official Announces Plans for Reagan Indian Policy," August 11, 1981, Bureau of Indian Affairs News Release.
3. Ibid., 2.
4. "BIA Official Will Negotiate Transfer of Schools to State System," February 8, 1982, Bureau of Indian Affairs News Release.
5. "BIA Announces Hearings on Proposed School Closures," March 15, 1982, Bureau of Indian Affairs News Release. Planned closures included Wahpeton, ND; Concho, OK; Southwest Indian Polytechnic, NM; Intermountain, UT; Mt. Edgecombe, AK; Sequoyah, OK; Flandreau, SD; and Phoenix, AZ.
6. Samuel Cook, "Ronald Reagan's Indian Policy in Retrospect: Economic Crisis and Political Irony," *Policy Studies Journal* 24, no. 1 (March 1996).
7. *Report and Recommendations to the President of the United States, Presidential Commission on Indian Reservation Economies*, November 1984. Reprinted in United States Congress, Senate, "*Federal Government's Relationship with American Indians: Hearings before the Special Committee on Investigations of the Select Committee on Indian Affairs*, Senate Hearing 101-126, Part 1, 101st Cong., 1st Sess. (Washington, D.C.: Government Printing Office, 1989) (hereafter Report to the President). Members of the commission included Robert Robertson (Occidental Petroleum Corporation, cochairman); Ross Swimmer (principal chief Cherokee Nation, cochairman); Daniel Alex (Athabascan); Ted Bryant (Cherokee-Choctaw); Manuel H. Johnson (assistant secretary of the treasury); B. Z. Kastler (attorney and president of the Salt Lake City Chamber of Commerce); David J. Mathews (chairman of the Coeur d'Alene Tribe); Neal A. McCaleb (Chickasaw); and Walter B. McKay (Cherokee).
8. Ibid., 25.
9. Ibid., 33–36 (tribal governmental obstacles); 47–52 (Bureau of Indian Affairs obstacles); 61–66 (federal obstacles); and 73–74 (local obstacles).
10. Ibid., 34.
11. Executive Order 12401, Presidential Commission on Indian Reservation Economies, January 14, 1983, Ronald Reagan, *Federal Register* 48, no. 12 (January 18, 1983).
12. Philp, *Indian Self-Rule*, 312.
13. An Act to amend the Internal Revenue Code of 1954 with respect to the tax treatment of periodic payment for damages received on account of personal injury or illness, and for other purposes, 96 Stat. 2605 (January 13, 1983).
14. An Act to authorize the purchase, sale, and exchange of lands by Indian tribes and by the Devil's Lake Sioux Tribe of the Devil's Lake Sioux Reservation of North Dakota specifically, and for other purposes, 86 Stat. 2515 (January 12, 1983).
15. "Western Indian Water Rights Negotiations," July 14, 1982, Department of the Interior News Release.
16. "Watt Seeks Negotiated Settlement for Indian Water Claims Suits; Will Create Negotiating Teams and Advisory Groups to Guide Settlements," July 14, 1982, Department of the Interior News Release (hereafter "Negotiated Water Settlements").
17. An Act to authorize the secretary of the interior to construct, operate, and maintain modifications of the existing Buffalo Bill Dam and Reservoir, Shoshone Project, Pick-Sloan Missouri Basin program, Wyoming, and for other purposes, 97 Stat. 1261 at 1274 (October 12, 1982). Title III is the Southern Arizona Water Settlement Act.
18. "Negotiated Water Settlements," 2–3. Several of these water settlements were executed: Mission Indians (San Luis Rey)—La Jolla, Rincon, San Pasquale, Pauma, and Pala Bands of Mission

Indians, 102 Stat. 4000 (1988), as amended by 112 Stat. 1896 (1998) and 114 Stat. 1441 (2000); and the Truckee-Carson Pyramid Lake Paiute Water Rights Settlement Act, 104 Stat. 3289 (1990).

19. "Interior Approves First Water Code Since 1975," October 9, 1986, Department of the Interior News Release.
20. Fort Peck-Montana Compact, Montana Code Annotated 85-20-201 (1985), Article III K.
21. *Handbook of Federal-Indian Law*, 13.
22. *Federal Register* 43, no. 39 (September 5, 1978): 361.
23. Office of Federal Acknowledgment, U.S. Department of the Interior, "Acknowledgment Decision Compilation List: Decided Cases Petitions Resolved by Department of the Interior." www.bia.gov/as-ia/ofa/decidedcases.
24. An Act to provide for federal recognition of the Cow Creek Band of Umpqua Tribe of Indians, to institute for such tribe those Federal services provided to Indians who are recognized by the Federal Government and who receive such services because of the Federal trust responsibility, and for other purposes, 96 Stat. 1960 (December 29, 1982); An Act to provide for restoration of Federal recognition to the Confederated Tribes of Coos, Lower Umpqua, and Siuslaw Indians, to institute for such Tribe those Federal services provided to Indians who are recognized by the Federal Government and who receive such services because of Federal trust responsibility, and for other purposes, 98 stat 2250 (October 17, 1984); An Act to settle certain claims of the Mashantucket Pequot Indians, 97 Stat. 851 (October 18, 1983); An Act to clarify the Federal relationship to the Lac Vieux Desert Band of Lake Superior Chippewa Indians as a distinct Indian tribe, to clarify the status of members of the band, to transfer title to trust lands, and for other purposes, 102 Stat. 1577 (September 8, 1988).
25. "Top Indian Official at Interior Submits Resignation," November 29, 1984, Department of the Interior News Release.
26. "New Indian Affairs Nominee Experienced in Tribal Leadership and Business," September 26, 1985, Department of the Interior News Release.
27. "Secretary Hodel Says New Assistant Secretary, Improved BIA Work to Strengthen Indian Tribes and Government-to-Government Relationship," October 7, 1985, Department of the Interior News Release.
28. U.S. Congress, House of Representatives, "Statement of the Secretary of the Interior Donald Paul Hodel before the House Subcommittee on Interior and Related Agencies, Committee on Appropriations," October 27, 1987 (Washington, D.C.: Government Printing Office, 1987).
29. U.S. Congress, House of Representatives, "Statement of the Assistant Secretary Ross Swimmer before the House Subcommittee on Interior and Related Agencies, Committee on Appropriations," October 27, 1987 (Washington, D.C.: Government Printing Office, 1987).
30. Ibid., 2–3.
31. Ibid., 4–5.
32. Seminole Indian Tribe v. Butterworth, 658 F.2d 310 (5th Cir. 1981).
33. Bryan v. Itasca County, 426 U.S. 372 (1976). See section 2(b) of Pub. L. No. 280, where Congress expressly precluded states from taxing Indian trust lands.
34. California v. Cabazon Band of Mission Indians, 480 U.S. 202 at 218 (1987).
35. Indian Gaming Regulatory Act, § 2710 (b), (2) (B).
36. Ibid., § 2202.
37. "Interior Announces Policy on Taking Indian Lands into Trust," February 6, 1986, Department of the Interior News Release.
38. "Swimmer Resigns; Ragsdale Named Acting Assistant Secretary," January 29, 1989, Department of the Interior News Release.
39. "Eddie Brown to be Assistant Secretary for Indian Affairs at Department of the Interior," April 13, 1989, Department of the Interior News Release.

40. "Brown Outlines Action Plan on Indian Affairs to Secretary Lujan," July 11, 1989, Department of the Interior News Release.
41. U.S. Congress, Senate, Final Report and Legislative Recommendations: A Report of the Special Committee on Investigation of the Select Committee on Indian Affairs, S. Rep. No. 101-216, 101st Cong., 1st Sess., November 20, 1989 (Washington, D.C.: Government Printing Office, 1989), 89–104 (hereafter Special Committee Report).
42. "Statement by Secretary of the Interior Manuel Lujan on Indian School Report," April 24, 1991, Department of the Interior News Release.
43. An Act to facilitate and implement the settlement of Colorado Ute Indian reserved water rights claims in southwest Colorado, and for other purposes, 102 Stat. 2973 (November 3, 1988).
44. "Assistant Secretary Eddie Brown to Keynote Conference on Economic Development of Indian Lands," March 12, 1990, Department of the Interior News Release.
45. "Secretary of the Interior Lujan, Leaders of Six Tribes Mark Agreements for Self-Governance Pilot Program," July 26, 1990, Department of the Interior News Release.
46. Special Committee Report, 16–17.
47. An Act to specify the terms of contracts entered into by the United States and Indian tribal organizations under the Indian Self-Determination and Educational Assistance Act and to provide for Tribal Self-Governance, and for other purposes, 108 Stat. 4250 (October 25, 1994). Tribal Self-Governance is Title II.
48. Ibid. See § 403 (b) (1) for Bureau of Indian Affairs programs, and § 403 (b) (2) for other Interior programs.
49. An Act to provide for the protection of Native American graves, and for other purposes, 104 Stat. 3048 (November 16, 1990).
50. *Indian Trust Fund Management: Hearing before the Select Committee on Indian Affairs, Oversight Hearing on the Management of Indian Trust Funds by the U.S. Government*, 101st Cong., 2nd Sess. (August 12, 1992) (Washington, D.C.: Government Printing Office, 1992).
51. "Interior Assistant Secretary Brown Outlines Plan to Improve Management of Indian Trust Fund," August 12, 1992, Department of the Interior News Release.
52. An Act to settle all claims of the Aroostook Band of Micmac's resulting from the Band's omission from the Maine Indian Claims Settlement Act of 1980, and for other purposes, 105 Stat. 1143 (November 26, 1991).
53. "Procedures for Establishing that an American Indian Group Exists as an Indian Tribe," *Federal Register* 56, no. 47 (September 18, 1991): 320.
54. "President Clinton Nominates Ada Deer as Assistant Secretary for Indian Affairs," May 11, 1993, Department of the Interior News Release.
55. "Interior Appropriations Conferees Gut the Bureau of Indian Affairs," September 20, 1995, Department of the Interior News Release.
56. See *Establishing Status of Indian Children: Hearing on S. 1448 before the House Subcommittee of Native American and Insular Affairs*, 104th Cong., 2nd Sess., (1995) on H.R. 3286 (statement of Congresswoman Deborah Pryce) (Washington, D.C.: Government Printing Office, 1995).
57. See H.R. Res. 3286 (Title III). *Adoption Protection and Stability Act of 1996: Hearing before the Senate Committee on Indian Affairs*, 105th Cong., 1st Sess. (1996) (Washington, D.C.: Government Printing Office, 1996).
58. "Congressional Bill Threatens Indian Children," May 8, 1996, United States Department of the Interior News.
59. Indian Reorganization Act, § 5. South Dakota v. U.S. Department of the Interior, 69 F.3d 878 (8th Cir. 1995).
60. Department of the Interior, Bureau of Indian Affairs, "Fee-to-Trust Handbook, Version II," (Washington, D.C.: Bureau of Indian Affairs, 2011), www.bia.gov/ots/fee-to-trust.

61. Department of the Interior et al. v. South Dakota et al., 519 U.S. 919 (1996).
62. County of Charles E. Mix v. United States Department of the Interior, 674 F.3d 898 (8th Cir. 2012); South Dakota v. United States Department of the Interior, 775 F. Supp. 2d 1129 (D.S.D. 2011); and South Dakota v. United States Department of the Interior, 487 F.3d 548 (8th Cir. 2007).
63. "Statement by Assistant Secretary for Indian Affairs Ada Deer," June 9, 1997, Department of the Interior News.
64. *Federal Register* 59, no. 38 (February 25, 1994): 9280.
65. *Federal Register* 65, no. 29 (February 11, 2000): 7052.
66. An Act to authorize the construction of a Wakpa Sica Reconciliation Place in Fort Pierre, South Dakota, and for other purposes, 114 Stat. 2868 (December 27, 2000). Title VII is Shawnee recognition.
67. "Assistant Secretary for Indian Affairs Ada Deer Announces Resignation; Secretary Babbitt Notes Accomplishments," January 19, 1997, United States Department of the Interior News.
68. "Interior Department Defends Tribal Self-Determination," March 10, 1998, Department of the Interior News.
69. "Assistant Secretary for Indian Affairs Delivers University of South Dakota Law School Speech on 'Indian Warriors: Then and Now'; Urges Responsible and Responsive Tribal Governments," March 19, 1998, Bureau of Indian Affairs News.
70. "Remarks of Kevin Gover at the Ceremony acknowledging the 175th anniversary of the BIA," September 8, 2000, www.tribal-institute.org.
71. "BIA and Tribes Sign an Agreement Establishing a Government-To-Government Consultation Policy," December 15, 2000, United States Department of the Interior News.
72. "Michael Anderson to Serve as Acting Assistant Secretary for Indian Affairs," January 5, 2001, United States Department of the Interior News.
73. "Neal McCaleb Sworn in as Assistant Secretary-Indian Affairs: Immediate Goals Include Meeting with Tribal Leaders," July 6, 2001, United States Department of the Interior News (hereafter "McCaleb Sworn In").
74. "Secretary Norton Praises Bush's Intention to Nominate Neal McCaleb as Assistant Secretary for Indian Affairs," April 17, 2001, United States Department of the Interior News.
75. "McCaleb Sworn In."
76. "Assistant Secretary McCaleb Calls on Tribal Leaders to Choose Prosperity over Poverty," June 20, 2002, United States Department of the Interior News.
77. *Confirmation of Neil A. McCaleb: Hearing before the Committee on Indian Affairs*, Senate Hearing 107-98, 107th Cong., 1st Sess., 12 (June 13, 2001) (Washington, D.C.: Government Printing Office, 2001) (hereafter *McCaleb Hearing*).
78. "McCaleb to Develop National Strategy for Improving Tribal Economies," October 11, 2002, United States Department of the Interior News.
79. *McCaleb Hearing*, 13.
80. "Remarks Prepared for Delivery by the Honorable Gale Norton, Interior Secretary, National Indian School Board Association Summer Conference," July 24, 2001, United States Department of the Interior News.
81. *McCaleb Hearing*, 15.
82. Ibid., 13.
83. Ibid., 19.
84. Ibid., 17.
85. Ibid., 18.
86. "Report to the President," 47–54.
87. Cobell v. Babbitt, 30 F. Supp. 2d 24 (D.D.C. 1998).
88. Cobell v. Norton, 226 F. Supp. 2d. 1 (D.D.C. 2002).

89. U.S. Congress, Senate, Proposed Reorganization of Major Agency and Functions Related to Indian Trust Reform Matters within the Department of the Interior, 108th Cong., 1st Sess., March 10, 2003 (Washington, D.C.: Government Printing Office, 2003).
90. United States v. Navajo, 537 U.S. 488 at 508 (2003).
91. "Secretary Norton Praises President's Intent to Nominate David Anderson as Assistant Secretary for Indian Affairs," September 12, 2003, United States Department of the Interior News.
92. "Dave Anderson Sworn in as Assistant Secretary for Indian Affairs," February 2, 2004, United States Department of the Interior News.
93. *Nomination of David W. Anderson: Hearing before the Committee on Indian Affairs, on Confirmation Hearing of the Nomination of David W. Anderson to be Assistant Secretary for Indian Affairs,"* 108th Cong., 1st Sess., 12 (October 22, 2003) (Washington, D.C.: Government Printing Office, 2003).
94. "Secretary Norton Lauds Senate Confirmation of David Anderson as Assistant Secretary—Indian Affairs," December 9, 2003, United States Department of the Interior News.
95. "President's Memo on Government-to-Government Relationship with Tribal Governments," *Weekly Compilation of Presidential Documents* (40:2016), September 23, 2004.
96. An Act to close the achievement gap with accountability, flexibility, and choice, so that no child is left behind, 115 Stat. 1425 (January 8, 2002).
97. "Gila River Indian Community to Benefit from Interior Secretary's Expansion of the BIA Land Consolidation Program," February 6, 2004, United States Department of the Interior News.
98. "Assistant Secretary for Indian Affairs Dave Anderson Announces His Decision to Resign and Resume His Entrepreneur Career," January 31, 2005, United States Department of the Interior News.
99. "Assistant Secretary Announces W. Patrick Ragsdale as New Director of the Bureau of Indian Affairs," February 7, 2005, United States Department of the Interior News.
100. "Carl Artman Sworn in as New Assistant Secretary for Indian Affairs," March 8, 2007, United States Department of the Interior News.
101. *Nomination of Carl J. Artman: Hearing before the Committee on Indian Affairs, on the Nomination of Carl J. Artman to be Assistant Secretary for Indian Affairs, Department of the Interior*, Senate Hearing 109-665, 109th Cong., 2nd Sess., 5–6 (September 14, 2006) (Washington, D.C.: Government Printing Office, 2006).
102. "Tribes, Native Organizations, Federal Partners to Gather in Phoenix for Groundbreaking Summit," May 8, 2007, United States Department of the Interior News.
103. "National Native American Economic Policy Summit Convenes in Phoenix," May 15, 2007, United States Department of the Interior News.
104. "Department of the Interior, Mashantucket and Seminole Tribes Sign Historic Partnership Project to Promote Indian Business Development," February 12, 2008, United States Department of the Interior News.
105. "Office of Federal Acknowledgment Guidance and Directive Regarding Internal Procedures," *Federal Register* 73, no. 30 (May 23, 2008): 146.
106. "Artman Announces Publication of Final Rule to Implement IGRA Section 20," May 20, 2008, United States Department of the Interior News.
107. The Assistant Secretary for Indian Affairs position was vacant the following dates: January 20, 2001, to July 4, 2001; December 31, 2002, to December 9, 2003; February 13, 2005, to March 5, 2007; May 23, 2008, to January 19, 2009. There were four acting assistant secretaries: James H. McDivit, Aurene M. Martin, Jim Cason, and George T. Skibone.
108. "Secretary Salazar Lauds Senate's Approval of Larry Echo Hawk as Interior's Assistant Secretary for Indian Affairs," May 20, 2009, United States Department of the Interior, Office of the Secretary.
109. An Act making supplemental appropriations for job preservation and creation, infrastructure investment, energy efficiency and science, assistance to the unemployed, and state and local fiscal

stabilization, for the fiscal year ending September 30, 2009, and for other purposes, 123 Stat. 115 (February 17, 2009).

110. *Nomination of Larry J. Echo Hawk to Be Assistant Secretary for Indian Affairs, United States Department of the Interior: Hearing before the Committee on Indian Affairs*," 111th Cong., 1st Sess., 14 (May 7, 2009) (Washington, D.C.: Government Printing Office).
111. Ibid., 15.
112. Carcieri v. Kempthorne, 555 U.S. 379 (2009).
113. An Act to settle Indian land claims within the state of Rhode Island and Providence Plantation, and for other purposes, 92 Stat. 813 (September 30, 1978); "Decided Cases—Petitions Resolved, Department of the Interior."
114. *Carcieri v. Kempthorne.*
115. U.S. Congress, Senate, "Amending the Act of June 18, 1934, to Reaffirm the Authority of the Secretary of the Interior to take Land into Trust for Indian Tribes," S. Rep. No. 111-247, 111th Cong., 2nd Sess., August 5, 2010, 5.
116. An Act to reaffirm that certain land has been taken into trust for the benefit of the Match-E-Be-Nash-She-Wish Band of Pottawatomi Indians, and for other purposes, 128 Stat. 1913 (September 26, 2014).
117. "Assistant Secretary Echo Hawk Charts Balanced Course for Off-Reservation Gaming Policy; Rescinds Guidelines Memo," June 14, 2011, United States Department of the Interior, Office of the Secretary.
118. "Decided Cases—Petitions Resolved, Department of the Interior."
119. "Tribal Consultation," *Federal Register* 74, no. 57 (November 9, 2009): 881.
120. "Secretary Salazar, Assistant Secretary Echo Hawk Launch Comprehensive Tribal Consultation Policy," December 1, 2011, United States Department of the Interior, Office of the Secretary.
121. "Assistant Secretary-Indian Affairs Larry Echo Hawk Moves Quickly to Begin Addressing Indian Country's Needs," United States Department of the Interior, Office of the Secretary.
122. An Act to protect Indian arts and crafts through the improvement of applicable criminal proceedings, and for other purposes, 124 Stat. 2258 (July 29, 2010). Title II is the "Tribal Law and Order Act."
123. An Act [that] may be cited as The Claims Resettlement Act of 2010, 124 Stat. 3064 (December 8, 2010).
124. White Mountain Apache Tribe Water Rights Quantification Act of 2010, Title III, 124 Stat. 3073 (December 8, 2010).
125. Crow Tribe Water Rights Settlement Act of 2010, Title IV, 124 Stat. 3097 (December 8, 2010).
126. Aamodt Litigation Settlement Act, Title VI, 124 Stat. 3134 (December 8, 2010).
127. Taos Pueblo Indian Water Rights Settlement Act, Title V, 124 Stat. 3122 (December 8, 2010).
128. "Secretary Salazar and Attorney General Holder Announce $1 Billion Settlement of Tribal Trust Accounting and Management Lawsuits Filed by More than 40 Tribes," April 11, 2012, United States Department of the Interior, Office of the Secretary.
129. "Assistant Secretary-Indian Affairs Larry Echo Hawk to Conclude Successful Term at Interior," April 9, 2012, United States Department of the Interior, Office of the Secretary.
130. An Act to amend the Act titled An Act to authorize the leasing of restricted Indian lands for public, religious, educational, recreational, residential, business, and other purposes requiring the grant of long-term leases approved August 9, 1955, to provide for Indian tribes to enter into certain leases without prior express approval from the secretary of the interior, and for other purposes, 126 Stat. 1150 (July 30, 2012).
131. "Salazar Applauds Senate Confirmation of Kevin Washburn as Interior Assistant Secretary for Indian Affairs," September 22, 2012, United States Department of the Interior, Office of the Secretary.

132. *Nomination of Kevin Washburn to be Assistant Secretary for Indian Affairs, United States Department of the Interior: Hearing before the Committee on Indian Affairs*, 112th Cong., 2nd Sess., 11–12 (September 14, 2012) (Washington, D.C.: Government Printing Office, 2013).
133. "Assistant Secretary Kevin Washburn to Conclude Successful Term at Interior, Return to Teaching," December 10, 2015, United States Department of the Interior, Office of the Secretary (hereafter "Washburn Resignation"). Craven v. Cobell, 2012 U.S. Lexis 8318 (2012).
134. "Interior Launches Land Buy-Back Program for Tribal Nations to Manage $1.9 Billion Trust Land Consolidation Fund," December 18, 2012, United States Department of the Interior, Office of the Secretary.
135. Match-E-Be-Nash-She-Wish Band of Pottawatomie Indians v. Patchak, 567 U.S. 209 (2012), 132 S. Ct. 2199 (2012).
136. "Washburn Proposes Changes to Land into Trust Procedures to Achieve Greater Transparency, Clarity, and Certainty for Tribes," May 24, 2013, Department of the Interior, Office of the Secretary. See Quiet Title Act, 28 U.S.C. § 2409a. The QTA's authorization of suit does not apply to "trust or restricted Indian land." The result is the plaintiff had no legal grounds to challenge the federal action. *Match-E-Be-Nash-She-Wish Band of Pottawatomie Indians v. Patchak.*
137. "Obama Administration Executes Ambitious Goal to Restore 500,000 acres to Tribal Homelands," October 12, 2016, United States Department of the Interior, Office of the Secretary; "Interior Approves Craig Tribal Association's Land-into-Trust Application," January 13, 2017, United States Department of the Interior, Office of the Secretary; "Assistant Secretary Issues Mashpee Wampanoag Tribe of Massachusetts' First Land-Into-Trust Decision," September 18, 2015, United States Department of the Interior, Office of the Secretary; "Secretary Jewell Announces Obama Administration's Largest Land-into-Trust Acquisition for Tribal Nations," January 15, 2016, United States Department of the Interior, Office of the Secretary.
138. "Secretary Jewell, Attorney General Holder Announce $554 million Settlement of Tribal Trust Accounting and Management Lawsuit Filed by the Navajo Nation," September 26, 2014, United States Department of the Interior, Office of the Secretary.
139. "Interior Proposes Reform of Federal Acknowledgment Regulations," May 22, 2014, United States Department of the Interior, Office of the Secretary.
140. "Federal Acknowledgment of American Indian Tribe," *Federal Register* 80, no. 37 (July 1, 2015): 865.
141. Ibid., 863.
142. An Act to reauthorize the Violence against Women Act of 1994, 127 Stat. 54 (March 7, 2013).
143. Ibid.
144. An Act to amend the Violence against Women Reauthorization Act of 2013 to repeal a special rule for the state of Alaska, and for other purposes, 127 Stat. 2988 (December 18, 2014).
145. Departmental Order 3335, "Reaffirmation of the Federal Trust Responsibility to Federally Recognized Indian Tribes and Individual Indian Beneficiaries," U.S. Department of the Interior, August 1, 2014.
146. "Secretary Jewell Stresses Self-Governance, Empowerment as Foundation for Successful, Culturally Vibrant Tribal Nations," December 3, 2014, United States Department of the Interior, Office of the Secretary.
147. "Interior Department Proposes Pathway for Reestablishing a Government-to-Government Relationship with Native Hawaiian Community," September 25, 2015, United States Department of the Interior, Office of the Secretary.
148. "Washburn Resignation."
149. "Alaska Native Leader Tara MacLean Sweeney Becomes First Female Native Alaskan Nominated for Assistant Secretary-Indian Affairs," October 17, 2017, United States Department of the Interior, Office of the Secretary.

150. Half of the top twenty poorest counties in the nation encompass Indian reservations. These include (1) Buffalo County, SD (Crow Creek Sioux), 81.59 percent Indian; (2) Shannon County, SD (Pine Ridge Sioux), 94.2 percent Indian; (3) Ziebach County, SD (Cheyenne River Sioux), 72.29 percent Indian; (5) Todd County, SD (Rosebud Sioux), 85.6 percent Indian; (6) Sioux County, ND (Standing Rock Sioux), 84.59 percent Indian; (7) Corson County, SD (Standing Rock Sioux), 60.8 percent Indian; (8) Wade Hampton County, AK (92.53 percent Alaska Native); and (9) Apache County, AZ (Navajo Tribe and White Mountain Apache), 76.88 percent Indian.

CHAPTER 11

1. Kvasnicka and Viola, eds., *Commissioners of Indian Affairs*, xv.
2. Cahill, *Federal Fathers and Mothers*, 6.
3. Case, *The Relentless Business of Treaties*, 7 (emphasis in original).
4. *Worcester v. Georgia.*
5. *Cherokee Nation v. Georgia.*

BIBLIOGRAPHY

ARTICLES

Berthrong, Donald J. "Legacies of the Dawes Act: Bureaucrats and Land Thieves at the Cheyenne and Arapaho Agencies of Oklahoma." *Arizona and the West* 21, no. 4 (Winter 1979): 335–54.

Cohen, Felix S. "The Erosion of Indian Rights, 1950–1953: A Case Study in Bureaucracy." *Yale Law Review* 62, no. 3 (1953): 348–90.

Collier, John. "Letter to General Eisenhower." *Nation*, January 10, 1953.

Connelly, Vera. "Cry of a Broken People." *Good Housekeeping*, February 1929.

———. "End of the Road." *Good Housekeeping*, May 1929.

———. "We Still Get Robbed." *Good Housekeeping*, March 1929.

Cook, Samuel R. "Ronald Reagan's Indian Policy in Retrospect: Economic Crisis and Political Irony." *Policy Studies Journal* 24, no. 1 (March 1996): 11–26.

DeJong, David H. "Unless They Are Kept Alive: Federal-Indian Schools and Student Health, 1890–1917." *American Indian Quarterly* 31, no. 2 (Spring 2007): 256–82.

Emmons, Glenn. "U.S. Aim: Give Indians a Chance." *Nation's Business*, July 1955.

Ickes, Harold L. "The Indian Loses Again." *New Republic*, September 24, 1951.

———. "Justice in a Deep Freeze." *New Republic*, May 21, 1951.

Koch, Lena Clara. "The Federal Indian Policy in Texas, 1845–1860." *Southwestern Historical Quarterly* 28, no. 3 (January 1925): 223–34.

Lindley, Lawrence E. "Why Indians Need Land." *The Christian Century*, November 6, 1957.

Lurie, Nancy Oestreich. "The Indian Claims Commission Act." *Annuals of the American Academy of Political and Social Sciences* 311, no. 1 (May 1957): 56–70.

"The Recent Change in the Indian Bureau." *Nation*, August 17, 1871.

Smith, Laura J. "Native American Trust Land Transfers in Minnesota." *CURA Reporter* 34, no. 2 (Spring 2004): 19–25.

Unrau, William E. "Politics, Bureaucracy, and the Bogus Administration of Indian Commissioner Lewis Vital Bogy, 1866–1867." *American Indian Law Review* 5, no. 1 (Summer 1977): 185–94.

Van de Mark, Dorothy. "The Raid on Reservations." *Harper's Magazine*, March 1956.

BOOKS

Abel, Annie. *The American Indian in the Civil War, 1862–1865*. Lincoln: University of Nebraska Press, 1992.

———. *The American Indian and the End of the Confederacy, 1863–1866*. Lincoln: University of Nebraska Press, 1993.

———. *The American Indian as Slaveholders and Secessionists*. Lincoln: University of Nebraska Press, 1992.

Adams, David Wallace. *Education for Extinction: American Indians and the Boarding School Experience, 1875–1928*. Lawrence: University of Kansas Press, 1995.

Bailey, L. R. *The Long Walk: A History of the Navajo Wars, 1846–1868*. Tucson: University of Arizona Press, 1988.

Berthrong, Donald J. *The Southern Cheyenne*. Norman: University of Oklahoma Press, 1979.

Brophy, William A., and Sophie A. Aberle. *The Indians: America's Unfinished Business, Report of the Commission on the Rights, Liberties, and Responsibilities of the American Indian*. Norman: University of Oklahoma Press, 1966.

Cahill, Cathleen D. *Federal Fathers and Mothers: A Social History of the United States Indian Service, 1869–1933*. Chapel Hill: University of North Carolina Press, 2011.

Calloway, Colin Gordon, ed. *Early American Indian Documents: American Revolution*. Vol. 18. Washington, D.C.: University Publishers of America, 1994.

Case, Martin. *The Relentless Business of Treaties: How Indigenous Land Became U.S. Property*. St. Paul, MN: Minnesota Historical Society Press, 2018.

Cohen, Felix S. *Handbook of Federal-Indian Law*. Charlottesville, VA: Michie, 1982.

Collier, John. *American Indian Life*. New York: American Indian Defense Association Bulletin, July 1930 and January 1933.

———. *From Every Zenith: A Memoir and Some Essays on Life and Thought*. Denver: Sage Books, 1963.

Debo, Angie. *A History of the Indians of the United States*. Norman: University of Oklahoma Press, 1970.

———. *And Still the Waters Run: The Betrayal of the Five Civilized Tribes*. Norman: University of Oklahoma Press, 1980.

"Declaration of Indian Purpose: The Voice of the American Indians. Proceedings of the American Indian Chicago Conference." University of Chicago, June 13–20, 1961.

DeJong, David H. *American Indian Treaties: A Guide to Ratified and Unratified Colonial, United States, State, Foreign, and Intertribal Treaties and Agreements, 1607–1911*. Salt Lake City: University of Utah Press, 2015.

———. *If You Knew the Conditions: A Chronicle of the Indian Medical Service and American Indian Health Care, 1908–1955*. Lanham, MD: Lexington Press, 2008.

———. *Plagues, Politics, and Policy: A Chronicle of the Indian Health Service, 1955–2008*. Lanham, MD: Lexington Press, 2011.

———. *Promises of the Past: A History of Indian Education*. Golden, CO: North American Press, 1993.

———. *Stealing the Gila: The Pima Agricultural Economy and Water Deprivation, 1848–1921*. Tucson: University of Arizona Press, 2009.

De Las Casas, Bartolomé. *In Defense of the Indians*. Translated and edited by Stafford Poole. DeKalb: Northern Illinois University Press, 1974.

Deloria, Philip, and Neal Salisbury. *A Companion to American Indian History*. Malden, MA: Blackwell Publishing, 2004.

Deloria, Vine, Jr. *American Indian Policy in the Twentieth Century*. Norman: University of Oklahoma Press, 1985.

———. *Behind the Trail of Broken Treaties: An Indian Declaration of Independence*. Austin: University of Texas Press, 1985.

———. *Custer Died for Your Sins: An Indian Manifesto*. New York: MacMillan, 1967.

———. *Of Utmost Good Faith*. New York: Bantam Books, 1972.

Deloria, Vine, Jr., and Raymond J. DeMallie. *Documents of American Indian Diplomacy: Treaties, Agreements, and Conventions, 1775–1979*. Vol. 2. Norman: University of Oklahoma Press, 1999.

Deloria, Vine, Jr., and Clifford M. Lytle. *American Indians, American Justice*. Austin: University of Texas Press, 1983.

———. *The Nations Within: The Past and Future of American Indian Sovereignty*. New York: Pantheon Books, 1984.

De Vattel, Emmerich. *The Law of Nations, or Principles of the Law of Nations, Applied to the Conduct and Affairs of Nations and Sovereigns*. Philadelphia: T & J. W. Johnson, 1883.

Documentary History of the State of Maine. Vol. 8. Portland, ME: Maine Historical Society, 1902.

Drinnon, Richard. *Keepers of Concentration Camps: Dillion S. Myer and American Racism*. Berkley: University of California Press, 1987.

Eastman, Charles. *My People the Sioux*. Lincoln: University of Nebraska Press, 1975.

Ellis, Richard. *General Pope and U.S. Indian Policy*. Albuquerque: University of New Mexico Press, 1975.

Farrand, Max, ed. *The Records of the Federal Convention of 1787*. Vol. 1. New Haven: Yale University Press, 1911.

Fixico, Donald L. *Termination and Relocation: Federal Indian Policy 1945–1960*. Albuquerque: University New Mexico Press, 1986.

Foreman, Grant. *Indian Removal: The Emigration of the Five Civilized Tribes of Indians*. Norman: University of Oklahoma Press, 1932.

Getches, David H., Charles F. Wilkinson, and Robert A. Williams. *Cases and Materials on Federal-Indian Law*. St. Paul: West Publishing, 1993.

Hagan, William T. *American Indians*. Chicago: University of Chicago Press, 1993.

———. *Indian Police and Judges*. Lincoln: University of Nebraska Press, 1966.

———. *The Indian Rights Association: The Herbert Welsh Years, 1882–1904*. Tucson: University of Arizona Press, 1985.

Hoig, Stan. *The Battle of the Washita*. Lincoln: University of Nebraska Press, 1976.

———. *The Sand Creek Massacre*. Norman: University of Oklahoma Press, 1961.

Holm, Tom. *Code Talkers and Warriors: Native Americans and World War II*. New York: Chelsea House, 2007.

Hoxie, Frederick E. *A Final Promise: The Campaign to Assimilate the Indians, 1880–1920*. Cambridge University Press, 1989.

Hurtado, Albert. *Indian Survival on the California Frontier*. Yale University Press, 1990.

Indian Reservations: A State and Federal Handbook. Compiled by the Confederation of American Indians. Jefferson, NC: McFarland, 1986.

Jackson, Helen Hunt. *A Century of Dishonor*. New York: Harper, 1965.

Kelly, Lawrence C. *The Navajo Indians and Federal Indian Policy, 1900–1935*. Tucson: University of Arizona Press, 1968.

Kvasnicka, Robert M., and Herman J. Viola, eds. *The Commissioners of Indian Affairs, 1824–1977*. Lincoln: University of Nebraska Press, 1979.

Leupp, Francis. *In Red Man's Land: A Study of the American Indians*. New York: Fleming H. Revell, 1914.

———. *The Indian and His Problem*. New York: Scribner, 1910.

Locke, John. *The Second Treatise of Government: An Essay Concerning the True, Original, Extent and End of Civil Government*. Edited by Thomas P. Pearson. New Jersey: Prentice Hall, 1997.

Madigan, La Verne. *The American Indian Relocation Program*. New York: Association on American Indian Affairs, 1956.

Manypenny, George. *Our Indian Wards*. Cincinnati: R. Clarke, 1880.

McCool, Daniel. *Command of the Waters: Iron Triangles, Federal Water Development, and Indian Water*. Tucson: University of Arizona Press, 1994.

McDonnell, Janet. *The Dispossession of the American Indians, 1887–1934*. Bloomington: University of Indiana Press, 1991.

Meriam, Lewis. *The Problem of Indian Administration*. Baltimore: John Hopkins University Press, 1928.

Morgan, Lewis Henry. *Ancient Society: Or Researches in the Lines of Human Progress from Savagery, through Barbarism to Civilization*. New York: Henry Holt, 1877.

O'Callaghan, E. B., ed. *Documents Relative to the Colonial History of the State of New York Procured in Holland, England, and France by John P. Brodhead*. Vol. 8. Albany, NY: Weed, Parsons, 1857.

Perry, Richard J. *Apache Reservations: Indigenous People and the American State*. Austin: University of Texas Press, 1993.

Philp, Kenneth R. *Indian Self-Rule: First-Hand Accounts of Indian-White Relations from Roosevelt to Reagan*. Salt Lake City: Howe Brothers, 1986.

———. *John Collier's Crusade for Indian Reform, 1920–1954*. Tucson: University of Arizona Press, 1977.

"Proceedings of the Lake Mohonk Conference of Friends of the Indian and other Dependent Peoples, 1912." New York: Lake Mohonk Conference, 1912.

Prucha, Francis Paul. *American Indian Policy in Crisis: Christian Reformers and the Indian, 1865–1900*. Norman: University of Oklahoma Press, 1976.

———. *American Indian Policy in the Formative Years: The Indian Trade and Intercourse Acts, 1790–1834*. Lincoln: University of Nebraska Press, 1954.

———. *American Indian Treaties: A History of a Political Anomaly*. Berkley: University of California Press, 1994.

———. *The Great Father: The United States Government and the American Indians*. Lincoln: University of Nebraska Press, 1984.

Robinson, Edgar Eugene, and Paul Carroll Edwards, eds. *The Memoirs of Ray Lyman Wilbur, 1875–1949*. Stanford: Stanford University Press, 1960.

Roosevelt, Theodore. *Theodore Roosevelt: An Autobiography*. New York: MacMillan, 1913.

Satz, Ronald N. *American Indian Policy in the Jacksonian Era*. Lincoln: University of Nebraska Press, 1975.

Schrader, Robert F. *The Indian Arts and Crafts Board: An Aspect of New Deal Policy*. Albuquerque: University of New Mexico Press, 1983.

Standing Bear, Luther. *My Indian Boyhood*. Lincoln: University of Nebraska Press, 1988.

Tibbles, Thomas Henry. *Standing Bear and the Ponca Chiefs*. Lincoln: University of Nebraska Press, 1972.

Tiller, Veronica E. *American Indian Reservations and Trust Areas*. Albuquerque, NM: Tiller Research, 1996.

———. *Federal and State Indian Reservations and Indian Trust Areas*. U.S. Department of Commerce, 1974.

Trennert, Robert A. *Alternative to Extinction: Federal Indian Policy and the Beginnings of the Reservation System, 1846–1851*. Philadelphia: Temple University Press, 1975.

Ulrich, Roberta. *American Indian Nations from Termination to Restoration, 1953–2006*. Lincoln: University of Nebraska Press, 2011.

Utley, Robert M. *The Indian Frontier of the American West, 1846–1890*. Albuquerque: University of New Mexico Press, 1984.

Vecsey, Christopher, and William A. Starna, eds. *Iroquois Land Claims*. Syracuse: Syracuse University Press, 1988.

Viola, Herman J. *Thomas L. McKenney: Architect of Early Indian Policy, 1816–1830*. Chicago: University of Chicago Press, 1974.

Williams, Robert A. *The American Indian in Western Legal Thought: The Discourse of Conquest*. New York: Oxford University Press, 1990.

LEGAL CASES

A Matter of Heff, 197 U.S. 488 (1905).

Bryan v. Itasca County, 426 U.S. 372 (1976).

California v. Cabazon Band of Mission Indians, 480 U.S. 202 (1987).

Carcieri v. Kempthorne, 555 U.S. 379 (2009).

Cass County, Minnesota, v. Leech Lake Chippewa Band of Indians, 524 U.S. 103 (1998).

Cherokee Nation v. Georgia, 30 U.S. 1 (1831).

Cherokee Nation v. Hitchcock, 187 U.S. 294 (1902).

Cheyenne-Arapaho Tribes v. Oklahoma, 618 F.2d 665 (10th Cir. 1980).
Chippewa Indians v. United States, 307 U.S. 1 (1939).
Choate v. Trapp, 224 U.S. 665 (1913).
Cobell v. Babbitt, 30 F. Supp. 2d 24 (D.D.C. 1998).
Cobell v. Norton, 226 F. Supp. 2d. 1 (D.D.C. 2002).
Colliflower v. Garland, 342 F.2d 369 (9th Cir. 1965).
Connecticut ex rel Blumenthal v. U.S. Department of Interior, 228 F.3d 83 (2d Cir. 2000).
County of Charles E. Mix v. United States Department of the Interior, 674 F.3d 898 (8th Cir. 2012).
Craven v. Cobell, 2012 U.S. Lexis 8318 (October 29, 2012).
DeCoteau v. District County Court, 420 U.S. 425 (1975).
Department of the Interior et al. v. South Dakota et al., 519 U.S. 919 (1996).
Donnelly v. United States, 228 U.S. 243 (1913).
Eastern Band of Cherokee Indians v. North Carolina Wildlife Resources Commission, 588 F.2d 75 (4th Cir. 1978).
Eells v. Ross, 64 F. 417 (12th Cir. 1895).
Elk v. Wilkins, 112 U.S. 94 (1884).
Ex Parte Crow Dog, 109 U.S. 556 (1883).
Hallowell v. United States, 221 U.S. 317 (1911).
Harrison v. Laveen, 196 P.2d 456 (Ariz. 1948).
Johnson v. M'Intosh, 21 U.S. 543 (1823).
Joint Council of the Passamaquoddy and Penobscot Tribes v. Morton, 528 F.2d 370 (1st Cir. 1975).
Lone Wolf v. Hitchcock, 187 U.S. 553 (1903).
Mashpee Tribe v. New Seabury Corp, 592 F.2d 575 (1st Cir. 1979).
Mashpee Tribe v. The Town of Mashpee, 447 F. Supp. 940 (D. Mass. 1978).
Mashpee Tribe v. Watt, 707 F.2d 23 (1st Cir. 1983).
Mashpee Tribe v. Watt, 464 U.S. 1020 (1983).
Match-E-Be-Nash-She-Wish Band of Pottawatomie Indians v. Patchak, 567 U.S. 209 (2012), 132 S. Ct. 2199 (2012).
Menominee Tribe of Indians v. United States, 101 Ct. Cl. 22 (1944).
Menominee Tribe v. United States, 391 U.S. 404 (1968).
Moe v. Confederated Salish Kootenai Tribes, 425 U.S. 463 (1976).
Oliphant v. Suquamish, 435 U.S. 191 (1978).
Perrin v. United States, 232 U.S. 478 (1913).
Reuben Quick Bear v. Leupp, Commissioner of Indian Affairs, 210 U.S. 40 (1908).
Seminole Indian Tribe v. Butterworth, 658 F.2d 310 (5th Cir. 1981).
Shivwits Band of Paiute Indians v. Utah, 428 F.3d 966 (10th Cir. 2005).
Solem vs. Bartlett, 465 U.S. 463 (1984).
South Dakota v. U.S. Department of Interior, 69 F.3d 878 (8th Cir. 1995).
South Dakota v. U.S. Department of Interior, 487 F.3d 548 (8th Cir. 2007).
South Dakota v. United States Department of the Interior, 775 F. Supp. 2d 1129 (D.S.D. 2011).
Tee Hit Ton Indians v. United States, 348 U.S. 272 (1955).
The Kansas Indians, 72 U.S. 737 (1867).
The New York Indians, 7 Wallace U.S. 761 (1866).
Trujillo v. Garley, New Mexico unreported (1949).
United States v. District Court for Eagle County, 401 U.S. 520 (1971).
United States v. Forty-three Gallons of Whiskey, 93 U.S. 188 (1876).
United States v. George Cook, 86 U.S. 591 (1873).
United States v. Holliday, 70 U.S. 407 (1866).
United States v. Jackson, 280 U.S. 183 (1930).

United States v. John, 437 U.S. 634 (1978).
United States v. Joseph, 94 U.S. 614 (1877).
United States v. Kagama, 118 U.S. 375 (1886).
United States v. Michigan, 471 F. Supp 192 (W.D. Mich. 1979).
United States v. Navajo, 537 U.S. 488 (2003).
United States v. Nice, 241 U.S. 591 (1916).
United States v. Rogers, 45 U.S. 567 (1846).
United States v. Sandoval, 231 U.S. 28 (1913).
United States v. Washington, 384 F. Supp. 312 (W.D. Wash. 1974).
United States v. Winans, 198 U.S. 371 (1905).
United States ex. Rel. Standing Bear v. Crook, 25 F. Cas. 695 (C.C.D. Neb. 1879).
Washington v. Fishing Vessel Association, 443 U.S. 658 (1979).
William McKay, et al. v. Agnes Kalyton, 204 U.S. 458 (1907).
Williams v. Lee, 358 U.S. 217 (1959).
Winters v. United States, 207 U.S. 564 (1908).
Worcester v. Georgia, 31 U.S. 515 (1832).

MISCELLANEOUS SOURCES

The American Presidency Project. John F. Kennedy. "Letter on Indian Affairs from Senator John F. Kennedy to Mr. Oliver LaFarge, President, Association on American Indian Affairs," October 28, 1960.
Hasse, Larry J. "Termination and Assimilation: Federal-Indian Policy, 1943–1961" PhD diss., Washington State University, 1974.
Montana Code Annotated 85-20-201 (1985).

NEWSPAPERS

Albuquerque Tribune.
New York Times.
Washington Post.

U.S. GOVERNMENT PUBLICATIONS

"A Study of the Need for Public Health Nursing on Indian Reservations." In *A Survey of the Conditions of the Indians in the United States: Hearings before a Subcommittee of the Committee on Indian Affairs, United States Senate, Part 3*. Washington, D.C.: Government Printing Office, 1929.
American State Papers: Indian Affairs. Vol. 2. Washington, D.C.: Gales and Seaton, 1834.
Annual Report of the Board of Indian Commissioners. Washington, D.C.: Government Printing Office.
Annual Report of the Commissioner of Indian Affairs, 1824–1964. Washington D.C.: Government Printing Office.
Annual Report of the Secretary of the Interior. Washington, D.C.: Government Printing Office.
Annual Report of the Secretary of the Treasury. Washington, D.C.: Government Printing Office.
BIA Profile: The Bureau of Indian Affairs and American Indians. Washington, D.C.: Government Printing Office, 1981.
Condition of the Indian Tribes. Washington, D.C.: Government Printing Office, 1867.
Congressional Globe. 46 vols. Washington, D.C.: John C. Rives, 1833–1873.

Congressional Record. Washington, D.C.: Government Printing Office.

Congressional Serial Set. 14,000+ vols. Washington D.C.: Government Printing Office.

Department of the Interior, Office of Indian Affairs. "Land Tenure, Economic Statistics, and Population Trends." Washington, D.C.: Government Printing Office, 1935.

Federal Register. Washington, D.C.: Government Printing Office.

Fitzpatrick, John C. *Journals of the Continental Congress, 1774–1789*. Washington, D.C.: Government Printing Office, 1904–1937.

Haas, Theodore H. *Ten Years of Tribal Government under the I.R.A.* Washington, D.C.: United States Indian Service, 1947.

Kappler, Charles. *Indian Laws and Treaties*. Vol.1. Washington, D.C.: Government Printing Office, 1906.

National Archives and Records Services. Record Group 75. Numbered Circular File.

Office Copy of the Laws, Regulations, etc., of the Indian Bureau, 1850. Washington, D.C.: Gideon, 1850.

Preston, Porter J., and Charles A. Engel. *Report of Advisors on Irrigation on Indian Reservations, Volume 1*. Washington, D.C.: Government Printing Office, 1928.

Progress Report of the Commissioner of Indian Affairs. Washington, D.C.: Government Printing Office, 1965–1969.

Public Papers of the Presidents of the United States: John Adams, Containing the Public Messages, Speeches, and Statements of the President, 1828. Washington, D.C.: Gales and Seaton, 1829.

Public Papers of the Presidents of the United States: Lyndon B. Johnson, Containing the Public Messages, Speeches, and Statements of the President, 1968–1969. Washington, D.C.: Government Printing Office, 1970.

Public Papers of the Presidents of the United States: John F. Kennedy, Containing the Public Messages, Speeches, and Statements of the President, 1961–1963. Washington, D.C.: Government Printing Office, 1964.

Public Papers of the Presidents of the United States: Richard M. Nixon, Containing the Public Messages, Speeches, and Papers of the President, 1970. Washington, D.C.: Government Printing Office, 1971.

Public Papers of the President of the United States: Harry S. Truman, 1946. Washington, D.C.: Government Printing Office, 1965.

Register of Debates in Congress. Vol. 6. Washington, D.C.: Gales and Seaton, 1830.

Richardson, James, ed. *A Compilation of the Messages and Papers of the Presidents*. Vols. 1 and 2. Washington D.C.: Government Printing Office, 1896–1897.

United States Code of Federal Regulations. Washington, D.C.: Government Printing Office.

United Statutes at Large. Washington, D.C.: Government Printing Office.

Weekly Compilation of Presidential Documents. September 23, 2004.

WEBSITES

Bureau of Indian Affairs News Release. www.bia.gov/regional-offices/western/pressreleases.

Department of the Interior, Bureau of Indian Affairs, "Fee-to-Trust Handbook, Version II." Washington, D.C.: Bureau of Indian Affairs, 2011. www.bia.gov/idc/groups/xraca/documents/test/ide-002543.

Department of the Interior Information Service (or Press Release or News Release) 1953–2009. www.bia.gov/regional-offices/western/pressreleases.

Minnesota Daily. www.mndaily.com.

"Native American Rights—Hunting and Fishing Rights." http://law.jrank.org/pages/8750/Native-American-Rights-Hunting-Fishing-Rights.html#ixzz3p3FQW0OP.

Office of Federal Acknowledgment, U.S. Department of the Interior. Acknowledgment Decision Compilation List: Decided Cases Petitions Resolved by Department of the Interior. www.bia.gov/as-ia/ofa/decidedcases.

"Remarks of Kevin Gover at the Ceremony Acknowledging the 175th Anniversary of the BIA." September 8, 2000. www.tribal-institute.org.
United States Department of the Interior, Office of the Secretary (2009–2017). www.bia.gov/regional-offices/western/pressreleases.
Upstate Citizens for Equality. www.upstate-citizens.org.

INDEX

Note: Page numbers in *italics* refer to tables and/or front matter.